anarchist prophets

Disappointing
Vision and
the Power of
Collective Sight

James R. Martel

anarchist

prophets

Duke University Press
Durham and London 2022

Designed by Aimee C. Harrison / Project Editor: Annie Lubinsky
Typeset in Portrait Text Regular, Antique Olive,
and Helvetica Neue by Westchester Publishing Services

Library of Congress Cataloging-in-Publication Data
Names: Martel, James R., author.
Title: Anarchist prophets : disappointing vision and the power of
collective sight / James R. Martel.
Description: Durham : Duke University Press, 2022. | Includes
bibliographical references and index.
Identifiers: LCCN 2021045554 (print) | LCCN 2021045555 (ebook)
ISBN 9781478015789 (hardcover)
ISBN 9781478018414 (paperback)
ISBN 9781478023043 (ebook)
Subjects: LCSH: Power (Social sciences)—History. | Anarchism. | Power
(Social sciences)—Philosophy. | BISAC: POLITICAL SCIENCE / History
& Theory | PHILOSOPHY / Political
Classification: LCC JC330 .M3398 2022 (print) | LCC JC330 (ebook) |
DDC 303.3—dc23/eng/20220118
LC record available at https://lccn.loc.gov/2021045554
LC ebook record available at https://lccn.loc.gov/2021045555

Cover art: Gustavo Díaz Sosa (Sagua la Grande, Cuba, b. 1983),
Huérfanos de Babel (Orphans of Babel), 2018. 160×114 cm (62.99"×
44.88"). Courtesy of the artist.

contents

acknowledgments

A BOOK ABOUT COLLECTIVE FORMS of vision and inter-
pretation would be seriously remiss if it didn't acknowledge the huge number of people whose thoughts, friendship, and insights are very much part
of this text alongside my own contributions. In my opinion, writing as an
anarchist, actually writing as anything or anyone at all, is always a group
project; arbitrarily determining that there is just one "author" seems to me
to reproduce liberal—and archist—forms of subjectivity.

With this in mind, I'd like to begin by thanking a series of reading groups
and one-on-one ongoing working sessions with a number of people who
have been very important for my thinking on this subject. I have had the
great fortune to participate in what I consider to be two dream teams of
wonderful coconspirators, comrades, and friends: First, a study group reading Benjamin with Karen Barad, Daniela Gandorfer, Max Tomba, Julia Ng,
Patricia Williams, Emanuele Pelilli, Isaac Jean-François, and AK Thompson
(as well as a previous one on Spinoza with many of the same people plus
Zulaikha Ayub and Stephen Engel). Second, a group organized by a grant on
International Law and the Challenge of Populism funded by the Australian
Research Council with Richard Joyce, Sundhya Pahuja, Andrew Benjamin,

Rose Parfitt, and Adil Khan. A lot of what is in these books is inspired by and amplified by these people.

I have also been engaged in separate readings with Emanuele Pelilli (on Furio Jesi) and Nick Thacker (on Pier Paolo Pasolini) and another reading group as well, originally San Francisco State University (SFSU) students of mine but afterward including a lot of other people I have been very fortunate to get to know: Alex Bouskos, Natasha Colette, Raphael di Donato, Lisa Walsh, and previously Alex McNeil, Lim Yeonjin, Keegan Quiroz, and Alejandro Pulido, among others.

Finally, I have been part of a wonderful and long-running reading group on law and contemporary theory with Marianne Constable, Ellen Rigsby, Yael Pittman, Tim Wyman-McCarthy, Angela Castillo, Linda Kinstler, David Lau, Alex Mabanta, and previously Bruno Ortiz, Chenxi Tang, Christopher Chamberlin, Daniela Gandorfer, Eva Vaillancourt, and many others.

I must also thank my students at SFSU, especially in my politics and literature class, where I usually teach the literary and filmic sources I happen to be working on, as well as a graduate seminar on Kafka. I want to especially thank Nick Doliber, Nick Thacker, C. S. Soong, Dennis Clisham, Simon Crafts, Zoe Clark, Luz Juan Garcia, Brad Bergman, Sammy Gatenby-Brown, Jared Kahlenberg, Zoe Yang, Swetha Pottam, and so many other great students.

I also have been experiencing some of the joys and travails of organizing as a union chapter president for my campus. What I've learned there has definitely influenced and continues to influence my thinking and writing. Special thanks to my comrades in arms Blanca Missé and Maureen Loughran.

Individuals who read or heard different parts of this book in different modes and offered invaluable feedback or who wrote or said things that I have incorporated into this work include Bonnie Honig (my forever comrade and fellow sister), Banu Bargu, Kate Gordy, Jodi Dean, Blanca Missé, Karen Barad (who has gotten me to rethink the concept of the universe as well as of immanence), Peter Burdon, Ricardo Sanín Restrepo, Marinella Machado Araujo, C.S. Soong, Peter Goodrich, Stacy Douglas, Kennan Ferguson, Angus McDonald, Kathy Ferguson, Jackie Stevens, Zulaikha Ayub, Mark Andrejevic, Andreas Kalyvas, Sara Kendall, Hyo Yoon Kang, Alison Young, Tiffany Willoughby-Herard, Naveed Mansoori, Başak Ertür (for whom I joyously switch my keyboard to Turkish just to get the right diacritic), Miguel Vatter, Agata Bielik-Robson, Mauricio Oportus Preller, Davina Cooper, Jacob Levi, Shalini Satkunanandan, Dan Matthews, Daniel McLaughlin, Daniela Gandorfer (for whom I am trying to learn to love Deleuze), Marc Crépon, Alex Dubilet, Kirill Chepurin, Diego Arrocha Paris,

Mick Dillon, Miriam Leonard, David Leach, Sam Weber, Keally McBride, Charles Barbour, Jennifer Culbert, Maria Aristodemou, George Shulman, Miguel Vatter, Maria Drakapoulou, Connal Parsley, Marinos Diamantides Max Tomba, Julia Ng, Alex Dubilet, Elena Louizidou, Dimitris Vardoulakis, Ben Golder, Jessica Whyte, Alberto Toscano, and many, many others. I often feel like the luckiest person on earth to have all these great minds to think and ponder alongside with. I even think with those who are no longer among us, especially with my dear, brilliant friend Nasser Hussain and the equally brilliant and dear Peter Fitzpatrick.

Tiffany MacLellan is the person who introduced me to the idea of the archeon. I spotted the word in her wonderful dissertation, for which I had the privilege of being an external evaluator.

I had many opportunities to present work from the book as it progressed. In reverse chronological order, I made a presentation on Spanish anarchism at a panel for the American Political Science Association (online) in September 2020. Thanks to Miguel Vatter, Alex Dubilet, and Inese Radzins for their participation and insights. I also got to present part of this book at the University of Kent in Canterbury, United Kingdom, in October 2019. Thanks to Maria Drakapoulou and Connal Parsley for making that happen and for the chance to think along with them, their fellow faculty, and their students. I presented a paper on Benjamin's angel of history at Northwestern University in May 2019. Thanks to Marc Crépon, Sam Weber, Mick Dillon, Michael Loriaux, and Jackie Stevens for their questions and insights. I also presented a paper on anarchist prophecy at a conference held at Humboldt University in Berlin in July 2018. Thanks to Alex Dubilet and Kirill Chepurin for organizing that conference and for their comments and comradeship. Thanks to Christina Tarnopolsky for the chance to present some of my work on Nietzsche at a conference at the National University of Singapore in April 2018. I also presented a paper on the archeon and the state at Griffith University in Brisbane, Australia, in December 2017. Thanks to Chris Butler and Karen Crawley for the invitation and their comments and thoughts. The initial paper that started this book was on Benjamin and prophecy and was presented at a conference on Benjamin at Oxford University in September 2017. Thanks to the organizers, panelists, and audience, and in particular to Julia Ng and Ben Morgan.

I feel so privileged to have gotten to work with Courtney Berger and the people at Duke University Press once again. Courtney is a dream editor. She always gets what I say to her and she pushes back in ways that always make the final results infinitely better than what I first present to her.

Thanks too to my two anonymous reviewers for their superb suggestions, all of which I took up.

As ever, I thank most of all my wonderful family: my husband, Carlos; my co-parents, Nina and Kathryn; my children, Jacques and Rocio; the "guncles," Elic and Mark; my mother, Huguette; my brother, Django; my sister-in-law, Shalini; my nephew, Shaan; and our beautiful, extended families. I dedicate this book to the memory of my father, Ralph Martel.

introduction

disappointing vision

Our ability to see means "forgetting" our inability to
see the gaze. We see, when we start seeing, without being able to see from the blind spot; unlike the
prisoners in the Panopticon, who are conscious of
being seen from the blind spot, most of us forget that
there is a point from which we are seen but which we
cannot see. —Maria Aristodemou, *Law, Psychoanalysis,*
Society: Taking the Unconscious Seriously

TWO PARABLES BY FRANZ KAFKA, taken in sequence, de-
scribe the creation and maintenance of what I call archism, that is, a form
of politics based on rule and hierarchy, on phantasmal authority structures
that supersede and replace any particular or horizontal and collective forms
of politics that I refer to as anarchism.[1] The first parable is called "The City
Coat of Arms." In that parable, Kafka describes a circle-shaped city built
around what is intended to be the foundations for the Tower of Babel, a "tower
that will reach to heaven."[2] Given that by definition this will be a multigenera-
tional undertaking, Kafka tells us that the planners of the tower were never
in any kind of hurry to build the tower itself but that in the end, this lack
of urgency meant that it never even got started. Anxiety and conflict about

how to build a perfect tower (given its exalted destination) proved fatal to the project. Kafka explains, "Such thoughts paralyzed people's powers, and so they troubled less about the tower than the construction of a city for the workmen."[3]

A circular-shaped city grew around the site of the proposed tower, never quite forgetting its collective and original purpose but not doing much of anything about it either. Kafka writes: "To this must be added that the second or third generation had already recognized the senselessness of building a heaven-reaching tower; but by that time everybody was too deeply involved to leave the city."[4] Kafka ends the story with the following passage: "All the legends and songs that came to birth in that city are filled with longing for a prophesied day when the city would be destroyed by five successive blows from a gigantic fist. It is for that reason too that the city has a closed fist on its coat of arms."[5]

In this parable, we see the power of collective phantasm and hence a possible origin story for archism. The nonexistent tower in the center of the city is the heart of the community, its veritable raison d'être. Without the tower, there would, it seems, be no city at all. In some sense, the dream (or perhaps desire) of the city to be annihilated by a giant fist represents a wish that the fictive basis of the city could be real. The community's worship of nothingness— the nonexistent presence that anchors its collectivity—apparently extends to seeking its own nothingness, its own annihilation, by a force that exists only in its collective imagination. By wishing its own destruction, the community is looking for some evidence that the emptiness at its center is real and manifest, that this emptiness is truly "higher" and "better" than the community is. The fact that the giant fist would act so manifestly in contradiction to the community's own desires for life and safety "proves" in a sense that this power is real and not just a figment of the imagination.

The second Kafkan parable to consider in this context is "The Refusal." This parable can be considered to be an effective sequel to "The City Coat of Arms," insofar as it shows not the birth of a city but its aftermath, the way that the archist authority represented by the blank center has moved elsewhere without ceasing to serve as an anchor for a political community based on an utter subservience to this invisible source.

The story that this parable relates takes place in a small unnamed town far from the center of power and authority. Most of the time this town is left to its own devices, but it remains in thrall to a capital city—perhaps Babel itself—whose existence is communicated purely through representatives who claim to speak on its behalf. Critically, the gaping hole at the center of the city is no longer in evidence, so the ephemerality of the power it generates is of a different kind, both less evident and more amorphous, yet no less powerful and compelling.

The top official in the town is the chief tax collector, who is also a colonel, a man whose link to the capital is extremely tenuous even as it is also absolute and unquestionable. Kafka says that the colonel "commands the town. I don't think he has ever produced a document entitling him to this position; very likely he does not possess such a thing."[6]

Presented with a petition by a group of citizens for some form of tax relief, the colonel whispers something in the ear of another official, who then tells the petitioners, "The petition has been refused. . . . You may go."[7] At that point, Kafka writes, "an undeniable sense of relief passed through the crowd, everyone surged out, hardly a soul paying any special attention to the colonel, who, as it were, had turned once more into a human being like the rest of us."[8] He further explains: "In all important matters . . . the citizens can always count on a refusal. And now the strange fact is that without this refusal one simply cannot get along, yet at the same time, these official occasions designed to receive the refusal are by no means a formality. Time after time one goes there full of expectation and in all seriousness and then one returns, if not exactly strengthened or happy, nevertheless not disappointed [enttäuscht] or tired."[9]

In this parable, as in "The City Coat of Arms," there is a desire on the part of the community to be dominated, ruled, and controlled by some outside, external agency. Whether it lies in the dreams of destruction of the city dwellers surrounding the empty site of the Tower of Babel or the relief that the people of the community in "The Refusal" feel when anyone's petition is denied, some anxiety is assuaged by the thought of a higher, archist authority that manifests itself precisely and only by going against whatever it is that the people in these communities might actually choose for themselves. In this way, there is a *need* for the townspeople to petition, to test the archist structure to make sure it is still intact, still willing and able to refuse what they ask for.

In part, the community's anxiety seems to stem from the simple fact that the power in question, that which they are subordinating themselves to, has no actual basis in reality. The Tower of Babel never exists except as an idea, and the capital city in "The Refusal" seems infinitely far away (Kafka notes that "whereas we do get news of the frontier wars now and again, of the capital we learn next to nothing—we civilians that is, for of course the government officials have very good connections with the capital; they can get news from there in as little as three months, so they claim at least"[10]).

In this way, we see that the citizens of both towns are deeply invested in making this invisible power as palpable as possible. With no actual physical object to see, nothing that *is* precisely that power or source of authority as opposed to its lieutenants and representatives, the citizens of these places "see" this power through those intermediaries. They understand in some sense how the thing they wish to see isn't there, but they invest the symbols of that authority with a visual power that serves, as it were, to link ordinary sight to the special sight required to see and believe in this other, higher power or place (the Tower of Babel, heaven, the capital, or whatever other agent of power they seek to obey).

Thus, in "The Refusal," Kafka writes that in fact "it does happen now and again that minor petitions are granted, but then it inevitably looks as though the colonel had done it as a powerful private person on his own responsibility, and it had to be kept all but a secret from the government—not explicitly of course, but that is what it feels like. No doubt in our little town the colonel's eyes, so far as we know, are also the eyes of the government, and yet there is a difference which it is impossible to comprehend completely."[11] In this way, when the colonel seems to return to his "human status" and actually grants an occasional petition, his edicts are understood as stemming from within the community itself, from the acts of a fellow, private individual (albeit a most powerful one). But wherever a petition is substantial enough to threaten the balance of power, it must be denied. On those times especially, the "colonel's eyes . . . are also the eyes of the government." He is not completely the same thing as that power itself ("there is a difference"), but he serves as the avatar, as it were, of that power, a tangible, audible, and perhaps above all visual—and visualizing—object that stands for a power that can't otherwise be seen and may not even (actually does not) exist at all.[12]

Critically, as we see in the passage just quoted, the colonel lends his own eyes so that the townspeople can see, as it were, through them. This becomes a way to render something magical and external into something entirely and banally human. In this way, the colonel offers his own imagined access and insight to a community that is otherwise wholly shut out from and deprived of those viewpoints. It is from such a perspective, from an assumed perch of judgment and knowledge, that the people come to see themselves. They are taught how to "see" what the state or other forms of archist rule want them to see, ordering their lives and the entire world accordingly.

Just as important, Kafka explains that the town's citizens, after experiencing one of these denials, return to their homes, "if not exactly strengthened or happy, nevertheless not disappointed or tired." It would be disappointing indeed if the colonel were to grant an important petition because it would hint at the very thing that these citizens seem to fear most: the absence of a power to order and determine them. In other words, they fear an absence that acts like an absence, a nothingness that is actually, and evidently, nothing. In this sense, it behooves us to think about what it would mean if these citizens *were* to be disappointed and what form that disappointment would take.

This book begins with this question of disappointment because it demonstrates the way that power—the same power that the citizens of Kafka's two parables project onto blank and unavailable spaces and which they receive in turn in an alienated form—is seen, related to, and also how that power is potentially resisted and taken back by that community.

Disappointment, in this instance, can be taken in at least two senses. First, it would be disappointing, in the emotional sense, to find out that the archist power that these citizens count on, a power that promises so much—including safety, health, well-being, and maybe even eternal life (or a semblance of it anyway)—could turn out to be nothing at all. Such a state of events would imply that human actors are forced to rely on themselves and on one another instead of on these forces that seem so perfect, so much stronger, better, smarter, and wiser than they are. This realization leaves people sad and dejected, even if it means they are freed from lies they have come to believe and count on, as well as from the violence and hierarchies they have incorporated as necessary for some kind of order.

But there is also the possibility of disappointment in a second sense, as in dis-appointment, removing the appointment or power that the townspeople have been giving to these invisible powers (and their visible representatives) all along. To take away that appointment is, in effect, to disappoint, not themselves but their would-be rulers, and, in that second sense of the word, disappointment takes on a radical and anarchist character.

There is even a third sense of disappointment if we leave the English language behind for a moment. The German term that Kafka uses, *enttäuscht*, is perhaps even more helpful than its English equivalent of disappointment because it suggests the taking away of an illusion. The German verb *täuschen* means to deceive and the prefix suggests taking that away, meaning something like "undeceive." Accordingly, we can think of disappointing vision as a way of getting people to recognize that what they've been worshipping, what they've been basing their entire existence on, is purely ephemeral. Exposing that ephemerality as such serves to ruin it as a fount of authority, to return it to its original nothingness, allowing the human actors who were in its thrall to see the world anew. More accurately they are able to return to their own ordinary forms of sight, to cease overwriting that sight, as the citizens in Kafka's parables do, with other sorts of vision.

Disappointment in this sense is not merely an emotional response but a political one as well. An archist form of vision is replaced by an anarchist one. Whereas the first form, one that is imposed by the colonel and the absent center of the city in Kafka's parables, is hierarchical and commanding, this other form is collective and open ended. This other vision, the power of collective seeing, what results from radical instances of disappointment, is what this book is all about.

Imagine if, for a moment, someone in the city of Babel said, "Did you all notice that the center of the city is absolutely empty, that there is no tower and never will be one? Why do we venerate an empty spot? Why do we obey those who claim to speak for that invisible power? Why do we wish that spot to materialize and actually destroy us?" Or if someone in the colonel's town said, "Why are we happy when our petitions are rejected? Why do we follow this person who is, after all, no different than any of us?" This person would not be speaking from any kind of divine inspiration or special sight. She would have no access to knowledge that anyone else didn't also have. She would not be "special" in any particular way, not predestined to save her community. And, because she was clearly embedded in the community, was "one of them," because she shared a language and vocabulary, a common and collective way of seeing, her fellow citizens would also tend to agree with her (even if they didn't want to).

Anyone could say this, and in fact it is far more likely that a random and average person would say this than anyone who had special powers or authority, since those figures tend to do very well under archist forms of politics and would have little incentive to ruin or expose the sources of that power and authority.

The main focus of this book is to recognize, recuperate, and foment this other kind of vision, the power of collective sight. As I will argue throughout this book, there is nothing special about collective forms of vision. They aren't "truer" than archist forms of vision per se; they aren't based on an obvious and absolute reality that archism ignores or hides. While it is the case, for example, that the center of Babel has no structures within it, the meaning of that space, even the determination that it is "empty," remains a collective decision. In this way, collective vision determines how a group decides to see something, how it takes it in, how it responds. And this response may well not be (usually is not) unitary and uniform the way that archist forms of vision always are. It is always a work in progress, a conversation, an argument, and even sometimes (actually almost always) a fight.

Collective forms of sight go on all the time, even under the strictest of archist regimes. This is a kind of sight that archism itself cannot utterly suppress because it is what actually makes life and human relations possible in the first place, something that archism, which is entirely parasitical, can never do. If archism were to eliminate or supersede this form of sight entirely, then human life would be as empty and as nihilist as archism itself.[13]

We engage in collective forms of sight every day when we collectively determine what, for example, our words mean and how they relate to what we perceive as happening in the world around us. We engage in collective vision when we treat certain objects in certain ways and not in a myriad of other ways that we could treat them. We do so in terms of how we relate to and treat one another. Collective vision amounts to what Hannah Arendt calls "a world," but this world is occupied territory, subject to a force—archism— that exploits and preys upon that world for its own purposes.[14] Even as it can never strip collective vision away from our eyes, archism superimposes itself over that form of vision, effectively transferring the concreteness or sedimentation of that vision to itself, as if it itself were part of or even the essence of that world. This is how archist vision manages to seem so "real" to us, actually becoming prior and superior to our own collective forms of sight.

The denizens of the city of Babel and the occupants of the unnamed village in "The Refusal" are neither unsighted nor crazy. They see the gaping hole in the center of power. They see the naked humanity of the colonel. But they also see something else. That something else is what archism commands them to see. It not only gets them to overwrite what they see together (that is, once again, what they collectively decide that they are seeing) with its own phantasms, but it further gets them to *want* that overwriting to occur, to the point where they become anxious that this overwriting may fail, that they might actually get what they want instead of what *it* (i.e., archism) wants them to want. Why does this happen? Why are the people in these narratives allowing, even facilitating, this transformation of vision?

Archism and archist forms of vision would not be as powerful and resilient as they are if they were based on fear and threat alone. Archism maintains itself by promising so much to so many people. Its promises include the promise of safety, of personal happiness, of success, and, perhaps most critically of all, the promise of eternal life, whether literally or symbolically. This latter promise reflects the way that archism, at least in its modern, Western variant, is based on a form of metaphysics that is inherently against the bases of human life. It holds up a vision of life that is entirely false and nonexistent yet deemed superior to the life that people actually lead; it even teaches us to hate our own life, our bodies, and our mortality, in favor of this false other way of being. The promise of eternal life then is a promise to the subjects of archism that they will somehow connect to or become this other, "better," and higher form of life, leaving their actual life behind. In this way, coming as it does out of nothing, actually being nothing itself, archism is not about life at all but about a form of death, one that is—unlike other understandings of death that are entirely compatible with collective sight—completely divorced from and implacably hostile to life. Consequently, even as it promises an exalted life for its subjects, it ceaselessly engages in causing death, in violence of both the physical and the metaphorical variety.

Of course, for many communities of color and in particular for Black and Brown people, for many women, for poor and working-class communities, for the queer, the trans, the undocumented, for those with disabilities and so many other forms of identity that are not privileged, the failure to deliver on these promises is far more evident, perhaps too evident at times, for the overwriting function of archism to entirely succeed. As opposed to the white, the rich, the male, the heterosexual, the cis-gendered, the nondisabled, such communities are, in some sense, always disappointed.[15]

This helps explain in part why the rule of archism is not utter and why there are times when archist forms of sight falter and sometimes even collapse. I am writing this book at a time of heightened awareness of the racism of the police in the United States given the brutal killings of George Floyd and Breonna Taylor, among many, many other Black people. Those participating in the current and ongoing insurrection are already deeply disappointed, and yet these power systems (so far!) remain intact. Even so—and even if this movement doesn't go any further than it already has—this moment represents something critical, namely a time when the lies and illusions of archist sight temporarily lose some of their grip, their overwriting power, not just on those who are directly targeted by archist power but also by others who do not face the same threat. Suddenly, the Minneapolis City Council considered abolishing its police department (although that did not actually come to pass). Suddenly, a many-decades-long stereotypical brand like Aunt Jemima pancake syrup—long recognized as racist by the Black community—became unthinkable by the (white) business community and was withdrawn. Suddenly, Black Lives Matter became extremely popular and more people said that the burning of a police station in Minneapolis by protesters was either partially or fully justified (54 percent) than anyone preferred either Donald Trump or Joseph Biden as presidential candidates.[16]

Yet, at the same time, we also experienced what appears at first glance to be a different form of collective vision, namely that of the right-wing fascists who attacked the US capitol on January 6, 2021. While this form of insurrection may seem to be similar to that which animated the somewhat earlier George Floyd uprising, I would argue that they are exact opposites; the George Floyd uprising is an example of collective (and anarchist) vision, a refusal to keep seeing the authority that stands over the community as anything but a predator and a killer. The attack on the capital shows the lengths to which some people—in this case almost entirely white people—may still hold onto archist forms of vision no matter what. The crazy paranoia of QAnon, the response to the COVID-19 pandemic (masks are a plot to enslave us!), and the absolute conviction that the 2020 election was stolen show the extent to which archist vision and, more particularly, the *desire* for archist vision and what it promises (power! superiority! superhuman status!) can supersede not so much "reality," because that is a thing that is itself always up for grabs, but a much larger sense of common vision.

Here, I am making a different argument than liberals do about the nature of this far-right-wing mob and their motivations. In the liberal claim, there is a clear-cut set of truths and the mob is either crazy or ignoring those truths in pursuit of its own agenda. In my understanding, even that original "truth" is itself a set of decisions that are often determined by archism itself. In my view, the very idea of truth is an endlessly political question, a site of contestation that is always in flux.

Furthermore, although it seems as if, yes, the ideas coming from Trump and "Q" are crazy, many ideas that are widely accepted are no less insane. For example, the idea that shareholders in a corporation should be privileged above all else even (or especially) to the extent that a corporation makes decisions that destroy human life, even causing the planet to become increasingly inhabitable, is just as crazy, just as pernicious (maybe even more so) than the idea that certain Democrats are pedophilic, cannibalistic Satan worshippers who congregate, among other places, in an underground chamber beneath a certain pizzeria in Washington, DC. The one idea (capitalist, certified, normative) strikes us—if we think about it at all—as objectionable maybe but not "crazy," while the other (given without the stamp of approval of most experts and authorities) seems nothing but pure lunacy.

This is itself a function of archist sight. There are innumerable candidates for the kinds of "truth" that archism pedals. Some succeed and some fail. The jury is out on the QAnon conspiracy as well as the "truths" that Trump is pedaling. There is nothing to prevent us from sliding into a society where those kinds of truths are widely held and acted upon. Or rather there is nothing except our own resolve to come up with counternarratives, based not on a verifiable and uncontestable reality but on a collective process of coming to terms with what we want our political and social lives to look like.

In fact, it is archism itself that is "crazy"; it involves, as Kafka shows, believing in things that aren't there and holding them in higher regard than things that are. Contra Samuel Johnson, the mere fact of existence does not in and of itself amount to a firm sense of reality. Here again, the determination of reality is a collective and political project. What makes QAnon (and capitalism!) crazy is not that it is unrelated to reality but that it seeks to supplant a general, collective, and ever-changing way of thinking about the world with some specific, permanent, and hierarchical ordering, thereby curtailing or eliminating any kind of public engagement (except for the adoring, obedient sort).

For this reason, rather than seeing the events following the 2020 election in the United States as a question of truth versus lies as liberals do (and, for that matter, the right-wing mob as well), I see it as a matter of truths that come from the top versus truths that are determined from within the larger community. The fact that this right-wing and fascistic vision is always oriented outside itself (this is what Trump/God/Q told us to do) is a sign that we are not dealing with what is often misleadingly called "populism" but a crowd in search of a master (and, paraphrasing Jacques Lacan, this is a master that they can readily find).

For all the threat posed by fascist modes of archist vision, this moment in time shows that archist forms of vision are not fated or absolute and that archism itself is vulnerable (the frenzy of that mob may suggest as much). Sudden changes in vision as we are currently experiencing, when things that are previously inconceivable suddenly become very conceivable indeed, point to the ephemerality and vulnerability of archist forms of vision, despite its claims to the contrary. These archist forms of sight are present, seemingly forever, seemingly absolute and unquestionable and then, quite suddenly, they are gone or at least severely weakened. Even the mayhem on the right suggests this vulnerability because the mental gymnastics required to remain faithful to some perceived truth has become increasingly and legibly grotesque, contorted and incredible. Whether this present moment leads to further leftist insurgency (as I certainly hope it will) or a fascist takeover (as I certainly hope it will not), it demonstrates that each moment is a chance for a radical rupture with archism as such.

Having said this, I must admit that the ways of seeing imposed by archism run deep and not just for those on the far right. Archist vision is hard to shake even to some extent for people who directly suffer from archism's inequities, its murderous violence. That's because, to quote Frantz Fanon, the realities produced by archism are "ontological." By this I do not mean, nor do I believe Fanon meant to suggest, that they are eternally and always true (although archism makes that claim) but that they are true to the point that they have a powerful, almost irresistible effect on what passes for reality itself.

Fanon tells us that "the black man has no ontological resistance in the eyes of the white man."[17] Here, he acknowledges the visual aspects of power, the way that seeing determines reality not just for the privileged white viewer but also for the Black person, the colonized subject or other particular targets of archist vision.[18]

For Fanon, there is no going back to an authentic past before the imposition of the white gaze; colonialism has taken up the past as one of its weapons, reshaping it to suit its own purposes. The only way to resist white ontology— or, as I would also put it, archist ontology, which makes whiteness one of its prime categories—is by resistance itself. He writes: "The colonized subject discovers reality and transforms it through his praxis, his deployment of violence and his agenda for liberation."[19]

For Fanon, "discovering reality" does not mean finding the truth that colonialism has buried beneath its lies. For Fanon, there is no "authentic" truth that the collective is returning to. Colonialism has ensured that even the past of a given community is thoroughly saturated with lies and distortions: in other words, yet more archism. By looking to resistance itself as the only form of collective decision-making, Fanon is acknowledging that the content of those decisions comes from nothing other than the collective process itself, a process that has anarchist implications as well: "Even if the armed struggle has been symbolic, and even if they have been demobilized by rapid decolonization, the people have time to realize that liberation was the achievement of each and every one and no special merit should go to the leader. Violence hoists the people up to the level of the leader. . . . When they have used violence to achieve national liberation, the masses allow nobody to come forward as a 'liberator.'"[20] Whether you choose to read Fanon's call to violence literally (he says it can be "symbolic" but he surely was not a pacifist), any break with the ontological involves a reclamation of authority and agency.

Violence—as well as resistance more generally—serves Fanon as both a strategy and a dramatization of the fact that collective life now recognizes only itself. Fanon shows us that the outcome of such acts of resistance does not readily allow for yet more hierarchy; collective forms of resistance enable and produce collective forms of judgment as well. The hallmarks of archism are abandoned only when that collective form of judgment is allowed its full expression.

If many communities are already disappointed by the violence and lies of archism, they are not, however, always disappointing, that is, they have not always learned to translate their perspective into a form that truly threatens archism in the way Fanon suggests. My claim in this book is that the disappointment of living under archism can only be fully achieved if those communities that live under it can better learn to decide for themselves what it is that they are seeing (and not seeing), seeking to transfer their disappointment from themselves to their archist oppressors. In other words, they might trade one form of disappointment, the disappointment of having their lives falsely determined by externalities (ones that don't even exist), for another, a disappointment in and of archism itself.

Archist and Anarchist Forms of Prophecy

This is a book about vision and prophecy, about organizing our experience of what we see in the world. The archist mode of seeing itself derives from a form of prophecy, what I would call an appointing form of vision, that has a long theological (and eventually secularized but no less theological) history. Such vision appoints not just the individuals who will stand in the name of the people they rule over but also the very foundations for that transfer of power and authority, the visual and effectively real bases of an illicit and ultimately empty—but no less powerful for being empty—form of control.

Appointing vision leads to the hierarchies and taxonomies that are the stuff of archist power. This is a way of seeing that gives archism a form of existence that appears to be greater than the actual life it rules over. We live in a world structured by such prophetic acts, whether they are theological or secular in nature (and, thanks to European colonialism and imperialism, very much including people who come from parts of the world where prophecy per se, as well as Abrahamic models of authority more generally that are connected to such prophetic origins, have no original purchase). Through this imposition of a globalized ontology (taking that word once again in its Fanonian sense), people "see" the power and authority of God, of nature, of reason, of the state, and of law even though at their origins these things have no empirical or material basis.[21] Like the colonel in Kafka's parables, we assume that the "eyes" of the representatives of that power are also the eyes of that power itself and so people, in turn, "see" the way they are told to see, always at their own expense and never in ways that accord with their own separate and collective understandings and experiences.

In discussing these forms of perspective, in some sense I am arguing for something different from what Michel Foucault talked about when he described the panopticon. In his telling, the panopticon is a guard tower with slender windows so that the person being viewed (initially a prisoner but later just about everyone) must always assume that the guard is watching them to the point where that guard is internalized and each person effectively watches (and controls) themselves.[22]

What I am talking about in this book is not quite the same thing. Here, the fear is not that you are being watched but the opposite; the fear is that at any given point, no one might be watching you. Falling out of the gaze of the ruler implies a kind of abyss of meaninglessness, the threat of which is a key part of how archism manages to maintain a hold on its subjects, how it gets them to desire their own submission to its ruling logics. Perhaps even more accurately, this fear is based on having adopted for oneself the view from that tower; people see themselves, as it were, through the guard's eyes, through what they imagine to be the perspective from inside the tower. The desire to be viewed then corresponds to a desire to *be* that guard, to be viewing from that perspective, taking it on as one's own.[23]

Because archism transfers the tangibility of human life to itself, our actual life begins to seem empty and shapeless and so we begin to project onto that life the very ephemeral nature of archism that now appears to us to be firm and utterly real, effectively swapping our life and agency for its deathliness and nihilism. This is a key way by which archism comes to dominate over anarchist life. Yet the fact that this transfer is not actual means that archism can never fully replace anarchist life because its own sense of tangibility is only generated from the transfer of that sense of reality from anarchist life itself. This is a transfer that is never complete but always ongoing and therefore reversible.

As a result of this, in the face of the desires that archism creates in its subjects, there is an answering anarchist form of desire as well: not so much a desire to be seen but to *see together* with others in one's own community. This other desire helps prevent archism from becoming totalizing. The desire to see together, to determine collectively what it is that is being looked at, what it all means, and what to do about it—even if a community doesn't end up producing some harmonious consensus (which is itself a phantasm of archism)—allows people to engage in anarchist politics even under conditions of archist power. This other desire, this other way of seeing, is always present but largely unrecognized because the mechanism of recognition is itself so deeply bound up with archism. In this book, I try to change the focus from the spectacularity of archism to the collectivity of anarchism as a way to trace this other way of seeing and wanting.

Accordingly, in what follows, I will try to think about a resistant and anarchist form of prophecy, one that has no special sight, that only sees what the community (also) decides that it sees. Such a form of seeing is messy; it does not have the top-down unity of archist forms of sight. It is never harmonious or fully coherent. For this reason, the insights of such a form of vision tend to be quieter and more subsumed than archist forms of sight. Anarchist vision is always present but usually overwritten by the spectacle and pomp of archist vision.

Collective sight is itself a form—really *the* form—of anarchist prophecy, but for much of this book I will focus on a transitional figure, not the anarchist prophecy of the community per se but of a specific individual within that community. The role of the individual anarchist prophet is to hold the form of collective sight when the community does not recognize it itself, much like the intrepid citizen of Babel that I previously envisioned. Her job is to spread disappointment, to ruin archist forms of vision, and to return the power of collective sight back to the community. This anarchist prophet brings such sight from the background to the foreground, so that it competes with and even displaces its archist rival and predator.

Yet I want to be clear from the outset that, although much of this book will focus on individual anarchist prophets, figures that I will draw from actual history as well as from literature and philosophy, they are not actually what lies at the heart of this book. For me, these prophets are only meant to counter the false, archist prophecy that has structured our sight for so very long. They are meant, like Moses, to get us to the promised land but cannot join us there themselves. They are a transitional figure. In fact, they *must* be transitional. To be effective, anarchist prophets often look very much like archist ones; they may even share some elements of archism itself. This gives them a critical advantage in that they (therefore) have the same access to the subjects of archism as their fully archist counterparts. Working from within the confines of archist authority, they can usurp that authority for anarchist purposes. Their form of vision seems to come from the same exalted heights as that of archist vision itself. In a sense, these prophets serve to betray and undermine archism from within and by its very own devices.

This ability, while critical, also poses a threat to the very collective vision that they serve to promote. For one thing, it is a very easy thing for an anarchist prophet to cease her subversion of archist vision and join the ranks of those who promote and perpetuate archism as such. I will provide a few examples of this happening in later chapters in this book. But even if she does not do this, even if she remains true to her original and subversive purpose, an anarchist prophet always poses a threat to her community. This is because if an anarchist prophet was always required for a community to see for itself, that would in effect make her an archist prophet after all. The community would effectively be seeing with her eyes instead of its own. For an anarchist prophet to really succeed, she must make herself entirely redundant. She holds collective sight for a community at a time when it fails to realize the way that it is itself continually engaged in such a form of vision, but she does not—nor could she—form that vision by or for herself. Insofar as anarchist prophetic sight is always collective, one person cannot by definition constitute that collective on her own. The anarchist prophet's role is to disappoint the community from the false sight, the lies and violence of archism, and, by that act, permit that vision to return to the people from whom it was stolen.

Layout of the Rest of the Book

In the chapters that follow, I describe the nature of anarchist prophecy, what it is, how it functions, and how it might be enhanced. Each chapter adds something distinct to the argument and, as the book develops, so does the overall argument about the nature and possibility of anarchist prophecy.

The following four chapters of the book form part I. In each of these chapters, I look at an anarchist response to and undermining of the theological and philosophical functions of archism.

Chapter 1 details archist prophecy, its connection to the Hebrew and Greek prophetic tradition, and the corresponding form of anarchist prophecy that arises in response to that tradition.

Chapter 2 is about how Thomas Hobbes—ordinarily considered one of the key architects of modern sovereignty and therefore the contemporary face of archism as well—demonstrates that language and theology, which are two main foundations for archism, are themselves actually anarchist and prophetic functions, reflecting the ferment of life itself in all its variety. In this way, Hobbes undermines his own archist tendencies. Hobbes also offers us one of the purest forms of anarchist prophecy in his understanding of the figure of the Holy Spirit, a figure that is wholly and only about interpretation and the refusal of one central and organizing truth.

In chapter 3, I argue that Friedrich Nietzsche's Zarathustra is a prophet who has all the appearances of being an archist prophet (and sometimes *is* an archist prophet) and who thereby manages to ruin that position from within, causing maximum damage. I also claim that the overman is a figure of ultimate disappointment in that so much is promised with this figure but we come to see that this is a messiah who will never actually arrive, depriving the would-be subject of their salvation of any hope and thereby throwing them to their own devices.

In chapter 4, I look at the way Walter Benjamin offers us both a disappointing prophet, the angel of history, and an understanding of a God who is herself anarchist so that the very origins of appointing vision become a basis for anarchist resistance. Benjamin's focus is always on what he calls "the living," that is, that vast ferment of anarchist life that is deeply connected to the material world around us.

In Part II of the book, chapters 5 and 6 demonstrate how the central promises that archism makes are undermined and disappointed by a series of real-life as well as literary (including television) prophetic figures.

Chapter 5 engages with the question of how anarchism can fight with and thrive under ongoing archist conditions, how anarchist prophecy deals with its own entanglements with archism. I look at four "case studies," as it were, to do this: anarcho-syndicalism during the Spanish Revolution of the 1930s; the contemporary Rojavan Revolution in northeastern Syria; and then, turning to literature, José Saramago's two-novel sequence, *Blindness* and *Seeing*; and Octavia Butler's two-novel Earthseed series. The two pairings, one political and one literary, are meant to contrast an ideal, or near ideal, case (Spanish anarchism; Saramago's *Seeing*, which describes a "plague" of anarchism) with a more compromised and problematic case (Rojava and the Earthseed series), demonstrating varying methods of resistance, with varying results as well.

In chapter 6, I also look at four case studies, this time focusing on the question of whether archism can be defeated and eliminated, at least for a time. Here again, albeit in reverse order, I pair more and less perfect examples of anarchism, focusing on how they reduce or eliminate archism entirely. I begin with a reading of Baruch Spinoza, who offers a homegrown Western form of resistance to archism via a doctrine of radical immanentism. I then look at the case of Yali, a prophet from the Rai Coast of New Guinea who lived in the first half of the twentieth century and whose culture had no sense of the transcendent, making the usual lies of archism difficult, if not impossible, to sustain. I then turn to two literary readings, first Mary Shelley's *Frankenstein*, which steals from archism its greatest conceit, that it can offer (and control) eternal life; and then the television show (and novel) *The Leftovers*, which imagines a complete breakdown of archism and what might possibly result from that loss. Here too, the somewhat more problematic or entangled case (Spinoza and *Frankenstein*) is paired with a more successful, "purer" example (Yali and *The Leftovers*).

In the conclusion, I argue that anarchism is the only possible source of political authority (archism merely steals or "borrows" from it) and then look at a few more real-life anarchist prophets who are, in each case, connected to some specific community or set of communities: José Carlos Mariátegui's notion of Inca communism, Emma Goldman and her connection to the US anarchist movement(s), and Frantz Fanon and his connection to the Black Power movement in the United States in the 1960s and today. Finally, I end the book by further considering the connection between anarchism and life as well as archism and death.

The anarchist prophets that I describe in these chapters are as different from one another as could be. Some of them are works of pure fiction, while others are very real, figures from anarchism's own long history. The mixture of philosophy, political theology, literature, and real-life analysis allows me to get at the phenomenon of anarchist prophecy from a variety of angles. The philosophical and theological readings allow me to get to the conceptual roots of archism and challenge it at that level. The real-life examples show us what is actually possible, how anarchism works and how archism can be, and has been, defeated, as well as what obstacles and limitations anarchism faces in its confrontation with archist power. The literary examples show how we can think differently about the nature and lastingness of archism, including imagining the death of archism, something that otherwise seems unthinkable from our own current position. Collectively, these chapters are intended to serve as a kind of map of the struggle with archism, the way that its seeming absolute grip on collective life may be thwarted, and also some of the dangers and pitfalls inherent to that struggle.

Seeing like an Anarchist

In order to set up the chapters that follow, some basic points must first be explained in greater detail. The first point has to do with modes of seeing and how anarchist sight actually works, what it "looks like." In *Seeing like a State*, James C. Scott shows how the state requires vast modes of enforced homogenization, to make the citizens, lands, and objects of the state uniform and thereby taxonomizable. In this way, the state can "see" all that it surveys; those homogenized bodies become legible to the state on its own terms and thereby more subject to its control.

I want to be clear from the outset that I do not consider the state to be the only or even the prime mode of archist expression. There are myriad forms that Western-style archism takes, ranging from capitalism and white supremacy to more amorphous things like particular forms of culture and ideology. But, at least for the time being, the state is a key example of archism and so its form of sight is important to understand and counter.

In this book, I will consider how to "see like an anarchist," that is, to see and engage with the messy, competing, contingent, and episodic moments of action, decision, and collective forms of vision that constitute the very same communities that archism seeks to control. In a sense, anarchist sight organizes just as much as archist sight does, but it organizes horizontally, among and between the community rather than from above. Rather than seek to homogenize all that it surveys, anarchist sight seeks to allow and incorporate the messiness of life, the complexity and heterogeneity of selves, to assert their own forms of mutuality and their own complexity (unlike archist vision, anarchist vision is never one but always many).

The good news about this point is that anarchist vision happens all the time; as Hobbes will show, communities are always engaged in collective, and prophetic, acts of seeing whether they want to do so or not. But with the overarching spectacle of archist authority eclipsing those forms of vision and sight, communities lose a sense of their own power to judge and see and defer to those archist modes of sight that always seek to replace and overwrite them.

The Naked Emperor

A second point to stress at the outset has to do with what, exactly, the individual anarchist prophet does through her act of seeing. As will become clearer in the subsequent chapters, the role of the anarchist prophet, the one who brings disappointment, is very challenging. It might seem as though her job is merely to point out that the "emperor has no clothes," but this is an overly simplified and misleading rendition of what she does. In fact, the point is not that the emperor has no clothes; it's that there is no emperor without their clothes. In his work on German *trauerspiel* (mourning plays), Benjamin tells us that when it comes to kings and other leaders, "the purple must cover it."[24] It is not their self or their body but the color purple in this case—a color associated with royalty—that makes the king or emperor an authority figure; it is their endowment with the transitive elements of authority and power that lets us know this person has been marked as special and "better" than the rest of us (just like the colonel in Kafka's parable is marked as superior in ways that are both visible and invisible).

There is therefore no "truth" revealed in the notion that the emperor has no clothes because in shedding his clothes, the emperor has also shed this marker. In some sense, a naked emperor is not an emperor at all, so that the king's authority is not actually about his body—all two of them!—after all but about the signs and markers by which that body is deemed to be kingly.

Here again, we see that the role of the anarchist prophet is therefore not to tell the truth ("the emperor is naked!") but to show how untruths are constructed around human bodies, architectural symbols, and other objects that become sites of archist projection. By identifying and exposing that projection, the anarchist prophet seeks to ruin or subvert the archist effect, canceling out its projective power with a counterprojective form of sight. Hers is less a power of seeing and more a matter of unseeing and teaching others how to unsee as well. Everything that follows, all the responses, decisions, and so forth—that is, the effects of disappointment—must occur at the level of the community as a whole and not, once again, at the level of the anarchist prophet herself.[25]

The Master Sense

One related point that I want to make concerns treating vision as the archon of human senses. As with all things archist, this form of sight does not involve the physicality of vision so much as a false sense that it superimposes over that and all other senses.[26] Here, as with all aspects of archism, a real thing (in this case, vision and seeing) becomes associated with an unreal thing so that the unreal steals its tangibility from the real, superseding it in the process. Hostile to and alien from all manners of human life, archism teaches us that sight is the most important and privileged of the senses even as it robs us of our own collective forms of sight in the process.

My focus on anarchist sight as a way to combat archist vision serves to get the master "sense" to be turned against itself. Since it is in fact no sight at all, archist forms of vision readily return to the nothingness from which they issue. But this nothingness is not easily achieved since we are all invested in it as the way that we "really" see (albeit not all to the same degree), and hence sense the world around us. Insofar as we are taught that sight organizes the world—"seeing like a state," among other variations—anarchist forms of vision, which we are never without, must nevertheless be made legible to us.

The difficulty here stems in part from the fact that anarchism as such never privileges one sense over the others. The anarchist alternative to archism is never as uniform or coherent as the archist model, and this means that, just as with everything else, sight is not dominant. Thus a spectacular and uniform mode of vision (archism) must be superseded by a medley of senses (anarchism) that does not possess this kind of character. Not unlike a former heroin addict who finds ordinary life to be without character compared to what their addiction supplies and must relearn to appreciate and respond to the world as such and how they might experience it, the archist subject too must learn to recognize and appreciate the sensorium itself, the material context within which human life is always suspended even as it does not always recognize it. More precisely, this subject must (re)learn to "see" in concert with others, not in a harmonious and transcendent way but in a way that recognizes human plurality and collective acts of interpretation (and prophecy). This transition is a key role for the anarchist prophet who both "sees both ways" (as we all do) and is in a position to do something about it (as we generally are not).

With the unmaking or at least diminishment of sight as the key sense, other senses and other ways of being political come to the fore. Peter Goodrich speaks of "proboscations," wherein smell gets its turn as a form of judgment and decision (he tells us, for example, that "the genius of the law is in its nose").[27] Kafka's work (as Benjamin points out) is full of vapors and stenches that strongly affect his characters and are key anchors of plot.[28] Other thinkers point to the power of sound and taste and touch; all form part of the human sensorium and are part of the ferment of anarchist life and exist (as Kafka ably shows) even amid the rule of archist vision and sight. In the pages that follow, I will pay attention to these other senses, including the actual, as opposed to the phantasmic, visual, as they come to the fore.

Archism and the Question of Blame

Another important point has to do with the question of whether communities are to be blamed for their own complicity with, or desire for, archism, something that may be suggested by Kafka's parables in particular. I think it would be a grave mistake to draw this conclusion. It is true that we are all in various and differing ways invested in archism even if we hate its effects and the power it has over us. Even Black, Brown, and Indigenous people, women, the poor, queer, trans, and disabled people, those who most suffer from the effects of archist lies, often participate to some extent in archist forms of vision (although I also think the overlay of that vision onto their own collective forms of sight is less convincing and far less alluring). It is precisely this double form of vision that Fanon sought to address and alter.

All of this is only to say that people are produced as subjects through a relationship to archism and so they come to want what it tells them to want, at least to a certain extent. In my view, it is not people's desires per se that are the problem insofar as what archism promises; safety, health, happiness, tranquility, fulfillment, and maybe even eternal life are not in and of themselves bad things. I think instead that the problem we have with anarchism is one of trust. Simply put, people do not trust in their own ways of doing things; their own judgments and powers and acts are not deemed to be valid in and of themselves. This is because people are taught that the only guarantor in the world comes from the externalities, phantom (but "higher, better") sources of authority and expertise, that serve as the basis for archist authority. Given the supersession of our own forms of collective judgment, interpretation, and vision by archist phantasms, those forms lose their own luster, diminished by the vampiric transfer of tangibility that is the basis for archism.

Archism perpetually reproduces itself by insisting that, were it not for the law, the state, and other archist institutions, we would all be stabbing each other within five minutes. In other words, our tendency toward peaceableness is taken as a sign of the success of archism in controlling us rather than something that people are capable of on their own.

There is no corresponding anarchist guarantor to counter archist promises of life, riches, and happiness. Anarchism offers no guarantees at all and in fact the very concept of a guarantee is itself a marker of archism as a system that is based on deception and illusion. I argue both in chapter 2 (on Hobbes) and in the conclusion that the anarchist answer to the problem of trust is not to offer more false guarantees but to recognize that the community is itself the only possible source of authority and that archism has stolen that authority and claimed it as its own. Thus, what we are "trusting" when we turn to the state and other archist structures is in fact only our own, now alienated, collective power, robbing ourselves of our ability to relocate that trust back where it belongs in the process.

The job of the anarchist prophet is to steal this authority back and return it to the community from which it was taken. The anarchist prophets that I will be describing are no less compromised than the rest of us when it comes to desiring what archism tells them to desire. These prophets must engage in the mechanisms of archism in order to be able to ruin it from within, but even as they do so, they feel and are drawn to its seductive power. For this reason, rather than show a series of perfect examples of anarchist prophecy, I will show a series of flawed and inconstant characters (especially in chapter 5). Some of the figures I will treat are ever on the verge of succumbing to archism themselves and some actually do succumb. None of them perfectly and purely manage the confluences of archist and anarchist forms of prophecy. Yet these characters, in all their complexity, show us that archism can be beaten at its own game. What issues from that defeat is not a perfect world free from archist temptation but just an opening, a moment when archism is not such a sure thing that it doesn't even need to have a name.

Why Talk of God (and Prophets)?

Another point I wish to consider here has to do with the question of theology and what kind of claims this book is making about the role of God and of Abrahamic understandings of God more specifically. In my view, this book is actually about what Maria Aristodemou calls "atheism," not the false secularity of liberalism—and of contemporary forms of archism more generally—but a form of politics that turns to human communities rather than external powers for the source of and inspiration for political life.[29] To the faux void that archism uses for its own purposes, I would counterpoise a different kind of void, a negation of the (false) negation, if you will. The anarchist readings of God that I am putting forth here offer two options: that God does not exist at all and the void is just that, an empty space that has no content whatsoever (Nietzsche's notion that God is dead may also suggest this way of thinking, although this is a complicated claim); or that God is herself an anarchist.

If the former is the case, then it becomes a matter of systematically finding all the places where a concept of God lurks (just about everywhere!) and negating them. If the latter is the case, God herself is seen as doing everything possible to prevent divine emanations from becoming hijacked by archist projections, an idea captured well by Benjamin's concept of divine violence. In either case, just as Benjamin offers a "real state of emergency" to counter the false emergencies that are the bases of archist forms of power, I would like to counterpose a "real void," a true negation, to the faux negative that archism requires in order to seem to stand outside itself and give itself a privileged perch from which to judge and rule the world.[30] The radical emptiness of the real void shows up the false emptiness of the archist version.

This book then takes a firmly agnostic stance on the existence of God, but I argue that in the end, it doesn't actually matter.[31] So long as the position that God is said to hold is seen as being utterly empty and without content, it serves to unmake the ultimate source of archism, regardless of the ways that we understand that emptiness. Insofar as God is taken as the ultimate archon, the heart of the emanations of archist projection, to radically void that space is to do an end run around the entire operation of archism, including its falsely secular models.

For this reason, we cannot leave a discussion of God out of the equation entirely because modern secularity, wherein any concept of God is simply dismissed, smuggles within itself an occult archist theology. Secularism therefore is not the correct model for a real atheology or atheism. As Aristodemou describes atheism, it consists in a form of "freedom from symbolic links, where the empty place is acknowledged and confronted in all its abyssal emptiness rather than being filled with idolatrous gods from laws to goods."[32] Some theological work must be done, some direct confrontation with the concept of God is required, in order to give us space from the mythic violence that is ceaselessly attributed to God (whether openly or stealthily).

The ubiquity of Abrahamic forms of understanding God and the divine more generally is a related issue of concern. I recognize that sticking to a language of prophecy, especially in terms of the way that I am approaching it, limits us to a largely Jewish or Christian approach to thinking about these issues. It involves Muslim viewpoints too, although the authors I engage with do not specifically evoke Islam. I do not think that the Western traditions I am drawing upon have any monopoly by any means on the nature and understanding of theology. My focus on the West and particularly its notions of prophecy, messianism, and God are a response to the fact that the West has spread itself via imperialism and globalism to false claims of universality, along with a concomitantly dominant form of Western archism. It is precisely this false Western universe that I would like to challenge, and so I go after its origins (its *arche*) in my response. Insofar as an Abrahamic God and, in particular, an Abrahamic understanding of prophecy, has become so widely globalized, it behooves us to look at the institutions of such prophecy to think further about how such worldwide hegemony can be beaten back (and by its own—prophetic—devices).

Furthermore, I do not mean to imply that Judaism and Christianity, the two main forms of Western theology I consider here, are inherently and only archist as such. Indeed, the authors I look to often find ways to subvert archism from within theological vocabularies that come from both traditions. Instead, I am trying to argue that these religions in particular have become the basis for contemporary archism through the process of translating from a religion to a particular political program and through the historical sedimentation of the historical relationships and effects of these religions on larger political communities.

We live in a time when so many of the world's religions are producing martial—and archist—forms of themselves. We see this in militant forms of Christian nationalism visible in Trump's United States, Vladimir Putin's Russia, Jair Bolsonaro's Brazil, and countless other examples. We see it too in Narendra Modi's promulgation of an intolerant and aggressive Hindutva; in militant Buddhism in Myanmar and Sri Lanka; in Benjamin Netanyahu's toxic form of Jewish nationalism; in militant forms of Islam, both associated with the state (Recep Tayyip Erdoğan) and without (Al Qaeda); and even in hybrid forms (the Islamic State in Iraq and Syria [ISIS]). We even see the aggressive promulgation of a kind of theocratic nationalism that has no formal religion associated with it, as in Xi Jinping's China.

I think it would be a grave mistake to lump all these forms together as simply variants of Western archism. Each religious tradition has its own trajectory and history and its own reception of and encounter with such archist forms. Yet the shared features—militant nationalism, extreme forms of racism, attacks on minority religions and communities, intense chauvinism—all point to a globalized phenomenon and are indications (as if we needed one!) that the theological is not yet done with us even if many of us are done with it.

As I read it, these various movements share a sense of threat wherein their own forms and degrees of archism are under assault. It makes sense to me that, as that sense of threat deepens—that is, after decades of neoliberalism, as the grave inequalities that untrammeled archism produces become more of a threat to its main functions in terms of capitalism and various modes of racial supremacy—the more its original and underlying theological nature comes to the fore. The disguise of secularism was always thin, but it may be especially so in our own time. For this reason, to avoid the language of God and prophets is, in some sense, to avoid the elephant in the room, the theological bases of our current dilemmas, and to miss an opportunity to think about what a true atheism (and corresponding anarchism) would look like.[33]

What Kind of Anarchism?

A final point has to do with terminology. In terms of making larger claims about archism per se, I am making no grand statement about archism in general, which has a long and variegated history. When I use that term, I will almost always be referring to Western archism. The archism that I am addressing here, with its roots in ancient Greece and Israel, is the archism of liberal capitalist universalism, the archism of contemporary modes of neoliberalism, state-sponsored racism, and other mechanisms that make up the contemporary world, recognizing that that world is changing and that other players like China, India, and Russia are working to alter that equation. I don't think this is the final and ultimate form of archism so much as the present and most pernicious form of archism in the world today.

The same is true for the anarchism that I am describing here, although in quite the opposite way. That is, even as use of the term *archism* seeks to locate and reduce the Western variant to its origins, my use of the term *anarchism* exceeds the normal use of that to become a kind of planetary, if not universal, point of reference. I recognize that my use of the term *anarchism* in this book may seem surprising to many readers as I associate it not just with the trappings of a particular political form connected to Mikhail Bakunin and Peter Kropotkin and on through Emma Goldman and into the contemporary moment of the antifa but with life itself. In doing so, I seek to unshackle the term *anarchism* from its narrow meaning (without, however, abandoning that connection entirely) and its entirely Western associations. In *Decolonizing Anarchism*, Maia Ramnath makes an important distinction between "the concept of anarchism and the Circle-A brand."[34] While the latter is specific to the Western left tradition, she explains that "with a small *a*, the word anarchism implies a set of assumptions and principles, a recurrent tendency or orientation—with the stress on movement in a direction, not a perfected condition—toward more dispersed and less concentrated power; less top-down hierarchy and more self-determination through bottom-up participation; liberty and equality seen as directly rather than inversely proportional;

the nurturance of individuality and diversity within a matrix of interconnectivity, mutuality, and accountability; and an expansive recognition of the various forms that power relations can take, and correspondingly, the various dimensions of emancipation."[35]

Using this other description, Ramnath can associate the term *anarchism* with movements and politics that have little to do with the West and in fact are often diametrically opposed to it (in her case, she describes a great deal of anarchist politics with regard to South Asia). I argue that this other, broader, "small *a*" anarchism is a condition that all of us on this planet share, that it is a matter of life itself and how that life is lived in all its messy and beautiful variety.

If the name *anarchism* can be used without necessarily invoking all the specific baggage of Western anarchist traditions, it helps draw our attention to our life as such in ways that do not automatically condemn us to just more archism. This kind of anarchism may go under different names and have very different forms. Some of the examples that I associate with this larger form of anarchism may raise some eyebrows in that their own authors use other terms (like communism in the case of Mariátegui and Benjamin) to describe themselves and their belief systems. And it might seem peculiar or even perverse to speak of Yali as an "anarchist prophet" when he has nothing to do with the tradition coming from Bakunin (nor Abraham, for that matter). But I think that the kind of collective behaviors I am talking about are, if not universal (because that is a claim that is too fraught with archist pieties, although I think Butler, among others, does some good work in challenging that universe on its own terms), then, once again, at least planetary.[36]

In speaking of anarchism in this way, I am talking about a phenomenon that comes directly out of life itself and, as such, goes by many names but which shares the quality of both being ruled by and resisting, by its very existence, archist predations. It is this life that anarchist prophecy addresses. To the extent that such prophecy melds into that life, it succeeds, whereas to the extent that it holds itself aloof from that life, it just becomes another iteration of archist predation, setting up the central challenge that this book proposes to address.

part i

chapter one

appointing prophets

Seeing like an Archist

TO BETTER ESTABLISH THE BASES OF MY ARGUMENT, let me first focus a bit more on the question of what this book is opposing, namely the appointing vision of archist prophecy. As we saw in Kafka's "The City Coat of Arms," the idea that a giant fist, a clear manifestation of actual and undeniable archist power and authority—just imagine whose arm is attached to such a fist!—comes in the form of a prophecy. Here, the prophecy tells us something deeply basic about the community as a whole; this prophecy serves as the site where the day-to-day life of a community (in this case, the city built around a central void) comes to meet the imagined source of authority (in this case, the void itself), giving the latter a similar sense of reality and, at least by analogy, a transference of its own palpability. The prophecy of a giant fist coming out of heaven helps articulate not just the ordinary ways in which authority is internalized and obeyed but also the most profound ways in which the material existence of this ghostly source of authority is needed, depended on, and effectively imagined—and visualized—into being. The giant fist's visitation to the city completes a process whereby reality itself is transferred from the material city to the celestial ruler, finally switching roles by reducing the city to the nothingness that originally belonged to the heavens (and presumably finally and wholly itself becoming real in the process).

This prophecy articulates an attitude that is being generated by the community as a whole but also serves to ensure that there is something in this wish that is *not* from the community, something that is above or beyond the people in question. We learn from Niccolò Machiavelli in his description of Numa, the second king of Rome—and the person that he considers to be Rome's true founder—that for people to obey a law, they must come to believe it has an external and transcendent source. In Numa's case, he lied and said that the laws he provided the Romans with were given to him by a goddess, making him an early practitioner of archist prophecy and appointing vision.[1]

For such an externality to actually work as a way to undergird human-derived law, it must be located beyond but not be utterly detached from the human sensorium; there must be some kind of anchor or attachment that connects the two realms in a way that makes it possible for people to effectively alienate their own authority and worship it in an external form. Acts of archist prophecy like Numa's—complete with the tablets that such laws are engraved on, the entire legal apparatus that it sets up, and even the tangible mental picture of Numa's claim to have actually met a goddess—are what allow the immaterial to take on a material form, to enter into something akin to what Louis Althusser calls the realm of ideology, wherein various actions, sites, speech acts, and the like form the material basis of this ghostly externalized source of authority (in a word, archism).[2]

Akin, but not exactly the same thing. It is important to speak of prophecy and not just a more secular term like propaganda or ideology, which, in its Althusserian form, might be considered to be an effect of prophecy. In speaking of prophecy, we are talking about the most basic foundations of what passes for and forms reality, for what, once again, Fanon calls "ontology." More accurately, I think this is what Althusser himself means by ideology, but to call this prophecy includes its historical and theological origins (something that Althusser himself recognizes), its longest lasting and deepest form that any specific ideology must accommodate itself to. From this perspective, the concept of reality as an unproblematical, apolitical, and wholly secular category may itself be one of the most phantasmic concepts there is.

The concept of prophecy points to the way that such a profound realignment of reality is possible: how it has changed over time and how it can be changed again. Secularism tends to hide its connection to the theological organization of its own sense of reality behind a show of empiricism (think of Samuel Johnson kicking his rock). Yet to think in terms of political theology openly admits of the ways that the world can be entirely remade, reenvisioned, and reseen at the most basic and profound level, at the very foundation of the way that "reality" gets organized and experienced. In a nutshell, the only way to get at the profoundly theological bases of archism is via a countertheology; archist forms of appointing vision must be met with anarchist forms of disappointment.

Learning to See Archism: *The Castle*

An example of how archist appointing power works can be seen in yet another of Kafka's writings, *The Castle*, which could be read as a book-length treatment of "The City Coat of Arms" and "The Refusal." In this book, Kafka shows not only the origins of archist prophecy but also the way that it actively organizes the world, the way that it commands us to see things we would not otherwise see. In *The Castle*, the main character, K., comes to a village that, it would seem—certainly we are told—is dominated by a great castle. We never actually get to see the inside of the castle (no one in the village does either), but it becomes increasingly questionable whether the castle is empty or, even more to the point, whether there even *is* a castle in this village at all.

When K. first arrives in the village, he cannot initially see the castle. Kafka writes: "There was no sign of the Castle hill, fog and darkness surrounded it, not even the faintest gleam of light suggested the large Castle. K. stood a long time on the wooden bridge that leads from the main road to the village, gazing upward into the seeming emptiness."[3] We dismiss this initial invisibility as irrelevant, due to the fact that it is nighttime. The void into which he is staring *must* contain a castle; the very title of the book demands as much!

The next day, K. makes a determined effort to actually get to the castle, but the roads he takes all lead him back down toward the village. Even from a relatively closer position and in broad daylight, try as he might, he can never really quite make out the castle's form. As K. approaches: "On the whole the Castle, as it appeared from this distance, corresponded to K.'s expectations. It was neither an old knight's fortress nor a magnificent new edifice, but a large complex made up of a few two-story buildings and many lower, tightly packed ones; had one not known that this was a castle, one could have taken it for a small town. K. saw only one tower, whether it belonged to a dwelling or a church was impossible to tell."[4] Here, it becomes increasingly possible that the castle doesn't actually exist, but in some sense it doesn't really matter if it exists or not: K. is busily organizing the visual field that he is presented with to "see" the castle no matter what.[5]

This visual organization does not come automatically or readily to K. He is shown to be learning to transform the scene before his eyes according to "higher" logics that he is continually incorporating. Indeed, in the very next passage, Kafka writes:

> Keeping his eyes fixed upon the Castle, K. went ahead, nothing else mattered to him. But as he came closer he was disappointed [*enttäuschte*] in the Castle, it was only a rather miserable little town, pieced together from village houses, distinctive only because everything was perhaps built of stone, but the paint had since flaked off, and the stone seemed to be crumbling. Fleetingly K. recalled his old hometown, it was scarcely inferior to this so-called Castle; if K. had merely wanted to visit it, all that wandering would have been in vain, and it would have made more sense for him to visit his old homeland again, where he had not been in such a long time.[6]

Here, we see that K. experiences a moment of disappointment in his attempts to see the castle. Left to his own devices, he makes his own decisions about what he is seeing. But this disappointment is not sustained; K. lives in a community that fervently believes in the castle. Such a castle cannot be disappointing; on the contrary, it must be everything that the villagers ascribe to it. It must be perfect, beautiful, magnificent, a suitably spectacular anchor for all their desires and phantasms.

K.'s training to see the castle in this way starts moments after the disappointing sight just mentioned. He runs into a schoolteacher who is a strict enforcer of village orthodoxy. They have the following exchange: "'You're taking a look at the Castle?' [the teacher] asked, more gently than K. had expected, but as though he did not approve of what K. was doing. 'Yes,' said K., 'I'm a stranger here, I only arrived yesterday evening.' 'You don't like the Castle?' the teacher said quickly. 'What?' countered K., somewhat baffled, but then, rephrasing the question more delicately, he said: 'Do I like the Castle? What makes you think I don't like it?' 'Strangers never do,' said the teacher."[7]

In this exchange, we see more than a hint of menace in the teacher's approach to K. Anticipating a fresh, undetermined approach to the castle, the teacher knows the kinds of impressions that K. will have (impressions that the schoolteacher may share even as he overrides that sight with archist forms of sight both for himself and for others). Without saying so directly, the teacher is, as may be appropriate to his profession, schooling K. in how to see or, perhaps more accurately, how not to see. That is, he is helping K. overcome his disappointment and replacing his own determination of what he is looking at with an externalized, appointing, and archist vision that the villagers all collectively enforce.

Accordingly, over the course of the novel, K. learns how to see the castle "correctly." Everything else that happens in the novel follows from his initiation into appointing sight. Much later in the novel, we see K. experiencing the castle in a way that reflects his own lessons in archist forms of seeing.

> The Castle, whose contours were already beginning to dissolve, lay still as ever, K. had never seen the slightest sign of life up there, perhaps it wasn't even possible to distinguish anything from this distance, *and yet his eyes demanded it and refused to tolerate the stillness.* When K. looked at the Castle, it was at times as if he were watching someone who sat there calmly, gazing into space, not lost in thought and therefore cut off from everything, but free and untroubled; as if he were alone, unobserved; and yet it could not have escaped him that someone was observing him, but this didn't disturb his composure and indeed—one could not tell whether through cause or effect—the observer's gaze could not remain fixed there, and slid off.[8]

Here, we see a description of the enforcing power of appointing vision at work. K.'s eyes now "demanded [to see signs of life] and refused to tolerate the stillness." What he sees is not the castle itself but the imagined gazer looking outward. It is, in fact, not K.'s eyes that produce the demand to see in this way but the imagined eyes of this observing figure. Seeing the world through this figure's eyes, K. is not the central object of that sight; he becomes just one facet in a vast landscape that is determined and ordered by this act of appointing vision. It is this other viewer's eyes, in fact, that "demand" to see the castle in a certain way, that is operative. Accordingly, countless moments of ordinary sight, on the part of both K. and the villagers, are ceaselessly given over to and incorporated by the archist gaze. Here we see that ordinary and anarchist acts of individual and collective vision become hijacked and reorganized by the centrality of archist vision.

In rendering the assertion of phantasm and desire so legible as a function of archist belief structures (as with Machiavelli telling the story of Numa), Kafka is engaging in a radical subversion of the truth-making power that the story might otherwise convey. Does it ruin the power of the castle if we catch it in the act of being produced as a visual object? Is there a way to extend and expand on the exposure of archist phantasm and the prophetic forms of sight that bring it into the world? And how much agency do the villagers—or political subjects more generally, insofar as in some sense we all live in the village at the foot of the castle—have in terms of taking charge of their own visual field?

To answer some of these questions, we must turn in a more explicitly theological direction than Kafka himself offers, at least on the surface of this text. There have been many attempts to read *The Castle* as either a theological or secular text. The very fact that this distinction cannot be successfully resolved may speak to the way that theology and secularity are themselves very hard to untangle in the modern Western mode. There are no mentions of God or prophets as such in the book, but the very idea of invisible things determining visible ones, of a metaphysics of higher and lower utterly determining a real and actual village, are in and of themselves inherently theological concepts. For this reason, if Kafka teaches us to look at how archism functions, we must look elsewhere, to earlier traditions that he draws upon (and gleefully subverts), to understand the mode of prophetic sight as such.

The Prophetic Origins of Archism

In terms of thinking about the theological and prophetic origins of archist vision, it is necessary to start with the specific traditions that it comes from, at least in its Western form. Archism may, once again, not be exclusive to the West; the West has no monopoly on hierarchy or rule, but through colonialism and global capitalism, the West has spread its model far and wide. This model in turn has a specific origin in two traditions, namely those of the ancient Hebrews and the ancient Greeks.

As a rule, those of us who have been subjectivized by Western forms of political and economic power tend to think of prophecy in strictly archist terms; prophets are the ones who can see what others cannot. This view reflects a long cultural and theological history. In the Jewish and Christian traditions—and, generally speaking, in the Islamic tradition as well—prophets are holy people, usually but not always men (think of Judith, Miriam, and Huldah, for example), who have access to forms of knowledge, judgment, and authority that are then given to the larger community. Usually it is held that the community in question is unaware of or even resistant to what the prophet sees, justifying the prophet's position above them. The prophet is understood to be speaking and acting for the greater good, sharing their special sight with the rest of the community for the sake of everyone. Finally, it is normally (but critically not universally) understood that the prophetic tradition has now largely ended, that we live in a "post-prophetic" time when God no longer speaks directly to us through emissaries and that we must strive to conform to God's laws and demands through a now largely absent prophetic history (in this way cementing the power of prophecy without the ongoing threat of new prophets that might disrupt the old orthodoxies).[9]

To be sure, the prophets that come through the Abrahamic tradition are not necessarily always in the business of shoring up their particular government or political form. The prophets of the Hebrew Bible often rail against the status quo. Even in our own "post-prophetic" times, modern figures deemed to be speaking with a prophetic voice (Martin Luther King Jr. and Nelson Mandela spring immediately to mind) often come from a leftist perspective, critical of power structures that are oppressive and hierarchical.[10] Archism and anarchism are intimately intertwined so even a prophet who speaks from the left is not immune to archist elements (and the reverse is also true).

Perhaps most critically, in thinking about such modern-day prophets, we should focus not on the views of the prophets themselves but on the way that they are regarded by a receptive community. To think that what these visionaries had to convey was specific to themselves and was something that other people could not see on their own, regardless of the context of their insights, tends to effectively put them in the camp of archist prophecy, at least in terms of the effects of their prophetic sight. If the insights that people take from a prophet seem to have come wholly from the prophet themselves or from whatever higher source they draw upon, this means that the community as such is effectively shut out from that wisdom except in the sense that they serve as its beneficiaries.

Put differently, archism is so good at adapting itself to every challenge that it can often absorb even direct rivals for its authority structures into itself. When we think that, were it not for this person/prophet, things would never have changed, or when we see their acts of prophecy as being part of "progress," a liberal narrative of teleology that is the direct opposite of anarchism, or an isolated incident never to be repeated again, we tend to lose the (anarchist) content for the (archist) form.[11]

The fact that, despite the claim that we no longer hear from God through the institution of prophecy, these prophets pop up every now and then anyway—often to the great detriment of archist plans—means that their insights have to be absorbed and co-opted into the archist web of power. This is often done, once again, by highlighting the way that *only* a Martin Luther King Jr. or a Nelson Mandela could have possibly understood and done what they did. This means the opposite too, of course, that *no one else* would have ever been able to think of these things on their own, rendering the communities in question further depoliticized even in the face of a claim for their rights and powers. To the degree that such narratives catch on (they don't always, fortunately), movements that might pose a real threat to established power systems can be co-opted and tamed, rendered into yet more fodder for archist vision and control. This is precisely where the question of anarchist prophecy and the way that it resists archist logics becomes so central. Prophecy can be both a source of ongoing orthodoxy and control or radical upheaval, depending on how these issues work themselves out.

Two Hebrew Prophets: Isaiah and Jeremiah

Of the two main sources of the Western prophetic tradition, the principal form is Abrahamic and, more particularly, the ancient Hebrew tradition as recorded in the Hebrew Bible. To better understand the Western form of archist prophecy, let me focus on two Hebrew biblical prophets, Isaiah and Jeremiah. Every Hebrew prophet brings something different, but these two might be considered exemplary figures, models for how (archist) prophecy is understood and enacted more generally. Critically, because God is undeniably *the* archon, the ur-archist, these prophets speak for a power that, though invisible, has an undeniable and irrefutable authority over the Earth, an understanding that some of the thinkers and writers that I treat—especially Friedrich Nietzsche, Walter Benjamin, and Octavia Butler—earnestly refute, often through the use of prophecy itself. The Hebrew prophets speak for (or as) the master of the universe and, in so doing, promote God's order, refashioning the world according to those models of divine vision.

The Book of Isaiah starts off with God speaking through the prophet, declaring that the Israelites have turned to sin. Isaiah says, "Ah, sinful nation, a people laden with iniquity, a seed of evil-doers, Children that deal corruptly! They have forsaken the LORD, they have contemned the Holy One of Israel, they turned away backward."[12] Here, the main sin of the Israelites is not their particular actions per se but a much graver sin as far as God is concerned, namely turning against God's rule, being disobedient subjects of divine authority.

As a consequence, Isaiah relates that the usual ways of appeasing God— offering sacrificial rams, burning incense, and the like—will no longer suffice. God speaks through Isaiah, stating that "your new moons and appointed seasons my soul hateth; they are a burden unto Me, I am weary to bear them."[13]

It seems clear that, given their rebellion against God's authority, the Israelites must become much more explicit in the way that they honor God; the nature of their subservience can no longer be demonstrated through symbolic gestures but must be delivered by decisive acts of contrition and servitude. Speaking through Isaiah, God makes it very clear that this kind of behavior is required or else the Israelites will be struck down. Isaiah states: "If ye be willing and obedient, ye shall eat the good of the land; but if ye refuse and rebel, ye shall be devoured with the sword; for the mouth of the LORD [that is to say, Isaiah himself] hath spoken."[14]

In reading this, we see an implicit promise being made by God. If the Israelites are with the Lord, they will be allowed to live (and not just live; they will "eat the good of the land"). If, on the other hand, they go against God, they will be smitten and they will die. This stark choice sets up the basis of archism's first principle, namely the promise of protection, of justice, and of a good life, but more basically just being allowed to live at all, if only one obeys. The promise also constitutes a fairly clear threat, the threat of death, destruction, and wretchedness if the Israelites do not do as they are told.

In this way, Isaiah's prophecy takes on an explicitly political form, setting up both political and legal modes of human authority and power even as it constitutes a pathway to obeying God (in the next chapter, I discuss how Hobbes considers the time of the Hebrew prophets, a period when God was in effect the king of ancient Israel). In this sense, the terrestrial political life of the Israelites is the site in which their theological obedience can and must be performed.

In a very well-known passage, Isaiah/God states:

It shall come to pass in the end of days, that the mountain of the house of the LORD's house shall be established as the top of the mountains, and shall be exalted above the hills, and all nations shall flow unto it and many peoples shall go and say: "Come ye, and let us go up to the mountain of the LORD . . ." For out of Zion shall go forth the law, and the word of the LORD from Jerusalem. He shall judge between the nations, and shall decide for many peoples; and they shall beat their swords into plowshares, and their spears into pruninghooks; nation shall not lift up sword against nation, neither shall they learn war any more.[15]

Here again, it seems like the purpose of this political order, the law and the word of God, serves not so much (or at least not only) as a way for the people to live a Godly life but also once again a way to demonstrate their fealty and subordination in all aspects of their life.

This passage also establishes the other key aspect of archism, namely God's power of judgment. God's judgment transcends all nations and even the world itself. No one is exempt from God's judgment (except for God, it would seem). That judgment produces peace—as the famous phrase about not "learn[ing] war any more" shows—but it also produces terror and pain, as when Isaiah says, "And the haughtiness of men shall be brought low; and the LORD alone will be exalted in that day."[16]

Ultimately the promise of life and the power of judgment become one and the same. God's judgment becomes the basis of life. God's judgment is not so much prepolitical as it is the stuff of politics, what politics is "made of," if you will. Isaiah's message is that there is no space on Earth that is free from God's power and obedience to God must be utter and unquestioned. Just as in the parables of Kafka, we know we are enveloped in this power when it goes against the things that we ourselves would rather do; there is a comfort here too in going against our own wishes, at least to some extent.

Jeremiah, another of the central prophets in the Hebrew Bible, also serves as an exemplar of the normative and archist mode of Abrahamic prophecy (as well as serving as the model for a particular subcategory of prophecy, the Jeremiad). The Book of Jeremiah helps us understand not only the exalted nature of God's power and judgment but also the visual regime that Jeremiah's relationship to God instantiates.

In this portrayal, the gift of prophecy (if a gift is the right word for what is an unwanted, unwilled, and absolute power) manifests itself as a visual power above all else. God asks Jeremiah what he sees, and as Jeremiah conveys the objects in his vision, God reinterprets and reenvisions these visions as being vehicles of divine agency.

> Moreover the word of the LORD came unto me, saying: "Jeremiah, what seest thou?" And I said, "I see a rod of an almond-tree."
>
> Then said the LORD unto me, "Thou hast well seen: for I will watch over my word to perform it."
>
> And the word of the LORD came unto me the second time, saying, "What seest thou?" And I said, "I see a seething pot; and the face thereof is from the north."
>
> Then the LORD said unto me, "Out of the north an evil shall break forth upon all the inhabitants of the land.[17]

Here, the seemingly neutral act of seeing becomes reorganized by God's words in such a way that the objects of sight become avatars of God's judgment. Telling Jeremiah that "I will watch over my word to perform it," God is explicitly testifying to the visual nature of divine power in the world. Accordingly, God will bring divine judgment into the world in a way that surpasses any form of human agency or resistance, once again rendering an otherwise intangible authority all too real and material.

God goes on to say that these visions will manifest themselves in terrible strife for Israel, which will in turn greatly resist this judgment. Yet, with God's power behind him, it seems that Jeremiah's prophecy is not only accurate but irresistible, a force to reshape—and revision—the world.

In thinking about these two prophets, we see exemplary instances of a form of archist prophecy that is repeated with some critical variations throughout the Hebrew Bible. Arguably, this remains the way that people in the West, and those subject to Western power (which is just about everyone else), think about what prophecy entails. It is one thing when this vision remains at an explicitly theological level; throughout this book, I give examples of how the Hebrew God has been radicalized, serving as a force for unmaking and resisting archism itself, not despite but because of the fact that it serves as a source for archist forms of authority. I will even argue through Hobbes that when God is "king" of ancient Israel, a much more anarchic kind of political community ensues. It is only when this doctrine becomes secularized and brought down to the human level—spoken for on behalf of human actors who claim the mantle of God's power and prophecy—that the fetishisms and projections of archism become deeply and horribly pernicious. Here, we are no longer really focusing on God per se but on God as an empty site upon which would-be archons project their own desires and phantasms, subjecting their fellow humans in the name of a God or other externality that they claim to speak for.

Privileging the kind of sight associated with such forms of prophecy contains within it the germ of Western archism, a model that ultimately supports hierarchical forms of politics, even when the politics being espoused may seem quite egalitarian. The original sight that sets up or alters these political forms, regardless of the content of its message, keeps within itself that basic distinction between the one who can see and the others who cannot. For this reason, the political results of such prophetic acts remain fundamentally archist and profoundly hierarchical as well.

Greek Forms of Prophecy

In speaking of the Western theological bases of archism, I would be remiss if I did not also mention the other—and non-Abrahamic—main source of appointing vision, namely the Greek tradition, which has its own prophetic modes (and, as we already saw, the Roman tradition had its own sense of prophecy as well). The Greek language is, after all, the source of the very word *archism* (and, by extension, of anarchism as well). This term comes from the Greek verb *arkein*, which means both to rule and to begin (to serve as an origin point).

Ancient Greece has a strong prophetic tradition of its own, ranging from the Delphic oracle to Tiresias the blind prophet of Apollo, who figures in several important Athenian plays. Sarah Iles Johnston tells us that the basic principle of Greek prophecy, especially for the Stoics, was based on the idea of *sympatheia*, the notion that the cosmos was held together by certain forces (for the Stoics it was *pneuma*, the divine breath) that caused disparate moments and events in time to be both interrelated and relatable.[18] In this way, acts of divination and prophecy are able to see the links between the divine determination of the objects and persons of the world, between the present and the future, and between acts that seem utterly disconnected but whose relationships become meaningful through the act of divination itself.[19] In this way too, the invisible becomes visible, the tangible becomes linked together via invisible threads, and people are taught how to see or read the world around them according to this prophetic and organizing logic.

In terms of the central and institutional structure of prophecy in ancient Greece, Johnston tells us that the most important thing about them was their location. She describes "[one] important characteristic that most ancient oracles shared: each was anchored to a specific place. Usually, there was a myth that told of how such a place was discovered, and what made each of them good for oracular activity."[20] Here, the location is critical because that space is somehow set aside from ordinary life and vision. It is understood that these acts of prophecy can only be uttered from that space. It is true that there was an entirely different category of independent prophets or *manteis* who were not bound to any particular spot, but the two main centers of prophecy of mainland Greece, Delphi and Dodona, were both sacred and unique, and generally the divinations that came from those places were considered far more prestigious and trustworthy than anything said by the *manteis*.[21]

Another key aspect of these major oracles was that their messages were ambivalent and had to be interpreted. Johnston cautions us that the popular modern idea that the Pythia, the oracle at Delphi, spoke in gibberish was not true; she spoke in normal sentences, either in prose or verse, but the meaning of these sentences still had to be interpreted. As information passed from the gods—at Delphi, the god in question was Apollo; at Dodona, it was Zeus—to the oracle and thereby onto the listener, there were many opportunities for alteration and confusion. One of the main fears around these oracles was that, given the power they had, they could be bribed or otherwise interfered with. Johnston writes, "Divination, as it played out at Delphi, was not so much a matter of *solving* a problem as it was of *redirecting* a problem out of a world that human enquirers could only imagine into a world in which their actions could have concrete effects."[22] In requiring human interpretation, oracular judgments entered into the world of politics, and so the question of how to read and interpret these sayings was of prime concern. If prophecy as such allows a kind of interface between the divine sources of authority and their human agents, in the end, some kind of human structure is required to redirect (or maybe just direct) those interpretations to form actual bases for human politics and law.

Here, we already begin to see a central vulnerability of archist forms of prophecy: language is never archist enough, never precise to the point that it can bypass human and collective interpretation (in the next chapter, I show that Hobbes has a great deal to say about this as well). Political leaders can and will insist that they and they alone understand the meaning of prophetic utterances, but they can't entirely deny the fact that ordinary people will judge these words for themselves, making them accessible to the vast anarchist networks that coexist with archist forms of seeing.

The Site of Archist Judgment: The Archeon

In thinking about the way that prophetic structures worked in ancient Greece, there seems to be a parallel and derivative structure in human politics even when it is removed from questions of prophetic sight per se. In *Archive Fever*, Jacques Derrida describes what he calls the "arkheion," a depository of state authority that existed in ancient Greece. Derrida connects the arkheion to the archive, both etymologically and conceptually, noting in both cases that something originary and authoritative is at stake (going back, once again, to the etymology of the verb *arkein*). Derrida writes:

> The meaning of "archive," its only meaning, comes to it from the Greek *arkheion*: initially a house, a domicile, an address, the residence of the superior magistrates, the *archons*, those who commanded. The citizens who thus held and signified political power were considered to possess the right to make or to represent the law. On account of their publicly recognized authority, it is at their house, in that *place* which is their house (private house, family house, or employee's house), that official documents are filed. The archons . . . do not only ensure the physical security of what is deposited and of the substrate. They are also accorded the hermeneutic right and competence. They have the power to interpret the archive.[23]

In this way, the arkheion (which I will henceforth anglicize as the archeon) is both the fount of knowledge and the origin or commencement of the power to interpret and disseminate that knowledge.[24] It serves, as with the Hebrew God, as a seat of judgment, a site from which such judgment could and did issue.

Like the oracles at Delphi and Dodona, the archeon, as Derrida describes it, is above all a "*place.*" It has a location that anchors it in a locality but which is distinct from the rest of the community. Here again, we see a kind of transitive vampirism occurring wherein, by locating archism in a particular place (and also in a particular time), archist authority structures gain the tangible substance that it requires in order to be credible. The physical tangibility and accessibility of a particular location no longer belongs to that place but is now the property of some higher (and otherwise invisible) agent. More accurately, this connection allows for an interface between an invisible and eternal power source and the mundane application of that power that prophecy provides more generally. Through that transference, we can come to believe in an invisible power as if it were as visible and tangible—only more so—as the places and things (and persons) that stand in for that power on Earth.

The archeon offers a place in space and time that is unique and superior to other spaces and other times, organizing reality accordingly. Thus (to connect this back for just a moment to the traditions of ancient Israel), just as in the Temple of Solomon, there is a spot, a holy of holies where God's invisible presence becomes expressed in reality, so too does the archeon (albeit according to the logic of Athens instead of Jerusalem in this case) pinpoint an inexpressible pervasive power so that it too can have a focal point, a way to believe that it is true and absolute and that nothing is prior to it even as it is also recognizable and locatable, taking on a seemingly solid and tangible form.

Most importantly of all, and connected to what I was saying earlier about the archist model of prophecy, the archeon provides a vantage point, a place from which to see (or perhaps gaze, to use a more Foucauldian term) in a way that is unidirectional. As the site of "hermeneutic right and competence," this is the seat of judgment; the archeon provides a privileged perch from which the world can be surveyed, known, taxonomized, judged, and controlled even as it is itself exempt from that very same gaze or judgment (very much like the judgments of the gods).

In some sense, we are commanded both to see the archeon as having this special status (much as K. learns to "see" the castle) as well as to see ourselves from and through the archeon's own perspective. The archeon is not simply its physical building or site that is invested with this power but the way that building or site is infused with a form of specialness that sets it aside from other places. This specialness is transitive; it can be moved around or even exist in multiple places at once. In modern times in the United States, such sites include the White House and the Capitol building, or in Germany the Reichstag, all of which serve as synecdochal manifestations of a power that has no true home or ontological source. This power becomes associated with this or that person, this or that edifice, but it never fully melds with any given person or place. It remains, as it were, a bit apart, from the buildings and even from the human beings (the archons) who claim its privileges, as Ernst Kantorowicz's notion of "the king's two bodies" attests to as well.[25] This manifestation in space and time serves as the basis of archist appointment.

Although Derrida treats the archeon as a largely secular phenomenon, the parallels with the formation of sacred sites of prophecy suggest its theological origins. After all, the position of absolute judgment, of "arkein," is modeled on a deity who occupies a similar perch in the transcendent realm. The gods' (or God's) absolute power as judges and origins of the world becomes reproduced in the power of the law and the state to judge and rule the rest of us. If the archeon is an earthly manifestation of that divine position, nothing short of divine interruption can disturb or undermine its privileged location (one of the vulnerabilities that I argue Nietzsche and Benjamin maximally exploit).

Archism and the Archeon

As a secularized manifestation of archist prophecy, the archeon becomes the basis by which the hierarchy inherent in the form of archist prophecy reproduces itself over and over into the world in which that prophecy initially occurs.[26] It is therefore not just a feature of archism but I would argue *the* feature, at least of its Western variant; it is that aspect of archism that can survive the death of any one iteration of its myriad forms.

As long as it has the archeon, archism can take an almost infinite number of forms; it can be liberal, it can be neoliberal, it can be fascist, monarchist, or just about any form that is based on rule and projection of authority over others. It can even appear that different forces within archism are involved in a kind of death struggle with one another (the contemporary struggle between liberalism and fascism is a version of this). Such struggles, while not exactly false (that is, not a pure contrivance), nonetheless serve to disguise the fact that, whoever "wins," the true winner will always be archism itself.

Foucault is famous for saying, "We need to cut off the King's head: In political theory that has still to be done."[27] This head, the thing we have yet to cut off, is the archeon itself, as opposed to the state or some other subunit of archist authority. An even better analogy might be to say that the archeon is like the beak of an octopus. An octopus can flatten itself to fit into virtually any space, pass through almost the smallest opening, as long as its beak can fit. Similarly, archism can take on any form, but it cannot live without the archeon, a site, transitive though it may be, from which it makes its judgments and from which we all see ourselves seeing it (and one another).

In this way, the archeon is both the source of archist power and its greatest vulnerability. As the king's head or the octopus's beak, the archeon survives in places both expected and unexpected. It lives in the fascist dictator who stands in for "the people." It lives in the way that liberal representative democracies, such as the United States and Australia, function—the way that political representation promises popular rule but delivers something quite different. It lives in the violence of warlords and debilitated "failed" states, and it lives in the algorithms that increasingly control and dominate international capital.

The Promise of Archism:
Representation and Immortal Life

If archism were only a purely negative force, if it were only in the business of predation or terrorism (which are its main activities, to be sure), I do not think that even its determination of reality would be enough to allow archism to reign generally supreme as it has for the last few millennia. There are at least two key "positive" elements that archism engages in that I think are critical for perpetuating its power that go beyond its violence and spectacularity. One is the principle of representation and the other is the promise of eternal life.

Let me begin with a discussion of archism's representational function (a subject that I revisit in chapter 5). Because its basis for power is so nebulous, it is vital that archism disguises itself. Archism rarely, perhaps never, presents itself as itself. This is one of the reasons that the term seems so unfamiliar to us; why would it need a name when it is just everywhere and always? The archeon is continuously standing for, speaking as, some larger group or community, that is, engaging in representation. In this way, it transfers its own nebulous nature onto a given (and tangible!) community and, in return, it receives back that palpable sense of reality that it has in fact stolen from the community it parasitizes.

Representation also allows a separation between cause and effect that permits archism to engage in its violence and its racism even as it purports—or rather the instruments that "represent" its power purport—to be neutral and just. Thus, to keep this in the parlance of the state for the moment (although this is, once again, assuredly not in any way archism's one "true" form), the state is not a killer, it is what protects us from killers; the state is not racist, it is what adjudicates and judges racists; the state is not capitalist, it is what protects us from, limits, and enhances capitalism, and so on. This separation of cause and effect serves as the basis for archism's representational function, giving it plausible deniability even as it also serves to further disguise its existence in the first place.[28]

The idea of representation serves to ensure that whatever archism is actually doing (ruling, killing, being racist, and so forth), it will never be read as such, not when the public eye is diverted by elections, parliaments and congresses, public opinion polls, and all the rest of the stuff of contemporary (archist) political life. Even the state form itself is one such diversion. Just as Althusser says that "ideology never says: 'I am ideological,'" so too does archism never say, "I am archist."[29] It is always something else even as it is only ever itself.

In this way, all the misrecognitions (to use another of Althusser's terms), prevarications, bifurcations, and the like that we read as often spelling the *end* of archism (the end of states, the end of sovereignty) are in fact ways of *perpetuating* archism by disguising and obscuring its ongoing forms of rule.[30] This is why it is important to restate that archism is not the same as the rule by states. The former can survive the death of the latter, arguably *is* surviving that death as we speak. Like the ark of the covenant, the archeon is portable and transferable. In all these ways, archism is a most insidious and ubiquitous phenomenon.

Through the device of representation, to be a subject of archism is to believe that one is somehow part of the very power apparatus that excludes them or, if they recognize their exclusion from that position, they are led to believe that but for the archist form, they would be subject to yet more dire consequences, to violence, to chaos, to what usually passes for anarchy. This of course depends on who this subject is. Given the racist character of the modern Western state, communities of color already understand the ways in which they are the subject of violence, whether from the state or other archist entities. Thus, when archism does show its real face, it usually does so with a display of maximum violence. Yet either way, the fiction of representation, the feint toward horizontal participation that is in fact a way to disempower and depoliticize those who are subjects of archist power, serves to obfuscate and calm any reaction. As long as people think, "I'm losing out in this system but my response must be made in terms of the system itself, via voting or lobbying or making appeals to those in political office," then archism has things covered.

The huge groundswell that we are seeing at the time I am writing this in response to the murder of George Floyd is something different from representation or a desire for inclusion. This is anarchism. This is life, specifically in this case Black life, responding with repugnance to the violence and racism of archism. Archism is good at incorporating that life into itself—and representation is precisely the mechanism that accomplishes that incorporation and co-optation—but it can never actually be congruent with that life and, for this reason, anarchism poses a perpetual threat to archism's control and determination.

Accordingly, there are times when life and anarchism (which, I argue throughout this book, amount to the same thing) respond. All such reactions to the predations of archism reflect this connection to life, although this particular uprising, as I'll discuss further in the conclusion, seems different even from many (but certainly not all) previous responses in the sense that it has briefly disturbed the representational function itself; the lies and faux reforms of liberal archism are, at least for the moment, not doing their job (nor is police repression, which is the other way that archism deals with uprisings of this nature). These are the conditions where revolution becomes possible, when anarchist vision supplants the representational function.

In terms of this moment in time (i.e., the moment when I am writing this), it remains to be seen what will happen—the January 6 attack on the Capitol is a sign of a deep and violent reaction to that uprising—but no matter what does occur, this is a sign once again that archist and appointing vision does not last forever and is not invulnerable to the life it reigns over.

It may seem to many that the moment of insurrection in the United States has already passed insofar as the Biden administration is arguably far more agreeable and moderate than the Trump administration was, removing some of the impetus for a left-wing response. However, I see the very fact that the Biden administration has itself swung so far to the "left," harking back to FDR and a pre-Reaganite mode of politics, comes not from itself (Biden is no radical!) but from the presence of a truly radical insurrectionary spirit that still remains in effect, pulling Biden way past what would normally be his comfort zone (Bernie Sanders's own candidacy was in some ways a vehicle for this effect as well). This is not to say that the more moderate politics of the Biden administration is itself in any way radical. It isn't (indeed, I would say that it is just more evidence of archist homeostasis, the swings of ideology that keep archism itself intact regardless of the actual policies in question).

But it reflects a magnetic pull from the far left, from the anarchist life that is always present, even as it comes in a most reformist and nonradical form.

How to Live Forever

In thinking further about the relationship between anarchism and life, about the threat that life as such always poses, we see that archism has an answer there too. Bereft of any actual life of its own, the other key promise of archism is to offer something *better* than life, that is, a higher, purer, and, above all, eternal form of life (a subject I return to in chapter 6) to replace the life that it commands and overwrites. The initial position of archism is always "do things my way or die"; archism threatens life in order to control and determine it. It is not "giving" up anything by letting people live but merely refraining from taking something away that does not properly belong to it in the first place. But if that was all that archism offered, it would not have the hold upon the world that it does. There needs once again to be a "positive" element to archism besides allowing people to continue to live, at least for those groups that archism favors. The positive aspect of archism is the promise that by associating themselves with it, by putting themselves under its "protection," at least some people will gain access to the kind of transcendent, superhuman life that they attribute to archism itself (abandoning their wretched and all-too-human embodied life in the process). The paradox here is that this "better" and "higher" form of life is actually only their own actual life that appears to the subject of archism in a stolen and alienated form. This is in fact a life that they already "have" but archism does not permit them to realize this.

In making this promise of eternal life, archism takes a literal (by going to heaven), metaphorical (by associating themselves with a state and other seemingly immortal institutions that exist beyond one's own individual death, or by taking part in some great, transhistorical array of "progress"), or transitive form. In the latter case, archism offers eternal life by giving the death of the privileged group to other nonprivileged people: Black, Brown, and Indigenous people; women, queer people, transgendered people, the disabled, the poor. Here, the violence of archism does a double duty as denying life to some, thereby perpetuating its threat and its power, even as it seems to confer immortality of a sort on those whom it seeks to protect and nurture, the basis of what Foucault calls biopolitics (and here, we see the theological origins of this concept as well).[31]

In a previous book, I read a short story by James Baldwin called "Going to Meet the Man" as speaking to this conferring of immortality, specifically in this case onto the white community.[32] The protagonist of this story, set in the U.S. South during the civil rights era, is a racist white sheriff. He is depicted as being in bed with his wife and impotent as he worries that his violent power over Black people is waning as they become increasingly organized and defiant (his sexuality and his political power are highly correlated in Baldwin's telling). In his thoughts, the sheriff goes back through his life, remembering various incidents where he dealt out death and violence to Black people, trying to rekindle his libido as he does so. He eventually recalls an early memory of his first lynching when a Black man is tortured, castrated and murdered in front of a crowd of white people who are having a picnic. He recalls the intense joy and sense of bonding that he felt with the other white people who were there. Such is his joy in this recollection that he is fully aroused at the end of the story and ready to subject his wife to some of the sexual violence that he has been subjecting Black people to his whole life.

I read this joy as indicating a sense that the white people at the lynching had in effect transferred their own death to this Black man (in another writing, Baldwin tells us that white people "do not believe in death").[33] Although we tend to think of antiblackness as a form of dehumanization, I see Baldwin as telling us that in fact, by being killed and abused so graphically, the Black man was actually being rendered all too legibly human and hence mortal, allowing his white tormentors to feel that they themselves had escaped the bonds of the merely human, becoming superhuman in the process. By abusing his body so tangibly, they were seeking to transcend their own bodies, allowing themselves, at least temporarily, to leave behind their own fleshy, mortal selves. This transcendence, a connection to the eternal source of archism's power, fulfills—again at least for a moment; Baldwin's story shows how the effects can wear off and so this violence needs to be performed over and over again—the promise of much of Western, and archist, philosophy. The desire for transcendental forms of subjectivity, the worship of abstractions like "mind" at the expense of material objects like "bodies" (where "mind" = white and "body" = Black), are the hallmarks of archist life, at least for those it privileges.

Transferring death, mortality, and fleshiness to other bodies promises to make a reality for the privileged white subject of the noumenal, higher self that they have always been told that they are (but which in fact does not and has never exist[ed]). It seeks to turn what is in fact the nihilism of Western philosophy—the worship of things that do not exist in preference over those things that do—into a positive and actual form of life, a goal that, were it to be achieved, would be the fulfillment of archism and arguably the end of any chance for anarchist resistance (a subject I return to in my treatment of *Frankenstein* in chapter 6). For everyone else, there is nothing but violence; there is representation, false hope, and perhaps the vaguest promise of an extension of immortality to them as well, at least some day in the far, far future.[34]

Living in(to) the Future

Representation and immortal life then are the two ways that archism both disguises itself and makes itself seem desirable, even indispensable, to various communities that live under it. Of the two, the promise of eternal life is perhaps the most important aspect, the thing that gets such widespread buy-in from privileged communities. This is because the concept of eternal life is critical, not just for the subjects of archism but the archons as well. It is the source of their own motivation at some point, what holds them in archism's grip. They may well know that representation is a farce, but eternal life is a different matter; it's the one thing that no amount of money or power can buy (that perhaps explains why so many billionaires want to have their brains frozen right before they die so that they can "cheat death"). Insofar as archism teaches us all to hate our bodies, to hate mortality and fleshiness, the promise of immortality offers the antidote to that hate and strings many, although certainly not all, of its subjects along via the promise of access to that transcendent state that it and it alone possesses.

The problem here of course is that archism is *not* a path to eternal life. It is once again nothing but death (as I explain throughout this book). Life is anarchic, and furthermore, life—any life at all—is not eternal but only ever mortal and ordinary. This may be archism's ultimate point of vulnerability: archism promises not only to offer life but once again to offer a better, truer, everlasting form of life even as it cannot offer any kind of life at all, even of the most ordinary sort. It can only steal life from its subjects. As such, anarchism poses a truly existential challenge to archism in all its forms.

This dynamic of false promises covered over by confident projections (and hence exposing yet another vulnerability) also extends into that all-important temporal direction that archism is always oriented toward, namely the future, the very dimension where this eternal life supposedly occurs. In its modern, Western-based variety, archism is always projecting itself and its power into the future, making itself retroactively inevitable. This is perhaps where the prophetic function of archism makes itself most apparent, insofar as one of the principal aspects of (archist) prophecy is the ability to predict and, in some sense, thereby to control the future. But as I argue further, this too is a lie. Archism is never really about the future as such. In fact, it does everything it can to make sure that there is no future at all, that is, no future that is any different from the present.

As I show further in chapter 4, Benjamin tells us that the archist (his word is *mythic*) understanding of the future amounts to what he calls "homogenous, empty time."[35] The future for Benjamin is not a blank canvas for the archons to fill with their own desires, nor is it some already accomplished space that the present unfurls itself toward in a predetermined and teleological manner. Instead, the future is empty and featureless (i.e., homogenous) in a different way, namely insofar as it is entirely nonexistent. As such, the archist predictions of the future are never about accurately connecting to some actual future time but are in the mode of what we tend to call "self-fulfilling" prophecies. They are, once again, not about the future at all but only ever about the present. Archist prophecy is about perpetuating some current power system with all its hierarchies and power relations into an imagined future so that it can be colonized by more of the same. It is self-fulfilling then, not in a guaranteed, absolute sense but in the sense that it hopes to perpetuate itself precisely by the act of appearing to make itself, once again, retroactively inevitable.[36]

Benjamin is once again helpful here because he describes something of this dynamic in his short essay "Fate and Character." There, Benjamin tells us that "it is . . . precisely the contention of those who profess to predict men's fate from no matter what signs, that for those able to perceive it (who find an immediate knowledge of fate as such in themselves) it is in some way present or—to put this more cautiously—accessible."[37] In other words, fate serves as a way to read what already is and to project the status quo, wishfully, into an as yet nonexistent future to force itself, as it were, into and over time.

Here too, we see an unexpected vulnerability to archism because this false and self-fulfilling form of prophecy is met, once again, by anarchist life in all its variety. Unless the entire human race is killed off (which is unfortunately all too possible), as long as this life persists, it is itself, and not archist lies, that will definitely enter into the future. When it arrives there, life may continue to be organized and degraded by archist parasitism but it also could live independently of such illicit forms of power. Insofar as archism has no life of its own, it must depend on that anarchist life to extend itself into the future, but here the guarantee that it uses to convince itself and to intimidate those that it rules over becomes a question rather than an answer.

Benjamin reminds us ceaselessly that capitalism, which may be the supreme form of contemporary archism, wants us to feel like we are breathlessly rushing into the future even as we are in fact always held in some static, unchanging hell.[38] Yet in fact, far from being inevitable, archism's determination to hold time hostage, even while masquerading as time itself, shows us that for all its promotion of its own immortality—and, by extension and invitation, the immortality of those it allows to associate with it—it too can, even must, die. And when archism dies (the subject of chapter 6), it does not die as we do. It does not remain held by the life that it had which connects it to other lives. Being a nonliving thing, when archism dies, it vanishes back into its original nothingness, taking all its lies, promises, and guarantees along with it.

A Definition of Archism

At this point, let me offer a provisional definition of archism—at least its Western variant—for the purposes of going forward in this book and summarizing what I've said so far. Given the fact that archism comes from the Greek verb *arkein*, which means both to begin and to rule, we can see that archism is that form of politics that claims to have no external origin but is itself the basis of its own authority. Because it must (therefore) always hide the empty—and theological—void at the center of its authority, archism is also inherently representational; it is always in this sense a lie. Just as critically, archism is about death instead of life. But it is once again not about death in the ordinary sense. For the living, death is an integral part of life. The death that archism consists of is of a different kind. It is the opposite, not the termination and transformation of life (as ordinary death is), an absolute nothingness, a thing that isn't, never was, and never will be. Finally, archism is always violent, akin to what Benjamin famously calls "mythic violence."[39] This violence comes from archism's own nothingness, the death that it always and only is.

Archism's nonexistence has a very strong impact on the way that it operates in the world insofar as the more insecure archism is about its own lack of reality, its own deathliness (and it never is wholly secure for reasons already explained), the more violent, the more aggressive and fascist it becomes. Archism is like King Midas, who may have had good wishes, but everything he touched turned to gold, killing all that he loved. Archism is the same way; it has lofty promises and visions of freedom and equality, but all that it touches turns to violence, death, rape, and robbery. This violence may often at times be physical; there is an enormous amount of death, genocide, and destruction dealt out by archism throughout its long and horrible history, but the basis for that physical violence is metaphysical, that is, archism is violent first and foremost in the way it projects itself into the world, the way it demands to be determinant of everything else even as it is itself entirely derivative. Itself a creature of projection, it insists on covering the terrain of the world (often literally) with projections of its own, as if to wipe out any space that might reveal the way that it is itself false, to avoid any space that might, in contrast to archist space, reveal its true (lack of) origins.

This definition of archism rules out some possible contenders that may, in other contexts, be considered archist themselves. For example, Hannah Arendt's idea of the "right to have rights" is considered by some to be an articulation of an *arche* in the sense that it is an originary position insofar as it is based on the "right of every individual to belong to humanity" (and thus related to one of the two main definitions of *arkein* as a form of beginning).[40] As Peg Birmingham explains, "Arendt is very explicit that the event of natality is an *ontological* event," suggesting a kind of rootedness in an absolute and unimpeachable truth.[41] And yet Birmingham also writes: "Arendt's ontology . . . does not describe an immutable order of essences; it does not seek enduring truths upon which to ground both thought and action; it does not posit a metaphysical notion of human nature or subjectivity in which human rights are inalienably inscribed. . . . By articulating this *principium*, Arendt does not give us an ontological politics; rather, she provides an ontological foundation for human rights."[42] Birmingham describes this position as an "anarchic event," suggesting her own understanding of how this kind of beginning does not implicate the full spectrum of archist authority.[43] I agree with her. The fact that Arendt's founding principle of natality is not metaphysical but based on the actual existence of human life in all its plurality means that this version of principium is anarchist instead of archist, as I understand these terms. For Arendt, there is no recourse to some transcendent beyond (what she calls "the absolute") but a simple acknowledgment of the existing world and the human life that exists within it. That, as I argue throughout this book, is the context and basis for anarchist life as such.

I would say the same thing for any number of other moral, political, or ethical claims wherein their source lies within the world instead of beyond it. One other interesting example of this can be found in Derrida's notion of a justice that is "to come" (*à venir*).[44] While this might sound like Derrida is invoking a language of transcendentalism, evoking a world that does not (yet) exist, I think it's more accurate to say that its existence is imperfect and ongoing yet entirely within this world or universe (i.e., immanent instead of transcendent). As Peggy Kamuf says of Derrida's understanding of the unconditional, which seems similarly transcendent (but is not): "To think the unconditionality of such concepts is not at all to remove thought from the practical experiences we wish to call hospitality, gift, forgiveness, or justice. On the contrary, this thinking registers the very desire to go on calling to these names for that which remains impossible as present experience."[45] In other words, the existence or nonexistence of these things does not depend on some godlike figure or nature to bring into the world but remains entirely and only within the realm of human possibility even if it does not currently exist in a tangible form. In this way, something that might look archist on the surface is actually not.[46]

This conversation may give a sense of the complex entanglements between archism and anarchism, including in terms of forms of prophetic sight. This mutual entanglement cuts both ways. On the one hand, it means that archism can never be free from anarchism. The contrast with anarchism reveals another of archism's abiding vulnerabilities, its need to be seen and read in a certain way, its need to hide what it is even as it is itself not wholly real. Although we can all plainly "see" the representations of archism, the archeon, the buildings, the presidents, the emblems, flags, and staffs, the corporate boardrooms, the algorithms (or at least the effect of those algorithms), etcetera, we can't actually ever see the magical source of its power. It is that source that archist prophecy commands us to see nonetheless, and it is that appointing sight that anarchist prophecy threatens with disappointment. Archism can never be free from this vulnerability because to see its true face (both its nothingness and its hideous violence) is to destroy its own basis for authority and power.

At the same time, it may seem as if anarchism is, by the same token, permanently saddled with archism, although as this book goes along, I argue that this is not true to the same extent as the converse. Anarchism lives and breathes amid archism; it is predated upon and parasitized by its nemesis. Yet, as I argue in chapter 6, anarchism has lived, does, and will live without archism (and, in particular, its Western variant). What it may never be able to shed entirely is the *threat* of archism, the possibility of its return in an infinite number of guises. The temptations of archism, the way it can project particular wishes as if they were universal, the promises it offers of privilege to some few elite and of comforting—but false—compensations for the rest, the harmony and peace it suggests (whereas in fact it is never anything but violence), makes archism a permanent feature of the political possible. For this reason, we cannot think of some kind of finish line that anarchism can cross and say to itself, "Finally, we are free once and for all." Instead, anarchism and, in particular, the collective forms of sight (but also hearing, smell, taste, touch, etc.) that it produces must never cease a certain kind of vigilance for signs of archism's return.

Anarchist Prophecy

In the chapters that follow, I argue for a very different political model that comes with a very different model of prophecy. Instead of being ancient and venerated, the form of prophecy I discuss is entirely contemporary (although it is at the same time far more ancient than archism) and profane. Instead of thinking about prophecy as something that the few possess, an insight that the prophet has that no one else can see, I argue for a form of prophecy that in fact entails quite the opposite: something that is available to everyone and which comes not in the form of special sight but in the form of distinguishing between collective and hierarchical modes of vision. More specifically, anarchist prophecy entails the two-fold operation of failing to see the false projection of state power and authority that we are otherwise told is really there even as it also means to pay attention to collective decisions about reality that a community is always engaged with (whether under conditions of archism or not).

Thomas Hobbes (the subject of the next chapter) tells us that in the presence of sovereignty, the power and agency of political subjects do not cease but are eclipsed and superseded by the sovereign's spectacularity. He writes: "As in the presence of the Master, the servants are equall, and without any honour at all; so are the Subjects, in the presence of the Soveraign. And though they shine some more, some lesse, when they are out of his sight; yet in his presence, they shine no more than the Starres in the presence of the Sun."[47] This metaphor may help explain how and why archist sight is so powerful. Given the apparent radiance of the sovereign, the smaller, dimmer light of the subject doesn't appear to shine at all (even though it is never wholly eclipsed). Yet there is one way in which I think this metaphor is misleading. It suggests that all light is the same and the sovereign just has more of it (in the same way as the sun is just another star but given its proximity to us appears so much brighter during the day). But this is not the case. The sovereign/archist light is a light that has been stolen from its subjects; it has no light whatsoever of its own. The magnitude of its light is proportional to the degree to which it has stolen it from the community (the "starres"). The role of the anarchist prophet is to steal back the field of visuality, redistributing that light to those it properly belongs to.

All the figures that I deal with in the ensuing chapters engage in complicated entanglements of archist and anarchist behavior, but in the end, I have chosen to focus on them because I believe that their anarchist aspects win out and ruin archism from within its maw. These characters demonstrate how people who are not only ordinary but thoroughly within the grip of archism can yet manage to subvert and ruin that power that controls and contains them. Furthermore, if archism is itself transitive, so is anarchism; the insights and acts of these characters are somehow contagious. Their subversive vision spreads from person to person like the plague of "white blindness" that Saramago describes in his novel *Blindness* (a plague that is followed by a contagion of anarchism in the sequel, *Seeing*).

In the world we live in, a world fabricated by archism, anarchism itself is never pure or innocent of archist power. It comes out of archist contexts; it grows and changes along with archism. But it has a major advantage over archism, one that I return to at several points in this book. While anarchism can and does exist without archism (the subject of chapter 6), archism cannot live without anarchism. Because of its vulnerability, its requirement that we see the invisible, because of the need for the archeon as a manifestation of that power and appointing sight, and most of all because it is death and we are life and it needs that life to exist at all, archism can never be free from the threat of disappointment. Although one cannot think that archism can be eradicated once and for all—as already noted, it can be killed off but it can also spring back to life at any time—it is just as true that we are not destined or fated to a permanently archist world.

The question that I focus on for the rest of this book is not to ask where anarchist prophets come from, since anyone and everyone can be an anarchist prophet, but how this potential for disappointment can be enhanced, connected to other sites of disappointment, protected from archist retaliation, and furthered in a way that causes maximum damage to archist forms of appointment.

The role of an anarchist prophet—taken as an individual—is therefore a critical one, but this figure does not come without risks: the risk of seduction into archism, the risk of her becoming just another archist prophet in the guise of overcoming archist forms of sight.[48] In light of this danger, a related question that I will come to again and again is why do (or just plain do) we need anarchist prophets at all? Isn't anarchism itself something that must exist horizontally and collectively and not be based on some individual person, even if what they are doing is wholly oriented toward the collective? My answer to this is that given the ubiquitous power of archism, a more horizontal solution where everyone comes into their collective vision together is relatively rare. Or rather in some sense, it happens all the time but it doesn't usually happen to the extent that archism is really threatened. Given that we all live double lives as archist and anarchist subjects, sometimes it takes an archist form to produce an anarchist outcome. And sometimes, when a groundswell is tentative (such as in our own moment), it takes a concentrated dose of anarchist prophecy to tip it over the edge. An example of this phenomenon is Mohamed Bouazizi, whose act of self-immolation brought on the Arab Spring and the downfall, virtually overnight, of many dictators who had been in power for decades.

Speaking of Bouazizi, anarchist prophets definitely don't have to be alive to be powerful. Not only can they be fictional, but they can also be persons who were once alive but are not alive any more. George Floyd, Breonna Taylor, Sandra Bland, Trayvon Martin, Michael Brown, and going all the way back to Emmett Till, and well before him too—all serve as Black anarchist prophets in their own way and their careers as such arguably began the moment they were murdered.

In an earlier writing, I wrote about a coconspiracy between the living and the dead, and I want to retain that analysis in this book as well.[49] It is important to remember that when I say that archism is death, I am not trying to connect it to the dead themselves. The dead, as a class of people who are intimately connected to the living (having once been alive), are able to resist the predations and projections of archism in ways that are often more effective than the living themselves who have the (unfortunate) ability to overwrite their own bodies with spectacular, and archist, projections. In their undeniable rotting materiality, the dead, especially in terms of their actual bodies, do not reflect the projections of archism but thwart and ruin those forms of vision. In this way, the living gain a great deal of freedom from archism simply by putting themselves into the path of the counterprojection of the dead. Accordingly, the dead are definitely part of the anarchist community that I am talking about here; in some way, they can all be seen as potentially (or already) being anarchist prophets.[50]

In terms of what any anarchist prophet has to offer, it is critical not to rule out any one as a possible candidate, no matter what outward subject position that person takes. No one is so pure of archism that they automatically make a good candidate for anarchist prophecy, and, by the same token (something that both Nietzsche and Benjamin stress in their work), no one is so far gone over to the side of archist power that they could never be an anarchist prophet, even—or maybe especially—despite their own desire only to rule and dominate.

In order to supplement and enhance ongoing moments of anarchist vision, we can turn to figures who engage with the form of archism (special sight, individuality, appointment) but who use that platform to generate the opposite of such things (ordinary vision, collectivity, disappointment). Given the way that archism always seeks to break its subjects up into isolated individuals in order to disempower them as a collectivity, or also makes them all "one" people as a whole, and therefore politically useless, mass, it makes sense that the antidote to this power is to have certain individuals or groups of individuals betray that identity and use it for the purposes of restoring or reinforcing anarchist forms of collective sight.

In the chapters that follow, I look at how the various forms of archism can be subverted to deliver an anarchist response, how the deep vulnerability of the archeon and the question of its visibility can be directly spotted and exposed, ruined through a different form of seeing that is as simple (but also as complex) as (re)encountering the world around us, a world that—like the circular city in "The City Coat of Arms"—people make together even when under the spell and allure of archist appointment. But I want to repeat the point that the purpose of anarchist prophecy is to make itself redundant; given that anarchist prophecy is often marred and complicated by the very archist elements it hijacks in order to enhance anarchist forms of vision, it cannot be a long-term solution but only a way to transition from archist to anarchist forms of authority and judgment.

chapter two

hobbes and
the holy spirit

The Word of God

WHEN IT COMES TO QUESTIONS of prophecy, of whether God ever speaks to, or through, human beings, Thomas Hobbes, normally all too ready to supply a definition or judgment, is surprisingly reticent about making a clear determination. He begins chapter 36 in *Leviathan*, titled "Of the Word of God, and of Prophets," by claiming that prophecy and the idea of God's words are almost never meant to be interpreted literally as suggesting that God spoke actual words to actual human beings. He writes:

> That which is here called the Word of God, was the Doctrine of Christian Religion; as it appears evidently by that which goes before. And [*Acts* 5.20.] where it said to the Apostles by an Angel, *Go stand and speak in the Temple, all the Words of this life*; by the Words of this life, is meant, the Doctrine of the Gospel; as is evident by what they did in the Temple, and is expressed in the last verse of the same Chap. *Daily in the Temple, and in every house they ceased not to teach and preach Christ Jesus.*[1]

In other words, for Hobbes the phrase "Word of God," when written in the Bible, does not mean that God literally speaks, even when speaking through prophets. Instead, Hobbes tells us that the notion of the Word of God and prophecy are generally meant more figuratively as an enthusiasm for God and a desire to study and learn the doctrine of Christianity (in this case). Hobbes makes this point quite clearly when he writes:

> Considering these two significations of the WORD OF GOD, as it is taken in Scripture [i.e., as a literal word that God spoke to human beings or as a sign of the Doctrines of Christianity], it is manifest in this later sense (where it is taken for the Doctrine of Christian Religion,) that the whole Scripture is the Word of God: but in the former sense not so. For example, though these words, *I am the Lord thy God, &c* to the end of the Ten Commandements, were spoken by God to Moses; yet the Preface, *God spake these words and said*, is to be the understood for the Words of him that wrote the holy History.[2]

Hobbes also states that the notion of the Word of God can be understood "sometimes *Properly*, sometimes *Metaphorically*."[3] He lists a vast number of cases in which the term is meant metaphorically and winnows down the times when God speaks "properly" to very few cases—and even in the case of Moses, the most exemplary of prophets, he says Moses was given "a more cleer Vision" but a vision nonetheless—almost down to nothing.[4]

Almost nothing but not quite. Hobbes will never actually say that God never speaks to human beings even as he questions virtually every instance that God is said to do just that in Scripture. In this way, the notion of prophecy presents Hobbes with a conundrum. He claims on the one hand that prophecy, and God's will more generally, serves as the basis of modern secular sovereignty, that it transmits an undeniable truth to human beings that anchors contemporary forms of political authority. Yet, at the same time, those moments of authorization seem to almost inevitably be instances of mere (that is, subjective) human interpretation. Whether we are dealing with the prophets during the period of what Hobbes calls the "Kingdome of God," a time, he tells us, when God was literally king of ancient Israel, or the time of the first Hebrew kings, when prophecy continued to periodically occur, or even during Hobbes's (or our own) time, when prophecy was thought to be gone but people still claimed to be prophets—with often devastating effect, in his view—for Hobbes, such forms of prophecy both advance and challenge a sovereign, or archist, politics by calling into question the degree to which its source of authority is certain (or not).

Accordingly, when it comes to the way he thinks about prophecy and God's words, Hobbes can be shown to be quite a bit more subversive than he is normally understood to be (generally speaking, he is understood as being the direct opposite of subversive). One of the most famous architects of the notions of sovereignty and state power, Hobbes is in a category of his own as a progenitor of archism, at least in its contemporary, Western form. And yet this seemingly most archist of thinkers demonstrates an unexpected and quite significant degree of resistance to precisely that kind of power when it comes to his political theology.

In this chapter, I show how Hobbes's secular and archist narrative is never far from, nor innocent of, a subversive political theology. Hobbes's discussion of prophecy offers us a glimpse of how a radical, and negative, political theology exposes and thwarts the otherwise confident and absolutist sovereign principle that Hobbes formally espouses. Accordingly, I argue that Hobbes demonstrates a critical and subversive element of archist prophecy, namely the fact that archist prophecy is also, and at the same time, a basis for anarchist sight. By looking at this most archist of modern thinkers, we see the fundamental structure of the archist order, the way it covers over voids that it derives its authority from, but also the way that it preserves within itself a kernel of resistance, that is, a kernel of that void, as a way to complicate, undermine, and subvert archist authority in all its variants.[5] Ultimately, I will argue that Hobbes shows us that prophecy itself is an anarchist activity and that, here too, the archist's role is only to steal that element and claim it for its own, reducing but never eliminating the radical element of collective prophecy in the process.

In his understanding of Hebrew prophecy, Hobbes evinces a very ambivalent attitude—if not consciously then at least textually—toward the way that such prophecy leads to and sets up subsequent secular sovereign authority. The theological genealogy of such authority both underpins and competes with the secular narrative that Hobbes would like to leave us with. When he describes specific instances of prophecy, they vary from subtly exposing the hollow core of sovereign authority to constituting a direct competition with and rejection of sovereign pronouncements. In all cases, prophetic power serves to bolster the power of collective—and anarchic—forms of interpretation and judgment that Hobbes, for all his archist tendencies, always seeks to preserve and protect from sovereign decision.

Although from an Abrahamic perspective, we now live, as Hobbes did himself, in a time when formal acts of prophecy are considered to have fallen silent, for Hobbes this does not mean that the prophetic authority, that interface between the divine and the human, is no longer available to us. Nor are we entirely bereft of its power to undermine and interrupt sovereign authority. In his own time—and ours as well—Hobbes offers us a modern-day version of prophecy in the figure of the Holy Spirit. This is a concept that, very much like the notion of the Word of God, Hobbes zealously purges of any specific meaning or content of its own, allowing for human collectivities to make their own unencumbered judgments in the face of a divine element whose own retreat from the world invites and produces anarchic human freedom in its wake.

The Holy Spirit is the key anarchist prophetic element in Hobbes's political theory, the one theological aspect that survives his attempt to secularize the religious bases of archist power and authority. The Holy Spirit's own emptiness allows us to see another emptiness as well, that of archism itself (the latter constituting an emptiness that is otherwise obscured by sovereign spectacularity, including some spectacularity of Hobbes's own devising).

In the two chapters following this one, I look at the way that Nietzsche and Benjamin radically subvert all forms of prophecy, presenting us with texts that appear to be far less ambivalent than Hobbes's own (especially for Benjamin) in terms of their anarchic, and theological, challenge to archist forms of authority. I begin with Hobbes rather than Nietzsche or Benjamin, however, not only because he comes first chronologically speaking but also because, as one of the best-known architects of modern, Western forms of archism, to start with him helps show that even in the beating heart of archist politics, there lays a radical anarchist spirit that can never be entirely ruled out or denied.

Furthermore, I think Hobbes is one of the best thinkers to lay out the bases of the anarchist alternative to sovereign power. For all his promotion of a sovereign authority, Hobbes is very consistent in counterpoising this to a collective form of value making and judgment that is inherent in what Aryeh Botwinick calls his "negative theology."[6] That such a key articulator of archism should also be someone who tells us about those alternative political practices that archism overwrites and attempts to suppress may indicate once again that Hobbes is more complicated than initially appears. It further suggests that the face of archism that he presents us with is less formidable and more variegated than we might initially think.

Hobbes's Dueling Genealogies of Sovereignty

In *Leviathan*, as well as in *De Cive*, Hobbes tells two origin stories of sovereign authority that do not always support one another and sometimes are directly contradictory. The first genealogy is well known and does not need much elaboration here. This is the story of the social contract, the rise out of the state of nature and the joining up of human beings under the aegis of a sovereign that is not itself bound by that contract. Everyone gives up their natural rights to the sovereign (although the sovereign itself is not a party to this bargain), gaining security, a way to avoid being arbitrarily killed by some fellow wild creature in the state of nature, in exchange for their obedience to the law and to the state.

As Hobbes famously states:

> The only way to erect such a Common Power . . . is, to conferre all their power and strength upon one Man, or upon one Assembly of men, that they might reduce all their Wills, by plurality of voices, unto one Will. . . . For by this Authoritie, given him by every particular man in the Commonwealth, he hath the use of so much Power and Strength conferred on him, that by terror thereof, he is inabled to conform the wills of them all, to Peace at home, and mutuall ayd against their enemies abroad.[7]

We see in this narrative a central articulation of the basic form of modern, Western archism. We also see one of the key promises of archism in its contemporary form: the promise of life or at least the avoidance of death, reiterating the kinds of promises that God made to Isaiah as well. Submit to archism, Hobbes argues, and you will get to live. The only true danger to your life, barring illness, accident, or, of course, the undeniable fact of human mortality—always an inconvenient truth when it comes to archist promises—arises if you move against the sovereign that has both the right to kill you and the means to do so since it maintains a monopoly on violence. The subject has the right to resist at that point, but it is unlikely that he or she will be able to save themselves from such a singular and powerful foe. The "terror thereof," the awful spectacle of sovereign authority that is armed with real weapons, akin to "the Generation of that great LEVIATHAN," is, for Hobbes, the basis for lasting peace, obedience, and authority.[8] This is a genesis story, then—although by no means the only one—for archism itself.

The second origin story starts with the covenant between God and Abraham. This covenant leads to the setting up of what Hobbes calls the "Kingdome of God," a state of affairs wherein the Levite clergy nominally ruled in God's name.[9] This was a form of rule that was frequently interrupted by prophets speaking as and by God, effectively bypassing the Levite clergy. Although Hobbes says explicitly that the covenant, the Kingdom of God, and the setting up of a human-ruled kingdom in ancient Israel that eventually replaced it set the pattern and source of sovereign authority for subsequent human kingdoms and other secular sovereign forms that follow, the way that he describes this period is markedly, even radically, different from the way he talks about the other, secular genealogy.

The most critical difference for the purposes of my argument in this chapter can be seen in terms of what Hobbes emphasizes in his two origin stories. In the secular genealogy, as is appropriate with archism more generally, the focus is on those things that stand in for and cover over the invisible power at the center of political and legal rule, that is, sovereignty's representative function. The idea of the Leviathan, itself a creature that has no real existence except as a vision that God conjures in the Book of Job, serves to distract from the void at the heart of sovereign authority, a void that was perhaps especially legible and vulnerable in Hobbes's time as the traditional theological bases of sovereign rule were being openly challenged.

In the secular narrative, Hobbes sets up the sovereign as a ruler who is both arbitrary and inviolable, a living incarnation of the Leviathan, or what Hobbes calls a "*Mortall God*."[10] This is a figure whose own violence promises not just imagery but real-life effects. Yet, although the sovereign as a human being, or set of human beings, is far more tangible than the figure of the Leviathan, the connection between that image and the person(s) at the basis of sovereignty points to the way that archism is, for Hobbes, always a matter of drawing the eye away from the void that it purports to stand in for. This is, once again, one of the reasons that archism is inherently representational, because every material manifestation of its power is always standing in for or covering over (i.e., representing) something immaterial.

The theological origin story that Hobbes tells is an entirely different matter. In that story, Hobbes focuses not on the cover-ups but on the void itself. When describing the original covenant God makes with Abraham, Hobbes writes: "The Father of the Faithfull, and first in the Kingdome of God by Covenant, was *Abraham*. For with him was the Covenant first made; wherein he obliged himself, and his seed after him, to acknowledge and obey the commands of God; not onely such as he could take notice of, (as Morall Laws,) by the light of Nature; but also such, as God should in speciall manner deliver to him by Dreams and Visions."[11] Rather than seeking to spectacularize and distract, here Hobbes is drawing attention precisely to the way that God can only be known via ephemeral and inherently unreliable measures.

Hobbes goes on to say that Abraham, like all other human beings, was already bound by moral law prior to the covenant. He explains that the real basis of the covenant came from and through the "Dreams and Visions" that Abraham had of God, that is, special insights that pertained to Abraham alone.[12] Here, we have a critical moment in the theological genealogy of sovereign power because Hobbes specifies that it came not from something palpably observable or evident but through an act of prophetic and appointing sight. The intangible and subjective experiences of dreams and visions serve as the basis for a lasting and binding power and obligation, the basis of politics itself.

In considering the story of the covenant, Hobbes argues that the power that Abraham was to yield in God's name is binding on all of Abraham's descendants even though God spoke only to Abraham. He writes: "They to whom God hath not spoken immediately [that is, all of Abraham's family and descendants, everyone but Abraham himself] are to receive the positive commandements of God, from their Soveraign; as the family and seed of Abraham did from Abraham their Father, and Lord, and Civil Soveraign. And consequently in every Common-Wealth, they who have no supernaturall Revelation to the contrary, ought to obey the laws of their own Soveraign, in the externall acts and profession of Religion."[13]

Thus, what is unique to and personal for Abraham becomes transmitted as a generalized and transmissible form of political power via Abraham's own patriarchal authority. The model of obedience and authority set up here is completely different from the one that operates in the secular narrative. It is based (at least initially) on family, and vision instead of consent and contract. It binds together a human person or set of persons with an intangible and invisible deity, whereas the terrestrial sovereign is, once again, not bound by the social contract at all.

While both stories sound definitively archist, there is a way that the theological story bucks its own archist tendencies inasmuch as, unlike the social contract narrative, the covenant has a mode of interruption—prophecy itself—which, given its uncertain provenance and the potential for multiple and competing forms of interpretation, can periodically alter or upset the political status. When he states that "they who have no supernaturall Revelation to the contrary" are bound forever by this covenant, Hobbes is allowing for an exception to the rule. Indeed, his subsequent descriptions of the Kingdom of God are full of acts of prophecy (i.e., "supernaturall Revelation") that trouble or interrupt the more quotidian forms of authority that follow God's revelation to Abraham, a state of affairs that extends into our own time.

This theologically based model of transmission of authority is far more unstable than the secular model, which treats all political forms as being more or less alike, hence offering the homogenization and uniformity that James Scott describes in *Seeing like a State*. In contrast to the social contract, the covenant between God and Abraham is marked by moments of quiet followed by other moments of prophetic interruption. Furthermore, unlike the secular transmission of authority, which is meant to be seamless ("the king is dead. Long live the king!"), Hobbes tells us that the covenant flickers in and out of existence as the Hebrews variously abandon or return to it.

In the biblical history that Hobbes adheres to, for a long period of time, the covenant is entirely suspended until it is restored by Moses. Hobbes acknowledges that, insofar as Moses is not a direct descendent of Abraham, the restoration of the covenant requires abandoning the model of hereditary descent that had been the basis of the transmission of authority to that point. Yet rather than see this as a flaw, Hobbes argues that it enables the Israelites as such to assert their own interpretive authority. He writes:

> Seeing Moses had no authority to govern the Israelites, as a successor to the right of Abraham, because he could not claim it by inheritance; it appeareth not as yet, that the people were obliged to take him for Gods Lieutenant, longer than they beleeved that God spake unto him. And therefore his authority (notwithstanding the Covenant they made with God) depended yet merely upon the opinion they had of his Sanctity, and of the reality of his Conferences with God, and the verity of his Miracles; which opinion coming to change, they were no more obliged to take any thing for the law of God, which he propounded to them in Gods name.[14]

Given the fact that the people have this power, a power to decide for themselves what they think and how they judge, it is vital to note what they do with this authority. In Hobbes's telling, initially the Israelites seek to give their interpretive authority away, offering it up to Moses. According to Hobbes:

> [Moses's] authority therefore, as the authority of all other Princes, must be grounded on the Consent of the People, and their Promise to obey him. And so it was: *For the people (Exod. 20.18.) when they saw the Thunderings, and the Lightnings, and the noyse of the Trumpet, and the mountaine smoking, removed, and stood a far off. And they said unto Moses, speak thou with us, and we will hear, but let not God speak with us lest we die.* Here was their promise of obedience, and by this it was they obliged themselves to obey whatsoever he should deliver unto them for the Commandement of God.[15]

Here, the link with archism becomes very explicit. The Israelites chose to obey Moses rather than strive to see for themselves what was happening on Mount Sinai. Not only could they not see what Moses saw, but they didn't want to; they were sufficiently terrified by the spectacle of thunder and lightning coming from the mountaintop to seek nothing but obedience and the promise to be allowed to continue to live, the basic compact of archism. In this way, an invisible power becomes directly translated into a terrestrial authority, not by people recognizing it as such but by refusing to do so.

This is part of why, for all the differences with the secular model, it is very important for Hobbes that this genealogy be read as conferring the same status upon modern-day sovereigns as the social contract genealogy does so that the two genealogies he tells appear to match up and come to the same final point. Thus he writes: "And notwithstanding the Covenant constitueth a Sacerdotall Kingdome, that is to say, a Kingdome hereditary to Aaron [Moses's brother] yet that is to be understood of the succession, after Moses should bee dead. For whosoever ordereth, and establisheth the Policy, as first founder of a Common-wealth (be it Monarchy, Aristocracy, or Democracy) must needs have Soveraign Power over the people all the while he is doing of it."[16]

Yet for all this turn to sovereignty, the prophetic transmission of authority and the popular interpretation of that authority do not cease in this transfer. Because the covenant as such only formally holds for Jews—and they are certainly not his main concern or interest—it is critical for Hobbes to allow the political model that it ushers into the world to survive, as it were, its own abandonment or its universalization to a more general model of political membership. This survival is only possible because of the prophetic nature of the transition from covenant to social contract. Exactly because the sources of authority are not fixed and determined by some clear and tangible source, there is leeway for Hobbes to insist that there is some kind of transitive principle at work in his genealogy. It is what allows him to compare communities ruled by fatherhood to those under the rule of the Levite priests and finally to kingship and modern sovereignty; each jump that he makes is enabled by the fact that the sources of that authority are invisible and prophetic, not connected to any particular human form of government even as it is subject to human interpretation (Hobbes's own interpretation very much included).

Negative Theology and Language

If that was all Hobbes had to say about prophecy, it might be fair to argue that the two origin stories, while quite disparate, eventually do come together, more or less. Yet for Hobbes, the fact of prophecy does not wholly reduce the Hebrews—and thereby the rest of us—to political obedience and quietude. On the contrary, the same acts of prophecy that help settle and determine the transmission of authority from God to human kings also produce an entirely different human response, an anarchist as opposed to an archist formulation. Because archism does not—and cannot—completely cover over the theological origins of its own authority, the remnant of the void that is, perhaps inevitably, brought along with the archist attempt to cover it up makes an entirely different relationship to the divine possible.

This other response is based on the way that for Hobbes the very void that is to be covered over by archist projections is itself a source of power for human beings. This power is not specific and individualistic, as sovereign, archist authority tends to be. Instead, it is collective and mutual. It comes not from speaking over and *as* God but from the way that the void tells us nothing, requiring but also enabling a human response in turn.

This source of collective and anarchic authority for Hobbes can perhaps be seen most clearly by looking at one of Hobbes's most important statements about his political theology (this is what Botwinick is specifically referring to in speaking of Hobbes's "negative theology"[17]). Hobbes writes that "the nature of God is incomprehensible; that is to say, we understand nothing of *what he is*, but only *that he is*; and therefore the Attributes we give him, are not to tell one another, *what he is*, nor to signifie our opinion of his Nature, but our desire to honor him with such names as we conceive most honorable amongst our selves."[18]

In thinking about God in this way, Hobbes seeks not to discover divine truth (which is impossible) but to use God as an opportunity for humans to think about their own power, about what they themselves value the most. Here, God's negativity is not a void to be covered over but a constant source of and invitation for new ideas, new values, and new judgments, a shifting and contingent basis for judgment that stems precisely and only from God's own silence.

Hobbes accepts the archist requirement of externalities as a basis for judgment, but in offering a wholly negative theology, he makes sure that externality does not offer a pure and unimpeachable archist form of interpretation. In his work, a negative theology takes a general tendency to look outward for its own sources of authority and redirects it back to the human community itself. Even when God's silence is breached, such as in a moment of prophecy, for Hobbes, those instantiations of God's will remain entirely on the level of human thought and response. Human agency therefore remains the sole basis for interpretation of that will.

Notice how closely this model resembles, at least on the surface, the standard operations of archism. In both cases, something is projected onto a blank canvas and received back as a form of authorization. The crucial difference between these modes lies in the different understandings of God each model conveys. When citing God as a way for people to be told stories about themselves and about the world that cannot be refuted or challenged because of its divine and mystical source, that is a recipe for archism. Here, the void of God's authority becomes overwritten, rendering it not a true void at all but just a screen to project archist wishes onto a divine (and unimpeachable) surface. When God is radically unavailable, however, when the boundaries between the divine and the profane are policed as stringently as Hobbes does—Benjamin is very similar in this regard—there is no ultimate and knowable archonic judge to attribute those things to and so it becomes a way for humans as a whole to discover and create their own values. This serves to subvert or bypass the fundamental bases of archism as a form of external orientation. When the ultimate externality (in this case God) is brought into the resistance to this process, it circumvents the archist basis for externality as such. Here, as with Hobbes's theological genealogy more generally, we are dealing not with a fake, archist void but a real, anarchist one.

Thus, whereas the sovereign speaks *as* God, effectively representing, replacing, and covering over rather than transmitting God's emptiness into the world, this other, collective form of power emerges from all the ways that God's silence is made legible. Here, once again, whereas the secular tale that Hobbes tells focuses on representation itself, the theological tale returns repeatedly to the void that such representation seeks to cover over. Accordingly, the anarchic response is not singular and decisive, as with the sovereign, but collective and multiple insofar as discovering what is valued most in the face of God's ongoing unknowability is a continual, nonharmonious, and undetermined process.

In making this distinction, it is critical to lay out the way that the anarchistic element that is inherent in Hobbes's negative theology is *not* representative (very much unlike Hobbes's understanding of sovereignty). Because God is utterly silent in this mode, *there is nothing there to represent*. People are forced to make their own decisions without recourse to God's ordering and approval. This puts the responsibility entirely on human actors. They are not speaking on behalf of anyone or anything—nor is anyone or anything speaking on behalf of them—but only as themselves. Without any recourse to a false (or even true) deity, the archonic nature of judgment is undermined and what you get instead is a kind of interpretive free-for-all in keeping with anarchist politics more generally.

Bereft of the archist device of representation, such a process must be collective. It is not and cannot be done among one or a few persons because to do so would reproduce the problem of archism, one or a few people deciding what God determines for the world. The only way to clearly signal that the judgments of a community are their own and not God's would be to have the entire community participate in that process, highlighting the way that this is a human attempt (hence involving all humans) and not a divine one. The very disagreements and plurality of readings that are inevitable with a mass response readily dispel any sense that the community is directly manifesting the divine will (an idea that Hobbes strenuously resists throughout his work).

Marks and Notes: The Anarchist Functioning of Language

This collective and anarchist response can perhaps be seen most concretely in terms of the way that Hobbes thinks about language more generally. For Hobbes, language is itself a collective (and I would add anarchic) enterprise. He tells us that human beings collectively decide on the meaning of words and form judgments through the engagement with meaning making that language entails. Although the sovereign is often considered the final decider for Hobbes, we can see that in fact language is not a power that the sovereign controls. Rather, the sovereign sits atop a vast network of human decisions about meaning that it is forced to recognize lest it becomes incomprehensible to its own subjects.

For Hobbes, the connection between language and theology is critical. He explains that the original author of language is not human beings (not even sovereigns) at all but God. He writes: "The first author of Speech was *God* himself, that instructed *Adam* how to name such creatures as he presented to his sight; For the Scripture goes no further in this matter. But this was sufficient to direct him to adde more names, as the experience and use of the creatures should give him occasion."[19]

Here, there is a divine source for a human power but once again that source does not eclipse but rather permits and enables human action and judgment (very much unlike human sovereign authority, which works quite the opposite way). Showing the same logic as his statements about the way that God's silence affects human beings in general, Hobbes goes on to say, "I do not find any thing in the Scripture, out of which, directly or by consequence can be gathered, that *Adam* was taught the names of all Figures, Numbers, Measures, Colours, Sounds, Fancies, Relations, much less the names of Words and Speech."[20] Thus, even in paradise Adam did not have to represent God's will when it comes to his acts of naming. He presumably comes up with all these names on his own.

God therefore is the source of language, but the practice of it is a wholly human phenomenon. God doesn't tell Adam what to name things; that remains something for Adam, Eve, and their descendants to figure out on their own (I talk more about Eve's possible subversive role, which Hobbes is far less interested in, in the conclusion). But even as they do this, it is God's original mandate to name things as well as God's ongoing silence that both require and allow and invite human judgment and decision.

In speaking further about the general practice of language, Hobbes writes:

> The generall use of Speech, is to transferre our Mentall Discourse, into Verbal; or the Trayne of our Thoughts, into a Trayne of Words; and that for two commodities; whereof one is, the Registring of the Consequences of our Thoughts; which being apt to slip out of our memory, and put to a new labour, may again be recalled, by such words as they were marked by. So that the first use of names, is to serve for *Markes*, or *Notes* of remembrance. Another is, when many use the same words, to signifie (by their connection and order,) one to another, what they conceive, or think of each matter; and also what they desire, feare, or have any other passion for. And for this use they are called *Signes*.[21]

Here we see the way that for Hobbes, language works as a vast anarchic network in which collectivities of people mutually agree on the significance of words and meanings. Signification itself, as Hobbes shows us here, is a form of collective value and judgment making, mutually laying down "*Markes*, or *Notes*" that guide people toward common but never uniform decisions (once again unlike sovereignty). Language facilitates this signage because, even before we can use words to mutually express our values, we must engage in a prior (and equally anarchic) form of collective work, agreeing on the basic sounds and meaning of words in the first place. This once again cannot be done by just a few people but must be a collective process.[22]

The anarchism of language formation also extends to the practice of language once it has been established. The meanings that are agreed upon are not anchored in some kind of ontological truth but reflect the shifting and contingent bases of human judgment. Hobbes notes, "When a man upon the hearing of any Speech, hath those thoughts which the words of that Speech, and their connexion, were ordained and constituted to signifie; Then he is said to understand it: *Understanding* being nothing else, but conception caused by Speech."[23]

Understanding then is for Hobbes only a recognition of some internalized rules of speaking (or "marks") that have been mutually agreed upon through the use of language and signification itself. Where sovereigns may seek to insist that the words they use have a definite and absolute meaning, Hobbes will never concede this point (even though it would seem to bolster the power of sovereign authority if he did). The power of words lies not in the thing itself—that is, the actual word as instrument or tool that not only conveys but in some sense constitutes a decision—but in its subjective and contingent usage, in what it is decided to mean at some given particular moment by the community that speaks and determines that language.

In this way, we can begin to see more clearly how Hobbes's concept of language connects to his concept of prophecy. Although the one is a case of humans speaking in the face of God's silence and the other is a case of God seeming to break that silence—albeit with human agents—in both cases, such speech acts serve not to bolster absolute truths but as moments of collective human judgment about what a community most values (and also what it most dislikes). Both speech acts are received into a larger community, and that community is the ultimate judge of whether that speech conforms with its own dynamic and contingent sense of meaning and value.[24]

In this way, these two phenomena, language and prophecy, both remain contingent and unsettled; they are always about their reception and not about whatever germ of truth or meaning they may (or may not) contain. This focus on understanding versus given truth is the radical and anarchic kernel of Hobbes's system of thought. Taken as a whole, these forms of collective meaning making and interpretation are a power that Hobbes will never give over to sovereign authority. While he frequently stresses that the sovereign must have the last word, even that word does not, finally, belong to sovereign authority; the sovereign is merely borrowing—stealing might be a more accurate word—that sign from the anarchic network that produced it.

Prophecy as a Collective Act

In order to look more closely at how the institution of prophecy works for Hobbes and furthermore how it is ultimately a much more radical institution than might at first appear to be the case, let me turn from a more general and abstract discussion to focus more directly on how prophecy worked in practice for Hobbes. Although it must be stressed once again that for Hobbes the formal purpose of prophecy is to produce archist political structures, I focus in what follows on the anarchist remnant that cannot be read out of these events as well as on the effect that such remnants have over the political order that derives from Hobbes's theological genealogy of political authority.

As mentioned in the very beginning of this chapter, Hobbes repeatedly stresses that instances of prophecy in Scripture should almost never be taken as an instance of God actually speaking to human beings. His insistence reflects in part his own view of the times he lived in, when, given the turmoil produced by the English Reformation and the civil war it helped produce, Hobbes saw a multitude of would-be prophets, speaking on behalf of God and spreading havoc as their various interpretations clashed with orthodox understandings as well as with one another.

Yet for all his anxiety about the dangers of widespread (and false) prophecy, Hobbes is also careful not to rule out entirely the possibility that God can speak to people. Such a possibility is itself the requirement for a great deal of human action (of both the archist and anarchist variety). A God who is present but largely silent is the indispensable basis of much of Hobbes's understanding of political authority. If God was completely absent from our world, if there was no possibility that God *could* speak to us if she so chose, the invitation to form meanings and judgments inherent in negative theology would also be withdrawn for Hobbes. By the same token, if she did speak, definitely and clearly to human actors, human decision would similarly be undercut, being trumped by a divine edict. It is precisely the ambiguity of God's speech, something that Hobbes preserves throughout his work, that allows just enough divinity to authorize human decisions and judgments without overwhelming and superseding them. In this way, Hobbes takes what is initially a problem, the ambiguous status of God's authority in the world following the 1649 execution of Charles I and the concomitant retreat from divine right authority as a basis for sovereign power, and turns it into a critical and ongoing and radical form of (anarchist) authorization.

In speaking of prophecy, in chapter 36 of *Leviathan*, Hobbes writes that "*Moses, Samuel, Elijah, Isaiah, Jeremiah,* and others were *Prophets.*"[25] He includes many others, such as the (Levite) High Priests, Abraham, and Miriam, in this category. But Hobbes also includes with this august list "they that in Christian Congregations taught the people" and, citing Scripture, describes "*every man that prayeth or prophecyeth with his head covered &c. and every woman that prayeth or prophecyeth with her head uncovered,*" effectively making virtually everyone (or at least every practicing Christian) seem to be a prophet.[26] He writes, "Prophecy in that place [of Scripture] signifieth no more, but praising God in Psalmes and Holy Songs."[27] He further explains that even poets have been considered prophets.

What does Hobbes mean by associating Abraham and Moses with a word ("prophet") that he also associates with common people and (secular) poets? Hobbes makes it clear that he considers Moses to be a kind of supreme prophet, along with the ecclesiastical hierarchy that Moses helped set up. Hobbes writes: "Onely to Moses hee spake in a more extraordinary manner in Mount *Sinai*, and in the *Tabernacle*, and to the High Priest in the *Tabernacle*, and in the *Sanctum Sanctorum* of the Temple."[28] Hobbes claims that God spoke to Moses "in such manner as a man speaketh to his friend."[29] Even so, after saying this, Hobbes almost immediately backpedals to add that even this speech was by mediation of angels and was "therefore a Vision, though a more cleer Vision than was given to other Prophets."[30]

Ultimately, for Hobbes the line between supernatural prophecy and ordinary moments of "natural" prophecy is very hard to distinguish insofar as dreams and vision shade into convictions and inspiration in all cases. He writes: "Seeing then all Prophecy supposeth Vision, or Dream (which two, when they be natural, are the same,) or some especially gift of God, so rarely observed in mankind as to be admired where observed; And seeing as well such gifts, as the most extraordinary Dreams, and Visions, may proceed from God, not onely by his supernaturall, and immediate, but also by his natural operation. . . . There is need of Reason and Judgment to discern between natural and supernaturall Gifts, and between natural, and supernaturall Visions, or Dreams."[31] Here, Hobbes is offering that the critical nature of prophecy lies, as with his discussion of language, not in the nature of the vehicle itself—that is, the question of whether the form of prophecy is clearly supernatural and transcending of ordinary modes of perception or not—but in the degree to which it is thought to accord with God's will. This is a complicated point since God's will is precisely that which is impossible to know, a will that is experienced only through the lens of subjective human experience.

Hobbes explains that accordingly, we have need of reason and judgment to adduce when a prophet is speaking for God and when she is not. More precisely, we need reason and judgment to adduce whether any kind of prophecy is godly or not, even in terms of forms that have no supernatural elements whatsoever.

This becomes even clearer when Hobbes follows this statement by cautioning that prophecy can often be false: "Consequently men had need to be very circumspect, and wary, in obeying the voice of man, that pretending himself to be a Prophet, requires us to obey God in that way, which he in Gods name telleth us to be the way to happinesse."[32]

False prophecy is, for Hobbes, a great temptation and a great danger to the community. The response to this danger must be engaged with at both the individual and the collective level: "If this examination of Prophets, and Spirits, were not allowed to every one of the people, it had been to no purpose, to set out the marks, by which every man might be able, to distinguish between those, whom they ought, and those whom they ought not to follow."[33] Here again, we see the notion of marks or notes, which are themselves the product of community decisions about what is valued and which serve as a set of mutually produced guidelines to help a community as it grapples with the appearance of prophecy. For Hobbes, the determination of whether a prophet is true or false is one of the key powers that he will always insist remains with the general public.

Although chapter 36 ends with an appeal to sovereign authority as the last word on questions of prophetic vision, it is really in the middle of the chapter that Hobbes lays out the key aspects of the politics of prophecy. As with the previous discussion of language as an anarchic network, when it comes to judging the nature and truth of prophecy, it seems clear that here too, the sovereign pronouncement only comes as an addendum to the ongoing collective process.

For the sovereign to declare a prophet false when the people have a different opinion suggests one of those breaking points between Hobbes's two origin stories. Whereas it seems clear that Hobbes would insist that the sovereign's will is determinant, given the way that God's authority serves as the bedrock of all that follows and given that all forms of interpretation rest ultimately on collective forms of decision, on marks laid down by said community, such a state of affairs would sorely try the modus vivendi between Hobbes's secular and theological tales (not to mention the authority of the sovereign in question).

In this way, we can see that calling ordinary people prophets and reducing prophecy more generally to a matter of interpretation serves not to denigrate the power of prophecy in a figure like Moses but to uplift the power of prophecy in ordinary persons. Prophecy for Hobbes, then, is not just a single person having a single vision; it is a collective act in which either one or many persons claim to speak for or with God—with that speech being taken in a variety of ways—and the entire community responding to either complete or terminate those claims through its collective acts of meaning and decision-making. Here, I reiterate a claim that I made earlier: prophecy, in Hobbes' view, *is only ever anarchic*. Its value comes not from the divine truths that it is thought to utter—it can never be said to do that in any kind of definitive way—but rather from the way that it serves to facilitate collective human forms of judgment. When prophecy is used to bolster sovereign authority and power, it is then in fact being redirected, stolen from the people's own prophetic abilities and transferred to a ruler who, by definition, will narrow and artificially freeze an ongoing and collective process into a dominating and unilateral one.

In this way, the term *prophecy* may well be the name given to this entire collective process of meaning and judgment making, and so we could indeed say that for Hobbes, everyone is a prophet (perhaps more accurately, everyone participates in prophetic speech). Hobbes offers here a means for human beings to speak of and engage with God in a way that is both deeply ordinary and still in some sense entirely sacred.

This sense of prophecy as a collective action can be further reinforced by considering Hobbes's discussion of the way that prophets predict the future. He offers that this ability in and of itself is no true sign of supernatural prophecy, even if what is predicted comes true.[34] He writes: "The woman of Endor, who is said to have had a familiar spirit, and thereby raised a Phantasme of Samuel, and thereby foretold Saul his death, was not therefore a Prophetesse, for neither had she any science, whereby she could raise such a Phantasme; nor does it appear that God commanded the raising of it; but onely guided that Imposture to be a means of Sauls terror and discouragement."[35] We see here more evidence that even evidently supernatural powers are not in and of themselves a sign of prophecy and that therefore ordinary people are not excluded from participating in prophetic acts simply because they do not possess such supernatural abilities (furthermore, archist forms of prophecy, especially modern ones, are not about predicting the future at all but are about ensuring that the status quo be projected onto the future, effectively determining it in advance). Indeed, by denying that the woman of Endor is a prophet, Hobbes is reinforcing the idea that isolated acts of divination are not in and of themselves prophetic. Prophecy, even when it comes from a single source, remains a collective and political activity.

Hobbes also notes in the following chapter on miracles that Egyptian magicians were able to perform magic tricks before the Pharaoh that, although certainly less impressive, were not necessarily all that different from the miracles that God was able to perform before the Hebrew people.[36] The focus then is not on a particular talent or trick but on a relationship with God that itself invites not an unimpeachable divine and singular response but a contingent, ever-changing human and collective one.

The central role of such public and collective forms of judgment in his political theory may be most apparent in a short set of comments that Hobbes makes about whether pagan forms of oracular sight can be considered to be instances of prophecy. In a nod of his own to the Greek heritage of prophecy, Hobbes writes: "For Incoherent Speech, it was amongst the Gentiles taken for one sort of Prophecy, because the Prophets of their Oracles, intoxicated with a spirit, or vapor from the cave of the Pythian Oracle at Delphi, were for the time really mad, and spake like mad-men; of whose loose words a sense might be made to fit any event, in such sort, as all bodies are said to be made of *Materia Prima*."[37] Although Hobbes seems to dismiss Greek prophecy out of hand (they "spake like mad-men"), we see that he recognizes the way that the oracles' words served as a kind of raw material ("*Materia Prima*") for public judgment. Outside the context of Judeo-Christian thought, the Greek example gives us a brief glimpse of the mechanics of prophecy without the sometimes obscuring architecture of Abrahamic religion. Without the burden of having to conform, or at least to attempt to conform, to divine truths—since nothing the pagan Greeks thought about theology is true for Hobbes—we see in this example a very clear case of a community learning about itself by projecting outward into what is most clearly and unambiguously (for Hobbes, at least) an empty void.

While the Greek prophetic tradition remains very much within the West, Hobbes's willingness to look beyond the Hebraic tradition itself allows us to speculate that what Hobbes says about truth and prophecy may not be limited, even to the West, but be more a feature of life as such, part of what could be called anarchism with a very small *a*.

Having considered these various aspects of Hobbes's concept of prophecy, it is striking how problematical a model this mode of political theology offers for a thinker who is thought to be wholly devoted to the promotion of archist power and authority. It would make far more sense for Hobbes to speak of a God who was an absolute and undeniable monarch rather than an invisible ghostly presence. Such a God would speak actual words and those words would have clear and indisputable meanings, ruling the world accordingly. This God would be the basis of an inviolable archism. What we get from Hobbes instead is a sovereign who is on the receiving end of a vast array of anarchist discourse and decisions. We see that language and theology, the two principal vehicles for the authorization of archist power, are also a source of its own challenge and undoing.

"A People Greedy of Prophets": Prophecy and
Interpretive Authority during the Kingdom of God

Despite this conundrum, it seems very clear that Hobbes can't and won't give us this other, more authoritarian kind of God. To do so would be to risk undermining the very archist secular power that he is purportedly seeking to promote. An active and tangible God would mean a weaker terrestrial sovereign. Such a God would not readily phase into sovereign power but serve as a permanent and inalterable rival for that power.

Here, we see quite readily the dilemma of archism more generally. Having none of its own, archism—in this case taking the form of sovereignty—steals its authority from the community (something that I return to in the conclusion, citing Hobbes specifically), and so it can't ever cut that community off or out. Insofar as prophecy itself can never come from sovereign dictates, it serves as a constant source of danger to, rather than the reinforcing of, sovereign authority more generally. Hobbes inherently recognizes and even accepts this basic fact even as doing so poses a permanent and existential threat to the archism that he is so often associated with.

The results of Hobbes's refusal to give us a truly archist and absolute deity become very clear when we look at some of the biblical history that Hobbes considers over the course of ancient Israel.[38] Here it is worth turning from *Leviathan* to the part of *De Cive* where Hobbes considers the effects of prophecy, first during the Kingdom of God itself and then (in the following section) during the period of time after the election of Saul and subsequent Hebrew kings when acts of prophecy continued to occur on a semiregular basis.

As in *Leviathan*, the key question in this part of *De Cive* is how the prophet's words are interpreted and, above all, whether and how the people decide that the prophet is true or false. Hobbes writes: "It cannot be known what *God's word* is, before we know who is the true prophet; nor can we believe *God's word*, before we believe the prophet."[39] Insofar as belief is itself subject to lies and seduction, Hobbes here repeats the argument that he makes in *Leviathan* about the use of marks and signs to distinguish between true and false prophets.

Moses was believed by the people of Israel for two things; his *miracles* and his *faith*. For how great and most evident miracles soever he had wrought, yet would they not have trusted him, at least he was not to have been trusted, if he had called them out of Egypt to any other worship than the worship of the God of Abraham, Isaac, and Jacob their fathers. For it had been contrary to the *covenant* made by themselves with God. In like manner two things there are; to wit, *supernatural prediction of things to come,* which is a mighty miracle; and *faith in the God of Abraham, their deliverer out of Egypt;* which God proposed to all the Jews to be kept for marks of a true prophet. He that wants either of these, is no prophet; nor is to be received for God's word, which he obtrudes as such.[40]

In this way, the tradition of faith and the covenant itself serve as a kind of bounded field within which prophecy must occur. Yet even that tradition remains something that comes from human collective behavior as much as it is said to be determined by divine authority (exactly as with Kafka's parable "The City Coat of Arms" about the Tower of Babel).

In terms of the development of prophecy during the Kingdom of God, Hobbes makes a fairly strong distinction between the time when Moses was God's "lieutenant" (or place holder) and the time that followed after his death. During Moses's own lifetime, Hobbes argues, there was little interpretive flexibility, especially at the collective level, and "it is manifest that this power [i.e., the power to determine the truth of statements accorded to God] during the life of Moses, was entirely in himself."[41] Hobbes also writes that "*the interpretation of the word of God* as long as Moses lived, belonged not to any other prophets whatsoever."[42] Furthermore, given that the Hebrews had pledged their loyalty to Moses specifically, allowing him to interpret God's words for them "lest they die," the fact of popular interpretation played a relatively small role in this period after the Hebrews' initial decision to let Moses interpret on their behalf.

Anyone who *did* claim to speak for God or even to challenge Moses's monopoly on this power was swiftly and definitively dealt with during this period. The story of Korah is an example of what happens when that monopoly is challenged; Hobbes records how Korah and his Levite followers were swallowed into the ground for having the audacity to question Moses's own authority and right to speak for God (Korah is a figure I return to in chapter 4).[43]

After Moses, Hobbes tells us that the power of interpretive authority became increasingly fractured and diffused. Nominally, this prophetic power henceforth resided with the High Priests who inherited Moses's prophetic authority. For Hobbes, this power remained relatively intact immediately after Moses's death but began to weaken subsequently. Thus Hobbes writes: "In Joshua's time *the interpretation of the laws,* and *of the word of God,* belonged to Eleazar the high-priest; who was also, under God, their absolute king."[44]

Anticipating the explicit linkage he will make between the authority set down during the Kingdom of God and later earthly sovereigns, Hobbes states that Eleazar "had not only *the priesthood*, but also the *sovereignty*."[45] Hobbes explicitly places the prophet Joshua himself under Eleazar's rule, explaining that "Joshua had not a power equal with that which Moses had. In the meantime it is manifest, that even in Joshua's time the supreme power and authority of interpreting the word of God, were both in one person [i.e., in Eleazar]."[46]

Following Joshua's death, a long period ensued of the Hebrew judges, lasting until the election of Saul as a human king. During this time, Hobbes writes, "the supreme civil power was therefore *rightly* due by God's own institution to the high-priest; but *actually* that power was in the prophets, to whom (being raised by God in an extraordinary manner) the Israelites, a people greedy of prophets, submitted themselves to be protected and judged, by reason of the great esteem they had of prophecies."[47] Here, we see that prophecy was explicitly set against the sovereign power of the state (such as it was).

Saying that the Israelites were "a people greedy of prophets" suggests that the Israelites were very devout and that they actively sought to have direction from their divine king, but it might also mean that they were "greedy" in a second sense as well, implying that they desired and enjoyed their own power to determine the truth of a prophecy and, in this way, sharing political power with the clergy that was formally appointed above them.

However we interpret this passage, this set of circumstances had the effect of diluting the power of the High Priests, effectively putting the people themselves in charge of determining whether the daily operations of government were going to be interrupted by prophetic interpretations of God's established will. For Hobbes, the Hebrews had access to an untrammeled form of collective interpretive authority that was not to be replicated again, with the possible exception for Hobbes of the period of the early Christian church when sovereigns were all pagans and the people—at least the Christian people—once again were relieved from having to compete with the sovereign, that great rival for interpretive authority.[48]

The extent of the people's access to this interpretive power during the period of Hebrew judges was marked not only by their de facto interpretive authority but even by their executive political authority. Thus Hobbes writes: "The reason of this thing was, because that though penalties were set and judges appointed in the institution of God's priestly kingdom; yet, the right of inflicting punishment depended wholly on private judgment; and it belonged to a dissolute multitude and each single person to punish or not to punish, according as their private zeal should stir them up."[49] As is evident here, Hobbes was not entirely sanguine about the nature of this collective power, offering that "if men were such as they should be, this were an excellent state of civil government; but as men are, there is a coercive power . . . necessary to rule them."[50] For Hobbes, this is the reason that God gave the Hebrews so many laws in the first place, to bind people within their otherwise fairly loose and shifting forms of self-government. Yet, in a way, this just begs the question since those laws are themselves of course subject to human judgment and interpretation.

Hobbes concludes his discussion of the Kingdom of God by reasserting the de facto power of the prophets over the High Priests: "If therefore regard be had to the *right* of the kingdom, the supreme civil power and the authority of interpreting God's word were jointed in the high-priest. If we consider the *fact*, they were united in the prophets who judged Israel. For as *judges*, they had the civil authority; as *prophets*, they interpreted God's word."[51] Here, Hobbes is leaving out any mention of his own earlier statements that, because the people had the ultimate power of deciding whether the prophet spoke truly for God, they had a lot of say—even the ultimate say—in terms of how God's word was adduced and interpreted. Even with this omission, however, insofar as Hobbes makes interpretation of God's law not only necessary but inevitable, and given that he denies that there is only one correct way to interpret that law, the implementation of human law in accordance with divine law during this period is markedly—and radically—distinguished from later forms of political rule and authority when it comes to the level of popular input into critical political questions.

Interrupted by God: Prophecy
during the Time of the Hebrew Kings

After the period of Hebrew judges ended with the election of Saul, a period of active prophecy persisted for quite some time. In this way, the Hebrew kings did not enjoy the monopoly of interpretation that Hobbes suggests is their right as well as the right of all future sovereigns. Like the High Priests before them, the Hebrew kings had to share power because they could not control or eliminate prophetic politics, just as modern-day sovereigns cannot serve as the sole arbiter of meaning in language. Because this period is the direct link that Hobbes makes between the power of God and the power of contemporary human kings in terms of his genealogy of sovereign authority, this transition period is critical for understanding what is preserved and what is lost in the change from divine to human sovereignty.

Whereas Hobbes might not have been as concerned with protecting the power of the High Priests against the rival power of the prophets—and, behind them, the power of the people themselves—one would not expect him to be as sanguine about that rivalry now that human kings have been introduced into the picture. Even so, Hobbes refuses to abandon the alternative forms of interpretive authority that he attributes to periods marked by prophecy, with important implications for the way that we think of popular versus sovereign forms of interpretive authority in Hobbes's time (as well as our own).

Hobbes begins his discussion of the period of Hebrew kings in *De Cive* by initially certifying that these rulers did have absolute political and civil authority: "Kings once being constituted, it is no doubt but the civil authority belonged to them. For the kingdom of God by way of the priesthood (God consenting to the request of the Israelites) was ended."[52]

Hobbes bases this kingly usurpation of priestly rule directly on the idea that the people acquiesced in subjecting themselves to the kings in a way that they did not when it came to the High Priests: "The oaths of the new priesthood and new sovereignty in Zadok and David, do testify that the right, whereby the *kings* did rule, was founded in the very concession of the people. The priest could rightly do only what God commanded him, whereas the king could rightly do to every man whatsoever every man could right do himself; for the Israelites granted him *a right to judge* of all things, and to *wage war* for all men; in which two are contained all right whatsoever can be conceived from man to man."[53] If this passage represents an attempt to bridge Hobbes's two genealogies of sovereign power that thread throughout his work, it must contend with the fact of ongoing prophecy—and thus popular interpretive power as well—during this period. God may no longer be king of ancient Israel at this point, but divine will always serves as a trump to the terrestrial power that is said to derive from it.

This is a tension that Hobbes grapples with throughout the text. In a very telling moment in this part of *De Cive*, Hobbes considers how law was propagated during the period of Hebrew kings. At first he says the kings had the absolute power of interpretation of the laws of Scripture. He even goes further—anticipating the creation of civil law in future kingdoms, the kingdom of England very much included—and says, "Forasmuch as the word of God must be taken for a law, if there had been another written word beside the Mosaical law, seeing the interpretation of laws belonged to the kings, the interpretation of it must also have belonged to them."[54] In this way, the kings have not only the power to interpret God's law but to also make up new laws of their own that similarly have to be obeyed. Here the transition from divine to human law seems to be complete.

Yet these secular laws remain troubled by the divine laws, which do not entirely disappear from the scene. Hobbes describes a moment when God's laws, which had been temporarily lost, were restored to the people and how that law was reinscribed.

> When the book of Deuteronomy, in which the whole Mosaical *law* was contained, being a long time lost was found again; *the priests* indeed asked counsel of God concerning that book, but not by their own authority, but by the commandments of Josiah; and not immediately neither, but by the means of Holda the prophetess. Whence it appears that the authority of admitting books for the word of God, belonged not to the priest. Neither yet follows it, that that authority belonged to the prophetess; because others did judge of the prophets, whether they were to be held for true or not. For to what end did God give signs and tokens to the people, whereby the true prophets might be discerned from the false; namely the event of predictions, and conformity with the religion established by Moses; if they might not use these marks?[55]

Here we see once again the specter of popular forms of interpretation rivaling or even displacing sovereign authority. Hobbes's immediate answer to this question is to reassert the power of kings. He writes that "the authority therefore of admitting books for *the word of God*, belonged to the king; and thus that book of the law was approved, and received again by the authority of king Josiah."[56]

Yet, even as he makes this claim, we see that there is a certain amount of ambiguity in his earlier statement that "others did judge of the prophets, whether they were to be held for true or not." Insofar as the "marks" that God set by to determine whether a prophet was true or false are not the exclusive property of the king and are readily available to everyone, it seems that Hobbes will not completely eclipse this other collective interpretive power in favor of the power of kings. Indeed, even when he explicitly says it is God who leaves these marks, for Hobbes such moments are still only ever expressed and responded to by human actors. In this sense, they aren't really "God's" marks at all but human marks seeking to set out the parameters of the way that divine agency can be read into the world.

With such marks in hand, Hobbes maintains the power of collective reading and interpretation in a way that specifically locates such power in the collective rather than in a sovereign body. If anything, one gets the sense, once again, that such marks serve to ensure that, should the king or sovereign decide to read God's words or acts in a way that went against those marks, the people would have a basis by which to reject and undermine that decision in favor of their own.

Hobbes reiterates this discrepancy when he writes that "prophets were sent not with authority, but in the form and by the right of proclaimers and preachers of whom the hearers did judge."[57] This statement too seems meant to convey the degree to which the prophets did not usurp sovereign authority. Yet here too, the very idea that "the hearers did judge" cannot help but include the people themselves who at this point seem to have dropped out of the conversation but remain present (as hearers), the veritable elephant(s) in the room.[58]

The final moment of the story of the Hebrews and their relationship to interpretive authority for Hobbes comes after the return from the Babylonian captivity. This period too is relatively anarchic and, for this reason, the disavowed (but not denied) power of popular interpretation returns in much greater force.

> After their return from Babylonian bondage, the *covenant* being renewed and signed, *the priestly kingdom* was restored to the same manner it was in from the death of Joshua to the beginning of the kings; excepting that it is not expressly set down, that the returned Jews did give up the right of sovereignty either to Esdras, by whose directions they ordered their state, or to any other beside God himself. That reformation seems rather to be nothing else, than the bare promises and vows of every man, to observe those things which were written in the book of the law.[59]

In contrast to the earlier period that he also considers to be a priestly kingdom, Hobbes argues that this period was relatively unstable and marked by great corruption. He writes: "Now, howsoever through the ambition of those who strove for the priesthood, and by the interposition of foreign princes, it was so troubled till our Saviour Jesus Christ's time, that it cannot be understood out of the histories of those times, where that authority resided; yet it is plain, that in those times the power of *interpreting God's word* was not severed from the supreme civil power."[60] One telling point here is that, although there continued to be prophets after the return from exile (Haggai, Zachariah, and Malachi specifically), they no longer really figure into Hobbes's narrative. The explicitly acknowledged power of prophecy—and through that, the implicit power of popular interpretation—becomes increasingly threatening to the edifice of sovereign authority and it may be for this reason that Hobbes generally ceases to even speak of it. Even as the Hebrews lose their own kings, other kings (foreign princes) are now involved and so sovereignty—human sovereignty, that is—seems like it is here to stay.

Yet here again, we see the same phenomenon that was previously noted; Hobbes takes the power of God almost down to the vanishing point but, when push comes to shove, he won't eliminate it. Referring to the power of *"interpreting God's words,"* Hobbes doesn't specify who is doing the interpreting but, based on his own understandings, he cannot and will not exclude popular and collective forms of reading. Even though for Hobbes there is a clear threat that prophecy and the popular forms of interpretation that it conveys pose to sovereignty, he will never explicitly repudiate it. Instead, he generally either stops talking about it or only refers to it obliquely. Sometimes too it reemerges in the text in new, often more secular, forms, perhaps most famously in the introduction to *Leviathan* with Hobbes's admonition to his readers to *"Read thy self,"* whereby "[the reader] shall thereby read and know what are the thoughts, and Passions of all other men."[61] Here the possibility of widespread and collective acts of prophecy becomes fully secularized as the act of reading itself. Yet, however secularized it may be, in essence the effects—along with the subversive political implications—are the same; whenever people are able to interpret (and they always are for Hobbes), an alternative source of interpretive authority is present and active. The sovereign may well try to appropriate this power for itself (and at times, Hobbes seems to explicitly seek for it to do so), but that power is only ever a stolen one and for this reason remains forever vulnerable to popular reappropriation.

This entire exercise of going through Hobbes's discussion of prophecy and its relationship to kingly as well as popular forms of authority is meant to demonstrate the myriad ways in which that coexistence is always fraught. We see here once again that the very acts that establish archist forms of rule (as Hobbes insists is the case) are also the basis for undermining that authority, effecting an archist appointment as well as a corresponding form of collective and popular disappointment. In this way archism is always haunted by anarchism and Hobbes shows us exactly how and why this is the case (I once again don't think the reverse is true, as I argue further in chapter 6). What you get in Hobbes is not so much a resolution but an ongoing struggle as the archist power is ever exposed, undermined by its own prime agent, the purely negative power of God.

Prophecy without Any Prophets:
Modernity and the Holy Spirit

In our own time—and Hobbes's as well—prophecy, at least in most of the Abrahamic faiths that have contributed to modern and Western archism, is seen to have fallen silent.[62] Yet there remains a way in which Hobbes keeps that prophetic interruptive element alive in the theological genealogy he presents us with. For Hobbes, we live in a time that is sandwiched between God's kingdoms. In chapter 41 of *Leviathan*, Hobbes tells us that Christ's mission is to restore the Kingdom of God. He was "to restore unto God, by a new Covenant, the Kingdom, which being his by the Old Covenant, had been cut off by the rebellion of the Israelites in the election of Saul."[63]

The two Kingdoms of God serve as bookends for the period of human rule and sovereignty that we currently inhabit. During this in-between time, the Kingdom of God is suspended. Instead of being ruled by God, we get ruled by a stand-in for that divine authority; in this time, God is represented in the world both figuratively and literally. For Hobbes, the figurative representations of God are the Father, the Son, and the Holy Spirit. He further tells us that each of these figures also corresponds to a literal "person," where God is embodied and acted for on Earth. Hobbes explains that God the Father is personified by Moses and God the Son is personified by Jesus. These two figures usher in the two Kingdoms of God. The third figure, God the Holy Spirit, which is the figure for our in-between time, is personified by "the Apostles, and their successors, in the Office of Preaching, and Teaching, that had received the Holy Spirit [and] have Represented him [i.e., God] ever since."[64]

Chapter 42, by far the longest chapter in *Leviathan*, is dedicated to the figure of the Holy Spirit and the persons it relates to. In that chapter, Hobbes tells us that the power of the Holy Spirit is explicitly *not* a political power: it works for "winning men to obedience, not by Coercion, and Punishing; but by Perswasion."[65] By the same token, Hobbes notes that this ecclesiastical power is itself resistant to coercive political power. He says that if a "King, or a Senate, or other Soveraign Person forbid us to beleeve in Christ . . . such forbidding is of no effect; because Beleef, and Unbeleef never follow mens Commands."[66]

Here, the tension between sovereign and people over religious matters that I alluded to earlier is brought out in the open; the violent and coercive power of sovereignty is set against the persuasive and collective power of belief and collective forms of valuation and is shown to be an ineffective power indeed. Although many read this passage and others like it as a justification for Hobbes's requirement that the clergy be subsumed to the secular sovereign power, it also can be read as a testament to the lasting power of that other political—and anarchic—form of popular decision.[67] Although here, and throughout chapter 42, Hobbes is talking formally about church officials and ecclesiastical doctrine, this ecclesiastical power—and the belief it is based upon—is rooted just as much in popular authority, in reading the "marks" left in the world to guide belief and in the kinds of collective conversations and decisions that anchor those marks and beliefs, than in any formal and hierarchical structure.

When it comes to the content of this belief, Hobbes winnows it down once again almost, but not entirely, to the vanishing point. In a subsequent discussion of martyrdom, he explains that there is only one tenet of faith that is worthy to die for and that is "*Jesus is the Christ*" (in the chapter that follows, he will repeat this point, saying that this doctrine is all that is needed for an individual to gain salvation).[68] Hobbes goes on to say, "To die for every [other] tenet that serveth the ambition or profit of the Clergy, is not required."[69]

Winnowing down all of Christian doctrine to such a simple statement may seem to suggest that Hobbes is not interested in Christian belief—as many have argued—at all, but I think in this instance too it could just as easily be the case that in so narrowing the critical basis for Christianity, Hobbes enhances the power of popular forms of belief over the narrow liturgical forms of expertise that church leaders themselves might seek to exercise.[70] If the "mark" set down for Christianity is simply that "Jesus is the Christ," then this works, as his negative theology does more generally to permit and even require a great deal of human innovation and response on a widespread and anarchic level so that here the "person" of the Holy Spirit is much broader than the Church and the Apostles and is embodied, in effect, by the entire community.

This sense of a broadening of the person of the Holy Spirit is perhaps suggested in the way that Hobbes seeks to reduce ecclesiastic authority even as he refuses, as ever, to surrender popular interpretive authority. Much of chapter 42 reads like a litany of powers that Hobbes takes away from the Church. He says, for example, that the Church does not have the right to refuse baptism to one who seeks it or to deem that a person's belief and repentance are insincere. Hobbes says of the latter issue: "Seeing no man is able to discern the truth of another mans Repentance, further than by externall marks, taken from his words, and actions, which are subject to hypocrisie; another question will arise, Who it is that is constituted Judge of those marks. And this question is decided by our Saviour himself."[71] In denying the Church this kind of power over its subjects, Hobbes is effectively keeping that power in the heart of each subject, both separately and together. This can be read as another example of negative theology; giving that power over to Jesus effectively leaves it up to the human community as a whole since Jesus is currently absent from the world. So empowered, those subjects, rather than the church per se, collectively form and develop the bases of belief. For this reason, although Hobbes will never say that the Holy Spirit is a popular entity—so that its person could once again constitute not just the apostles and the church ministers but all members of the community—at least by implication, the Holy Spirit is personified by each subject both separately and taken as a whole and not just by an ecclesiastical elite.

Hobbes further reinforces this possibility when he points out the example of Paul's coming to a synagogue in Thessalonika and seeking to convince the Jews there, based on their own scripture, that Jesus is the Christ. Hobbes says that although all believed in the Jewish scripture itself, some believed his arguments and some did not. Hobbes writes: "Whosoever perswadeth by reasoning from principles written, maketh him to whom hee speaketh Judge, both of the meaning of those principles, and also of the force of his inferences upon them. If these Jews of Thessalonica were not, who else was the Judge of what S. Paul alledged out of Scripture?"[72] Here again, the "hearers" are the people rather than the clergy or other leaders. And this is in the face of not just any officer of the Church but of the Apostle Paul himself! Each person judges for herself what she believes and collectively a sense of the larger boundaries of belief systems—such as constitute Judaism or Christianity—are mutually established.

In perhaps his clearest word on the subject, Hobbes cites the Bible and comments upon that citation, writing: "Our Saviour himselfe saith to the Jews (*John 5.39*) *Search the Scriptures; for in them yee thinke to have eternall life, and they are they that testifie of me.* If hee had not meant that they [i.e., the Jews] should Interpret them, hee would not have bidden them take thence the proof of his being the Christ. He would either have Interpreted them himself, or referred them to the Interpretation of the Priests."[73] Interpretation itself then is the basis for the power of Scripture and, by extension, for the power of the Holy Spirit. Power does not come from office or station but through belief and persuasion; it is not a power to make one uniform reading true—although Hobbes implies that Christ does have that power—but, on the contrary, it is a power to make multiple, even conflicting interpretations possible.

This is an indication that the interpretive power that Hobbes discusses throughout *De Cive* and *Leviathan* is anarchic, not only in the sense of being collective but also insofar as it does not create one harmonious whole but a mutually contradictory, contingent, and ever-changing engagement with belief. The "marks" that Hobbes repeatedly refers to suggest a general baseline for discourse (such as "Jesus is the Christ"), but on a day-to-day level, there is more difference than agreement in these kinds of collective decision-making processes—in a sense the paucity of a concept like "Jesus is the Christ" is precisely what admits so much diversity and fluidity of interpretation. The anarchist life that Hobbes depicts is thus a lot messier but also a lot more dynamic than is offered by the homogenized and determined subjects of a standard archist understanding. Here again, Hobbes's version of anarchism—if I have been persuasive—refers to life as such and not to any edict or rule that stands outside and above it.

Accordingly, given that the Holy Spirit offers an interpretive power, Hobbes takes great pains to ensure that the idea of being inspired by the Holy Spirit is not to be taken literally as some kind of uniform and undeniable truth that enters the body wholesale as some of his contemporaries, and in particular, some Puritan thinkers of his time, were arguing.[74] He writes, for example: "Where St. Peter (2 *Pet.* 1.21.) saith, that *Prophecy came not in old time by the will of man, but the holy men of God spake as they were moved by the Holy Spirit*, by the Holy Spirit is meant the voice of God in a Dream, or Vision supernaturall, which is not *Inspiration:* Nor when our Saviour breathing on his Disciples said, *Receive the Holy Spirit*, was that Breath the Spirit, but a sign of the spirituall graces he gave unto them."[75] Here, as with the previous discussion of Christian doctrine more generally, Hobbes seeks to narrow the meaning of the term *Holy Spirit* to avoid making it a literal possession of a person by some kind of tangible, albeit holy, ghost. To think in that way would be to colonize the alternative form of collective interpretive power with the unifying and homogenizing archist sovereign power that it is always in tension with throughout Hobbes's texts.

In perhaps his most important passage of all on the question of the Holy Spirit and its radical emptiness, Hobbes explicitly argues that to think of the Holy Spirit as anything but a collective and interpretive enterprise is to turn it into an idol. He says this in part IV of *Leviathan*, which is devoted to combatting all forms of devotional and representational idolatry.[76] There, Hobbes writes:

Whereas there be, that pretend Divine Inspiration, to be a supernaturall entring of the Holy Ghost into a man, and not an acquisition of Gods grace, by doctrine, and study; I think they are in a very dangerous Dilemma. For if they worship not the men whom they beleeve to be so inspired, they fall into Impiety; as not adoring Gods supernaturall Presence. And again, if they worship them, they commit Idolatry; for the Apostles would never permit themselves to be so worshipped. Therefore the safest way is to beleeve, that by the Descending of the Dove upon the Apostles; and by Christs Breathing on them, when hee gave them the Holy Ghost; and by the giving of it by Imposition of Hands, are understood the signes which God hath been pleased to use, or ordain to bee used, of his promise to assist those persons in their study to Preach his Kingdome, and in their Conversation, that it might not be Scandalous, but Edifying to others.[77]

Here again, we see a discussion of marks and signs, guideposts—but nothing more than that—to assist humans in their own attempts to make sense of the world around them. Hobbes also tells us that the Holy Spirit is called "an *Assister*."[78] The Holy Spirit—or ghost, in this case—is manifested in "doctrine, and study"; it is present in both the marks of faith (doctrine) and the interpretive response to those marks (study).

In a sense, the Holy Spirit is for Hobbes the terrestrial avatar of negative theology, the incarnation, as it were, of the pure void that is God. It has no content of its own whatsoever; instead, it serves to bring that radical emptiness that it represents into the world, to stand in contrast to the faux readings and truths that are constantly being projected onto God as well as other sources of authority. Accordingly, the Holy Spirit for Hobbes represents the idea that no text has an absolute and clear meaning that is given on its face. Through its negation of absolute truths, the Holy Spirit allows for individual and collective and multiple acts of interpretation and response to be both possible and necessary.

And in this case, the form of representation that we see in the case of the Holy Spirit is of a radically different sort than how representation normally operates in the time after prophecy. Without God as king or prophets to speak on behalf of God, the modern age perforce turns to a certain form of representation to stand in for a God that has become silent. This is the basis for modern archism since a silent God cannot interrupt or interfere the way that modern archons use the concept of divine will as a means to realize their own desires, power, and authority.

The Holy Spirit is different. In its pure emptiness, it makes God's own radical negative theology present in the world in a way that it would not otherwise be. This is a form of negative representation—maybe de-presentation would be a better word—that dispels and interferes with the faux forms of representation that we find in other mechanisms of authority in the world.

In its very blankness, the Holy Spirit keeps open that negative space that God offers human beings as an invitation to their own interpretive power (we see the radical possibilities of evoking such blankness in chapter 5 when I consider Saramago's novel *Seeing*). In this way, the Holy Spirit works very much as Benjamin's notion of divine violence does, a purely negative force that interferes with attempts to fetishize and control the idea of God's own will—or whatever secular manifestation of that will is in question—as a force in the world.

As the figure of our own time, the Holy Spirit, therefore, thwarts the absolutism of archist forms of authority that it is often evoked to serve and bolster. Devoid of any truth content of its own, the Holy Spirit acts to counteract or undermine the confidence that Hobbes displays in other parts of *Leviathan* about religious doctrine, science, and natural law as the basis for some kind of certain and enforceable truth. Any decree by any terrestrial archon—but also by a purportedly celestial one as well—is instantly put into question when faced with the radical void that the Holy Spirit (de)represents. In the face of such a void—that is, in the face of God's silence—everything is subject to conversation, interpretation, and possibly resistance too.

Perhaps most critically of all, insofar as Hobbes offers us this figure and the corresponding persons of the Holy Spirit, this means that even though formal prophecy has gone silent, the prophetic function that we all partake in has not. The community retains its interpretive authority—once again as suggested by Hobbes's admonition to "*Read thyself*"—even or perhaps especially after the rival archist forms of prophecy (that is, "real" prophets who "really talked to God") have long since ceased. It could indeed be said that the Holy Spirit is even an improvement upon earlier prophetic forms as far as its radical anarchist potential is concerned. Unlike earlier prophetic figures like Moses or Jeremiah, the Holy Spirit cannot be read to offer any formal value of its own; with no content or agency of its own, it cannot be seduced into the powers of archist prophecy that it might seem to convey. In this way, as a wholly negative figure, the Holy Spirit is perhaps a more pure vehicle for the kinds of popular forms of interpretation that prophecy constitutes more generally. In this sense we might say that even though formal prophecy has fallen silent for Hobbes, the radical implications of prophecy are, if anything, enhanced in our own "post-prophetic" age.

The Holy Spirit ensures that this widespread collective interpretive power will be with us as long as we remain between Kingdoms of God. And, given that this period is the time marked by human sovereignty, Hobbes ensures in this way that, so long as we are stuck with sovereigns, we always have the Holy Spirit as a way to ensure that its decrees do not totalize and determine either us or the world around us.

The anarchist and collective power that comes from such a source is easy to miss in the face of sovereign authority (recall, once again, Hobbes's point about the sun outshining the stars). It is true that Hobbes will always formally insist that when resistance occurs, it happens only within the heart of each individual and so appears to be only a minor and private form of resistance. Yet over the course of *Leviathan* in particular, one can see how this is not actually the case. For Hobbes, individuals do not exist in isolation from one another; everything we think and say comes out of the vast anarchist ferment of language and meaning making that we all participate in. This extends once again even to the interpretive power of the sovereign (if we take that creature as an individual as well), insofar as it is itself always a creature of and a response to that conversation. The sovereign has no separate vocabulary or basis of power, nor does it have a separate prophetic power of its own; everything it says and does comes out of the same linguistic ferment as larger collective decisions. The sovereign's interpretation is therefore more like the tip of an iceberg than a separate force and entity. Its claims to own and determine this entire production of meaning and judgment rings hollow in the face of the vastness and complexity of that anarchist ferment that it stands over and draws from.

Given all the above, the Holy Spirit is the remnant of the prophetic power that Hobbes discusses in earlier moments in his theological genealogy. Just as during the time of active prophecy, the words of prophets became an opportunity for a community to decide what it thought (in all the variety those thoughts came in), so too does the Holy Spirit permit these same kinds of conversations in our own time. Only what was once a kind of waiting game, wherein the people had to be presented with the opportunity of an act of prophetic sight in order to be able to determine their own response, in our time becomes acts of common and collective prophesying, which can and do happen all the time.

Once again, whereas formal prophecy has disappeared from the world, the kind of collective discussions and decisions it instantiates has not. If I have been convincing that prophecy itself is a collective—and anarchic— phenomenon, then the Holy Spirit is a form of prophecy without the prophet, or perhaps more accurately, it is a reflection of the generalization of prophecy from specific individuals (be it Moses, Miriam, Jeremiah, etc.) to the general population.

Furthermore, in insisting on the separation of the power of the Holy Spirit from any kind of sovereign authority, which is a big part of what he argues for in chapter 42, Hobbes may be offering us a glimpse of an anarchist response without its necessary entanglement with the sovereign form. If for Hobbes archism and anarchism can be said to be mutually produced through the exercises of asserting political authority, the Holy Spirit allows us to see what anarchism might look like when it is clearly separated from that archist or sovereign aspect. The Holy Spirit could therefore be taken as the name of the prophetic and anarchic element in our own time, a time when God is no longer king and hence a time when humans are, at least potentially, left to their own devices, left, that is, with the possibility of having no kings, no archons at all.

We Are All Prophets Now

Given these various claims, we should take seriously the possibility that Hobbes means it when he tells us that anyone can be (in fact already is) a prophet, just as he explains that we are all authors too.[79] If we are all prophets, at least potentially, then even in our own times—which are also Hobbes's time—when the kinds of formal modes of prophecy that I have been discussing are no longer available, there will still be some form of prophecy, however diffused, to challenge sovereign forms of political authority. If we are all prophets, guided by the Holy Spirit—and thereby returned to our own devices—then this radical alternative has become a permanent feature of the modern political landscape even despite the move to ever greater secularization. Such secularization can never hurt the Holy Spirit; having no content of its own, there is nothing in it to disprove or lose faith in. Through the figure of the Holy Spirit, Hobbes offers a way to circumvent the requirement that all human meaning and value be processed via an externality. Or rather he makes sure that the externality in question is the Holy Spirit itself, a portal to a transcendent realm that tells us absolutely nothing at all but does accurately reflect its own void-like qualities, qualities that archism is forever trying to paper over. In this case, the externality that the Holy Spirit gives us access to serves to turn the human agents who are seeking answers right back to themselves and to their own discursive and meaning-making practices.

In order to think a bit more about the possibility of everyone being a prophet, let me once again cite an earlier passage in *Leviathan*, chapter 36 (but in an expanded form) in order to consider the degree to which this assertion ought to be taken as a serious challenge to archist forms of interpretation. Recall that Hobbes wrote:

> In the same sense, the Prophets that came down from the High place (or Hill of God) with a Psaltery, and a Tabret, and a Pipe, and a Harp [I. *Sam.* 10.5, 6.] and [vers. 10] Saul amongst them, are said to Prophecy, in that they praised God, in that manner publiquely. . . . So it is also to be taken [I. *Cor.* 11.4, 5.] where St. Paul saith, *Every man that prayeth or prophecyeth with his head covered &c. and every woman that prayeth or prophecyeth with her head uncovered*: For Prophecy in that place, signifieth no more, but praising God in Psalmes, and Holy Songs: which women might doe in the Church, though it were not lawfull for them to speak to the Congregation.[80]

If every person is both praying and prophesizing whenever they make a public display of praising God, then prophecy is indeed a rather common event, part of the everyday aspect of contemporary life. Hobbes extends this power to women even while they are not formally allowed to speak to the congregation, another sign that the hierarchies of Hobbes's own time (and ours) could not trump the fully collective nature of prophecizing as such. This point could even be extended past Hobbes's own formal claim that only Christians proclaiming about God can be said to be engaging in prophesizing. Perhaps this activity could be said to be something that people engage with whenever they think about what they most value, making those values public to others and enabling them to think collectively about what kind of life and polity they wish to have, whether they are Christian, Muslim, Jewish, Hindu, Sikh, Buddhist, agnostic, atheist, or any other form of belief (or disbelief).[81]

But surely, one could argue, this is not what Hobbes means in this passage. Surely he is only reducing prophecy down to the point where its political potency—a potency that we have seen Hobbes directly contrast to sovereign power—is nearly eliminated. My response to this is to say that to nearly but not entirely eliminate this power is effectively to keep it intact, hiding it in plain sight. This remnant of the divine power of prophecy—which for Hobbes in modern times is once again present in the figure of the Holy Spirit—is all that people need in order to be able to maintain their ability to pose challenges to sovereign forms of rule. This is the case even when theology has been formally left behind, as my comments about prophecy and language as both being forms of collective value creation might indicate.

Therein lies the paradox that we find in Hobbes's writing on prophecy; because he seeks to almost, but never entirely, eliminate prophecy in favor of secular forms of power—leaving a tiny remnant of the divine void intact in the form of a negative theology—the very operation of trying to eliminate prophecy as a political force by restricting and watering it down becomes the basis by which that force is maintained and preserved in the heart of the process of political interpretation. Every time Hobbes seems to diminish prophecy, calling it "only" metaphorical or what have you, he is also spreading that power to the larger community and, in this way, actually diminishing the absolute power of sovereign interpretive authority instead, revealing how it is in effect a wholly derivative and parasitical power. In the end, interpretive authority is in fact, for Hobbes, the only kind of authority that really matters, perhaps the only form of authority that exists, period.

This unacknowledged but persistent core of Hobbes's understanding of interpretation, the radical prophetic kernel that lies under all that secularization, means that Hobbes can never escape the more radical implications of his own work. In a nutshell: without a spark of prophecy, there can be no sovereignty, but with that spark, sovereignty is permanently endangered by this other and competing mode of interpretation that this spark (or "spirit") also permits; in this way, the two genealogies of political authority that Hobbes offers us never come to the same point but remain in perpetual and irremediable tension. And here, we come to the subversive heart of Hobbes's understanding of prophecy and all that it entails.

IN THE FOLLOWING CHAPTERS, on Nietzsche and Benjamin, I explore the idea of having God abandon the position of archon, either by "dying" in Nietzsche's case or giving up the role of ultimate judge in Benjamin's. For these thinkers, the tension between archism and anarchism is much more overt than it is with Hobbes himself. While Hobbes remains resolutely silent on the nature of God, for Nietzsche and Benjamin, even God is enlisted in an anarchist political project. Accordingly, what is only suggested in Hobbes's text comes fully to the surface, changing from a permanent potential to an active and openly revolutionary force in the case of the latter two thinkers, particularly for Benjamin. If Hobbes shows us that even in the heart of archism, we find the preservation and nurturance of a radical anarchist kernel, with Nietzsche and Benjamin—and many other authors and thinkers I consider in the pages that follow—we get something more akin to a full-fledged revolution in political theology.

chapter three

a most disappointing prophet

Nietzsche's Zarathustra

OF ALL THE THINKERS AND WRITERS that I treat in this book, Nietzsche is probably the one with the greatest willingness to disappoint. Nietzsche himself often gloats about the way he betrays, deceives, and lets down his readers, as, for example, when he writes in *The Genealogy of Morals*, "As regards my *Zarathustra*, I think no one should claim to know it who has not been, by turns, deeply wounded and deeply delighted by what it says."[1] To read a text of Nietzsche's is to be by turns led to the height of hope and possibility and then, moments later, to have that hope dashed cruelly and utterly (and not just once but over and over again). Nietzsche could be thought of less as a philosopher and more as someone who commits a series of psychic exercises, the purpose of which is to break us (and him!), once and for all, from our hope for archist salvation.

Through these highs and lows, Nietzsche's *Thus Spoke Zarathustra* works in cycles of appointment and disappointment. At times, Zarathustra appears to be the epitome of an archist prophet, offering life, wisdom, and access to "halcyon heights" to his readers. He starts out in a famous statement to the sun in which he says:

Great star! What would your happiness be, if you had not those for whom you shine!

You have come up here to my cave for ten years: you would have grown weary of your light and of this journey, without me, my eagle and my serpent.

But we waited for you every morning, took from you your superfluity and blessed you for it.

Behold! I am weary of my wisdom, like a bee that has gathered too much honey: I need hands outstretched to take it.[2]

We see here that Zarathustra is duplicating in this moment the bases of archist appointment. He sees a remote externality—in this case, the sun—and determines that it is, in effect, working on his behalf. He takes its "superfluity," it's excess of wisdom, and uses it to preach, to go among other human beings and teach them what he has learned. In this way, Zarathustra is appointing himself (via his imagined relationship to the sun) as a kind of urarcheonic figure. He is up high and he has to now "descend into the depths: as [the sun does] at evening" to dispense his precious wisdom to the masses who are otherwise ignorant and incapable of gaining such wisdom on their own.[3]

Zarathustra even evokes an explicitly visual model for his relationship to the sun, although the sun itself, as the basis for all light and vision, is already deeply imbued with the supremacy of vision as a master sense. He says, "So bless me then, tranquil eye, that can behold without envy even an excessive happiness!" (at the very end of book 4, Zarathustra says another version of the same greeting, this time calling the sun the "eye of happiness").[4] The sun itself becomes an "eye" whose vision scans the world. It does so "without envy" since the sun is so much above the sin and fleshiness of the world. By identifying himself with the sun, effectively seeing that world through the eye of the sun, and therefore from the greatest possible height, Zarathustra sets up a basis by which he and he alone has something to tell the rest of the human race.

In this mode, Zarathustra is entirely in keeping with the model of archist prophets described in chapter 1 of this book. He promises a bright, shining future and the ability to be redeemed. Yet, at the same time, and sometimes in the exact same sentence, Zarathustra undermines and ruins this very same archist stance. Even in his ode to the sun, we see a small hint of this insofar as, by acknowledging the fact that the sun, like Zarathustra himself, has highs and lows, it also may suggest that in addition to serving as a basis for appointment, the sun might also set up Zarathustra for disappointment (as will indeed be the case in this book). In this other, anarchist mode, Zarathustra himself is, above all, one who disappoints.[5]

Perhaps the clearest example of the way Zarathustra disappoints his would-be followers (one that I have commented on several times in past writings) comes in the part of *Thus Spoke Zarathustra* called "On Redemption."[6] This is probably the section that most epitomizes Zarathustra's unique version of prophecy. In that section, a series of ill and disabled people come up to Zarathustra while he is crossing a bridge. They beg him to heal them. Were he to be more of the usual variety of archist prophet, he undoubtedly would have done so insofar as performing apparent miracles is a key way that archist prophecy announces its connection to truth. Yet Zarathustra refuses to do as they ask, forcing these people to be (and possibly love) themselves as they are. Not only does he refuse to heal them, but he even identifies with them, saying he is "a seer, a willer, a creator, a future itself and a bridge to the future—and alas, also like a cripple upon this bridge: Zarathustra is all this."[7]

In describing himself this way, Zarathustra is once again using the language of archist prophecy. In this setting, he and he alone can see the path forward; he and he alone knows the future and what it portends as well as how best (or maybe the only way) to move forward toward that future. From a Nietzschean perspective, this version of Zarathustra is a hater of life; he really does think these people (and all other people, himself very much included) are horrible as they are, that they need to be "saved" from being themselves. In this view, these people need someone better and higher than they are to replace their own awful selves with some higher, better versions of themselves. In this way too, Zarathustra seems to parrot the nihilism that Nietzsche sees in Western philosophy more generally, in the way that figures like René Descartes and Immanuel Kant seek to eradicate the existing subject or at least subjugate it to higher, better, but utterly nonexistent notions of another self (hence nihilist).

But Zarathustra also says he is "a cripple upon this bridge"; he sees the shining perfect future, he wants to get there—he is not immune to the lures and seductions of archism, by any means—but he is unable to go forward, unable to help and save those who would like to go forward with him. And, precisely because the people believe that they need the prophet to show them the way (in the archist hierarchy that prophecy of that type sets up), if *he* can't get over the bridge, no one else can either. His failure becomes the failure of everyone else as well.

Here, then, is a key instance of bitter disappointment. Not only has Zarathustra refused to save this community, but he has in effect ruined its chance of ever being saved by anyone else either. Whereas, before he showed up, there was always at least the possibility of a messianic figure coming along to save the community, now that possibility has been removed by Zarathustra's actually showing up and refusing to do anything. Without the hope of future redemption, the people on that bridge must remain as themselves now and quite possibly forever.

In keeping with the double (or even triple) sense of the term *disappointment* described in the introduction to this book, Zarathustra has also unmade his own appointment as a prophet with a higher vision. Refusing to heal these people, Zarathustra offers that he is no different from them, with no special insight that they don't also, on some level, also have access to.

This disappointment seems awful, even cruel.[8] Yet, through this disappointment—in fact *only* because of this disappointment—we see the possibility of a more positive outcome as well. In this inversion of the function of the prophet, Zarathustra effectively saves himself and the community he is amid from salvation. In that way, in a very complicated sense, he *is* a prophet after all but one who uses his gifts to undermine his own office, his appointment. What he sees and is ultimately drawn to—and what he in turn draws his audience to as well—is not the shining future that does not exist; in fact, the future does not exist in any way. Instead, he sees the present; he sees the bridge where they are all standing: *that* is his prophetic gift.

The people who are on the bridge with him effectively see the present too—they are, after all, standing there with him—but they don't want to recognize what they are looking at; the whole time he is speaking, a hunchback, who is one of his prime interlocutors, is actually covering his face with his hands, presumably including his eyes.[9]

In one of his statements to this crowd, Zarathustra tells a blind man, "If one gives eyes to the blind man he sees too many bad things on earth: so that he curses him who cured him."[10] This seems impossibly cruel (and very disappointing), but, as I discuss further in chapter 5, prophetic sight is not purely connected to actual vision. Just as the blind are not immune to "seeing" the emptiness posing as substance that is the basis of archism, so too are they capable of seeing the present moment that they are part of as much as anyone else. The kind of anarchist sight that I am talking about is once again not so much a matter of opening one's eyes and seeing what is plainly there (since what is evident is itself a political question) but a form of collective reading and interpretation of that world.

In this sense, it could be said that Zarathustra is not condemning the blind man to blindness so much as he is helping him avoid false forms of sight. Insofar as archism has invested so much in "proving" its existence by placing its authority in tangible structures—that is, in the archeon itself—if Zarathustra were to allow the blind man to see, he would condemn this man to believing that what he saw contained what it was said to contain; he would be forced to see what isn't there through his renewed faith that now that he had been saved, he was "really seeing" the world. Zarathustra won't do that, leaving the blind man able to interpret and engage with the world around him on his own terms and in conjunction with his fellow all-too-human sufferers.

When Zarathustra says to these people that "to redeem the past and to transform every 'It was' into an 'I wanted it thus!'—that alone do I call redemption," he is explaining that redemption does not come in the form of magical transformations and the annihilation of the self, its replacement with something else.[11] Instead, it comes from choosing one's life and afflictions, that is, choosing and thus seeing and interpreting the present (once again in ways that are not exclusively visual).

Another way to say this (and in keeping with the arguments I made in chapter 2 about Hobbes) is that Zarathustra seeks for his followers to choose to see what they individually and collectively decide they are actually seeing. That is, he asks them to refuse to see what they are told to see, what archism demands of them, and instead see something of their own devising. "Seeing the present" only means that they respond to their own context; what they determine they are seeing, how they respond to that sight, is entirely up to them. To have such sight at all is only possible when people have been stripped of the false hope (what Lauren Berlant calls "cruel optimism") that they will somehow be rescued from having to make these kinds of choices at all.[12] Like the townspeople in "The Refusal," having the responsibility to decide for yourself what you think and see is a burden and a responsibility, but it is the price to be paid for having a political life, for being actually (as opposed to nominally) free.

Although Nietzsche is often depicted as a radical individualist (and in many ways he is), there are several ways that Nietzsche actually requires some level of collectivity nonetheless—not, however, in the harmonious way that collectivity is often imagined to be by archism—aligning him, however unexpectedly, with Hobbes's understanding of anarchic and collective decision-making processes. For one thing, as Nietzsche explains in the section "Of the Friend," we require other people than ourselves in order to avoid sinking into self-obsession. In that section, Zarathustra tells us that in terms of the conversation each of us has with our self, "the friend is always the third person: the third person is the cork that prevents the conversation of the other two [that is, me and myself] from sinking to the depths."[13] Without an outsider, there is a kind of solitary madness that settles in without the interference, even the enmity, of the friend, hence the fact that collectivity for Nietzsche is once again not harmonious but actually adversarial.

It could be said that we need a collectivity for Nietzsche because each of us is in fact already a collective; we do not have a single self in his view but many. In this way, the presence of an apparently separate, third self, set apart from the myriad internal selves that we always are, serves to anchor each of us, to give the self an outside view of itself that helps it remain coherent if still in deep internal and external tension.[14] Collectivity then offers Nietzsche a kind of externality that serves not to overwrite us with archonic whims but to situate ourselves in larger contexts and conversations.

It is to this anarchist, discordant, multiply divided ferment that Zarathustra addresses his disappointing call. Zarathustra may occupy the position of an archist prophet, but he ruins this form of prophecy from the inside. He takes on the role of the prophet to eviscerate it and, in that way, causes it to cease competing with the anarchic forms of collective and multiple prophecy—the decisions, clashes, and arguments of the community itself—that are otherwise overshadowed and overruled by false displays of unifying archist vision.

Yet at the same time—and I think this is equally important—Nietzsche, more than even Hobbes in some ways, allows himself to be seduced by archism, lets it go deep into his heart.[15] In doing so, he comes dangerously close to merging with it, but there is one critical advantage to him taking this risk. It means that Nietzsche, and through him his prophet Zarathustra, learns so much about how archism functions, how it works, and, just as critically, how it can be attacked from deep within itself. Whereas Hobbes always has his two sides, his archist side and his anarchist side, for Nietzsche, these are far harder to pick apart, but in that very closeness we get a view of archism from within that we could not otherwise get, and this is in and of itself a singularly important contribution to thinking about anarchist prophecy and the way that it can resist archist triumphalism.

A Different Kind of Prophet

To show how radical Zarathustra is as a prophet, and how much he stands in contrast to a more conventional, archist prophet, it is helpful to look at a figure in *Thus Spoke Zarathustra* that Zarathustra encounters in part II, in a section called, fittingly enough, "The Prophet" (this section comes immediately before the section "On Redemption," already described). Here, Zarathustra encounters a self-styled prophet who is quite dreary and defeatist. He is purportedly based on Arthur Schopenhauer, at least in terms of what he preaches.[16]

This prophet says, "Everything is empty, everything is one, everything is past!"[17] The prophet further says, "Truly we have grown too weary even to die; now we are still awake and we live on—in sepulchres!"[18]

In this section, it is not immediately clear whether the prophet is actually saying these things or if Zarathustra is just hearing the nihilism behind the prophet's actual words (then again, Schopenhauer was famous for being pessimistic).[19] From Nietzsche's perspective, the kind of authoritative visions that this prophet utters constitute a kind of deep nihilism even as his words may be formally meant to convey the opposite. If he is really an avatar of Schopenhauer, this other prophet speaks on behalf of the Enlightenment, of reason and truth and other such constructions (albeit with some particular variations for Schopenhauer himself). Insofar as he therefore asks us to believe in something that does not exist (the truth in some form or other), such prophecy is actually a vision of deep despair, a denial of life and a seeking of death, that very same nothingness that archism always comes from.

By hearing this other prophet's platitudes as being wholly and only negative (via an act of radical mishearing, if that is what is really going on), Zarathustra is already encountering this form of prophecy through the lens of disappointment: whereas we all think and want this and other archist prophets to be talking about truth, he is really telling us nothing at all (which is why Zarathustra hears his words as conveying only death and loss).

Even though he hears what the prophet is actually saying and recognizes how empty his words are, Zarathustra can't help falling into despair anyway. Hearing the prophet's words, Zarathustra himself becomes "sad and weary; and he became like those of whom the prophet had spoken."[20]

Zarathustra falls into a deep sleep and has a (prophetic) dream. He says, "I dreamed I had renounced all life. I had become a night-watchman and grave-watchman yonder upon the lonely hill-fortress of death."[21] Here, Zarathustra seems to have given up and joined the belief system of the other prophet, becoming a fellow night watchman at his "hill-fortress of death."

If you think of this fortress as a kind of archeon, a site that is meant to give order and tangible authority to life but is in fact a sepulcher or a tomb, you can see that for all his despair, Zarathustra does not entirely give up on the people who remain suspended between life and death, that is, all of us, we who are alive but who act as if we are already dead. Indeed, he tells us that "life overcome [*überwundenes*] regarded me from glass coffins."[22] In this way, even a life that is "overcome" is still a life, still available for other ways of seeing.

And Zarathustra is not helpless in this dream; he has with him "the rustiest of all keys" so that he could "open with them the most creaking of all doors," that is, the door to the fortress of death.[23]

As Zarathustra attempts to open the door, he hears evil croaking and presumes that whatever lies within the crypt "did not want to be awakened."[24] Yet he perseveres, albeit unsuccessfully, at which point "a raging wind tore the door asunder: whistling, shrilling and piercing it threw to me a black coffin: And in the roaring and whistling and shrilling, the coffin burst asunder and vomited forth a thousand peals of laughter."[25] This was followed by "a thousand masks of children, angels, owls, fools, and child sized butterflies."[26] This is a veritable storm blowing out of the space of death, from the archeon, releasing all that was held prisoner in that foul place (in the next chapter, I connect this storm to two other storms that Benjamin describes as blowing out of paradise).

In relating his dream to his disciples, Zarathustra himself claims not to understand what his dream signified, but one of his disciples tells him that "your life itself interprets to us this dream, O Zarathustra! Are you yourself not the wind with a shrill whistling that tears open the doors of the fortress of death?"[27] Hearing this, Zarathustra seems to come back to himself (even though he shakes his head at the disciple who interpreted his dream).[28] He even invites the prophet to go to his cave and wait there for dinner (the start of a long line of invitees, as it turns out).

In this act of interpretation of his dream, we see both a resolution and a danger. The resolution is clear; Zarathustra simply unmasks the prophet as a phony. His own life stands as a testimony to another way of being, and he overcomes the despair that comes with Western forms of nihilism. Zarathustra thus unsees and unhears (that is, disappoints) what the prophet wants us all to see and hear, making anarchic prophecy possible for himself and for the rest of us in the process. Once again, we can see that Zarathustra has no special sight or hearing. Even if he was initially able to hear what the prophet was *really* saying (that is, to hear the dark nihilist message behind what might have been sunnier sounding words), this only means that he does not overwrite those words with what he wants him to be saying.

Yet Zarathustra himself is not, once again, immune to the temptations of archism, nor is he immune from the crushing weight of disappointment.

To really come to terms with this other prophet's words, Zarathustra can't merely expose them for what they are but has to first accept and go through them, akin to what Lacanians call "traversing the fantasy," to experiencing all the temptation and despair that the cycles of disappointment produce in him (and in us) in order to break him (and us) of a habitual subservience to our own desire for salvation.[29]

This is all well and good, but this is where the danger comes in. The danger is that Zarathustra himself has become nothing more than a prophet himself—taking this term in the normative and archist sense—wherein his disciples see themselves as depending on him to serve as the wind to blow apart the fortresses of death. Their interpretation of his dream as suggesting his—and only his—power to save the day very much suggests that danger. If that were the case, then Zarathustra would really only be replacing one archist prophet with another. He may seek and preach life, but in fostering dependence on himself, his followers would only be living his life and not their own, and so death and nihilism would reassert itself in the guise of being overcome.

The Cry of Distress

Zarathustra may be alluding to the danger of becoming just another (archist) prophet in another encounter with the same prophet much later in the book in part IV, in a section titled "The Cry of Distress." In that encounter, Zarathustra is once again deeply affected by the nihilism of the prophet. He calls him a "preacher of evil" even as he recognizes this evil as a form of "human distress."[30]

In responding to this distress and sympathizing with the prophet's plight (and the plight of all mortals who do not wish to be only what we are), Zarathustra feels a great temptation to agree with the prophet's position. In this sense, not only does Zarathustra feel the allure of hearing the call of archism, but just as critically he feels the allure of making that call himself—that is, the temptation of being *that* kind of prophet—believing that he actually *must* save those around him, and thereby condemn them to death, after all.

Indeed, in this section, the need for that call is manifested as an actual cry that the prophet and Zarathustra hear while they are talking.

> "You preacher of evil," said Zarathustra at last, "that is a cry of distress and a human cry, perhaps it comes from out [of] a black sea. But what is human distress to me? The ultimate sin that is reserved for me—perhaps you know what it is called?"

"*Pity!*" answered the prophet from an overwhelming heart and raised both hands aloft—"O Zarathustra, I come to seduce you to your ultimate sin!"[31]

Here, we see that the prophet's plan is to use Zarathustra's love of the people, his pity for them, as a way to get him to join the ranks of those who would assign them to death. Clearly, Zarathustra isn't always subject to this pity; he certainly didn't show any to the disabled people he encountered on a bridge in the earlier section "On Redemption." But the temptation of pity is not something one can turn against once and for all. A fallible human being himself, Zarathustra will always be subject to its lures.

The prophet tells Zarathustra that the cry is for him, and, when Zarathustra asks who is emitting the cry, he tells him, " It is the *Higher Man* who cries for you!"[32] The Higher Man is an avatar of perfection, the promise of the kinds of redemption that archism eternally promises but never actually delivers upon.

Zarathustra is horrified at hearing this and breaks out in a sweat, saying, "The Higher Man? . . . What does *he* want?"[33] Strangely enough, it is the archist prophet who delivers the disappointing message to Zarathustra; he tells him that he will never find happiness in finding the Higher Man, effectively acknowledging that the cry he makes as well as the perfection he promises are merely lures and seductions. The prophet says:

> Anyone who sought *him* [i.e., the Higher Man] here would visit these heights in vain. . . . Happiness—how could man find happiness with such buried men and hermits! Must I yet seek ultimate happiness upon blissful islands and far away among forgotten seas?
>
> But it is all one, nothing is worth while, seeking is useless, and there are no blissful islands any more.[34]

After hearing this, following a renewed bout of despair, Zarathustra once again brushes aside the effect that this prophet has on him, saying, "No! No! Thrice No! . . . I know better! There still are blissful islands! Do not talk about such things you sighing sack-cloth!"[35] He then determines to go into the forest to search for the Higher Man.

In this exchange, it is almost as if the two prophets have changed positions, with the archist prophet exposing the empty lies of archism and Zarathustra refusing to give up hope for further, better places and times. Zarathustra reinforces this ambiguity when, taking his leave of the prophet, he says, "But I too—am a prophet."[36]

This last remark could once again mean that Zarathustra is an equal to the other prophet, in which case they might not be as different as either of them think, potentially relegating Zarathustra to the ranks of an archist prophet after all. Or it could mean the opposite, that Zarathustra occupies the rank of prophet but only once again to ensure that this position is ruined from within, wrecked as a vehicle for salvation (and perhaps with some help from the other prophet as well).

The ambiguity of this entire exchange between Zarathustra and the prophet suggests not only that Zarathustra is not immune to archist longings—we already knew that—but also that archist prophets are not immune to anarchist views either. This reinforces the possibility that *anyone* can be an anarchist prophet, even the most committed archist. As is often the case in *Thus Spoke Zarathustra*, this complex and dizzying interplay of engagement with and resistance to the lures of archism is not resolved. In this case, the whole question is put off by the prophet's promise to wait for Zarathustra in his cave (a question I return to shortly).

Conversation with Kings

Much of this discussion thus far has been somewhat speculative in terms of the political nature of Nietzsche's treatment of prophecy. However, in the very next section after "The Cry of Distress," called "Conversation with Kings," Nietzsche seems to touch directly on archism as a project of state power.

In this section, Zarathustra, who is out of sight of the road, sees two kings, highly ornamented with regalia, who are passing by with a donkey. He remarks, "I see two kings—and only one ass."[37] The kings hear but do not see Zarathustra. They speak together about their low opinion, not only of the masses but of kings too, saying:

> Everything is false and rotten with us. Nobody knows how to be respectful anymore: it is from precisely *this* that we are running away. They are honey-mouthed, importune dogs, they gild palm-leaves.
>
> It is this disgust that chokes me, that we kings ourselves have become false, arrayed and disguised in the old, yellowed pomp of our grandfathers, show-pieces for the stupidest and the craftiest and whoever today traffics with power!
>
> We are *not* the first of them [i.e., the masses] yet we have to *pretend* to be; we have at last become tired and disgusted with this deception.[38]

Here, the kings themselves have seen, from their unique perch at the apex of power, that there is nothing to see, that the archeon is empty and the archon—that is, themselves—knows nothing at all. We see here that even kings are not immune to the contrast between what they are supposed to be seeing and what they might decide to see instead.

Yet, for all their realization, the kings remain in some sense captive to the hope and power promised by archism—they are kings, after all—so that their disappointment is not complete. Or, putting it another way, they have not quite given up on their appointment. The kings tell Zarathustra that they too are searching for the Higher Man (spoiler alert: he never quite shows up; Nietzsche is endlessly disappointing).[39] In this way, Zarathustra therefore still has something to offer to (or take away from) them. He invites the kings to his cave, where the other prophet is still waiting for dinner.

Waiting for Redemption

Over the course of the latter part of the book, Zarathustra collects a variety of people (all men) who he invites to his cave. By the end of part IV and the book as a whole, Zarathustra's cave is absolutely jammed with characters who are waiting for him. The question is, what are they all waiting for? It appears that both Zarathustra and his guests are expecting something more than dinner. Zarathustra is effectively collecting candidates for his own salvation. Among their numbers are a sorcerer, a pope, the two kings, and the prophet himself. He is perhaps hoping that one or all of them will turn out to be the Higher Man/Men. The people he invites in turn seem to be hoping that Zarathustra himself will turn out to be the Higher Man. In the end, they are all sure to be disappointed.

In the meantime, these people all settle in to wait. For the kings specifically, after telling them to wait, Zarathustra notes, "The whole virtue still remaining to kings—is it not today called: *being able* to wait?"[40] As usual, this can be read on several levels. Whereas in a fully archist context, waiting may seem to be infused with hierarchy and domination—one person waits for someone higher and better than them—it can also take on a new meaning in terms of this other, anarchist kind of prophecy that Zarathustra is engaging in. Waiting—especially in a Nietzschean context where waiting is never awarded with redemption—could mean being forced to live in the present after all (just like the life that the man from the country lives while "waiting" for entry into the gate of the law in Kafka's parable "Before the Law").[41]

When attending to a prophet or a messiah who has already come and done nothing, and who wouldn't change a thing if she does come back, the act of waiting becomes something different, at least potentially. As long as there is the hope of redemption, waiting is just a way to extend the endless torturous nature of archist prophecy. Through an act of disappointment, however, this same action becomes transformed into a kind of radical presentism, a chance to realize that the kind of higher person—in this case the "Higher Man"—that one is waiting for is not going to show up and that any further actions can come only from oneself and one's own community.

Waiting for Salvation

If the point of all this waiting is to achieve a state of disappointment (not necessarily intentionally since all the figures, including Zarathustra himself, once again seem to be hoping for the Higher Man to show up), that disappointment must go deep. To be effective in combatting the false hopes of archism, such a disappointment can't simply mean that those who wait become dissatisfied with the practice of archism; if that were all that was needed, archism would be in big trouble. Even if they don't like the way archism is being practiced—and a lot of people do not—that doesn't mean that someone who experiences some level of disappointment won't hold out for a greater archon to come and save them from whatever way a local archon has let them down. This chain of salvation ultimately leads all the way to God, the ur-archon; surely that deity, if no one else, won't be disappointing!

The fact that the kings and even Zarathustra continue to wait for the Higher Man is not in and of itself a bad thing; it just sets them up for disappointment all the more. Being compromised by archism in general is not a fatal state, as much as archism would like it to be. Indeed, in a sense a certain degree of commitment to archism is a prerequisite to the possibility of disappointment in the first place. A call to "come to my cave and meet your anarchist disappointment!" would not, I suspect, fare as well under these circumstances. If people think they are getting saved, they might put themselves into a situation where a "real" salvation—that is, a salvation from salvation—could actually take place.

Furthermore, by gathering various archist subjects (including a prophet, two kings, a pope, and many others) together, Zarathustra is allowing them not only the chance to realize that they are waiting for nothing but also a chance to engage in that kind of collective and anarchic relationship that is the answer to or next step after that deep disappointment they might experience. Together, they have at least a chance to realize the anarchist life they already are living while they think they are waiting for redemption.

The Return of the Prophet

As *Thus Spoke Zarathustra* continues toward its conclusion, we get little sense that any of his interlocutors have been radically altered by their encounters with Zarathustra (here is another spoiler: this realization never actually happens for any of them). Or rather, they *have* been transformed but not in a way that accords with the radical disappointments that Zarathustra is calling them, and himself, to. Zarathustra realizes this when he comes near his own cave and hears once again the cry of distress. This time, Zarathustra discovers that it is emanating from his own cave. Nietzsche writes: "It was a protracted, manifold strange cry . . . and Zarathustra clearly distinguished that it was composed of many voices: although, heard from a distance, it might sound like a cry from a single throat."[42]

Zarathustra rushes inside and sees all the various people he has invited over by that point in the narrative (ten in all). He says:

> You despairing men! You strange men! So it was *your* cry of distress I heard? And now I know, too, where to seek him whom I sought today in vain: *the Higher Man.*
>   —he sits in my own cave, the Higher Man! But why am I surprised! Have I myself not enticed him to me with honey offerings and cunning bird-calls of my happiness?[43]

Here, it is Zarathustra himself who offers that these people are perhaps themselves the very persons—the Higher Man, presumably one or all of them; henceforth he begins to speak of "Higher Men"—that they have been waiting for, indicating once again that he himself might have been waiting for this eventuality even while they were waiting for him.

This is a radical and actually unwelcome message. The people in the cave do not want to find out that they are their own saviors. They know themselves too well and know that they are nothing of the kind. Redemption can't look like *that* for these people. It must be external; it must involve someone who isn't them, someone like Zarathustra himself. Here again we see the preposterousness of this process: Zarathustra hopes that these men will be the Higher Men to him. They want him in turn to be the Higher Man for them. And even if he or they *are* the Higher Man/Men, there is an ongoing fear that they will not be "high" enough. Disappointment is built into this system.

The archist prophet answers Zarathustra's claims directly, arguing in effect that neither he nor the rest of them could be the Higher Men (for the reasons I've already suggested) but that Zarathustra must either be that figure himself, or somehow presage that figure's coming. The prophet says:

And that we despairing men have now come into your cave and are already no longer despairing: that is only a sign and omen that better men are on their way to you;

for this itself is on its way to you, the last remnant of God among men, that is: all men possessed by great longing, great disgust, great satiety,

all who do not want to live except they learn to *hope* again—except they learn from you, O Zarathustra, the *great* hope![44]

Zarathustra's response to this is to reject the notion that he could possibly be their savior and, more importantly, that they cannot possibly be his savior either. He replies, "Truly, you may all be Higher Men . . . but for me—you are not high and strong enough."[45] Here, he is disappointed by these men and he disappoints them at the same time. He tells them they are not handsome or pure enough, that they are "crooked and malformed."[46] Later he complains that the air in the cave smells bad too now that all these people are sitting around in it. This is one of those rare moments where a sense other than sight gets its due (the cry of distress is another), but it is no small thing; the stench of these archists drives Zarathustra out of the cave and into the fresh night air, helping separate him from these figures who neither understand Zarathustra nor help him in any way except by negative contrast.[47]

As *Thus Spoke Zarathustra* heads to its final conclusion, we see, right up to the end, Zarathustra's tendency to wildly mix hope and despair, his raising of expectations and promises only to disappoint/be disappointed. After this exchange, they all settle down to a very long dinner (the very one that Zarathustra initially promised the prophet). During this time, a series of songs, speeches, and the like ensue, sometimes punctuated by the donkey, who periodically interjects by saying—it turns out that it can speak—"Yea-a."[48]

The speeches and songs are all attempts, whether by Zarathustra or his followers, to nail down the nature of truth, to finally determine what can be known and said and what cannot. Zarathustra makes a speech to the Higher Men—he is apparently back to believing that is who his guests are—that expounds on their superiority to the masses; this is him in his most archist guise. For people who want to read Nietzsche as a fascist, he gives plenty of ammunition in moments such as this. To paraphrase Lacan, if you are reading Nietzsche looking for a master, you will find one. If, on the other hand, you buck his authority as author, something he strongly encourages, you get a much more radical—and anarchist—Nietzsche as a result.

Following Zarathustra's speech, there are several other speeches by the Higher Men. A figure called the sorcerer makes a speech about truth. Then a figure known as the wanderer makes a speech about his need for Zarathustra (and also, it would seem, about white supremacy). Throughout these speeches, Zarathustra keeps leaving the cave during this period because he once again finds the air too close; he requires fresh air and solitude. When he does come back, he often does so to chide the other speech givers and singers about their own messages. He tells them (and maybe also himself?) that they are wrong and don't understand what he is trying to say to them.

A Kingdom of the Earth

This chiding by Zarathustra culminates when he comes back after one of his temporary departures and sees that the Higher Men have begun to worship the donkey (shades of the Golden Calf of the Bible). The various people in the cave explain to Zarathustra their reasons for this worship. The figure known as the pope says, "Better to worship God in this shape than in no shape at all."[49] Others inform Zarathustra that God has come back to life.

Zarathustra's response to this is telling. At first he is furious and sees this as a betrayal of everything he has taught until now. He calls his followers children and tells them it is time to leave the cave, saying,

> "To be sure: except you become as little children you shall not enter into *this* kingdom of heaven" (And Zarathustra pointed upwards with his hands.)
>
> "But we certainly do not want to enter into the kingdom of heaven: we have become men, *so we want the kingdom of earth*."[50]

This is a critical moment for my purposes because it exemplifies the difference between archist and anarchist forms of sight. In his absence, Zarathustra's followers reproduce archist logics. They resurrect God (who Zarathustra claimed was dead) and insist on seeing a form of this God in the flesh via the donkey. When the pope tells Zarathustra, "Better to worship God in this shape than in no shape at all," he is attesting to this double desire: both to be ruled by an invisible, perhaps even nonexistent deity, and to have a tangible avatar of that deity to facilitate that worship, some version of the archeon once again even if in this case it takes on a most humble, and asinine, form.

When Zarathustra says it is time to seek a kingdom on Earth, he is expressly refusing this kind of logic. He goes from attacking and vilifying his followers to offering them a different way to see. What he offers is not the future, not perfection, not even something higher but only where they are and what they are capable of thinking both together and alone, on Earth instead of in heaven.

These "Higher Men" therefore have the opportunity—but only that—to realize that they are not Higher Men after all, something they already know but appear to have forgotten. The very idea of being "higher" evokes heaven and an aspirational kingdom, an archeonic perch from which to judge, order, and control the world, whereas the kingdom they already occupy is neither higher nor lower but simply *here* where they stand, a place whose content is forever being determined and redetermined. Rather than direct these people to a higher, better future—although he certainly has done that in the past, including that very evening—Zarathustra tells them to "redeem the graves, awaken the corpses!" indicating an orientation that looks not up but down, even into the ground and not to a shining future but to those who have already lived and, in this case, died.[51]

And, in fact, despite his anger as to the worship of the donkey, Zarathustra does not utterly condemn the so called "Higher Men." As Shalini Satkunanandan pointed out to me, after all of his vitriol, Zarathustra ends by saying "Do not forget this night and this ass festival, you Higher Men! You devised *this* at my home, I take that as a good omen—only convalescents devise such things. And if you celebrate it again, this ass festival, do it for love of yourselves, do it also for me! And in remembrance of *me!*"[52] Satkunanandan reads this as indicating that Zarathustra in fact recognizes that, although what they have done is terrible, even fetishistic, it is also something that they have done as themselves, without any help from Zarathustra himself (nominally, this is what he has been asking from them all the time). In this way, it could be said that even as he condemns them for their fetishism, Zarathustra also recognizes the way that they are in fact living and acting on their own. That is, he recognizes the anarchist elements of the Higher Men—the way that they developed a religion in tandem—even as he sees them as devoted to archist phantasm. This simultaneity of archist belief and anarchist life here speaks to the way these things are merged more generally in our lives, not just with the "Higher Men," but all of us. Although in this case, the Higher Men chose to create something seemingly archist (Zarathustra appears to think so anyway), they could also have chosen to create something anarchist amongst themselves; their collective act points to this ongoing possibility.

For all of this, in the immediate aftermath of this insight, Zarathustra despairs of these disciples. It becomes clear to Zarathustra that his words are wasted on his followers. The next morning, when he wakes up and goes outside by himself, he thinks, "*They* [the Higher Men] are not my rightful companions! It is not for them that I am waiting in my mountains."[53] He asks them, "What do you think, you Higher Men? Am I a prophet? A dreamer?

A drunkard? An interpreter of dreams?"[54] In contrast to when he said, "But I too am a prophet," here the very question of what kind of prophet he is, if he is one at all, comes to the fore.

Asking for a sign, a huge lion appears out of nowhere and nuzzles against Zarathustra. When the (so-called) Higher Men try to come out of the cave to greet him, the lion roars and they scatter and disappear deeper into the cave, presumably never to be seen again. Here, Zarathustra renounces the pity for others that the prophet told him would seduce him. He recognizes that the pity he felt for the Higher Men is now gone: Nietzsche writes: "*Pity! Pity for the Higher Man!*" he cried out. "Very well! *That*—has had its time!"[55] Alone again and turning back to himself, he says, "This is *my* morning; *my* day begins: *rise up now, rise up, great noontide!*"[56]

A Prophet for Everyone and No One

In thinking about the book in general, I don't think we should put too much store on the end of this book per se as determining the true "meaning" of *Thus Spoke Zarathustra*.[57] To read the ending as a conclusive point is to subject the text to an archist reading wherein the final moment of the book is its truth; everything else is seen as leading up to that culminating event. The cyclical nature of this book suggests that we can derive our own judgments about the book from innumerable earlier moments in the text as well. Indeed, the end of the book isn't much different from any other part of the text; it ends with Zarathustra descending once again down from his halcyon heights, suggesting just another repetition of highs and lows, of appointments and disappointments.

We haven't really learned anything at the end of the book that we didn't know before. The Higher Men are not really "higher," although they never quite figure this out. By failing to do so, they lose an opportunity to recognize who they are on their own terms as occupants of "a kingdom of earth." As for Zarathustra himself, although he ends on a happy note, it is not particularly happier than any of the earlier numbers of revelations and insights that periodically occur to this prophet; we already know that he will soon be down again, facing—and fostering—a new round of disappointment.

Furthermore, we know almost from the very beginning of the book that Zarathustra will never have disciples that understand him, disciples that don't try to turn him into someone who can save them from being themselves. His best disciple probably remains his very first, a tightrope walker who dies, falling from his rope, right at Zarathustra's feet. For a time, Zarathustra carries his corpse around with him and this, it could be said, was the one disciple who didn't try to turn Zarathustra into something he was not.[58]

Perhaps it could be said that Zarathustra has no real followers because he is not the kind of prophet that invites such a relationship; the very idea of "following" is itself redolent with archist hierarchy. Back when he decides that having a corpse for a follower is insufficient, Zarathustra says to himself: "I need living companions who want to follow me because they want to follow themselves."[59] In other words, the only kind of follower he wants is someone who renders him (i.e., Zarathustra) redundant, who doesn't depend utterly on him for her own insight.

For all his highs and lows, Zarathustra is very consistent in terms of seeking to avoid having traditional disciples. He ceaselessly works to undercut his own authority with his followers, even including those moments when he succumbs to archism himself. Unlike other figures in the book such as the prophet and the sorcerer, Zarathustra doesn't lie to or try to manipulate any of the people he talks to; he doesn't even necessarily try to dissuade them from their delusions of salvation or, if he does, he usually doesn't try all that hard.

Unlike those other kinds of prophets, Zarathustra won't make a choice about salvation for them, nor will he demand that they make such a choice themselves. He doesn't have to do these things; the power to see or not see lies with each of them separately and together and very much independently of Zarathustra's own form of sight. Because his own preaching is so erratic (follow me to the halcyon heights! Never mind, there are no such things! No wait, there *are* such heights after all! etc.), Zarathustra works hard to buck the devotion of even his most ardent disciple. Instead of asking people to follow his lead, all he can do is disappoint them, even from believing in his own vision, leaving the rest up to them.

If the people in the cave, the false prophet and the kings very much included, realize this, so much the better. If not, they remain entrapped in illusions of archist power and authority, waiting for something that will never come, seeing things that aren't there (and pointedly not seeing things that might be).

The fact that at the end of the book—but also in the middle—the Higher Men do not understand any of this is of no importance. This is a book, as Nietzsche tells us in the subtitle, for "everyone and no one." Everyone could learn to stop seeing falsities, the determining structure of archist vision, or no one could. Zarathustra can't and won't make that determination for other people because if he did, they would have succumbed to a yet deeper—and more hidden—form of archist appointment, one in which they might have thought themselves to be fully in the present even as that present was wholly determined by Zarathustra himself.

Zarathustra is very explicit about his desire to shrug off his followers. As he famously states at the end of part I:

> You say you believe in Zarathustra? But of what importance is Zarathustra? You are my believers: but of what importance are all believers?
>
> You had not yet sought yourselves when you found me. Thus do all believers; therefore all belief is of so little account.
>
> Now I bid you lose me and find yourselves; and only when you have all denied me will I return to you.
>
> Truly with other eyes [*mit andern Augen*], my brothers, I shall then seek my lost ones; with another love I shall then love you.[60]

We see here in no uncertain terms how little belief matters for Zarathustra. It is not belief that he is interested in but experience and individual—but also collective—forms of sight (and not just sight but sound, smell, etc.). In denying belief, Zarathustra is challenging a major tenet of archism. Even when it is formally absent, such as is the case with modern secular positivism, we see the power of belief in an archist polity. The modern subject doesn't believe that she is believing; she asserts that she is merely acknowledging what is. Yet this too is a belief system and Zarathustra is offering something different. He is offering a form of unbelief that doesn't establish any truths but works to always call any truths into question in the same way that Fanon ends *Black Skin, White Masks* by saying, "O my body, make of me always a man who questions!"[61] Zarathustra seeks to subject all contenders for truth to the anarchist ferment of decision and interpretation that for Nietzsche, as for Hobbes, is the actual stuff of life, even as it also allows those communities the chance to tell their own accounts of what they are encountering.

When Zarathustra says, "With other eyes . . . I shall then seek my lost ones," we can see in effect a refutation of the kinds of logic that we saw being expressed in Kafka's parable "The Refusal." Kafka, in describing the archist "colonel," who effectively runs the town in the name of some mysterious far-off and unseen capital, tells us that "the colonel's eyes, so far as we know, are also the eyes of the government, and yet there is a difference which it is impossible to comprehend completely."[62] Here, the eyes of the colonel do not quite belong to him. He is seeing with the eyes of the state, at least in the way that he is popularly interpreted. When Zarathustra then says he will see "with other eyes," he may in fact be referring not to someone else's eyes at all but actually to his own. Zarathustra, as a prophet, *is* expected to see with other eyes, just as Jeremiah in the Bible is portrayed as seeing through God's eyes. In refuting this model, Zarathustra can be said to be seeing with his "other other eyes," that is, his own. Refuting a sense of a higher source of vision, Zarathustra is seeing with his all-too-human eyes and what he sees is his "lost ones," that is, his fellow humans who are lost because they do not (yet) realize that they too are currently seeing with a pair of eyes that do not belong to them. By reminding them of this fact, however cryptically, Zarathustra may well be inviting them to join him in an act of collective and earthbound sight.

Zarathustra backs up those words with deeds all meant to dissuade his followers from seeing in any other way than as and by themselves, both separately and together. This includes endlessly leaving his followers behind (even his dead one), giving them impossibly contradictory messages, alternatively enticing them with hope and then dashing those hopes, sounding like a fascist one minute and an anarchist the next. Paradoxically, leaving the disciples to their own devices—even abandoning them—in a sense invites them into that collective vision, joining him if they choose to see from their own perspective. This reflects the fact that not only Zarathustra's eyes but his love too could be transformed from a force of seduction, pity, and destruction— something his disciples latch onto as a way to "save" themselves—into something else, something more like what he elsewhere calls *amor fati*.[63]

The Life and Death of God

There still remains one other key element in thinking about Zarathustra's relationship to archism, namely his relationship to God. If Zarathustra plays havoc with terrestrial archons of all sorts, if he refuses a conventional relationship with disciples and other forms of archist authority structures, what about his relationship to God? If we think once again of God as an ur-archon, then it seems that none of Zarathustra's attempts to undermine archist authority structures would matter insofar as the final authority, God, is still able to trump any kind of radical, anarchist alternatives, can still organize the world through an ultimate, and divine, appointing vision.

This is why Zarathustra's famous claim that God is dead is so critical. God is dead doesn't mean that God never was. The existence of God, at least in terms of a belief structure, is effectively presupposed by any form of archism.

Even the most secular form of archist authority has at its core a theological root and ultimately, at least in its Abrahamic mode, a connection to God.

Saying that God is dead means that whereas that archist structure once emanated from this one central node, that original guarantor of archism is no more and so archism itself is at risk. Critically, for Zarathustra, God may have died, but the deity doesn't necessarily stay dead, as the Higher Men try to remind him. Toward the end of the book, back in the cave after the example of worshipping the talking donkey, Zarathustra confronts another character, the ugliest man, accusing him of having resurrected God, asking him, "Is it true what they say, that you have awakened him again? And why? Was he not with reason killed and done away with?"[64]

The ugliest man responds, "Whether *he* still lives or lives again or is truly dead, which of us two knows that best? I ask you" (this exchange occurs immediately before Zarathustra evokes the "kingdom of earth").[65]

If God's "death" can be only temporary, if furthermore, as the ugliest man suggests, we can never truly know if God is dead once and for all (or if God never existed in the first place), then there is never going to be a point where Zarathustra can safely avoid his ongoing struggle with archism. And not just his struggle: the idea that God might not stay dead serves as a warning to us all. It tells us that we must never fall into the trap of thinking that archism, even if it is vanquished, can never come back again. Archism is a permanent temptation; like God, it does not necessarily stay dead. Rather than think of a once-and-for-all finish to archism—akin to G. W. F. Hegel's end of history, an archist concept if there ever was one—it is better, perhaps, to think in terms of a constant struggle against archism as a tendency. Even if the universe itself may tend toward anarchism, we can never be entirely free of the shadow of archism. For, as Nietzsche also writes in *The Gay Science*: "God is dead; but given the way of men, there may still be caves for thousands of years in which his shadow will be shown.—And we—we still have to vanquish his shadow, too."[66]

In this way, the question of whether God is alive or not does not make all that big a difference. Given that God casts a shadow whether alive or dead, that shadow haunts archism and anarchism alike. The mere possibility that there is or isn't a God is enough to call into doubt the possibility of an absolute (and archist) political order as well as an anarchist order that is free, once and for all, from the threat of archism.

Indeed, if Zarathustra could know with absolute certainty that God was really dead or had never existed in the first place, he wouldn't have to bother with prophecy and anarchist forms of sight at all; he certainly wouldn't have to bother with inducing states of disappointment in either himself or others. He would merely have to point out the absence at the center of all political forms and leave it at that. As long as God is possible, archism is possible—and, perhaps anarchism too, at least in the mode that I have been discussing here—and so disappointment is the only possible response, drawing out our secret desires for redemption in order to dash them over and over again.

What saying that God is dead *does* accomplish is to sow doubt in the heart of archism so that the very same element that makes it impossible to rule out archism also makes it impossible to, as it were, rule it in. If archism can't rely on this ultimate trump card, if it can't confidently know that there is a final judge and a final source of its ghostly authority, it can never be secure, never free from the possibility and rival authorities of anarchism. In fact, a living God can also serve to unmake archism. The archist God is meant to be living but silent, tacitly acquiescing to all the false projections that archons will make. If she turns out to be an anarchist after all, if she somehow interferes with the projections that have been placed on her (via unauthorized forms of prophecy or, as Benjamin offers, via a general and ongoing revolt of all materiality against archist forms of power, just to give two examples), she spectacularly fails to fulfil this role.

There is one final and critical aspect to note about the particularly negative theology that comes from Nietzsche's contention that God is dead. At one point, a bit later on in *The Gay Science* from the passage just cited, a madman jumps into a crowd and cries out, "Whither is God? . . . I will tell you. *We have killed him*—you and I. All of us are his murderers."[67] This singular statement is vital for my argument because it suggests not only that God "died" but also that human beings are complicit in that death. Suggesting, however obliquely, that human beings have killed God—and not just a single killer but each and every one of us—means that there is no going back to full-blown archism. Not unlike the way that Fanon understands the radicalizing power of violence on the colonial subject, here too, our collective guilt in the death of God helps produce our own possible freedom from all that has been attributed to divine rule.

Indeed, the madman goes on to explicitly link human freedom to having killed God. He says: "But how did we [kill God]? How could we drink up the sea? [shades of the Leviathan!] Who gave us the sponge to wipe away the entire horizon? What were we doing when we unchained the earth from the sun? Whither is it moving now? Whither are we moving? . . . Do we not feel the breath of empty space? Has it not become colder?"[68]

Here we see an articulation of the awesome, even terrifying responsibility and freedom that comes with the end of the power of celestial deities over human life. More accurately, we see the virtue of ceasing to have a permanent blank canvas upon which worldly archons can project their wishes; if God, as a figure that permits such projection, can come back to life she can also be killed over and over again. The specter of the kinds of freedom that stem from such a prospect is as overwhelming as it is thrilling, akin to what Arendt calls "the abyss of freedom."[69]

As scary as it may be, this is a choice that Nietzsche makes fully visible for us. If the death of God is possible and if that death was brought about by the entire human population, it means that in some sense a prophet like Zarathustra is not *required*. Once again, just as Fanon's notion that collective acts of violence against colonial power render everyone effectively equal, if everyone killed God, then no one special exalted person is needed to save the world from mythic violence.[70] Everyone has already saved everyone from salvation. This idea that everyone killed God—even if not forever but for a time—is probably one of the most anarchist things Nietzsche ever wrote down.

Zarathustra the Assister

This last idea raises an important question: if Zarathustra is not required per se, what do we need an anarchist prophet for in the first place? If we have all already collectively killed God, what can the prophet add to what we've all already accomplished? Furthermore, if in fact Zarathustra is only offering those around him and the readers of this book access to what they already know, isn't it rather archist to suggest that we still would benefit from a specific person or force to allow us to see what we decide we see rather than what the archists decide we see?

The answer to this question is complicated, and I return to it in subsequent chapters as well as the conclusion of this book. For the time being, I repeat an earlier argument: the subjects of archism themselves—that is, everyone—are, like the citizens depicted in Kafka's parable "The Refusal," deeply invested in maintaining their own subordination, albeit to different degrees. As a rule—that is, the rule of archism—people do not trust themselves as themselves to be their own basis for judgment and decision. A prophet like Zarathustra helps us in such a case because he appears to be made of the same stuff as the archist prophets we seek to follow. If we can't trust ourselves the fact that we do trust Zarathustra—he looks and talks like a prophet, after all—allows him to do an end-run around that issue, at least potentially.

For this reason, Zarathustra remains useful. He hides in plain sight, arriving with all the markings of archist prophecy, just like the marks Hobbes talks about that announce true versus false prophets. He is, by his own terms, exalted above us, seeing the future and so forth. Yet Zarathustra uses his power to undo his own authority and the authorization that makes others want to follow him. He is therefore akin to the "hair of the dog that bit you," a *pharmakon* that uses its own poison to nullify other poisons, to give people a chance to avoid being poisoned in the first place, as it were.

This is not to say that anarchist sight doesn't happen without the interference of an anarchist prophet. It happens everywhere and all the time, even under conditions of the most dire and severe archism. There are countless instances where that power asserts itself over and above the archist authority that seeks to determine and control it.[71] Zarathustra doesn't have to invent this sight, in fact he cannot do so; such a form of vision doesn't belong to him. But he can undo the overriding archist forms of sight that interferes with that form of collective vision.

Hobbes calls the Holy Spirit "an Assister." I think the same thing can be said here of Zarathustra. An anarchist prophet like Zarathustra is not himself the cause of our vision or our freedom; we do that on our own. He merely assists us in recognizing the vision we already have engaged with—perhaps the result of our having killed God—through the exercise of disappointment. He is able to do this because, for all his appearance to the contrary, Zarathustra is, above all, *one of us*. He is not other, not made of some other thing, not above or better than everyone else. Although he looks like the prophets of the Bible, and he often talks like one too, he tells us he is "a cripple at this bridge," just another wayfarer trying to find his way in and to the present. This is perhaps the key to Zarathustra's prophetic power, the fact that in the end, he doesn't have any power that doesn't also belong to everyone else ("a book for everyone and no one").

Nietzschean Revelation

In *Ecce Homo*, one of Nietzsche's very last writings, he reflects on *Thus Spoke Zarathustra*, among others of his works, and offers perhaps his final thoughts on the nature of Zarathustra's prophecy, how this figure has affected Nietzsche and the world itself (with the caveat once again that we should not put too much stock in final thoughts and words insofar as it is archism that teaches us to take the end of narrative more seriously than the parts that lead up to it).

In the section of his autobiography devoted to *Thus Spoke Zarathustra*, Nietzsche explains that, while he was sojourning in Italy, Zarathustra *"stole up on me."*[72] Describing his inspiration, which initially came in the form of a single sentence—"6,000 feet beyond man and time"—Nietzsche writes: "If one had the slightest residue of superstition left in one, one would hardly be able to set aside the idea that one is merely incarnation, merely mouthpiece, merely medium of overwhelming forces."[73]

Here, Nietzsche seems to be saying that *he* didn't write Zarathustra but that, in a way, Zarathustra wrote *him*. This sense of Zarathustra being external to him—and not only external but in some sense prior to his own agency—suggests that even for this singularly disappointing author there is yet a need, or at least a desire, for such an externalized prophet, one with special sight to guide him in order to be able to guide the rest of us.

Yet, as is often the case with Nietzsche, this assertion is troubled, in this instance by his saying, "If one had the slightest residue of superstition [*aberglauben*]."[74] It suggests that perhaps Nietzsche *does* have such a residue, at least potentially, and that the seeming helplessness he portrays here, even the involuntary nature of Zarathustra's arrival, is not quite what it appears to be. Perhaps there is a sense in which Zarathustra is both of and not of Nietzsche's own devising (and vice versa).

This complex interaction between other and self-determination is further suggested by the next sentences, where Nietzsche writes: "The concept of revelation, in the sense that something suddenly, with unspeakable certainty and subtlety, becomes *visible*, audible, something that shakes and overturns one to the depths, simply describes the fact. One hears, one does not seek; one takes, one does not ask who gives; a thought flashes up like lightning, with necessity, unfalteringly formed—I have never had any choice."[75]

In speaking of revelation, in this case the revelation of Zarathustra himself, we see once again a process by which something invisible—at least to us—becomes manifest, apparent, and authoritative. Becoming *"visible,"* there is a kind of ipseity, an undeniability to what is presented to Nietzsche; as he tells us, "I have never had any choice."

Such a view of revelation may not at first glance appear to be all that different from the archist variety where truth unfurls itself into the visible world and similarly insists on its undeniability. Yet it seems that the revelations of what Zarathustra has to tell us are not of the usual sort nor with the usual effects. We see this more clearly when Nietzsche writes:

Everything is in the highest degree involuntary but takes place as in a tempest of a feeling of freedom, of absoluteness, of power, of divinity. . . . The involuntary nature of image, of metaphor is the most remarkable thing of all; one no longer has any idea what is image, what metaphor, everything presents itself as the readiest, the truest, the simplest means of expression. It really does seem, to allude to a saying of Zarathustra's, as if the things themselves approached and offered themselves as metaphors. . . . This is *my* experience of inspiration.[76]

There is a kind of merger or at least concurrence between the objects of the world and the interpretive power by which to receive them. This revelation wherein "the things themselves approached and offered themselves as metaphors" is not something to be meekly accepted as occurs in an archist sense. Rather, it produces Nietzsche's own ability to judge and decide, his own interpretive power.

The author is not a master but a coconspirator, as it were; the objects of the world come forward to serve as ways to turn visibility into language. Quoting a line from Zarathustra to elaborate on this point, Nietzsche writes: "Here all things come caressingly to your discourse and flatter you: for they want to ride upon your back. Upon every image you here ride to every truth. Here, the words and word chests of all existence spring open to you; all existence here wants to become words, all becoming here wants to learn speech from you."[77]

This concept is remarkably close to the way that Benjamin understands the relationship between human beings and the world around them; it harkens to the latter's description of Adam, whose job it was to name the things in the Garden of Eden and also the way that, following the Fall, the objects of the world exhibit an "other muteness," a sadness due to no longer being so named.[78]

For Benjamin, in response to the Fall and the fetishism that follows, the objects of the world are in constant and endless—but silent—revolt against what he calls mythic violence and I call archism. The coconspiracy that Benjamin speaks of—and that Nietzsche too seems to subscribe to here—allows human beings to take their own stand against what otherwise totalizes and dominates them. This is a slight variation on the absolute silence of God that we get with Hobbes. Here, even as we reach toward God, God and the universe that God created are also, in some sense, reaching back toward us too. While this is also true with Hobbes—his concept of prophecy is precisely attuned to whatever form that reaching back might take—Hobbes's tendency is to focus entirely on the human side of things, whereas both Nietzsche and Benjamin look at the relationship, as it were, from both ends. With Nietzsche, of course, it is not God per se that does this reaching back since God is (currently) "dead." Rather, it is materiality itself that offers itself as a metaphor, not as a passive instrument for us to use—for that would be simply the reinstatement of archism—but as a set of objects that fight side by side with human actors.

In looking at this passage, it becomes unclear whether the things of the world seek to "ride" the author or if the author in turn is "riding" the things. This indistinction may be due to the fact that we tend to read things through the vocabulary of archism—one must be riding the other; they can't both be riding at the same time, after all. But if we read this through an anarchist lens—the kind of lens Nietzsche offers throughout *Thus Spoke Zarathustra*—we can see this as a model for a relationship between subjects and objects as well as between objects and objects and between subjects and subjects; these distinctions become less clear thanks to Zarathustra's revelation. This is a relationship that invites and even demands a collective and contingent, and messy, and contradictory, response.

When we cease to ask the question "who is the master?" we begin to see the way that we don't have to choose between Zarathustra's agency and Nietzsche's own, or to decide what is absolutely true and what is absolutely false. In his view, nothing is so wholly itself that it is unrelated to and isolated from everything else. By the same token, we don't have to determine whether objects rule us or whether it is the other way around, nor to decide which human among us will rule over the others, based on esoteric truths that become visible by the act of revelation. This is a different kind of revelation.

This model of revelation helps explain better how anarchist communities interact with their environment. This relationship lies somewhere between two poles, one being a straight-up empirical response that dictates its meaning directly via its physical presence—which, under conditions of archism, becomes a handy way for archons to determine what those objects "mean" and do—and the other pole being one where objects are totally obscure and we are cut off from them entirely, only making guesses (and bad ones at that) at what they are and how we are to treat them.[79]

To put this back in the lexicon of Zarathustra and the way that he, like those around him, is radically present, the "real world" that he is facing is indeed "here," but its meaning, what to make of it, only comes from an interchange between the community of interpreters and those objects themselves. In other words, "here" is not simply a self-evident site. It is full of objects and relations, overlaps and contradictions, and all of that must be engaged with, contested, fought alongside with or against. This process, akin to the forms of inspiration discussed in chapter 2, is contingent and ongoing. Revelation in this sense, like prophecy is for Hobbes, becomes a collective process, one that draws human agents into a much vaster web of interpretation that involves all the physical matter of the world around them (and the universe too).

We can see how revelation, the operation of having something manifest itself out of a void to become visible, can serve not just archism but—and by the very same operation—anarchism too. This is another example of Nietzsche robbing the building blocks of archist power and turning them into something that subverts and defies that authority. The objects that we have been pursuing as truths, the things we seek to master through archist logics, emerge into the present as something for our individual and collective pondering. They are autonomous and can be said to have an agenda of their own. Here, the external, that ultimate workhorse of archism, is engaged (or conspired) with to deny archism its perch from which to judge and order the rest of us.

This is not a form of revelation that reveals us as being something of God's making or that shows us some big Other that undergirds all of existence; instead, it shows that we already have all the externalities we need right here in the world, even within ourselves and certainly with one another and the objects we live amid. Zarathustra shows us why we don't need to turn to God to get outside ourselves; we are always outside ourselves (and inside ourselves too).

Such a form of revelation enables the kind of radical presentism that I have been arguing Zarathustra's prophecy is all about, once again akin to what Aristodemou calls atheism. Under normal conditions of archism, we think we already understand the entire world and the way all objects and subjects are ranked in that world and related to one another. We have received what Foucault calls a "grid of intelligibility," and everything must pass through that filter.[80] What Zarathustra does for Nietzsche is to call this "grid" into question. When that happens, a revolution in perception is already underway. This does not mean that we start over in terms of perception, as if encountering the objects of the world for the first time. We have always been engaged in anarchist forms of interaction with the world. What changes is that the grip that archism has over us is shaken, weakened, perhaps even ruined.

And, in the same way that what Zarathustra has to say is thereby revealed to Nietzsche, so too is Zarathustra's revelation transmitted to us, the readers of Nietzsche's texts. If Zarathustra "steals" upon Nietzsche, he also steals upon his readers who, perhaps assuming that they will be finding a master explainer in this text—as is sometimes promised by Zarathustra himself—find instead a disarticulation of precisely that mastery. In this sense, it could be said that Zarathustra has nothing to show us; all he has to do, all he does, is remind us that the world is out there staring us in the face—and actively demanding our attention—even when we do our best to hide from its insistent gaze.

Early on, in the prologue of *Thus Spoke Zarathustra*, Zarathustra meets a holy man, a hermit who lives in the woods. Fully in his archist mode, he tells the holy man, "I am bringing mankind a gift," implying that he has a store of knowledge and truth to offer the world.[81] The holy man replies, "Give them nothing. . . . Rather take something off them and bear it with them—that will please them best."[82] Although the holy man seems to be confused—he doesn't know, for example, that God is dead—it turns out that what he said was correct. Zarathustra doesn't give anyone anything. He only removes the certainties of archism. Now that he has "revealed" what was always before us, the absence of any overriding and organizing truth, Zarathustra can go on his way and we on ours.

chapter four

a prophet who can't see the future

Benjamin's Angel of History

All Prophets Are False

IF BOTH HOBBES AND NIETZSCHE offer us complicated visions of
the intermixing of archist and anarchist forms of prophecy, Walter Benjamin
perhaps offers us the closest thing to an unadorned anarchist response. Benjamin speaks of the possibility of being *"useless for the purposes of fascism,"* giving
a sense of how to avoid the otherwise ever-present danger of being co-opted
by archist politics.[1]

It's not that Benjamin doesn't evince some of the same archist tendencies we see in Hobbes's and Nietzsche's texts. He too understands the ways
that archism—which I think corresponds quite well with his own concept of
mythic violence—is deeply insinuated in the world, the way that fetishism
and false forms of representation, the stuff of archism and myth, are ubiquitous and actually unavoidable to some extent. For Benjamin, this state of
affairs is not, however, determinant; we are not doomed to an endless archist
past, present, and future. Yet, by the same token, Benjamin's work cautions
us against any kind of once-and-for-all victories; as with Nietzsche, for Benjamin, we may be able to defeat archism (the subject of chapter 6), but we
can never be assured that it won't come back. Hence the need for ongoing

vigilance, a way of life and a state of being that is inherently, and continually, anti-mythic.

This sense of continual struggle with archism (my word, not his) is built into all of Benjamin's work. In *Critique of Violence*, he famously contrasts mythic violence, the violence of projection and self-assertion, of empty power posing as ontologically based truth, with divine violence (Godly violence is perhaps a more accurate translation). This may, at first blush, seem to suggest that the solution to human archism is divine archism, and—here, Benjamin's own ambivalence shows itself most clearly—there are moments where this seems to be the case. But of the three practitioners of radical negative theology (Hobbes, Nietzsche, and Benjamin) discussed so far, I think Benjamin goes the furthest in ensuring that the solution to archist/mythic violence does not involve an archist God—whether by killing her or by displacing her—and theology but an anarchist one (in the next chapter, I discuss the way that Octavia Butler's own version of radical negative theology, as articulated by her character Lauren Olamina, may go farther still in imagining what such an anarchist God would look and act like).

Benjamin sees God as being neither almost entirely absent from the world (as Hobbes does) nor "dead" (like Nietzsche). Instead, Benjamin offers us a God that is very much present in this world—albeit in a way that is completely opaque to human beings—and who is ultimately on the side of anarchism. This is a God that acts in ways that counteract the archism that is promulgated in her name. Indeed, for Benjamin, that's what divine violence is all about.

In this chapter, I argue that Benjamin's political theology is fundamentally opposed to archism in all its guises even as it is intimately connected to it. Like Hobbes and Nietzsche, Benjamin recognizes the power of externalities, the way that they both lure and support human endeavors. For Benjamin these lures are not just tempting but are, once again, unavoidable. Benjamin's own work is marked by a particular cosmology, one influenced by Jewish and, in particular, kabbalistic sources, wherein myth and fetishism, the creation of authority out of nothing, is endemic due to the fact of the Fall of Adam (here a certain Eurocentric or at least Abrahamist-centric viewpoint is revealed on Benjamin's part).[2] Given that for Benjamin there is no alternative but to engage in some form of fetishism, his focus is on how to turn those very same practices into their opposite, how to engage, that is, in an anarchist form of archism, as it were.[3]

If Benjamin's theology is truly to be "useless for the purposes of fascism," it must be so in the full knowledge that it is also fetishistic, itself a form of false prophecy. But whereas other forms of false prophecy are the ground for mythic violence and archism, in Benjamin's hands, even false prophecy can potentially become a basis for the undermining and overcoming of the archism that such forms of prophecy ordinarily produce.

Here again, we see one of the fundamental building blocks of archism turned into its opposite. Perhaps particularly in Benjamin's case, there is a refusal to ever write off any form of prophecy, any phantasm, as hopelessly archist, or mythic, to stick to his own language. Not unlike Nietzsche too, rather than having two parallel tracks, one archist and one anarchist, as we see with Hobbes, Benjamin always shows the anarchism within the archist. He offers the notion that prophecy as such is never to be dismissed merely because it is false. If that was the case, from a Benjaminian perspective, there would never be anything but archism insofar as all prophecy is, in some sense, false. In this way, I think he is an especially subversive thinker, stealing from archism the very heart of its power and source of (false, stolen) authority.

In order to show how this works in Benjamin's theory, let me turn first to a consideration of how Benjamin thinks about prophecy in general. I then focus on what I consider perhaps the preeminent prophetic figure in Benjamin's opus, the angel of history, with a brief consideration of Satan as well. Finally, I turn to a consideration of the anarchist God that Benjamin sees as subverting archism from its very heart (from the supreme archon herself). Collectively, these understandings produce a potent and ongoing response to incipient archism in all its guises.

Benjamin and the Prophetic Tradition: Foreseeing the Present

In terms of his relationship to prophecy, you would be fairly hard-pressed to find all that many overt references in Benjamin's work to the Hebrew prophets or to the prophetic tradition as such more generally.[4] Although some writers have connected his work to the tradition of Hebrew prophecy, Benjamin himself rarely cites them by name.[5] Instead, you mainly get indirect references to prophets, such as when Benjamin tells us, at the end of "On the Concept of History," that "the soothsayers who queried time and learned what it had in store certainly did not experience it as either homogenous or empty. Whoever keeps this in mind will perhaps get an idea of how past times were experienced in remembrance—namely in just this way. We know that the Jews were prohibited from inquiring into the future: the Torah and the prayers instructed them in remembrance. This disenchanted the future, which holds sway over all of those who turn to soothsayers for enlightenment."[6] This can be read, perhaps, as an oblique reference to the aforementioned Jeremiah, who warned sternly against the appearance of prophecy that was actually just fakery (or "soothsaying"). For most people, the difference between soothsaying and prophecy itself might seem to depend on whether the prophecy actually came true or not, but Benjamin has very different criteria of judgment. Just as with Hobbes, in Benjamin's view, what matters is not the accuracy of the prophecy per se—since the very question of truth itself is always at issue for Benjamin—but the way that temporality is affected and disrupted by a particular act of seeing.

In part, for Benjamin, this comes down to a question of whether the prophet is looking toward the future (like a "soothsayer") or looking to the past ("being instructed in remembrance"). In "On the Concept of History," Benjamin describes the angel of history, whose "face is turned toward the past."[7] While this angel might not otherwise seem particularly prophet-like—he neither says nor does anything so far as we know; all he can do is look—it is critical to note that in an earlier version of this essay, the figure who is looking toward the past is not called the angel of history but is simply referred to as a seer or a prophet. There, Benjamin writes: "The seer's gaze is kindled by the rapidly receding past. That is to say, the prophet has turned away from the future: he perceives the contours of the future in the fading light of the past as it sinks before him into the night of times. This prophetic relation to the future necessarily informs the attitude of the historian as Marx describes it, an attitude determined by actual social circumstances."[8] Rather than peer into a future that is merely "empty homogenous time"—because, as previously noted, it does not yet exist in any way—the role of the prophet must be resolutely backward looking. In another section of the notes, Benjamin elaborates further on this question when he writes:

> The saying that the historian is a prophet facing backward [referring to a fragment from Friedrich Schlegel] can be understood in two ways. Traditionally it has meant that the historian, transplanting himself into a remote past, prophesies what was regarded as the future at that time but meanwhile has become the past. . . . But the saying can also be understood to mean something quite different: the historian turns his back on his own time, and his seer's gaze is kindled by the peaks of earlier generations as they sink further and further into the past. Indeed the historian's own time is far more distinctly present to this visionary gaze than it is to the contemporaries who "keep step with it." The concept of a present

which represents the intentional subject matter of a prophecy is defined by Turgot—not without reason—as an essentially and fundamentally political concept.[9]

In this contrast, we see a key difference between what Benjamin will refer to as historicism in the completed "On the Concept of History" essay versus historical materialism. Both stances seem similar, but the first (historicist) stance involves projection of oneself into a previous time. This historian, to some extent, can be said to cheat by "predicting the future" from a position when it had already come to pass and hence partake in a form of mythic violence and soothsaying.

The historical materialist, by contrast, turns her back on her own time, not to face the future—which remains empty and homogenous—but in order to get a clearer sense of the present by engaging that moment into a constellation with past moments. As opposed to those (i.e., historicists) who "keep step" with their own time, which is to say those who insist they know exactly what their time is about and who try to foist that temporal certainty onto other periods of time as well, this other mode of temporality makes one's own moment "far more distinctly present to this visionary" and is thus prophetic. As such, one's own time becomes no longer a sure thing but something in question, something that might be affected by the juxtaposition of different temporal moments. It is not therefore the stance of looking toward the past that is decisive—since historicists do it too—but the way that one allows the past to interfere with a sense of the present that ultimately matters for questions of prophecy.

Most critically—and here once again, Benjamin approaches Nietzsche, in this case in terms of the latter's treatment of revelation—the historical materialist is distinguished from the historicist by her direct engagement with the materiality of any given temporality. In Benjamin's own version of materiality, the objects of the universe are in a constant state of revolt against the fetishism that human beings project onto them. This revolt is, as I read it, the main manifestation of divine violence, the principle way that an anarchist God fights back against mythic violence. Historical materialists then are those who recognize not only the effect of materiality on any given subject but also the way that materiality has, as it were, an independent agenda, as with Nietzsche, something that human beings can (but also might not) be in conspiracy with.

Benjamin goes on in the above passage to further cite Turgot as writing that "politics is obliged to foresee the present."[10] Insofar as under archist notions of time we remain—as Turgot suggests as well—always one step behind a reality that is always eluding us (because it is phantasmic), an engagement with the past becomes the only way to break through that phantasm. This breaking through does not constitute getting a "true" sense of the present so much as to allow past materialities to interfere with one's own material present.

Accordingly, as with Hobbes, prophecy is not, for Benjamin, a matter of discerning things that others cannot see but a matter of discerning things that everyone can see. But Benjamin takes this beyond the scale that Hobbes is interested in. Insofar as materiality itself, in Benjamin's cosmology, is once again not inert but active in this process, it is not purely up to human beings to decide what materiality is or what it means; we can only do that in conjunction—or conspiracy—with materiality itself. In this way, acts of prophecy necessarily tap into the kinds of collective decisions and arguments that are the stuff of anarchist political life only that anarchism is expanded beyond the purely human to include (literally) the whole world around us. This amounts to what Benjamin calls "the dreaming collective," the subconscious expression of people in all their multiplicity, a product of their myriad experiences, their deepest wishes and responses to those experiences and material contexts, with critical imput from those material contexts themselves.[11]

The Prophet as Historical Materialist

It is a peculiarity of Benjamin that very often modalities of Jewish and kabbalistic doctrine are overlaid, however unexpectedly, with Marxist and other leftist forms of politics.[12] In this case, the juxtaposition he presents between prophecy and historical materialism serves to infuse a radical political agenda with a form of messianic possibility. By turning prophets into historical materialists, that is, into people who encounter and engage with the material nature of time, Benjamin is also turning historical materialists into prophets. In this way, Benjamin is giving a form of messianic sight to figures that normally are considered to be utterly secular and hence bound by the temporalities that are formed within a secular universe. Perhaps we could call this merging of categories prophetic historical materialism.

For Benjamin, a prophetic element is necessary to sharpen the powers of historical materialism because the human relationship with the material world is complex and heavily fraught with theological elements.[13] One could argue that Benjamin's notion of materialism is itself a theological concept. In his essay "On Language as Such and on the Language of Man," Benjamin writes, as Hobbes did before him, that Adam was tasked in the Garden of Eden with giving spoken names to the objects (including animals and even himself) in the garden. The name that Adam gave these objects corresponded to the silent name that God had already given them through the act of creation. He writes, "God's creation is completed when things receive their names from man."[14] In Eden, Adam engaged not in representation but in what might be called presentation, a direct recognition of things as such and in their own right.[15]

This aspect of naming is disrupted (to put it mildly) by the Fall. Benjamin writes: "After the Fall . . . when God's word curses the ground, the appearance of nature is deeply changed. Now begins its other muteness, which is what we mean by the 'deep sadness of nature.'"[16] Nature (that is, the objects found in the world, including human ones) is sad because it is no longer completed by the act of naming. According to Benjamin, human language becomes random and unconnected from what it seeks to name: "To be named—even when the namer is godlike and blissful—perhaps always remains an intimation of mourning. But how much more melancholy it is to be named not from the one blessed paradisiacal language of names, but from the hundred languages of man, in which name has already withered. . . . In his creative word, God called [things] into being, calling them by their proper names. In the language of men, however, they are overnamed."[17]

Here, we see a premonition that the paradisiacal state was not meant to last (even in the godlike state, there is "an intimation of mourning") and also a sense of how human language overcompensates for its postlapsarian failure to truly name. Instead of giving one true name, there are now hundreds of false names—in other words, "overnaming"—none of which accord with the material entities that are being sought after.[18]

For Benjamin, human language and human thought are, for this reason, always fetishistic, seeking to produce truth by fiat, offering a connection that can only be given by God's command—shades here of an archist deity—and which are hence no longer available. Because of this, all human endeavors are, to some extent or another, mythic, that is, projecting onto a screen of reality, a series of phantasms and delusions about what is really "out there."

Because prophecy is itself a linguistic and human activity, it is necessarily false, itself an example of overnaming, and for this reason alone we should never be too sanguine that we can always or accurately distinguish soothsaying from prophecy. Yet this does not mean that prophecy is entirely without some kind of communicative power. It is suspended, as we are all suspended, within a material context that, as previously noted, is not itself bereft of some spark of the divine.

For Benjamin, after the Fall, the objects of the world enter into a "new muteness," which is to say a kind of silence imposed on them by human beings' inability to name them properly. But they never lose their own original connection to God, their own silent name that they retain. The idea of them having a "mute sadness" reflects the fact that they are still animated by a name so they can be sad, among other things, even if silent. Because of this other name, Benjamin tells us, "they can communicate to one another . . . through a more or less material community. This community is immediate and infinite. . . . It is magical (for there is also a magic of matter)."[19] This "magic of matter" is something that human beings, for all their mythic fetishism, can't control or displace. It is the source of the rebellion that I spoke of earlier, serving to actively combat and diffuse the effects of that fetishism, acting as a permanent source of resistance that humans can draw upon in their own struggle with mythic violence, the prophetic tradition very much included.[20]

Benjamin offers us a deeper understanding of the kinds of mutual and horizontal forms of speech and judgment that I have been looking at throughout this book. Not only are these forms of action mutually engaged with between human beings, but those engagements are in effect occurring within the context of an even vaster network of mute material communications. The "magic of matter" is therefore an all-inclusive practice of anarchism that goes well beyond its human participants but, insofar as we are bodies (that is, objects) we partake in that rebellion as well, even if we are not always aware of it.

What Kind of Materialism?

Benjamin's understanding of a suprahuman network of materiality is critically important because it means that even if human beings no longer have the capacity to name the objects around them with their proper or true name, we do have the capacity to let ourselves be affected by the larger network that we are suspended within, a network which does not share our perceived alienation from reality (insofar as it constitutes reality as such). Although this material community is infinitely vaster than us, and although it surrounds us entirely—indeed it *is* us—this network also sustains us. Reversing the parasitism of archism, the material universe lends us its own independence and solidity, making our own anarchist response possible in response (in very much the same spirit as Nietzsche's understanding of revelation).[21]

While the explicitly theological origins of Benjamin's concept of materialism might seem to suggest a kind of occult transcendentalism that makes the material universe something entirely ethereal and hence available for human determination and domination, I would argue the opposite. In my reading, it is precisely Benjamin's theology of materialism that keeps his politics rooted in an actual world and universe. Exactly because it *is* theological, there is an element of Benjamin's materialism that is not entirely up to human beings to determine, that is not entirely subject to representation. This is in contrast to the supposed materialism that comes from liberal philosophy, which claims (falsely) to be entirely secular and based on empiricism, on a real encounter with the world around us. In the latter case, materiality is, as with all things archist, a screen upon which archism projects its desires, rendering materiality entirely passive. In the former, anarchist case, materiality exists and even acts independently of our projections and our collective acts of interpretation—and prophecy—can and must reflect that opacity. Here, a false, archist externality is replaced with a real, anarchist one (although the nature of that reality is radically different and far less determinant than the archist forms we usually subscribe to).

As Max Tomba explained it to me, Benjamin's texts are full of references to struggle (*kampf* in German), wherein we must confront or even fight not only one another but also our encounter with historical moments, events, things as they appear to us over the course of time.[22] The struggle or confrontation demonstrates how human beings precisely can *not* control or determine the material world. As we saw in the question of who is riding whom in Nietzsche's text, the resolution for Benjamin is not some clear form of mastery but an endless and highly productive tension, akin to what Peter Fitzpatrick calls a "productive failure."[23]

Here, we see an interesting thing: human interpretation forms around the material world that we are surrounded by. In a sense, this looks a lot like archist forms of meaning making, the way that, for example, the city of Babel forms around the void of the tower. Human interpretation also occurs in a field peppered with material objects whose own truth is withheld from us but which we seek to engage with nonetheless. But there is an absolutely crucial difference; whereas the archist mode is formed around a nothingness that poses as something, the anarchist mode is formed around something that remains otherwise opaque to us. That thing is in some ways as mysterious as the void, but since it actually exists, it is available to shape us as much as we shape it (this is an idea that Butler's work will help make clearer).

Our interactions with the material world, even when we think we are its masters, involves forms of interaction and recognition that we can choose to ignore or override, but those interactions are always available to us as a way to resist the archism that we otherwise help instantiate. In my reading of him, divine violence is not purely an act of God for Benjamin but is also the name for the way that the material world itself refuses our fetishization of it; it is in a constant state of revolt that we can conspire with or not but can never overcome.

This spatial relationship to materialism works in precisely the same way in relation to time. Because the past actually and materially exists, it can and does affect us. Since the future, like the void at the center of Babel, doesn't exist, it cannot affect us at all; it can only serve as a blank slate by which to bounce off archist desires. Archism chooses empty spaces, towers that will never be built, ideas of heaven and God, temporalities like the future, because it doesn't have to risk the competition of actual externalities interfering with its phantasms. Anarchism, on the other hand, is all about that risk; it seeks rather than hides from the encounter with materiality, the way it shapes us even as we try to shape it. It constitutes a deep engagement, not only with one another but also with the world around us—including our own bodies—that remains, for Benjamin, in a paradisical state even if we ourselves remain fallen.

This means that when anarchist prophets steal things back from archism, what they steal will have the same form that one sees in archist renditions, once again expressing the proximity—even the identity!—of soothsaying and prophecy.[24] In a way, this should not be surprising since archism is a purely parasitical thing. But it shows us once again that we cannot assume that just because something has archist associations, it means that we must jettison it. By the same token, it also means that we should never assume something is perfectly safe from archism. Benjamin's idea of something being "useless for the purposes of fascism" is not a matter of keeping a list of what is "safe" and what is "unsafe"; it means instead that any object, any relationship, any historical event, and any person or group of persons must ceaselessly be encountered, confronted, challenged, and changed by that encounter (in chapter 5, I show that this is the epitome of Lauren Olamina's religion in the Earthseed series).

What this means in the end is that human interpretation is not all powerful, a set of fabulations that we can impose on any surface whereby any and all interpretations are equally viable. Instead, interpretive communities struggle with and confront what they encounter, not a black box but a series of contestations, sedimentations, and narratives, a human materialist history of prophetic vision. We are fortunate indeed that the material world resists our attempts to determine it. In its ceaseless rebellion, the universe itself can be said to model and sustain our own ability to resist, to engage in a revolution. This struggle once again includes our encounter with one another, but it also encounters a deeper form of confrontation, one with a material world that we neither own nor control, one that ceaselessly rebels against our idolatry and which we are fortunate indeed to find ourselves amid for that very reason.

Navigating Revelation

Accordingly, we can see that just as with Nietzsche, who, as already noted is a fellow traveler in terms of his theologically inflected form of materialism, Benjamin has his own understanding of revelation as well. His version of revelation shows that, even though fetishism is a permanent feature of the postlapsarian world, we can begin to see how that is not the end of the story, a dead end leading to the fullest expression of archist/mythic violence, but the beginning, a way to resist that is built into the most basic fabric of phantasmic and fetishistic power. Given that the material world is a permanent source of resistance to that fetishism, we always have the chance to understand that our attempts at grasping at truth are necessarily failures, and in this one way, we do have a version of redemption—as much redemption as Benjamin is willing to give us, anyway—after all.

A false prophecy that recognizes itself as such understands that even though it is inevitably engaging in overnaming, the name that it gives is both an abject failure and a way to reach out to what is also reaching back toward us. This potentially even includes soothsaying itself insofar as both soothsaying and prophecy are attempts at regaining the sight—and voice!—of the original prophet, Adam himself (and presumably Eve too, although Benjamin doesn't talk about her in this regard). Soothsaying is not made of different stuff than prophecy; it is just marked by a failure to understand that it is already and necessarily a failure. It is a grasping at what can't be grasped and for this reason turns outward toward an empty direction (the future), turning its back on the material forms of communication that it is always embedded within.

To recognize our position in a material network, to acknowledge the magic of matter even if we don't necessarily share in this magic (except insofar as we are objects as well) is to take part in Benjamin's own version of revelation. In "On Language as Such and on the Language of Man," he writes:

> The equation of mental and linguistic being [*Der Gleichsetzung des geistigen mit dem sprachlichen Wesen*, where "mental" is a somewhat problematic translation for *geistigen*, which means intellect or consciousness but also has an aspect of spirit] is of great metaphysical moment to linguistic

theory because it leads to the concept that has again and again, as if of its own accord, elevated itself to the center of linguistic philosophy and constituted its most intimate connection with the philosophy of religion. This is the concept of revelation—Within all linguistic formation a conflict is waged between what is expressed and expressible and what is unexpressible and unexpressed.[25]

For Benjamin, as for Nietzsche, revelation is not what it is conventionally said to be, the exposition of God-given and self-evident truth. Rather, for him it consists in the navigation between what can be known by human beings and what cannot. What is "revealed" is simply the presence of materiality. Revelation in this view tells us nothing at all, yet that nothingness, as I've shown before for Hobbes and Nietzsche, can be very powerful. Benjamin says:

> The expression that is linguistically most existent (that is, most fixed) is linguistically the most rounded and definitive; in a word, the most expressed is at the same time the purely mental [*geistige*]. This, however, is precisely what is meant by the concept of revelation, if it takes the inviolability of the word as the only and sufficient condition and characteristic of the divinity of the mental being that is expressed in it. The highest mental region of religion is (in the concept of revelation) at the same time the only one that does not know the inexpressible.[26]

We see here that language in its most materialist form, the sounds it makes, the marks we use to inscribe it on a page, is perhaps the clearest expression of what it actually cannot express, but which is nonetheless the source of any possible connection to what it seeks to name. This has nothing to do with the "meaning" of words; for Benjamin, as for Hobbes, that part of language is an entirely human and arbitrary set of conventions. Instead, expression for Benjamin lies, in this sense, not in the power of the wielder of language but in the material form that language takes. Revelation, one could say, is happening all the time, all around us. It is present in every word we say or write, in everything we talk about. In one sense, we are cut off from what is being revealed, that is, the world itself, the present moment, the objects that surround us, and even the object that we are ourselves. Yet we are not entirely disconnected from this world; it anchors and holds us even as we seek to determine and dominate it. The words we speak are empty, but the fact that we speak them at all points them toward that which we cannot otherwise (can no longer) name.

In this way, it can be said that for Benjamin, as for Hobbes (and Nietzsche too), we all engage in some collective form of prophecy, in responding to what has been revealed to us. But whereas Hobbes, at least formally, restricts prophecy to speaking about religious matters, for Benjamin it seems clearer that it can be extended to engaging in language in any way at all: to speak, perhaps even to think, actually even to *be*, is in effect to prophesize.

For this reason, even the most ardent fetishist—once again there is no one who is not in some way a fetishist, but some are less ardent than others—is not entirely wrong when she thinks she has access to the world. She is a false prophet, a soothsayer, but in that falseness, the world is revealed nonetheless (only not to her). The appropriate stance vis-à-vis the world then is to recognize not only our failure to know it but the fact that we respond to it, and prophesize about it, nonetheless.

In one of his clearest statements about the nature of representation in a postlapsarian world, in "Konvolute H" of the *Arcades Project*, Benjamin advises us that "the true method of making things present is to represent them in our space (not to represent ourselves in their space). . . . We don't displace our being into theirs; they step into our life."[27] He is giving a sense of how to engage with the material community that surrounds us. We should not seek to invade and colonize its space—since that space is entirely inaccessible to humans—and think that our overnaming projections have given us access (the attitude of historicism). Instead, we should engage in representation, yes, but a form of representation that shatters our certainties, that allows the material world to invade us rather than the other way around, perhaps therefore once again being a form of de-representation.

This point reflects back to Nietzsche's discussion of whether language is "riding" on our back or we are riding on it, on questions of our "mastery" of language as such. In the case of Benjamin, as with Nietzsche, this is not the right way to think about language, not the right question to ask. In abandoning the struggle for mastery, we cease to project and instead stand in the light of the magic of matter and see with other eyes—actually with our own eyes for a change—all that has been revealed to us.

The "Now" Time

Even with such guidance, for Benjamin, the distinction between prophecy and soothsaying is highly fraught precisely because the differences between them are vanishingly small, virtually nonexistent. As with archism more generally, soothsaying as a kind of emblematic form of mythic violence can take on almost any form, can co-opt almost anything that seeks to exclude it. If we are all prophets, we are also all soothsayers as well.

For Benjamin, historical materialism—a Marxist concept that Benjamin overlays with his own theological constructions—is his response to the difference between soothsaying and prophecy. As I've been suggesting, the attitude Benjamin expresses here is not simply to say soothsaying is bad and prophecy is good, because that fails to understand the way these categories overlap. Instead, he sees historical materialism as a way to navigate this relationship. This leads to certain questions. How do these two radically different modes, one prophetic and one secular, work in tandem? What does prophetic historical materialism look like in practice?

We can observe the way Benjamin sees these two modes as being in some kind of alignment most clearly in both "On the Concept of History" and the preparatory notes that preceded it. In the final, completed essay, in section 14, Benjamin writes:

> History is the subject of a construction whose site is not the homogeneous, empty time, but time filled full by the now-time [*Jeztzeit*]. Thus, to Robespierre ancient Rome was a past charged with now-time, a past which he blasted out of the continuum of history. The French Revolution viewed itself as Rome reincarnate. It cited Rome exactly the way fashion cites a by-gone mode of dress. Fashion has a nose for the topical, no matter where it stirs in the thickets of long ago; it is the tiger's leap into the past. Such a leap, however, takes place in an arena where the ruling class gives the commands. The same leap in the open air of history is the dialectal leap Marx understood as revolution.[28]

We see once again that Benjamin is animated by a distinction between prophecy and soothsaying, wherein fashion is generally a form of the latter. In much of his writing, Benjamin cites fashion as a device that gives a sense of headlong progression through time, which disguises the fact that capitalism is in fact a temporally static system, changeless in the same way as hell is.[29] Fashion promises that both the past and the present are part of a rush toward the future and so seeks to co-opt this temporality into the maw of mythic violence itself.

Yet, here we also see more evidence of how close soothsaying and prophecy can be. Fashion is perfectly capable of seeming to be oriented toward the past as well as the future. Fashion is endlessly recycling itself, turning "retro," and thus retrieving an item from the past only to place it into the sequential forms of teleological time that is the hallmark of capitalism and archism more generally. In this way, both prophecy and soothsaying can once again look and act identical, actually *are* identical in some sense. The same gesture, in this case turning to an item from the past, can, in one context, produce nothing but reaction, whereas it can be a way of breaking open that reactionary stasis in another.

What fashion and other forms of soothsaying miss in their headlong rush toward the future and mythic engagement with the past is an engagement with what Benjamin calls the "now-time" (*Jeztzeit*). Although this term might appear to have a very mystical connotation, the now time might be interpreted as simply meaning our experience of time when it is released from the obfuscations and overshadowing that come from teleological usages of temporality. The now time is not a "true" intimation of the moment we are actually in but is an awareness, but only that, of the material context that time is revealed within; it once again reflects our immersion in a material world, our own bodily materiality in communion with other bodies, including inanimate ones, and the way that this materialism stands independently of our own grasping at truth. The "now-time" then could be considered the human apperception of that material community, our recognition of this environment, and our part in it, however fleeting and overnamed our experience of it might be. Here too, it's not quite that soothsaying is wrong so much as it does not allow itself to be inflected with the true direction of prophecy, not the future but the now time, not the eternal and harmonious truth but the material envelope that contains us in all its diversity and contradiction. The role of the historical materialist is therefore to allow this complex context to be manifest, both to herself and to others (recognizing that this manifestation does not come from her; she only draws our eye toward what is already visible and present).

For Nietzsche too, with whom Benjamin has an admittedly complicated relationship, the present is an elusive quality that can only be experienced—to the extent that it can be experienced at all—by stripping away the falsehoods and delusions that usually prevent us from recognizing this moment.[30] Nietzsche's metaphor of someone who hears the twelve strokes of noon but gets distracted and loses count, therefore having no idea what time it is, serves as a helpful illumination of this principle.[31] His notion of the future serves as a lure to draw the distracted subject toward what they think they are looking for. The future itself does not exist, but we all desperately hunger for it. He tempts us with this false mode and then, when that appears as empty, in our disappointment, we get an unwanted but tangible sense of the present.

For Benjamin too, the now time may only seem mystical to us because our focus is on anything but this moment. The mystical feeling we associate with the now time may reflect the fact that the kinds of time that we *do* experience are themselves actually mystical in the sense of being false and phantasmic. From the position of this false time, the now time has the appearance of being ephemeral and impossible, but it is actually the other way around; our experience of the now time is a necessarily false intimation of the concrete form of time, whereas our experience of archist time is a false intimation of nothing at all.

In this way, the historical materialist really *is* a kind of prophet for Benjamin because she can see what the rest of us are overriding so long as we cast our eyes to the future, or even the fake, immaterial past, as in fashion. We need the now time, Benjamin tells us, because it is the only possible moment for action, for revolution. So long as we are prevented from recognizing this moment that is always before us, we remain quiescent and passive in the face of capitalist predations. Thus we turn to prophets—not spiritual ones but (historical) materialist ones—to break up teleological time and offer us access to the time that we inhabit, allowing us a kind of collective agency that archism is devoted to overshadowing and co-opting. Where soothsaying and other forms of unacknowledgedly false prophecy "takes place in an arena where the ruling class gives the commands," the prophetic vision of the historical materialist allows for "the dialectical [and I would add antiteleological] leap Marx understood as revolution."[32]

Although Benjamin largely removed the language of prophecy from the final version of "On the Concept of History," it is useful to keep the implicit parallel between the historical materialist and the prophet in mind. This connection does not just serve as a metaphor for how historical materialism works; it also represents the basis by which historical materialism engages with the messianic—and material—forces that Benjamin did choose to acknowledge in the final text.

To give an example of how this works, let me revisit another passage from "On the Concept of History" by keeping the parallels between historical materialism and prophecy in mind. In section 16, Benjamin writes:

> The historical materialist cannot do without the notion of a present which is not a transition, but in which time takes a stand [*einsteht*] and has come to a standstill. For this notion defines the very present in which he himself is writing history. Historicism offers the "eternal" image of the past; historical materialism supplies a unique experience with the past.

The historical materialist leaves it to others to be drained by the whore called "Once upon a time" in historicism's bordello. He remains in control of his powers—man enough to blast open the continuum of history.[33]

If one can manage to contend with the awful sexism of this passage ("drained by the whore"?), we can see that if one simultaneously reads the term *soothsaying* along with historicism and reads *prophecy* along with historical materialism, we have a much clearer sense of what is involved here. We see that the reality of time is quite the opposite of what capitalism tells us it is. When we focus on the future, we find that, rather than rushing breathlessly along, time actually comes to a standstill. Homogeneous empty time comes to invade our own time, and we are stuck in a static moment where the present is suspended and unavailable to us. Even the past becomes a chimaera ("Once upon a time"), and the present is nothing at all (not distinguishable in any way from any other moment). By "blast[ing] open the continuum of history," the historical materialist/prophet manages to give us a different experience of time so that we have "a unique experience with the past" and, in that way, a unique experience of the present as well. Here, we become reconnected, however falsely and inadequately, to the material context that always serves as our home; thus the historical materialist is prophetically engaged with the act of revelation.

This way of thinking also helps us better understand the rather cryptic statement toward the end of "On the Concept of History," in appendix A, when Benjamin writes: "The historian who proceeds from this consideration [of joining 'events that may be separated . . . by thousands of years'] ceases to tell the sequence of events like beads of a rosary. He grasps the constellation into which his own era has entered, along with a very specific earlier one. Thus, he establishes a conception of the present as now-time shot through with splinters of messianic time."[34]

The prophetic element is once again what makes the now time visible to us. Even if we don't actually have access to true and ontological time, for Benjamin, we have a way to break apart the stranglehold of empty homogenous time that is produced by the temptations of soothsaying. For this reason, by "now-time" Benjamin is perhaps not strictly referring to the present as such but to the whole matrix of time that has and does exist, giving us access to any point in materially present time.[35] By acknowledging other moments and other materialities, we gain, if not a genuine perspective, then at least an inkling of our own connection to time as such. We get a sense of the material granularity of a given moment even if, once again, this materiality is not itself available to us and this, as Jews sing on Passover, is (has to be) enough ("Dayenu").

Modern Prophets

Insofar as the Fall is for Benjamin the signal moment that divides human forms of vision into their pre- and postlapsarian varieties, he does not quite share Hobbes's notion that there is a divide between an ancient time of human history when God was active in the world (was king, in fact) and prophecy was a common feature and a modern time in which God is formally silent (but is represented by the Holy Spirit). Nietzsche doesn't necessarily share this vision either, although his choice of the name Zarathustra, an ancient Persian prophet, suggests that he was, at the very least, seeking to draw upon that earlier tradition as a way to bolster his prophet's bona fides.

For Benjamin, however, all time since the Fall—that is, all time, because time as such did not exist in Paradise—has been marked by an absence of true prophecy, and ancient times are no more "authentic" than modern ones (Brian Britt speaks of Benjamin as offering a "negative messianism" in addition to a negative theology).[36] It is perhaps for this reason that Benjamin is less interested in the ancient Hebrew prophets such as Isaiah, Jeremiah, Miriam, and Ezekiel (although he had quite a bit of knowledge about these figures too) and more interested in modern and contemporary prophetic figures.[37]

Benjamin's prophets therefore are principally modern and early modern figures such as Kafka, Baudelaire, and the many authors of the *trauerspiel* (the German baroque mourning plays that were the study of his *Origin of German Tragic Drama*). These figures are able to "foresee the present," gaining an insight about their own time through the way that they connect to the past as well as the way they connect to materiality, which turns out to be much the same operation. In this way, they help turn the subject of time from being a passive passenger along for the ride of teleological development into an active participant, a prophet herself, however false, who can connect disparate temporal moments via revealed materiality in a way that maximizes the possibility for revolutionary change.

To help flesh out this idea more clearly, let me give a brief reading of one such modern prophet in a Benjaminian mode, namely Franz Kafka. Of all the modern-day prophets that Benjamin considers, Kafka must be one of the most important in his view. Insofar as prophecy and soothsaying come perilously close to one another, for Benjamin, Kafka, perhaps more than anyone else, demonstrates best how to negotiate that complicated relationship.

Part of the way that Kafka does this, according to Benjamin, is that he attempts to reconcile the failure of representation with the mystical tradition that seeks to overcome that failure. He does this by treating with the materiality of that tradition rather than its purportedly sacred content. In his June 1938 letter to Gershom Scholem, Benjamin explicitly connects Kafka to the mystical tradition, as when he writes, "What is actually and in the precise sense *crazy* about Kafka is that this absolutely new world of experience comes to him by way of the mystical tradition."[38] Yet Benjamin adds, "This could not have happened, of course, without devastating occurrences within the tradition itself."[39] In other words, that which the mystical tradition seeks to address is not itself available to the modern prophet and was not even available to those who partook in it in earlier times. The connection to what that tradition seeks must be elliptical, even *"crazy."*

Addressing the nature of Kafka's prophetic vision directly, Benjamin explains that in fact Kafka "was not far-sighted, and he had no 'visionary gift.' Kafka listened attentively to tradition and he who strains to listen does not see. This listening requires great effort because only indistinct messages reach the listener. There is no doctrine to be learned, no knowledge to be preserved. What are caught flitting by are snatches of things not meant for any ear."[40]

In this view, to try to "see" at all involves a deep form of misperception. Appropriately, Benjamin switches away from visuality and focuses on auditory cues as offering a different relationship to the mystical tradition. But even "listening" does not actually tell us anything definite (as we see, it can itself interfere with perception insofar as "he who strains to listen does not see"). In telling us further that "Kafka's genius lay in the fact that he tried something altogether new: he gave up truth so that he could hold onto its transmissibility, the haggadic element," Benjamin articulates the way that prophecy understands it is speaking truth even when it doesn't know what it is saying (or why).[41] Saying that Kafka has no "visionary gift" does not mean that he is not prophetic; rather, it suggests that he is a different kind of prophet, one who sees—and hears—without the assumptions about truth and the future that normally come with that role.

A few years before he wrote that letter to Scholem, in the essay "Franz Kafka: On the Tenth Anniversary of His Death," Benjamin wrote in a similar vein: "The gate to justice is study. Yet Kafka doesn't dare attach to this study the promises which tradition has attached to the study of the Torah. His assistants are sextons who have lost their house of prayer; his students are pupils who have lost the Holy Writ [*Schrift*]. Now there is nothing to support them on their 'untrammeled happy journey.'"[42] Given the collapse of ancient traditions of thinking about God and truth that once may—or may not—have undergirded any attempt to think about politics, the characters in Kafka's stories must engage in similar behavior but with an entirely different form of methodology. They continue to read and study, but having "lost the Holy Writ," they do not and can never understand what they are studying.

Rather than condemn them for their ongoing devotion to the empty gestures of a lost tradition, however, Benjamin sees that Kafka's characters fully revel in their failure. These students' ongoing devotion to a tradition that can tell them nothing is not wholly futile. Instead, it allows for two things. First, by copying and gesturing in the same direction as the lost tradition, Kafka's characters are acknowledging the political theology that remains buried beneath the ruins of modernity. Without this obeisance, we would effectively abandon any attempt at "foretelling the present" and give ourselves over to the phantasms of our time and hence, no time at all.

But the opposite is equally true. If we don't understand that these links are severed, we risk thinking that in performing the rituals of study and reading, even of prophecy, we actually *are* connecting with that ancient tradition, or more accurately with the truths that tradition claimed access to, in which case we would be fully indulging in the kind of (bad) fetishism that is the hallmark of what Benjamin—citing Karl Marx—calls the "phantasmagoria." In fact, given that the ancients thought their tradition did offer a connection to God and truth, these modern students are in a much *better* position vis-à-vis their own fetishism; it is only by losing the Holy Writ that students have a chance to approach what cannot be understood. Here it is their focus on the material aspects of that transmission (Haggadah) rather than the law or truth that transmission is supposed to instantiate in its readers (Halakhah) that matters for Kafka.

By engaging in a ritual that has no real basis, both dangers mentioned previously can be averted. We acknowledge our relationship to the mystical tradition but we equally acknowledge that this tradition is lost to us (was *always* lost), that the tools that we use to discern the past and the present are broken and useless, and that this endeavor can only lead to failure. Or rather, these tools are broken and useless when it comes to telling *truth* but are in fact critical for connecting us to our own time, for giving us a sense of a wide revelation of materiality without any particular content. Indeed, these are not even tools at all but material coconspirators.

In thinking further about how best to occupy a space marked by failure and loss, Benjamin relates a Talmudic story that answers the question of "why Jews prepare a festive meal on Fridays."[43] The story, and Benjamin's interpretation of it, are as follows:

> The legend is about a princess languishing in exile, in a village whose language she does not understand, far from her compatriots. One day this princess receives a letter saying that her fiancé has not forgotten her and is on his way to her.—The fiancé, so says the rabbi, is the Messiah; the princess is the soul; the village in which she lives in exile is the body. She prepares a meal for him because this is the only way in which she can express her joy in a village whose language she does not know.—This village of the Talmud is right in Kafka's world. For just as K. lives in the village on Castle Hill, modern man lives in his own body: the body slips away from him, is hostile towards him. . . . The air of this village blows about Kafka, and this is why he was not tempted to found a religion. The pigsty which houses the country doctor's horses; the stuffy back room in which Klamm, a cigar in his mouth, sits over a glass of beer; the manor gate which brings ruin to anyone who knocks on it— all these are part of this village. The air in the village is permeated with all the abortive and overripe elements that form such a putrid mixture. This is the air that Kafka had to breathe throughout his life. He was neither mantic nor the founder of a religion. How was he able to survive in this air?[44]

This is one of the best passages to understand not only Kafka's plight but the condition we all live in. We live ensconced in the fumes of the "village," that is, the world around us. Here the master sense of visuality is displaced as olfactory logics take precedent over visual ones. The material world is everywhere, but we are not at home in it. Or perhaps more accurately, we *are* at home—we can even *smell it*—but we don't recognize (don't see) that fact.[45]

Kafka's gift is to allow himself to be affected by the stenches and airs that emanate from the village, the material community that surrounds us notwithstanding our own alienation from that landscape. Similar as with Hobbes's understanding of God, he doesn't know *what* this real world is, only *that* it is. Yet, for Benjamin, it could be said that Kafka adds one extra bit of substance to this relationship. We don't know the village per se but we do live amid and are deeply affected by what could be called its off-gassing, those emanations that reach out from the material world to affect our senses, to make us insistently aware that they are all around us.

Benjamin once again clarifies that Kafka is not "mantic," not prophetic or religious in the ordinary (archist) sense. He doesn't have that kind of sight. Instead, his prophecy, if you will, is simply to show us our material context, what we all already know but continually refuse to adequately acknowledge. This context can only be experienced once again as a kind of off-gassing of "the real thing." The fumes and stenches of reality are all we have access to and even these can be (to some extent will be) mis-smelled.

It makes perfect sense that for Kafka the mystical and the divine only come to us in the most ordinary and banal of forms. Looking for God in a vision of pure perfection, we miss the fact that the divine is actually present in the stench of a pigsty, in the pulsing of our own blood in our bodies. When we try to own and control these things, they are purely phantasmatic and wholly unavailable to us. When we try to *see* these things, we are subject to all manner of delusions; smells and sounds are ways to bypass our own ensconcement in the visual regimes of appointing sight, but even those are not direct pathways to what is being expressed.

It is only when we acknowledge our suspension in something much larger than ourselves that we can at the very least make a feast, cook a dinner to honor (as Hobbes counsels as well) what we can never truly know. Accordingly, it seems most fitting that the best way to acknowledge the material community around us is not by projections and phantasms but by our own ordinary and everyday acts, our own engagement, however flawed, with the material world that surrounds us. Not just speaking but cooking, eating, walking, engaging, making, and breaking things alone and together constitute the fabric of our anarchist life, the very same life that is the object of divine violence.

In this way, ordinary life becomes a form of worship, a connection to a lost tradition. Whereas the archons of the world seek to project fantastic images of God and state, it is in fact people making dinner or doing other aspects of daily and regular life who are much closer—as close as we can come—to what the archons too are seeking out. The archons are hence the true soothsayers of this world, while ordinary life is itself sanctified by what it honors, by the miasmic (but in a good way) interchange between human life and the material world that such acts allow for. In this way too, ordinary life itself can be considered to be a form of collective and ongoing prophecy, perhaps its most enduring and critical form.

Storms out of Heaven: Angels and God
as Anarchist Prophets

If Kafka is an example of a prophet for Benjamin, albeit a prophet who is not "mantic" in any traditional understanding of that term, there remains a figure of prophecy that lies much closer to what is usually meant by that word. This is the angel of history, who is simply called a "prophet" or seer in earlier versions of the essay "On the Concept of History." In the completed essay, Benjamin famously evokes a storm of history blowing out from paradise, helplessly witnessed by the angel. Taking his cue from a painting called *Angelus Novus* by Paul Klee that Benjamin had purchased and displayed in his own home, Benjamin writes that the angel's "eyes are wide, his mouth is open, his wings are spread. This is how the angel of history must look."[46]

In a very well-known passage, Benjamin writes:

[The angel's] face is turned toward the past. Where a chain of events appears before *us, he* sees one single catastrophe, which piles wreckage upon wreckage and hurls it at his feet. The angel would like to stay, awaken the dead, and make whole what has been smashed. But a storm is blowing from Paradise and has got caught in his wings; it is so strong that the angel can no longer close them. The storm drives him irresistibly into the future, to which his back is turned, while the pile of debris before him grows toward the sky. What we call progress is *this* storm.[47]

It is true that the angel of history remains primarily a visual creature. His main contribution in the short passage describing him is that he sees all that is before him. "His eyes are wide" and "his face is turned toward the past." It also seems to be true—at least at first glance—that the angel sees things that the rest of us do not, or at least sees them in ways that others do not: "where a chain of events appears before us, *he* sees one single catastrophe." And like some of the prophets of yore, this is a reluctant prophet; Jeremiah and Moses, for example, both expressed fear and reluctance when they found that they would have to be God's mouthpiece. Similarly, the angel's wings are pinned back and "the storm drives him irresistibly into the future."

For all these similarities, this prophet is otherwise utterly unlike the earlier biblical models. For one thing, this angel faces backward, toward the past. The future, the usual realm of prophecy, is nothing for him—everything that matters, the key to seeing what is, comes from the past and from the storm that is blowing out of heaven.

It's not that this angel is necessarily rebelling on purpose. As we saw, "the angel would like to stay, awaken the dead, and make whole what has been smashed." In other words, this angel would like to act as a prophet is supposed to act—an archist prophet at least—making whole, or appearing to make whole, what has been smashed, looking forward to future redemption, even to waking the dead. But the prophet cannot see these things, not only because he is facing the other direction but because he *knows*—that is, he *sees*—that such outcomes are phantasmic; in front of him (the past) is nothing but debris, behind him (the future) there is nothing at all.

Upon closer inspection, it turns out that this most unlikely of prophets is not actually seeing something special after all. We are all being blown by the same wind and seeing the same pile of debris as the angel; that wreckage is, in fact, the same material communion that Kafka espies in his own way. The fact that we call that pile of debris "progress" shows the power of archism to reorder and indeed *re-see* the existing world in its own image, reminiscent once again of God's own power in Jeremiah to reorder the objects that Jeremiah saw.

The difference between the angel of history and the rest of us is that his position as an angel allows him to see what we all see but do not recognize. His seeing itself isn't different; he has eyes that work like everyone else's, at least everyone who can physically see. Yet, precisely because he is an angel, because he is supposed to have some inside scoop or knowledge—shades of the archeon—that the rest of us do not have access to, the fact that he sees nothing but debris and emptiness means that he *knows* there is nothing else there. The rest of us rely on the archon, some authority figure, to tell us, "I see this or I see that" because we believe—that is, we desperately hope—there *must* be something else there. The angel of history knows otherwise; he has no one above him who can stand in as holding onto archist forms of vision. He himself would be the one to ask.

Thus, the fact that the angel doesn't really do anything but look—he would like to do other things but his wings are pinned back and one imagines that his eyes are forced open à la *Clockwork Orange*—is not in and of itself a problem in terms of thinking of him as an effective anarchist prophet. It is the angel's unknowledge and unsight—that is, the fact that he knows and sees that there is nothing else to know or see—that he can gift to the rest of us. Very much like Zarathustra as well, given his own privileged position, the angel is the one who can inform us that the archeon is empty, that there is no site of judgment (for Benjamin, that seat of judgment is not so much eliminated as it is vacated; it is endlessly, perhaps permanently, postponed). Given access to his field of vision, from his point of view, we are forced to confront what we see as well. We might not believe it if one of our fellow humans reported a similar sight, but he is an angel and he's supposed to know better and more. This angel is a disappointing prophet, to be sure.

The storm that the angel of history is witnessing reminds me of an earlier storm. Recall Zarathustra's dream in "The Prophet" in which, having opened up the fortress of death, Zarathustra is subject to a powerful storm, a "raging wind" that blew out "a thousand masks of children, angels, owls, fools, and child sized butterflies." It seems that these kinds of divine storms—perhaps themselves avatars of divine violence—are required to liberate us from our tendency to see the way we are told to see (i.e., as "progress," in this case). We also see in Nietzsche's words that angels are among the things blown toward us by such storms. Perhaps these are even one and the same storms (and one and the same angels too).

We might prefer the comfort of a fortress of death or a prophet who tells us nothing but lies. Yet anarchist prophets such as Zarathustra and the angel of history fail to perform their function as proper avatars of archist rule. In doing so, they betray their privileged positions and give away the secrets of God, nature, and the state. Furthermore, they force the rest of us to occupy our own sight and, just as critically, our own relationship to our material context. We, the subjects of their prophecy, already know what they show us to be the case; we are just as much subjects of divine revelation as the prophets themselves, even as we desperately want to be convinced otherwise.

The Dark (Other) Angel

A discussion of prophetic and anarchist angels in Benjamin's work would be incomplete without mention of another angel that emerges elsewhere in Benjamin's writings, namely Satan.[48] To read Satan as having some positive and prophetic function requires even closer textual reading than when it comes to the angel of history, insofar as this fallen angel has a very ambiguous status for Benjamin. In many ways, Satan serves as an avatar of his—and our—own time; Benjamin connects the timelessness of the phantasmagoria with the stasis of hell.[49] Evil and temptation are modes that Benjamin often evokes to describe not just Satan's reign but the capitalist world that Satan helped create (in part via his role in the Fall). In some sense then, Satan represents the acme of archism; he lies, he projects, he deals only in death. Yet for Benjamin, Satan has an anarchic element as well, one that is often intimately entangled with his archist persona.

There are two key texts where Benjamin's complex view of Satan is perhaps most clear and the contrast between them—and within each of them—helps set the tone for his treatment of this figure more generally. The first text to consider, going out of the chronological order in which they were written, is his very short piece "Agesilaus Santander" (of which there were two versions; I'm focusing on the second). Scholem noted that the name of this piece is a near anagram to Der Engel Satanas (the angel Satan).[50] If Scholem is right, the narrator of this short piece might be Satan himself. He tells a story of hiding his two secret names—presumably Agesilaus Santander / Der Engel Satanas—as well as the fact that he is a Jew. He suggests that he lived an ordinary human life until he reached maturity, at which point his secret names were revealed and he lost "the gift of appearing human."[51] In this way, the angel comes into himself by receiving his (true?) name. He goes on to tell us: "In the room I occupied in Berlin, even before that person [presumably his angelic self] emerged fully armored and accoutered from my name, he had fixed his image to the wall: New Angel" (usually taken as a reference to, and thus a connection with, Angelus Novus, the angel of history painted by Klee that hung on Benjamin's wall).[52]

The narrator then describes a struggle that he, as well as the New Angel, has with God, writing: "The Kaballah relates that, at every moment, God creates a whole host of angels, whose only task before they return to the void is to appear before His throne for a moment and sing His praises. The new angel presented himself as such before naming himself. I only fear that I had kept him excessively long from his hymn. Aside from that, he has paid me back."[53] If the final "he" in this story is God, it might seem as if the deity is exacting revenge on ("pa[ying] back") Satan for making the new angel late for his praising of God (or maybe not, since the phrase "aside from that" suggests that there were maybe other things that God has paid Satan back for instead).

The text goes on to say that the narrator was "born under the sign of Saturn—the planet of the slowest revolution, the star of hesitation and delay."[54] Here, the narrator is himself eternally late and waiting, perhaps explaining the delaying role that he plays with the New Angel.

If God makes Satan into an angel that waits—if that is indeed his punishment—Satan has occupied that waiting according to his own terms (not unlike Zarathustra). The narrator goes on to write, "He [i.e., God] may have been unaware that in doing this he brought out the strength of the man against whom he was proceeding—namely his ability to wait. . . . Nothing could overcome the man's patience."[55] The narrator then describes what he has been doing ever since: waiting for souls to capture. He depicts, for example, waiting patiently for a woman to get old and presumably die so he could get his "pinions" in her.[56]

What starts as a punishment thus becomes a mode of operation for the dark angel, one that he extends to the New Angel as well. Although the narrator tells us that the New Angel "resembles everything from which I had to part [i.e., his own humanness]," there is some way that the New Angel resembles Satan too: "he, too, has claws and pointed, razor-sharp pinions."[57] The New Angel also seems to be a kind of harvester of souls (although perhaps for a different purpose than Satan's). The narrator says, "[The New Angel] makes no attempt to fall upon whomever he has his eye on [because he seeks to] draw him after himself on that road to the future along which he came, and which he knows so well that he can traverse it without turning round and letting him whom he has chosen out of his sight."[58] Here we see that, even if he appears to be heading toward the future, the New Angel continues to, as it were, fly backward, keeping his eye on the past.

Thinking of the New Angel as having satanic qualities draws him into the ambivalent status of Satan himself. If he's flying backward, his regard is in the correct direction but perhaps for a problematical reason (to harvest souls). Yet in reading this text, our presumption that Satan is evil conflicts with the way that he seems to expand the realm of freedom and possibility against a God who serves as the ur-archon. Rather than merely praising God, Satan and the New Angel do something different. Even as an ambivalent text, "Agesilaus Santander" therefore suggests that there is space in the world for alternative forms of vision and that waiting itself, that space of messianic expectancy, need not be passive but can instead be a space of action both individually (for the dark angel) and collectively (in terms of his relationship to the New Angel). This all begs the question of what is being done with this agency. If it only serves for more archism (lying, cheating, death, etc.), then the rebellious nature of Satan—and, by extension, the New Angel—is not "useless for the purposes of fascism," and hence not helpful for our own purposes either.

When we read this short piece in conjunction with a passage from the very end of The Origin of German Tragic Drama, which was written about eight years before "Agesilaus Santander," we see a bit more evidence for the anarchist possibilities of the figure of Satan (and, by extension, for the New Angel).

The section of The Origin in question comes at the very end of the book. It plays with the same ambivalence that we may have about Satan as both figure of ultimate, archist evil and anarchist rebel against an ur-archonic God. In that section, Benjamin speaks of "three original satanic promises," saying further, "What tempts is the illusion of freedom—in the exploration of what is forbidden; the illusion of independence—in the secession from the community of the pious; the illusion of infinity—in the empty abyss of evil."[59]

Here is an almost perfect alignment of the figure of Satan with the false promises of archism. Both promise freedom, autonomy, and a kind of immortality ("infinity"), and neither deliver on these things. Yet, even here, we are puzzled by the fact that Benjamin precedes this passage by telling us that the dominant mood of evil is "that of mourning, which is at once the mother of the allegories and their content."[60] Tying Satan to allegory appears to align him, not with the most reactionary and archist of forces, a basis of mythic violence, but the opposite.

This possibility is reinforced when Benjamin writes:

> As those who lose their footing turn somersaults in their fall, so would the allegorical intention fall from emblem to emblem down into the dizziness of its bottomless depths, were it not that, even in the most extreme of them, it had so to turn about that all its darkness, vainglory, and godlessness seem to be nothing but self-delusion. For it is to misunderstand the allegorical entirely if we make a distinction between the store of images in which this about-turn into salvation and redemption takes place, and that grim store which signifies death and damnation. For it is precisely visions of the frenzy of destruction, in which all earthly things collapse into a heap of ruins, which reveal the limit set upon allegorical contemplation, rather than its ideal quality.[61]

The apparent doom and destruction attributed to Satan are also ways to "turn" and redeem, only in this case, Benjamin refuses to allow the positive elements that emerge to be separate in any way from the destructive elements; this is not about transcendence and an ethereal floating above that results from the encounter with and cancellation of worldly evil. Benjamin further tells us that all the signs of fallenness, the "bleak confusion of Golgotha," and the general dismay displayed in allegory are ultimately a matter of resurrection.[62] He states, "Ultimately in the death-signs of the baroque the direction of allegorical reflection is reversed; on the second part of its wide arc it returns, to redeem. . . . For even this time of hell is secularized in space, and that world, which abandoned itself to the deep spirit of Satan and betrayed itself, is God's world."[63] In fact, Satan is doing God's work without necessarily even realizing it. All the sin, despair, and death that Satan causes align human beings not with eternal damnation but with the possibility of resurrection via the structure of allegory. Here, their failures become a basis for undermining the very lies that Satan is normally associated with (which he may even actively seek to promote).

A similar sentiment can be found in "Agesilaus Santander" as well, insofar as that short work ends with the following statement: "He [the New Angel] wants happiness—that is to say, the conflict in which the rapture of the unique, the new, the yet unborn is combined with that bliss of experiencing something once more, of possessing once again, of having lived. This is why he has nothing new to hope for on any road other than the road home, when he takes a new person with him. Just like myself; for scarcely had I seen you the first time than I returned with you to where I had come from."[64] Directionality is once again called into question; is this a call for evil or for good? Are they going forward or backward? In an archist or an anarchist direction? It appears that in effect all roads lead to the same place in the end, to whatever (and wherever) is "home," once again suggesting that these angels are not necessarily as in control of their own destinies as they might think, insofar as they remain subject to the power of divine violence. While Satan might think he has lured the New Angel to hell—the negative pole that helps structure archist judgment—it might turn out that neither of them are going to hell but once again toward a radically present materiality (the "bliss of experiencing . . . having lived"), which is to say, "home," the now time. And, in this way, they could be said to be potentially taking human beings along with them despite their own (archist) intentions to have a very different outcome.

As I read these sections, they are of a piece with Benjamin's points about the German baroque dramatists who were the main subject of his study in *The Origin*. These dramatists too may be motivated by bad intentions; they want to promote false, archist ideas about Gods and kings, but they do such a clumsy job of it that they produce not persuasive and "realistic" dramas— like their contemporaries William Shakespeare and Pedro Calderón—but allegories that serve to subvert the very things they want to promote. It is the same with Satan. He has the worst possible intentions, and he, far more than the angel of history / New Angel, wants to achieve all the lies of archism—or at least have them be believed in—but he too fails to make these lies fully ontological and irrefutable. In his failure, we see the success or at least the possibility for God's unmaking of mythic violence.

Even if Satan has successfully seduced the "New Angel"—let's assume that this is the same angel as the angel of history for the moment—it doesn't matter in the end. We already saw that that angel would like to "save" us, to do what archist prophets do and see the shining future, just as Satan does, or says he does. But God does not allow this. God pins the angel's wings back with a divine storm, an act once again of divine violence, forcing the angel to witness the pile of rubble that was meant to serve as the basis for satanic—and archist—lies.

I'm not sure if that quite allows me to claim that Satan is therefore an anarchist prophet. In a way, it could be argued that if Satan is an anarchist prophet, it would seem that every other archist prophet is as well, which is not something I'm quite ready to concede.[65] Even so, I would hold out the possibility for this claim, insofar as Satan is such an extreme version of archism—in some ways, he lies at the heart of mythic violence—that his own self-subversion, or perhaps more accurately his subversion by God, serves to radically and, as Benjamin says elsewhere in *The Origin*, "unsurpassedly" ruin the very archist lies that are the basis of his power and authority.[66] In that very limited way, we could say that the dark angel is an anarchist prophet as well and that the fact that he becomes one does maximal damage to the whole structure of mythic violence from its most awful and violent, death-seeking source.

An Anarchist God: That Constantly Postponed Day

If even Satan is inadvertently serving God's agenda, even if his intentions are archist and evil, what does it mean that God the ur-archon is herself a source of subversion and anarchist possibility? Insofar as we have seen several instances of God serving anarchist ends, how precisely does Benjamin understand the workings of this deity and the radicalizing acts of divine violence she engages in? Whereas normally God is understood as the ultimate pinnacle of archism, the enforcing archon, the judge and ruler who serves as a model for earthly rulers too, Benjamin's God abandons this role, opening up a space for human judgment and anarchist prophecy in the process.

It is true that on the surface of things, for all her own anarchist tendencies, Benjamin's God appears at times to be very archist indeed. After all, the key story that Benjamin tells in "Critique of Violence" to distinguish divine violence from mythic violence is the biblical story of Korah. As Benjamin tells us—in a story that Hobbes repeats as well—Korah was an idolator who, along with other of his Levite followers, rejected the rule of Moses and Aaron (two prophets) in favor of their own right to determine what was sacred and what wasn't, potentially meaning that everyone was or could be a prophet.

As Benjamin tells it, God's response to this challenge is decisive. Benjamin writes: "God's judgment strikes privileged Levites, strikes them without warning, without threat, and does not stop short of annihilation. But in annihilating it also expiates."[67] In this way, Korah's sin is utterly removed along with Korah himself and his followers by an act of divine violence. Benjamin famously goes on to write, "Mythic violence is bloody power over mere life for its own sake; divine violence is pure power over all life for the sake of the living. The first demands sacrifice; the second accepts it."[68]

Even a generous reading of this passage cannot avoid the sense that God is clearly an archist ruler who brooks no disobedience whatsoever. What Korah was calling for, resisting the political and theological authority of Moses and Aaron, is perhaps more akin to an anarchist position than that offered by Moses or Aaron themselves. Even if Korah seeks only to establish the interpretive power of the Levites, as we see in Hobbes's analysis, any broadening of who gets to judge and interpret opens in turn a door to popular interpretation as well. In this view, even if God's divine power is different and better than the pseudo-divine power of mythic violence, it remains potentially archist. Just like its secularized mythic imitation, divine power tolerates no resistance, demands recognition, and judges all in its view.

It's also true that much of the rest of the "Critique" shows that the human response to the absolute power of God need not be the false imitation of such power that we find in all instances of archism. Even if God is an archist, Benjamin strictly polices the boundary between the divine and the human worlds so that as far as human beings are concerned, God's will and judgment are largely unknowable (so that it doesn't readily translate into mythic violence). Benjamin tells us shortly after the passage quoted above that even a divine commandment that is as seemingly black and white as "Thou shalt not kill" cannot be read literally, insofar as "no judgment of the deed [of killing] can be derived from the commandment."[69] He furthermore says that the commandment "exists not as a criterion of judgment, but as a guideline for the actions of persons or communities who have to wrestle with it in solitude and, in exceptional cases, to take on themselves the responsibility of ignoring it."[70]

A human and anarchist response is still called for, but this in and of itself does not alter the fact that, up to this point, Benjamin's God *qua* God can appear to be quite archist indeed, commanding, determining, and judging as such a deity is wont to do. The anarchism comes not from God herself but from the way that human beings are thrown to their own devices in the face of God's absolute power and absolute silence (hence, very similar to Hobbes's own "negative theology").

Yet, in other writings, we see that Benjamin's God may not be as archist as initially appears or, perhaps more accurately, Benjamin shows us a God who abandons and withdraws from the very archist authority that her presence seems to otherwise instantiate. A key place where this happens occurs in a well-known fragment titled "The Meaning of Time in the Moral Universe." In that essay, which was written roughly at the same time as the "Critique," Benjamin offers a very different understanding of God.

There, Benjamin discusses the meaning of the Last Judgment, the time when human beings finally get their due reckoning from God as supreme judges. Benjamin writes: "The Last Judgment is regarded as the date when all postponements are ended and all retribution is allowed free rein. This idea, however, which mocks all delay as vain procrastination, fails to understand the immeasurable significance of the Last Judgment, of that constantly postponed day which flees so determinedly into the future after the commission of every misdeed."[71] In speaking of the Last Judgment as "that constantly postponed day," we see a dichotomy being set up between the power of God to judge and the question of whether God will actually ever do so.

Yet another divine storm is brewing here. Benjamin speaks of a "tempestuous storm of forgiveness which precedes the onrush of the Last Judgment."[72] This storm—I would wager that it is the same storm that is blowing back the angel of history's wings and perhaps even the same storm blowing out of Nietzsche's fortress of death, all manifestations, perhaps, of divine violence—is forever putting off the Last Judgment so that human beings are de facto located in a suspended sort of time where the teleologies and determinisms of God and nature still apply but are never actually enforced, leaving room for human agency and our anarchic response. In the gap produced by this storm, the falsities of archist appointment recede and the present, the now time, becomes more possible, or at least less impossible.

Interestingly, the storm of forgiveness looks quite a bit like the act of divine violence God commits against Korah, as described in the "Critique." In "The Meaning of Time in the Moral Universe," Benjamin writes, "This storm is not only the voice in which the evildoer's cry of terror is drowned; it is also the hand that obliterates the traces of his misdeeds, even if it must lay waste to the world in the process."[73] This is very reminiscent of the way that the divine act of violence against Korah "does not stop short of annihilation. But in annihilating it also expiates." In both cases, God's overwhelming power seemingly wipes away human agency, leaving no trace.

But notice the difference between the story of Korah and Benjamin's description of the storm of forgiveness. In the latter case, God is endlessly postponing the very judgment that gets so decisively delivered in the "Critique." If we return to a consideration of the archeon as that perch from which judgment issues, we see that in effect for Benjamin, in "The Meaning of Time in the Moral Universe," God has abandoned the archeon. That is, God *could* judge everything and settle all scores once and for all but, in this telling, God evacuates that seat of judgment, making it available for no one else and thus leaving it empty.

One can begin to see how subversive this story is in terms of human politics. For if all mythic formations are ultimately based on an archist theology, then to have God evacuate that core of authority serves to undermine all the imitations of that authority as well. That is how even an ur-archist like Satan can unknowingly serve an anarchist agenda; the archist core of the universe is eviscerated when God herself turns against her own power and authority.

Perhaps the true meaning of divine violence is that it describes when God abandons her own ultimate archist position. If God is not sitting in judgment, securely perched on the archeon, then the very hermeneutic power that Derrida attributes to the secularized (and Greek) version of that space, the power of judgment itself, is undermined, or, perhaps more accurately, redistributed among the people from whom that authority is otherwise normally taken in God's name.

In looking at God in this way, we see that for Benjamin, this deity works in tandem with the angel of history and possibly with Satan, God's unwilling yet ultimately anarchist prophet(s). Rather than abandoning the world and the archeon within it or dying, this God actually colludes with the angel to force him to see what he sees (or perhaps also forces him to stop seeing the progress, teleology, and redemption that isn't there). In this way, the angel of history becomes a kind of unwilling historical materialist—or at least a basis for historical materialism in human beings—and a disappointing prophet.[74] As for Satan, his function as an anarchist prophet is probably a great deal thinner than the angel of history, but due to his exaltedly evil position, his own subversion by God might have an even greater anarchist effect than the angel does.

In this portrayal of a God who is both archist and anarchist at the same time, we can see that this is a tension that never gets fully resolved for Benjamin. After all, the very notion of a God who forces angels to be anarchists—against, it would seem, their own will—seems like a very peculiar merging of archist and anarchist features. And there are times when God acts directly archist (as with Korah) and anarchist (as with the storm that constantly postpones Judgment Day). This irresolution does not mean that Benjamin is indifferent to God's nature but only that, as with all things in this universe, Benjamin recognizes the mutual entanglement of archism and anarchism, mythic and divine violence. If God serves as a force in the universe to undo and push back archism, she is, at the same time, an ultimate archon. She is both at once.

On the whole, however, in my reading, the anarchist features that Benjamin attributes to God greatly outweigh the archist features in a way that roughly equals what we find with Nietzsche's political theology as well. In particular, the image of a storm blowing out of heaven serves to demonstrate the general direction of God's work. Those storms—and maybe Zarathustra's storm too—are all instances of divine (or Godly) violence, and always serve to expose and reduce the power of archism. Whether it pins back the wings of the angel of history or postpones judgment, this storm offers that the basic quality—and direction—of the universe is anarchist, that the forces of mythic violence are always going against the grain, and that the cosmos moves in sync with distinctly anarchist rhythms.[75]

In a critically important way, we are all in the same position as the angel of history, subject to the same storm and only able to see what is in front of us—that is, what lies in our past and present—even though we imagine we are looking into the future. For this reason, Benjamin tells us in "On the Concept of History" that the working class is "nourished by the image of enslaved ancestors rather than by the ideal of liberated grandchildren."[76] The past, and the directionality of time more generally, serve as a current within which we operate and which archism operates against. This all serves as the context, the material backdrop, and the network that human beings are embedded within, enabling our own anarchism, our own horizontal forms of collective prophecy, in response.

We Are All Experts

Having laid out Benjamin's understanding of prophets and of God and the universe, I would put to Benjamin the same question that I put to Nietzsche: Are the prophets he treats, whether it's Kafka, Baudelaire, or the angel of history (or even Satan), required for the rest of us to see differently? Or, to use a more Marxist vocabulary, do we need historical materialists as such or are we perhaps all already historical materialists who don't, therefore, need any help or advice from an expert?

Much of Benjamin's work is set expressly against the notion of expertise, of the idea that the vast majority of people need other (implicitly better, smarter) people to figure things out for them. In "The Work of Art in the Age of Its Technological Reproducibility," Benjamin shows how endless reproduction, particularly in terms of the medium of film, far from being a loss for art, actually allows art to complete its mass character. Benjamin writes: "The masses are a matrix from which all customary behavior towards works of art today is emerging newborn. Quantity has been transformed into quality: *the greatly increased mass of participants has produced a different kind of participation.*"[77]

The technological reproducibility inherent in film, for example, allows for the kinds of collective decisions and struggles over meaning and value that I've been describing to emerge into plain view to that community itself. As one moves from painting to film, the authority and sense of the expertise of the artist begins to melt into larger and collective forms. This possibility may suggest how things work with the prophets and historical materialists (who are one and the same thing) I've been describing as well. In the case of film, it is not anarchic prophecy but anarchist technology that permits the move from singular to collective forms of authority. In the case of someone like Kafka, their role, not unlike the angel of history, is to transfer back their own interpretive authority to the community from which that authority has originally emerged. Kafka's focus on ordinary life—on laundry being hung and cabbage soups being cooked in courthouses and the crushes that people have on secret figures like Klamm in *The Castle*, even the stenches of the pigsties in the village at the castle's feet—allows him to help make that transition legible. In fact, nothing is actually being transferred in these kinds of moments; it's just that credit is being returned to an anarchic and collective process that is always underway. In this way, once again, Kafka touches on how ordinary life is not distinct from a connection to the divine—including in terms of its anarchist implications—but is instead precisely the only way that that connection exists at all. That is, this connection does not reside with "experts" and their special knowledge but with everyone in their very ordinariness, asserting a different sort of expertise, that of the collective itself. A collectivity that prophesizes together necessarily also knows, as a whole, all that it needs to know. There is no "special knowledge" required to make this collective function; so-called expertise is merely the stolen form of this kind of knowledge.

When Benjamin says that God, unlike the forces of mythic violence, serves the "living," I read him as pointing to the same vast anarchist ferment as Kafka depicts in his writings (this is a subject I return to in the conclusion). This is more evidence for my claim that anarchism is about life as such. Benjamin's primary focus in that passage is living human beings, but the concept of the living can in some sense be extended to animals, plants, and even rocks and bagels and all the rest, insofar as we are all suspended in a vast intercommunicating web that Benjamin once again calls the "magic of matter."

I think it's fair to say that for Benjamin, as for Nietzsche, these kinds of mass anarchist responses do not *need* the kinds of prophets that I've been talking about to have access to their own vision, their own collective forms of interpretation. They have these things with or without those prophets. But, so long as archism steals credit from these collective forms in the name of expertise, so long as it raises spectacles and makes promises by which those forms are hidden or relegated to the background, these figures, drawn from archism itself, are helpful (are "assisters"). These prophets and angels—including dark ones—this anarchist God, the historical materialists, and even the authors and artists of our world all serve to turn against their own, and hence our collective, ensconcement in phantasmic power.

While for Benjamin the possibility of prophecy is perhaps even more generalized and widespread than it is for Hobbes or Nietzsche, inherent not just in speaking but in all forms of material communion, this comes to nothing if such prophetic sight is ignored or overwritten. We *are* all prophets just as we are all experts, but (how) do we know that? Sometimes it takes special sight to see that there is no special sight. Sometimes it takes one (prophet) to know (every) one.

AT THIS POINT IN THE BOOK, I leave part I, a consideration of the important radical political theologies of Hobbes, Nietzsche, and Benjamin, and move to part II, toward treatments of historical and contemporary examples of anarchist practice along with literary and filmic (in this case from television) forms of prophetic sight. I want to emphasize that in doing so, I don't consider that the "theoretical" part of the book has ended but only the canonical part. I consider each one of the real-life examples, literary texts and (one) TV series (and one philosophical text too, for that matter), that I consider in what follows to be in and of themselves contributions to an understanding of both archist and anarchist forms of prophecy. This is therefore life and literature not just "illuminating" theoretical models but contributing to those models. In what follows, I engage with a series of examples and texts that collectively spell out the complex relationship between anarchist life and the parasitic archist authority that sits astride it. The following, chapter 5, picks up on the question just raised about whether we need anarchist prophets or whether they might in some way interfere with the very anarchist forms of sight they are meant to help recover. It also looks at how the conflict between archism and anarchism can best be navigated, how it can be maximized under circumstances of coexistence. And in chapter 6, I ask whether, given the deep mutual entanglement I have described in the first three chapters, anarchism can ever be free of archism. My answer is yes. Not only can anarchism be free of archism, but it already has been and is free, depending on which context we are talking about.

While the value of the historical and contemporary examples of anarchist practice that I look at may not need any defending or justification, before turning to these chapters it is helpful to briefly describe what a turn to literature as such helps accomplish in this regard. Literature is once again not just useful because it offers examples of theoretical claims; it also performs its own kind of analytical function by its very nature of being fictional. Through fiction, seemingly impossible situations can be considered nonetheless (such as the moment in Saramago's *Seeing* when nearly an entire city casts blank ballots or Tom Perrotta's depiction of the "Sudden Departure" in *The Leftovers*). Insofar as part of the lasting power of archism is to limit the sense of the possibility of its own nonexistence (so as to rule out any rival forms of politics and authority), fiction, by its very speculative and imaginary nature, allows such limitations to be breached. The guise of fiction also permits a kind of explorative engagement with issues that are not burdened by a need to "tell the truth," which, in archist societies, usually means to accept the various phantasms of life as if they were accurate and real. As Benjamin notes too, literature and film (and, by extension, TV) have a subversive quality by definition; by turning their back on the authority of truth, they get at other sorts of authorities and other kinds of truths, the kinds that are more in keeping with a Nietzschean view of the "homespun, severe, ugly, obnoxious, un-Christian, unmoral" truths he discusses in *Genealogy of Morals*.[78]

Finally, and I think most critically of all, literature gives us a sense of the richness and nuance of life in a way that works of political theory or philosophy cannot. When read in tandem with real-life examples, as is the case in what follows, literary treatments allow us to supplement readings of actual life in all its complexity with imaginations about that life that go beyond what is toward what could yet be. Since life as such—the anarchist ferment we are all living—is what emerges in the aftermath of disappointment, the intention of the following chapters is to help bring that life and all its possibilities to the fore. In this way, these literary treatments not only help undermine and subvert archism, exposing its false promises and its vulnerabilities, but they also give us a thick sense of the anarchist lives that are being led while all this resistance and subversion (and suffering and oppression) is going on.

Of all the figures that I look at in the next part of the book, only one fictional character, Octavia Butler's Lauren Olamina, and one real-life figure, Yali, a man from the Rai Coast of New Guinea, could properly be called prophets. Yet all the characters that I look at are seers of a sort. They all emerge out of the anarchist context I've been examining throughout this book. Some of them, perhaps especially the monster in *Frankenstein*, desperately want to believe in the promises of archism, but in their various ways they are too injured, ambivalent, angry, or simply too decent to become either the kind of subject or the kind of prophet that archism demands. Accordingly, they help model what resistance looks like from within the maw of archism, beginning with the question of resistant forms of sight but including models based on other senses as well.

The figures that I look at diverge greatly from one another, yet in that divergence, they give a strong sense of the variety and resilience of life in all its complexity and rich characteristics, something that philosophy and political theology can only gesture at but not depict. Of the real-life examples, someone like Buenaventura Durruti, an important anarchist figure from the Spanish Revolution, seems to come close to an ideal of a merger between his own agency and sight and that of the larger anarchist community. In the case of Abdullah Öcalan, the leader of the many contemporary Kurdish resistance movements, and Yali, the Melanesian prophet, their relationship to their own authority is more complicated and problematic (and even Durruti struggled against his own desire for leadership and authority).

In my literary examples, among the many figures that I treat, the monster in *Frankenstein* perhaps in particular takes disappointment to a new level. The monster is horrible; he is hideously ugly, violent, and vengeful. He spitefully murders many innocent people just out of his own rage at being abandoned and rejected. Other literary figures are damaged beyond repair: Nora Durst, in *The Leftovers*, hires prostitutes to shoot bullets at her while she wears a bullet-proof vest (the only way she can bear the fact that she lives in a world where her husband and children vanished in a split second). Lauren Olamina herself is bone weary and traumatized. The doctor's wife in Saramago's *Blindness* and *Seeing* is amazingly resilient but doesn't otherwise seem special in any way.

These are not the figures that you would want as poster children for anarchist resistance, and yet they are the kind of figures who exemplify that resistance and that vision precisely through the ways that they are so compromised, so weary, and so disappointing and disappointed. Heroic figures produce heroic outcomes; they are the stuff of archism. These figures are, if anything, antiheroic, although I think nonheroic may be an even better term since antiheroes are, after all, secretly just the same as heroes. Such a stance prevents a strong distinction being made between these prophets and anyone who would follow their vision, even as there is a strong desire, as with Zarathustra, that people come into such vision of their own accord. This ambivalent quality may be critical for helping ensure that anarchist prophets don't slide into archism after all, the central subject of the next chapter.

part ii

chapter five

navigating
(and fighting)
archism

Anarchism in Practice

IN MOVING FROM a more purely theoretical model of what anarchist prophecy might look like to the application, both in real life and in
the literary imagination about such prophecy, it becomes necessary to think
about a central problem that was brought up in the earlier chapters but remains unresolved: namely, how do anarchist communities manage to come
into their own, and even thrive, in the face of archist predation? What role
do the anarchist prophets play in this drama and how can their own archist
tendencies be prevented from reproducing the archism that they assist the
community in resisting in the first place? The first part of this book looked
at theoretical models of resistance, but in this, the second part, I focus on
the actual experience of living amid and fighting archist power and authority, without, however, abandoning the theoretical analysis that comes along
with these case studies.

The role of anarchist prophecy in these narratives is both critical and
complex. The very ambivalences that we see in figures like Nietzsche's Zarathustra and Benjamin's angel of history are lived out in both real-life and
literary examples. One cannot engage with archism, even with the intention

of resisting it, without feeling its siren call, and anarchist prophets, like the communities that they come out of, are not immune to that call and its temptations. My focus in this chapter is on how best to navigate archism, how to beat it at its own game without succumbing to its horrible and seductive power. Insofar as anarchist prophets must take on the mantle of archism in order to perform their task of ruining it from within, there is always a risk of becoming the very thing that they are fighting. And this temptation happens not only to the anarchist prophets themselves but to entire communities as they too grapple with their archist parasite.

In this chapter, I visit these kinds of questions using a variety of sources, both actual and literary. I have four examples in all, two from real life and two literary. In both pairings, I contrast a perfect or near-perfect case of anarchism, Spain in the 1930s and José Saramago's *Blindness* and *Seeing*— especially the latter text—with a more compromised, and therefore perhaps more typical, example of anarchism coexisting with or navigating archism: Rojava and Octavia Butler's Earthseed series.

In terms of the real-life examples, I begin with what might be the ultimate moment of collective anarchist prophecy, namely, the decades-long experiment with anarchism in Spain that culminated in the Spanish Revolution and then its violent defeat by fascism in 1939. In this example, I show how the Spanish anarchists organized themselves in such a way as to make their collective reliance on any one person or some group of persons redundant, something to be held in suspicion. The anarchists of Spain had their heroes and leaders, to be sure: Buenaventura Durruti, Francisco Ascaso, and the Haymarket martyrs figure prominently in anarchist discourse of the time. But there is a particular way that these figures are linked into the larger Spanish anarchist community that is distinctive in no small part because of the concern for and guardedness against what I call incipient archism— and which is sometimes referred to as "leaderism"—that counteracts, at least partially, both the allure and the stealth presence of archist models.

A second real-life and much more recent, in fact contemporary, model that I draw upon is the case of Rojava, the Kurdish region of Syria that has gained autonomy from the authoritarian state that still nominally controls it. The case of Rojava is interesting because it suggests a case in which a more conventional leftist movement led by Abdullah Öcalan began to transform itself into a more anarchist model (officially called democratic confederalism). As the story goes, Öcalan began his career as a Marxist, but while in a Turkish prison—where he remains to this day—he studied the work of the American anarchist writer Murray Bookchin, among others. Here we may seem to find a case where an archist prophet, even if from the left, turned himself into an anarchist one, although the degree of his own anarchism, as well as the anarchism of Rojava more generally, is not a settled fact.[1] That vision in turn was translated—and perhaps facilitated by the fact that Öcalan himself was prevented from having any direct political power due to his jailing—into a more widespread form of anarchist practice. The full story is, once again, more complicated than this, and Rojava is neither free from sovereign power nor perfectly anarchist—then again, neither was Spain in the 1930s—but here too we see a tension between archist and anarchist elements that, at the very least, may have resolved themselves more in favor of the latter than of the former.

In terms of literary texts that engage with this same dynamic, I begin with two books by José Saramago, *Blindness* and *Seeing*, and then look at two books that constitute Octavia Butler's Earthseed series (*The Parable of the Sower* and *The Parable of the Talents*). Both sets of books are sequels. In these books, we see a similar overlapping of anarchist and archist aspects, with the former set once again displaying anarchism as a "purer" form.

In the Saramago novels, we see something that approaches an utterly anarchist model, wherein there really are no leaders of an anarchist movement that rejects the state entirely, albeit in a context where archism is not dead but simply at a remove. If there is a singular anarchist prophet in those books, it is a character known only as the doctor's wife. Yet in a sense her role as leader is mostly a reflection of the archist state's desperate attempt to find a leader of the entirely collective anarchist movement that threatens them. They reason that by identifying, intimidating, and killing her, they can in effect stop the movement itself. Yet, in her very ordinariness, and in her connection with that collectivity that she is only part of, we see the complete failure of that mission.

In Butler's novels, Lauren Olamina, the heroine of both books, is unquestionably a singular figure in a religion that she begins called Earthseed. In this way, she looks and acts a lot like an archist prophet would. Yet her religion is itself highly anarchist and may serve to combat some of its leader's— that is, Lauren herself—own archist tendencies.

In all these readings, I am arguing that the fact that anarchism and archism remain intimately intertwined does not mean that we are always fated to archist victory. In fact, I think the opposite is true, that the universe itself tends toward anarchism and that it is archism that must fight against the current in order to persist. What the examples I look at show is that while anarchism can itself be a source of archism—especially in cases where an anarchist prophet is singular or part of a small elite group—there are ways to combat incipient archism. I also claim that ultimately, for anarchism to succeed and thrive, anarchist prophecy must become entirely collective, or it will eventually succumb to archism all over again.

The fact that those rare moments of anarchism emerging into the open inevitably seem to bring the harshest possible archist response does not in and of itself mean that an anarchism that has overtaken its archist entanglements can never be more than a fleeting and temporary experience. Part of the purpose of this chapter is to see lessons that can be learned and applied to future (and past) anarchist endeavors, to fight, as Benjamin would say, for the sake of the living and the dead alike.

The Spanish Revolution

It may seem not only strange but downright obnoxious to equate the anarchists involved in the Spanish Revolution of the 1930s with any theological terms such as prophecy, insofar as one of the signature aspects of that revolution was a sound rejection of any form of religion whatsoever. Hostility to the Catholic Church and its connection to corrupt and dictatorial forms of control in Spain was rampant among the anarchists who took part in the Spanish Revolution. This is one of the places in which it becomes helpful to speak of archism, rather than sovereignty or statehood, as a foundational aspect of modern life. Archism is itself a theological phenomenon; even its most secular face preserves a certain kind of theological orientation, and so the remedy to that theology must be a kind of countertheology, the kind that I have been describing as anarchist prophecy.

To think about the Spanish Revolution in theological terms does not condemn the anarchists of that time to yet more religion but finally and actually achieves what Maria Aristodemou calls "atheism," a reckoning with and then final break with theological externalities once and for all.[2] I think therefore that the Spanish anarchists of this period can be considered atheists rather than secularists with their a-theism aligning with their an-archism. In both cases, the "a" in question is not a pure negation—so not just "not theistic" and "not archist." It is also, and perhaps more critically, a positive model, one that replaces and supersedes the archist models with other forms of political, social, and economic organization that reflects the anarchism of everyday life, albeit in a way that is far more evident and far more dangerous for the forces of archism than what archism itself normally permits us to see and act upon.

To begin this inquiry, let me first give a bit of background for what most people call "the Spanish civil war" but anarchists, and I, being one of them myself, will stick with this practice, call the Spanish Revolution. The names are important because most of the famous revolutions that we talk about—the French Revolution, the American Revolution, the Russian Revolution, and the Chinese Revolution, to give only some of the most famous examples—are either liberal capitalist or communist in their structure. There are certainly anarchist aspects to all these revolutions, as Arendt attests in her book *On Revolution.* There, she describes moments when small workers' councils—the Soviet workers' councils in Russia, the clubs and societies in France, and so on—were organizing at the local level, but as she shows, in each case, these "elementary republics" were overcome by parties (the Bolsheviks, Jacobins, etc.), which led these revolutions in a different, generally archist, direction.[3]

The Spanish Revolution was different. Arguably this was the closest that any revolution has come to having a real anarchist takeover of power. Perhaps more accurately, it was not a takeover of power but a removal of archist power over anarchist life. In his book *Insurgent Universality,* Max Tomba argues that anarchism does not need to literally replace archism (my word, not his). All it needs to do is to create a fully viable alternative to the state and to the market which readily replaces and renders obsolete those state and market functions.[4] This is precisely what the Spanish anarchists did. Although ultimately the anarchist revolution in Spain was crushed by a combination of archist forces, we should not take this to mean that the revolution was a failure or that it indicated anything about anarchism per se that suggests a weakness or an impracticality. In fact, the opposite might be true: the Spanish Revolution was so successful, even in its prewar mode, that it threatened capitalism—and archism itself—to its very core. This led to a violent fascist counterrevolution that was initially effectively supported by nominally liberal and antifascist democratic powers such as the United States and Great Britain, a fact that should not surprise us when we realize that archism is above all about supporting its main economic form, namely capitalism.

Key to the reception of this revolution was the fact that it was, and remains to some extent, either widely ignored or, if paid attention to, treated as a bit of an anomaly rather than as a major revolution in its own right (hence the importance of what we call it). As Bookchin said of the revolution: "What so few of us knew outside Spain, however, was that the Spanish Civil War was in fact a sweeping social revolution by millions of workers and peasants who were concerned not to rescue a treacherous republican regime but to reconstruct Spanish society along revolutionary lines. We would scarcely have learned from the press that these workers and peasants viewed the Republic almost with as much animosity as they did the Francoists."[5] In many ways, this reminds me of another largely anarchist revolution—at least by my own definitions—that was also deliberately forgotten, at least as far as the West was concerned, namely the revolution in Haiti at the turn of the nineteenth century (certainly this revolution was not forgotten in Haiti, nor was it forgotten in the Black communities in the rest of the Caribbean, as well as in North and South America).[6] The imperialist powers of the West acted as if the Haitian Revolution had never happened because of the challenge it posed to Western narratives of white and European supremacy. The fact that an army of slaves could overthrow the combined power of Napoleonic France and many of his erstwhile enemies—then, as in the case of Spain in the 1930s, you had de facto alliances between mortal enemies when it came to the common defense of capitalism—proved impossible for the West to fathom, much less admit to. That is once again why I think it's important to call the event in Spain in the 1930s what it was, a revolution, and not just a "civil war," and an anarchist revolution at that.

The roots of the Spanish Revolution can be traced to a mixture of Indigenous and external factors. Bookchin cites the influence of Giuseppe Fanelli, a supporter of Mikhail Bakunin, who came to Spain in 1868 to spread the doctrine of anarchism.[7] Yet Fanelli didn't arrive in a vacuum. Bookchin himself argues that "the resiliency and tenacity that kept Spanish Anarchism alive in urban *barrios* and rural *pueblos* for nearly seventy years, despite unrelenting persecution, is understandable only if we view this movement as an expression of plebian Spanish society itself rather than as a body of exotic libertarian doctrines."[8]

Spanish society at the time was marked by a strong resentment of the caciques, local strongmen, along with an antagonism to the power of the Church and the state, which was often seen as corrupt and self-interested. Thus, Fanelli arrived at a place that was very ready to receive his message. He gave a name, a sense of united purpose, and a set of organizational strategies to a movement that was already nascent long before his arrival.

The chief aspect that distinguished Spanish anarchism, especially when it really came into its own in the 1920s and 1930s, was its connection to unions. The concept of "anarchosyndicalism" is a good term to use for this particular anarchist manifestation because, in effect, the main anarchist union, the Confederación Nacional del Trabajo (CNT, National Confederation of Workers), an organization that had as many as one and a half million members at its height—and the anarchist movement were effectively one and the same.[9]

Many recounters of the revolution, ranging from Murray Bookchin to Juan Gómez Casas, use the terms *anarchist* and *anarchosyndicalist* interchangeably in this regard.[10]

The CNT also had a strong relation to an alliance of affinity groups called the Federación Anarquista Ibérica (FAI, Iberian Anarchist Federation). This group worked in tandem with the CNT for much of its history. It has often been accused of "leading" or ruling the CNT, but in fact its purpose was quite the opposite: it served to ensure that the CNT itself did not succumb to what some call "leaderism," a tendency for organizations, even radical anarchist ones, to develop a leadership that tends to undermine its own rank and file, to make common cause with other leaders of the state and industry.[11]

Here, we can already see evidence of the struggle between archism and anarchism that this chapter is focused on. Even an anarchist union like the CNT was subject to archist tendencies within itself. Recognizing this tendency and acting to counter it as much as possible is one way that anarchist movements can maintain horizontal forms of vision.

Throughout its history, the CNT was under attack from both external and internal foes. Externally, it had to fight off the predations of many communist and socialist organizers who had their own intentions for the union. From its inception, the CNT had to resist attempts to merge it with the other main union at this time, the socialist Unión General de Trabajadores (UGT, General Workers' Union), which did not share the CNT's concerns about leaderism and was far more reformist and collaborative with the Spanish state. The CNT also had its own internal battles, including the moderate and reform-oriented "treintistas" led by Ángel Pestaña, who favored more common cause with other unions and with republican and Popular Front forces.

Despite these challenges, a generally collective form of anarchist commitment sustained the CNT in these battles even before the FAI came into being. Juan Gómez Casas writes: "The CNT . . . had a sufficiently strong ideological foundation to correct errors and maintain its course. It could neutralize or expel bodies that were foreign to the nature of the organization. It was the anarchist character of the CNT that closed the door to the partisans of Moscow even though there was no specific organization of the anarchists at that time."[12] In other words, what kept the CNT going, what preserved its anarchist structure, was anarchism itself. It remained anarchist therefore not because of but despite its own leadership. Its anarchism was located in its vast membership and in their collective forms of vision. Let me therefore detail a bit more precisely how that collective form operated and was preserved.

Organization of the CNT

The CNT had many deliberate organizing features designed to combat incipient leaderism in its upper ranks. This was done in ways that were both formal and informal. One key element of this organizational structure was the concept that there should be one union (*uno sindicato único*), which would be composed of various sections across all sorts of trades that operated more or less independently from one another even as they were coordinated by the union apparatus. In this way, the union as a whole could stand united against capitalist predations, but at the same time, the CNT had a federalist structure that allowed maximal diversity of views and actions.[13] This is typical of a pattern of what might be called decentralized planning, a key feature of anarchist organization, whereby the parts are separate but coordinated, allowing for a best-of-both-worlds combination of decentralized creativity, experimentation, and talent along with the benefits of unity and coordination as far as other organizations and institutions were concerned.

Relatedly, the CNT practiced a unique kind of solidarity in its ranks. Sections that were not as bought into anarchism were not excluded from membership but were engaged with, allowing for a great deal of ideological diversity so long as the basic principles of organizing from the ground up was maintained.[14]

Another key tenet of the CNT, held for much of its existence until the struggle against Francisco Franco, was that its leaders would not participate in state politics or direct its members to participate in parliamentary elections and other liberal—and archist—models of political participation. This tenet was reneged upon in 1936 when four members of the CNT leadership became ministers in the republican government, creating a storm of protest and criticism among the rank and file.[15] This may reflect more the steady erosion of anarchist solidarity and morale in the face of war than an internal problem within anarchism as such. As Vernon Richards points out, just two months after an essay in *Solidaridad Obrera*—one of the main anarchist journals and a publication of the CNT—condemned any thought of coalition with the government as leading to the "rapid destruction of our capacity for action, of our will to unity," the same journal praised the fact of bringing four CNT ministers into the very same state, insofar as the latter had "ceased to be an oppressive force against the working-class."[16]

Another key element in fighting leaderism was the attempt to limit the scope and number of positions that could become the basis for centralizing tendencies. Positions of authority were only open to those who actively practiced trades that were included in the CNT (i.e., no "professional union activists" were allowed).[17] To resist a tendency for men to dominate and form cliques, women were deliberately included in all steering committees as well.[18] Finally, leaders, such as they were, were limited to short terms and were not paid. In practice, however, these last points were not always adhered to, leading to some difficulties over time.[19]

Radical Practices and Institutions

In addition to its organizational models, there were also some institutional and conceptual aspects of the CNT that also helped hold back leaderism. Perhaps the key point here is that the CNT was devoted to the idea of direct action, a concept that came from French anarchosyndicalists. Direct action permitted the rank and file to take matters into their own hands. It also meant that union demands were not to be negotiated but either taken as is or rejected.[20] This meant that there was no bargaining team to make side deals. The demands themselves came from general assemblies of the rank and file so that, to the highest degree possible, there was no "middleman" between the workers and the bosses.[21]

Another way to call the leadership into question was through the enormous and flourishing anarchist press of that period. Some publications, like *Tierra y Libertad*, were directly associated with the CNT, as was *Solidaridad Obrera* (although on at least one occasion, militant workers, noting that the editors were all in jail, took over the press and wrote their own issue).[22] Other journals, such as *Redención, Iniciales*, and *La Revista Blanca*, were more independent. In general, these newspapers and other publications were freewheeling and open sites of collective discourse—even the ones operated by the CNT itself—that allowed for a great deal of criticism and debate within the anarchist ranks.[23]

The development of the FAI, and even within the FAI certain subunits such as Nosotros (Us), was another way to avoid the ossification—or really the archization—of the CNT. The FAI, which was formed in 1927, was a collection of affinity groups that came together to coordinate with the CNT. In one of the preliminary congresses that led to the formation of the FAI, it was stated that "the two organizations [i.e., the FAI and the CNT] could complement each other, the unions and the ideological groups, and . . . they should be joined in a federal structure, each maintaining its autonomy, with joint representation of the groups and their federations with the unions and their federations at all levels."[24]

Here again, a typical anarchist solution, informal but coordinated, with confederal unity at the macrolevel with a devolvement into smaller independent groups at the microlevel, is maintained both within and between various anarchist organizations. As Gómez Casas argues, the informality of this structure was both a blessing (because it once again allowed maximal experimentation and flexibility for these organizations as they worked together and apart) and a curse (because it allowed anti-anarchist forces to say things like the FAI was "leading" the CNT, among other archist characterizations of this organization).[25]

Finally, anarchist economic models were also deployed, in terms of both collectivization and worker self-management, in ways that were analogous to the anti-leaderist methods of political organization already mentioned. In the case of both rural collectivism as well as urban and industrial collectivism, the pattern was quite different from the sort of centralized planning-based collectivization that was undertaken in the Soviet Union. In Spain, families remained in their own homes but worked together to achieve economies of scale. In some places, wages were paid, and in others, profits were shared, once again showing the diversity and experimental nature of anarchist practices.

The same political model used to organize people in general was used in rural collectivization—often constituting the same bodies, in fact—wherein small independent individuals and groups organized themselves into larger groups and then went on to form extremely large unitary organizations that nonetheless preserved their internal diversity. One estimate is that during the main period of collectivization, during the struggle with Franco, up to three million rural people may have been involved in anarchist collectives.[26] As a rule, peasants were not forced to collectivize if they didn't want to, leading to a kind of patchwork of collective and noncollective rural activity. Those who chose not to collectivize were still invited to participate in the group economy, as they were able and willing to do.

What was true for rural farming was also true for urban collectivization. Here, larger firms with more than one hundred workers were generally collectivized while those with fewer than one hundred workers were allowed to remain capitalist if their owners chose, but even in such cases, their workers were guaranteed certain rights, while cooperation with the collectives was also encouraged.

In all these models of organizing, one principle was key: the idea that the people in their variety and own experiences collectively knew far better what was right for them, whether in terms of political or economic questions, than any politicians or managers. All they need is a forum in which they can encounter one another to collectively decide on their own work practices, a situation that archist work systems do everything in their power to avoid.

Stripping off this parasitic, archist layer and allowing them such a forum returned the workers and peasants to their own knowledge (i.e., expertise) and agency, and, as such, this system flourished before the fascist victory cut it dead. Here we can see very clearly how anarchist vision ultimately comes not from some externality but simply from its removal.

The Fight against "Leaderism" in the CNT

Despite all these precautions and institutional barriers, corruption and co-optation in the leadership was an ongoing problem for the CNT, especially after 1936 when the struggle against Franco began and when some CNT officials became members of the government. Richards quotes the French anarchist Gaston Leval as explaining:

> Some anarchist delegates, who had become ministers or official personages in different capacities, took their tasks seriously: the poison of power took effect immediately. But what was saved was the potential of the Spanish anarchist movement. It had thousands of seasoned militants, in all or almost all the villages of Aragon, the Levant, and Andalusia. Almost all the militants of the CNT had a solid experience of practical organisation in their own trades or in the life of a village and enjoyed an indisputable moral ascendency. Furthermore, they were gifted with a strong spirit of initiative.[27]

Here, Leval is attesting to the principal strength of anarchist forms of vision, their rootedness in locales and communities. The CNT militants who formed the rank and file were once again reflecting the ordinary and anarchist life that we all take part in. Only in this case, they were allowed to use that vision for meaningful political and economic purposes; the organizing structure of the CNT and the various forms of collectivization that the Spanish anarchists engaged with more generally allowed for an actualization of that anarchist potential, giving people a voice and a place from which to speak to and hear from one another, largely minus the overarching competition of archist forms of organization and vision.

This preservation and enhancement of anarchist forms of vision allowed the rank and file to anticipate and attempt to counter any archist tendencies in their leadership. Vernon Richards offers one example of how this worked out when, in February 1938, the Generalitat, the elected governing body of Catalonia, announced that it intended to take over the public entertainment industry in the region. In order to gain support for this, the Generalitat appointed three CNT officials to oversee this sector, thereby seeking to co-opt the leadership. When the government nonetheless began to get re-sistance to this move from rank-and-file union members as well as the anar-chist newspapers, they decided to just strong-arm the situation and declare it a done deal. That led to a general strike by workers, who clearly saw the attempt to buy off union leadership for what it was.[28]

Another more critical example of this kind of situation came when the republican government sent in troops to take over the Telephone Exchange building in Barcelona in May 1937. They only succeeded in taking over the first floor, while CNT militants barred them from going any further upstairs. This takeover was rightfully seen by the CNT rank and file as the bourgeoisie try-ing to take over power in Barcelona, long a center of anarchist resistance. The CNT leadership at the time was eager to broker a deal, whereas the rank and file had no intention of doing so. In sequence, two of the leadership's best orators were sent to make appeals to the workers, who had lined barricades around the building. This included Juan García Oliver, a highly regarded militant with strong anarchist credentials. As it was recorded, García Oliver gave an "oratorical masterpiece which drew tears but not obedience."[29] This helps show that there were limits to how much the CNT leadership could manipulate the rank and file, although ultimately, at the end of the day, they did make a deal and it did betray the rank and file.

Anarchist Prophets and the Question of Vision

It seems clear that anarchist leaders are not immune to the seductions of power. But what about those anarchists who were killed before those seductions could fully take hold or who managed to hold out and remain committed to the larger forms of vision held by the anarchist rank and file? Does their status in any way threaten the collective vision they help instantiate?

Perhaps the most critical person to discuss in this regard is Buenaventura Durruti, who has a near legendary status in the annals of the Spanish Revo-lution. If anyone can claim the mantle of anarchist prophet for the Spanish Revolution, it is Durruti.

A metallurgy worker from León, Durruti was from an early age adamant about imposing organizational limits to stop even a figure such as himself from abandoning his connection to collective forms of power, vision, and authority. Durruti always insisted that theory take a back seat to action; he saw politics as emerging from the decisions and actions of people on the ground and held that only in that way could there be revolutionary change.[30] He sought, for example, to forbid anyone from FAI or related groups from becoming a leader of the CNT. He states:

No anarchists on the union committees unless at the ground level. In these committees, in case of a conflict with the boss, the militant is forced to compromise to arrive at an agreement. The contacts and activities which come from being in this position, push the militant towards bureaucracy. Conscious of this risk, we do not wish to run it. Our role is to analyze from the bottom the different dangers which can beset a union organization like ours. No militant should prolong his job in committees, beyond the time allotted to him. No permanent and indispensable people.[31]

One writer, Abel Paz, whose account of Durruti is certainly hagiographic, tells us that "the cult of personality should never be encouraged, but neither Durruti nor his comrades like García Oliver and Francisco Ascaso could escape from the influence they exerted against their will. This influence could be pernicious and Durruti was tormented by this more than anyone else. He was perfectly conscious that his comrades at work looked up to him: this wasn't caused by the aura which he spread unknowingly but by a sort of gratitude which they felt for the way in which he had given himself so entirely to his work."[32]

Paz suggests a paradox. The more a figure like Durruti is devoted, body and soul, to the revolution—Paz notes that Durruti barely saw his family and his partner was forced to raise their daughter effectively single-handedly—the more they become venerated, threatening in a sense the very openness and horizontality that they are devoted to creating.[33] Such devotion to the collective seems to produce a mixture of reverence both for the figure themselves and for the anarchist collectivity that they help instantiate, and these two forms of reverence may at times work at cross-purposes.

Not all of the best-known anarchists shared Durruti's hesitations about taking on a leadership role. García Oliver, for example, was one of the handful of CNT members appointed to ministries during the struggle with fascism. García Oliver was also far more open to models of organization that looked very much like archist ones. At one point, he and Durruti argued over the formation of paramilitary forces. García Oliver was for creating such a force as a way to combat Franco's troops. Durruti wanted only guerilla fighters, fearing that a paramilitary force would lend itself to supporting some form of statism within the anarchist ranks.[34]

It may therefore be conjectured that part of Durruti's mass appeal was precisely that he did not try to stand in for the anarchist power he was devoted to. The masses, seeing that he did not try to replace their vision with his own, could afford to appreciate him while being more wary of people like García Oliver. In this way, they could allow Durruti to serve in a purely mimetic fashion, not as a leader but as a model for what every anarchist subject could be or was: maximally open to collective decision-making.[35] Durruti in this way could serve as the site where leadership would occur and ensure that that site was kept maximally open to the vastness, experience, and diversity of the rank-and-file anarchist members.

These attitudes toward Durruti can be seen as being reflected in the anarchist press, which often wrote about him and his exploits. In a November 1936 issue—the month when Durruti was killed—*Boletín de Información*, a CNT publication, had an essay in which the author wrote: "Victor Hugo and Lenin rest in pantheons, in superb mausoleums. Our comrade Durruti is not in a pantheon; he is more modest and offers us only his name and his work, giving him a privileged place in our estimations. Resting by his side is the other great fighter [*luchador*], his brother, our brother too, the great Ascaso."[36] Francisco Ascaso, who had been killed earlier that year, is another key figure who was highly regarded by the anarchist rank and file (other anarchist heroes included Federica Montseny as well as August Spies and the other Haymarket martyrs).

It is true that in the case of a major figure like Durruti, he is clearly given his due. The same article in *Boletín de Información* also notes: "None other [than Durruti] to our eyes has the height of this giant, none other can replace his mission. . . . There is no one who is so intimately connected to the substance of the Iberian revolution."[37] Here he does seem to be seen in an exalted sense, as someone above the rest.

And yet the essay continues, "But there is yet here something in this death that serves to raise—frenetically and ardently—our energies." Connecting the death and legacy of Durruti once again with Ascaso, the article explains: "These two had a fate which was tragically equal. The two fell in the field of honor, killed by homicidal bullets . . . but nothing, neither men nor events nor time itself, could extinguish the great light they projected into the shadows of an ill-fated past. Nothing could stop their ideas and examples from fertilizing the conscience of men to disseminate the ideas that sustain and set the foundation for the society of the future."[38]

Here, as is often the case in these archival sources, the greatness of these figures is seen mainly insofar as it serves as a catalyst for collective greatness. In these tributes, the role of heroic figures and martyrs, rather than being set on a kind of pedestal, is always brought into a collectivist project, seen as models for and examples to all individuals who take part in these forms of struggle, suggesting once again a largely mimetic function for the anarchist leaders, at least for those like Durruti and Ascaso who fought the tendency to idolize them.

This relationship to leadership was not uniquely related to the men of the revolution either. Federica Montseny was also a major figure among anarchist leaders (she was one of the deputies appointed to the Popular Front government and, perhaps for this reason, much of the anarchist scholarship seems to downplay her role). There were also anarchist women who formed their own collectives and affinity groups. As Martha Acklesberg writes in *Free Women of Spain*, Lucía Sánchez Saornil, Mercedes Composada, and Amparo Poch y Gascón founded the group Mujeres Libres (Free Women), which worked with the CNT and other anarchist organizations. As Acklesberg tells us, "What was necessary was an organization run by and for women, one committed to overcoming women's subordination in all its facets, whether in their home, in the workplace, or in the anarcho-syndicalist movement itself."[39] This giving voice and concrete political structures to communities within the larger anarchist community—the community of women being obviously the most important and numerically largest—was another way that the anarchists sought to fight against archist forms of hierarchy (the democratic confederalists of Rojava engage in similar practices).

From Heroes to Anarchists

A key takeaway for thinking about how to preserve anarchist vision under conditions such as those experienced by the Spanish revolutionaries might be to look at how they redirected and repurposed archist tendencies. If hero worship can be said to be one of the bases of archism, then turning heroes into anarchist subjects involves a conscious and steady engagement with the bases of such worship. What is held "high" becomes held "sideways"; the directionality of admiration becomes horizontalized, perhaps akin to what Machiavelli has in mind when he speaks of glory.[40]

If we think of "charisma" as being a quality that is held not by leaders themselves but by the community as a whole, then we can see that ordinarily—that is, under conditions of archism—this form of authority is monopolized by leaders, being effectively stolen from the community that produces it and claims it as its (i.e., the leader's) own. When a community reappropriates that charisma back into itself, sometimes with the help of anarchist prophets, it experiences its own collective form of authority in a no-longer-alienated form.

As to the question of whether we "need" anarchist prophets, as far as the example of the Spanish Revolution is concerned, I would say that the answer is a qualified no. The anarchist model in the Spanish Revolution shows that, when left to its own devices, a community readily adopts its own collective forms of sight, even as nonheroic leaders like Durruti definitely played their part in fomenting and assisting those actions. The very idea that the people are "stupid" or need help figuring out what they actually want as a community is belied by the fact that on those occasions where real forums are created that allow people a chance to engage with one another on a political, social, and economic level, they already know what they need to do. They don't have to be told anything.

This connects back to a point I made in chapter 1, that politics may be one of the key activities for which human beings all have an automatic expertise. If anarchist politics is about life, then all of us who are living are in fact already "experts"; the way that archism has turned politics into a profession—and an exclusive one at that—only serves to convince other people that they are better off not taking part in their own political existence. To the extent that those of us who live under the full control of archism, as opposed to the partial control afforded by the Spanish Revolution, it is good to remember that we too have that form of vision even when anything but archist logic and vision appear to be unimaginable.

Rojava's Incomplete Revolution

Turning now to a contemporary moment of anarchist practices, the current situation in Rojava—meaning "the West" in Kurdish since this area of Syria is considered to be western Kurdistan—is highly unstable, but then again so was the situation in anarchist Spain in the 1930s. Even so, Rojava offers us another important example of the resilience of anarchist models of authority as well as the complex way in which anarchist and archist modes both coexist and interact. The very question of the "anarchism" of Rojava is not accepted by everyone and this is, at best, a deeply imperfect model, perhaps especially in comparison with the Spanish Revolution. But for this very reason, the contrast between Spanish anarchism in the 1930s and Rojava today allows us to see how resistance to archism works in a variety of contexts and with a variety of different results, how even a partial anarchism allows some critical elements to flourish, elements that archism is normally entirely oriented toward stamping out.

In the chaotic aftermath of the Arab Spring uprising that challenged Bashar al-Assad's rule in Syria, the civil war that followed, and the subsequent rise—and fall—of ISIS, the Kurds of northeastern Syria, along with many multiethnic partners, managed to carve out a kind of state within a state. More accurately, because in fact the Syrian state has never renounced or abandoned its rule, at least de jure, of this region, and the Partiya Karkerên Kurdistanê (PKK, Kurdish Worker's Party), the Kurdish political party, which, along with its partners the Partiya Yekîtiya Demokrat (PYD, Democratic Union Party) and the Yekîneyên Parastina Gel (YPG, People's Protection Units), is ideologically opposed to statehood, one could say this is more of an antistate within a state, albeit imperfectly so.

The PKK is one of several Kurdish political parties that follow the ideology of Abdullah Öcalan, a former Marxist who has since embraced a version of anarchism that is called democratic confederalism.[41] Öcalan and many of the Kurdish resistance movements that he is connected to underwent a major political and ideological transformation beginning in the 1980s and culminating in 1999 when Öcalan was captured by Turkish authorities, sentenced to death—since then commuted to life imprisonment—and held in solitary confinement in a prison on İmralı island in the Sea of Marmara.

While in prison, Öcalan intently studied the works of the anarchist writer Murray Bookchin, among others (Fernand Braudel, Immanuel Wallerstein, and Foucault were also important influences).[42] Originally, the Kurdish resistance movements were committed to the same Marxist-Leninist ideologies as the larger Turkish left. Later, however, these movements abandoned the centrally planned and organized models that this form of thinking tended to entail. As the radical activist Ercan Ayboğan describes this transformation: "[The PKK] rejected the existing Marxist-Leninist structure as too hierarchical and not democratic enough. Political and civil struggle replaced armed struggle as the movement's center. Starting in 2000, it promoted civil disobedience and resistance (the Intifada in Palestine was also an inspiration). Further, the movement gave up the aim of establishing a Kurdish-dominant state, because of the existing difficult political conditions in the Middle East and the world; instead, it advanced a long-term solution for the Kurdish question within the four states Turkey, Iran, Iraq and Syria: democratic confederalism."[43]

Bookchin's influence on Öcalan is significant, although it should not be overstated.[44] Based in part on Bookchin's philosophy of libertarian municipalism—where Bookchin's use of the word *libertarian* is not to be confused with right-wing pro-capitalist libertarianism that is rampant in the United States—Öcalan helped develop the bases for democratic confederalism, which sought to make small local communes the basis for all political power and authority.[45] In order to promote this vision, Öcalan created the Koma Civakên Kurdistanê (KCK, Union of Communities in Kurdistan).[46] This movement began a broad-level experiment in locally oriented political forms. Their mission also included commitments to ecology and a form of feminism called Jineolojism.[47] These experiments resulted in the current-day practices we now see in Rojava itself.

"Eroding the State"

In an essay titled "Eroding the State in Rojava," the anarchist activist and writer Ali B. describes the degree to which democratic confederalism has been achieved in Rojava. Although he claims that the movement in Rojava is more successful as an antistatist entity than as an anticapitalist one, Ali B. nonetheless concedes that this example has vitally important connotations for thinking about anarchism as an actual and enduring practice. Among those practices is a deep commitment to overcoming narrow ethnic and nationalist identities. As Ali B. describes it, despite claims in the media of ethnic cleansing of Arabs in Rojava, in fact it is a mistake to think of this as a purely Kurdish project. He writes that the fact that "Kurds, Arabs, Assyrians, Syriacs, Chaldeans, Armenians, Chechens and Turkmens; Christians, Shia, Sunni and Alevite Muslims are sharing governance in one of the most sectarian regions of the world . . . might be revolutionary in and of itself."[48]

This is in keeping with Öcalan's own antinationalism, part of the reason he does not advocate for an independent Kurdish state (and, since Rojava has not formally declared independence from Syria for this reason, it allows the strange coexistence of sovereign and antisovereign bodies that we see there). In his booklet *Democratic Confederalism*, Öcalan explains, "The call for a separate nation-state of the Kurds results from the interests of the ruling class or the interests of the bourgeoisie, but does not reflect the interests of the people."[49]

Ali B. also describes the way that Rojava is politically organized. He writes:

> The most basic unit of society in Rojava is defined as the commune. Communes are found in different sections of society, on both the local neighborhood level, as well as in workplaces and in accordance with other groups, such as women or youth. They are meant to be the vehicle of self-governance. Visiting some of the neighborhood-based communes (in Qamishlo City, for example, there are around 100), as well as their higher

level organizational structure the *Mala Gel* (People's houses—of which there are 7 in the same city), illustrates the challenges captured in the opening quote of this article [i.e., the challenge to creating an anarchist-based society in the context of the Syrian Civil War]. While attempting to provide the foundation for a self-managed society, there are still remnants of the prior regime that threaten to return the Rojava revolution to what it replaced.[50]

The communes are the first level of response in Rojava. Given the fact that the Baathist regime is still nominally in charge in the region, one scholar describes the communes—citing Bookchin too—as a "decentralized, radical democracy *within or despite the given nation-states*," reflecting the ways that the communes can coexist, at least to some degree, with archist elements.[51] The communes serve to "decentralize decision-making and realizing self-rule." They "ha[ve] the power to determine how electricity and food would be administered," among other matters.[52] Each commune sends delegates to city or local councils (delegates also come from political parties, women and youth groups, and others).[53] Each such council in turn has to have at least 40 percent of its members be women.[54]

Yet, as Ali B. points out, these communes are not entirely self-directed. Cadre from the PKK serve as a kind of "professional revolutionar[y]" institution in regard to organizing Rojava.[55] There are also so-called peace and consensus committees, which serve as a kind of parallel legal system that was developed by leftist Kurdish insurgents over many years of struggle with the Turkish state.[56] There is also what Ali B. calls a "parliamentary superstructure," the Tev-Dem, which represents the various people's assemblies.[57] Furthermore, the Charter of the Social Contract of Rojava (Syria), which serves as a constitution, enumerates several levels of governance, including a governor, a legislative council, an executive council, and a separate judiciary. The preface of that document states: "The areas of the democratic self-management, does not accept the concept of state nationalism, military and religious. It accepts the centralized management, central rule and it is open to the forms of compatibility with the democratic and pluralistic traditions, to enable all social groups, cultural identities, the Athenian and national to express themselves through their organizations, and respect the Syrian border and human rights charters and preserve civil and international peace."[58]

Here, we see an attempt to live with both archist and anarchist elements. The Social Contract, whose very name, with its Rousseauvian overtones, speaks of that same kind of coexistence, does not accept "state nationalism," but it does recognize some centralizing—and hence archist—features of government. In Article 2 of the Charter of the Social Contract, it states that "people are the source of authorities and the sovereignty exercised through institutions and elected assemblies, and not to any contradiction of the social contract of the democratic self-management." Asserting that there can be no "contradiction" does not of course ensure a smooth coexistence, but it at least expresses a hope that such coexistence is possible.

In his own thinking about the issue, Ali B. notes the incongruity of the situation in Rojava. He tells us, for example, that when it comes to the communes, "Many people still treat these structures as if they were a typical government agency; they knock on the door of these new political forms asking for bureaucratic signatures, permissions, and requests, as opposed to utilizing them as a means and resource for self-organization."[59] Similarly, there are offices for the still intact (but not effectively functional) Syrian government, including certain ministries and airports and even a bakery, islands of Baathist authoritarianism scattered amid an otherwise fairly anarchist space.[60]

In this mixture of archist and anarchist elements, what emerges is, as Ali B. puts it, an "eroding state," not a vanishing one. The state persists and, as with the Spanish anarchists, one can see traces of "leaderism" both among the leadership itself and even, as we see, among the people, as the example of ordinary Rojavans treating communes as if they were government agencies shows.

This balance is perhaps even more problematic when it comes to the economic practices in Rojava. Ali B. offers that while on the ideological level, the Rojavan Revolution seeks a real and meaningful break with economic forms of archism, in practice this quasi-anarchist system does not effectively function to contain capitalism.

> The Kurdish proposal for Rojava, and in fact for the whole region, is genuine. But the transformation it seeks is arduous and impeded by both an ongoing war and pre-existing social relations. One thing which is clear upon visiting Rojava is that the revolution, in its capacity to abolish today's world, is much more anti-state than anti-capitalist. To be more specific, three types of property are present in Rojava; communal, public, and private. Private property, including factories and land holdings, is permitted. The wage system still exists in the streets of Qamishlo, but the main constitution-like document, the Charter of the Social Contract of Rojava, states that there must be limits set on private property

and enterprise. On the flipside, the state as a landholder is being abolished and decisions effecting the lives of those living in Rojava are made increasingly through the commune structures. But despite this, and perhaps due to wartime conditions, certain conventional functions of the state are still assumed by Tev-Dem and with it come tensions.[61]

In this way, we could perhaps speak of "eroding" rather than eliminating capitalism, just as Ali B. speaks of eroding the state. In my own view, capitalism is more critical for archism than the state per se, which in its contemporary form works mainly as a way to bolster and protect capitalism. Accordingly, the fact that the Rojavan Revolution has had more success with antistatism as opposed to anticapitalism may suggest serious problems with the model from an anarchist perspective. Yet this discrepancy was also true of the Spanish Revolution, where in some areas capitalism was left more or less intact while in others it was almost completely eliminated. The point to stress here is that the destruction of the capitalist core of archism is the ultimate, but not yet achieved, goal of an anarchist polity and that in both revolutionary Spain and Rojava, a spirit of experimentation and localism helps us see which means of self-organizing and structuring economic and political life best lead to that result.

Not a Prophet

In thinking about the upshot of the Rojavan Revolution, it is important to stress the relatively short time it has existed as well as its great precarity. The situation in Rojava is very unstable; already at the time of writing this, Turkey has seized a large amount of territory along the northern strip of territory, forcing the Rojavan forces to retreat deeper into their territory. The strain of dealing with Turkey and with ISIS—not entirely eliminated to this day—the threat of Assad's own reassertion of his power over the area; the perceived treachery of the United States, which cut a deal with Turkey's Recep Tayyip Erdoğan to allow his seizure of territory along the Turkish border; and other ongoing threats all mean that the Rojavan Revolution is operating under conditions of major duress. Then again, every anarchist experiment, the Spanish Revolution very much included, has occurred under such conditions, not once again because anarchism doesn't work but precisely because it does; its success poses an existential threat to archism that archism cannot tolerate.

It may be that by the time this is published, Rojava in its current form will be no more, although I certainly hope that is not the case. Yet, in its very existence, Rojava, like the anarchism of the Spanish Revolution, speaks to the possibility of pushing back upon, if not eliminating, archism and, in the process, demonstrating models of anarchist politics that can serve both present and future manifestations of anarchist life.

One key question to raise in this case is the role of Öcalan in all this. He is clearly the major figure leading this form of resistance, but does that mean Öcalan is an archist prophet who became an anarchist one? And, if so, how does his relationship to those who follow him change? David Graeber, for one, rejects the notion that Öcalan is any kind of prophet at all. In his introduction to Öcalan's *Manifesto for a Democratic Civilization*, volume 1, Graeber writes: "Öcalan's work, over the last fifteen years of his captivity, has been nothing if not ambitious. True, he carefully avoids taking on the role of the prophet. The latter would be easy enough under the circumstances: to speak ex cathedra in epochal declarations like some latter-day Zarathustra. Clearly he does not want to do this."[62] Leaving aside my own claims that Zarathustra is a very different kind of prophet than what Graeber might have in mind, we can see that there is, at the very least, a desire on Öcalan's part—and Graeber's part as well, clearly—to avoid his determining and controlling the various formations of democratic confederalism (which are not limited to Rojava, by any means).

In his transformation from a more conventional Marxist to an anarchist, Öcalan argued that the original Marxist-Leninist structure of the PKK was "too hierarchical and not democratic enough."[63] Creating the KCK was intended as a way to create an independent set of bodies that would be relatively immune to their own party leadership (including Öcalan's own authority, presumably). In his own introduction to *Manifesto for a Democratic Civilization*, Öcalan states, "The [KCK] will be the entity of the role of resolving the problems with the rigid nation-states that surround it. KCK can be the leading model for the Middle Eastern democratic confederalism."[64] Even if Öcalan is the one who conceived of this model and set it into place, it is made to run itself and in this way function separately from any will or direction from Öcalan himself.

Furthermore, the fact that Öcalan has been in jail throughout the entire period of the Rojavan Revolution—in solitary confinement, no less—is another factor that may help minimize his own control over and determination of what occurs in Rojava. Öcalan has been extremely prolific in jail, writing volumes of books (although he is not always allowed to have paper and pen).[65] Yet his writing is a far cry from the kind of leadership he might have engaged in had he been physically present to direct operations in Rojava and elsewhere in Kurdistan.

In this way, a mixture of fate and Öcalan's own ideology have helped reduce the degree to which he himself serves as an impediment to furthering democratic confederalism. It is true that Öcalan has a larger-than-life status in the Kurdish movement. His followers are called Apocu based on his own nickname of "Apo"—uncle, in Kurdish—and his movement is called Apoculuk (Apoism). But in a very real sense, Öcalan's success has been to make himself relatively irrelevant to the day-to-day choices and actions of the communes of Rojava. In this way at least, he can be considered to be an anarchist prophet even if in ways that are not necessarily always voluntary (but that is not atypical of anarchist prophets more generally). The imperfect rollout of an anarchist polity in Rojava may in part reflect the fact that this transition from archist prophet to anarchist prophet and onto collective forms of prophecy has not been entirely successful, but it also suggests that even an imperfect, episodic, and fragmented anarchist polity demonstrates the absolute challenge that anarchism more generally poses to archism.

Furthermore, the need for absolutes and totality may itself be a marker of archism. In both the Spanish and the Rojavan Revolutions, there has been an acceptance that popular forms of authority can be piecemeal, can come and go, and can be here but not over there. It is archism itself that requires every inch of space and every moment of time be occupied by its own authority structures. In considering these experiments, we should be careful to avoid using archist measurements to gauge the success or failure of these revolutions. We see then that the admixture of archist and anarchist elements that are visible in both the Spanish and Rojavan Revolutions speaks less to the fact that anarchist elements seem to generally always be tied up with their archist counterparts—including in terms of the institution of prophecy—and more to the fact that despite this mixture, anarchism is able to thrive and even dominate in some cases.

This ability may reflect an asymmetry between these two forms of power. Precisely because archism must be everywhere and forever, any kind of mixture with anarchism threatens it absolutely, whereas anarchism as a political form has long existed within archism's embrace. In this sense, because anarchist life exists even in the most absolute of archist societies—to stamp it out would be to stamp out life as such—the archist system is under a continual state of threat. In a nutshell, anarchism can readily live without archism, but the reverse is not true. Archism, which is only death, needs anarchist life to predate upon; when that life declares itself independent of such a predator, archism has no response but more violence, lest it be returned to its own original nothingness.

Saramago's *Blindness* and *Seeing*

Turning now to a set of literary analyses, I look first at *Blindness* and *Seeing*, written by the Portuguese author José Saramago. These novels offer a perspective on anarchism, prophecy, and sight through the double action of removing first physical sight (in *Blindness*) and then phantasmic, archist sight (in *Seeing*).[66] These twin novels are interesting for my purposes because they describe the subversion, but not quite elimination, of a key standard of archism, the concept of representation. In *Blindness*, Saramago's first novel, (almost) everyone goes blind with what Saramago calls a plague of "white blindness," wherein people can only see a uniform whiteness, as if the medium of representation itself has washed over its limits and made any kind of actual vision impossible. In *Seeing*, which is set in the same (unnamed) city four years after everyone has recovered their sight, a large majority of members of that community turn in blank ballots in a general election. That is the first action in an anarchist rebellion against the strictures of archist forms of vision and rule. The casting of blank ballots, by those that Saramago calls the "blankers," makes everything go topsy-turvy; normally the vote is a way that archist subjects feel they are participating in their own political life (even though by voting for someone, they are allowing that person to live their own political life on their behalf). Here, however, the vote becomes a form of defiance and so, once again, the stuff of archism becomes turned into a weapon to undermine and subvert it.

The one common figure in both novels is the singular character known only as "the doctor's wife" (Saramago avoids proper names and also uses a very anarchist style of punctuation). She is the only one who does not go blind in *Blindness*, and in *Seeing*, she is the one who is accused by the archists of fomenting a vast conspiracy (because from their perspective, someone has to be leading it!).

In *Blindness*, in all her ordinariness, the doctor's wife exemplifies what a prophet who is not about herself but is instead about a communal form of sight that she alone holds onto might look like. In *Seeing*, in the face of an attempt to entrap and frame her, the doctor's wife continues to hold onto that vision and in fact to spread it to the very person who is responsible for catching her out (a character known only as the Superintendent).

It might seem too much to call the doctor's wife in this sense an anarchist prophet—although in both *Blindness* and *Seeing*, she displays a high degree of vision, courage, and resolve—but that may be precisely why she succeeds in that role. She cannot become the voice for the blankers, despite the archons' insistence that she play that role, because she is so clearly just one of many. The fact that the doctor's wife has no special sight (just the regular kind) and doesn't have inside, special knowledge (because there is nothing special to know) is precisely why her anarchic vision is so critical and resistant to archist predations.

Blindness: Seeing Too Much

In her own brilliant reading, Maria Aristodemou treats *Blindness* in particular as depicting an encounter with the Lacanian Real; the sudden and swift catastrophe of mass blindness in the book marks an eruption of the Real into human life. She writes: "The Real is not, as sometimes assumed, something that does not happen; what is horrific about the Real is that, unimaginable as it is, it nevertheless does happen, or more accurately *strikes*. But what renders it 'Real' is that it exceeds our capacity for representation; since we do not have the words to represent it, it remains unassimilable in our experiences."[67] As Aristodemou further puts it, the entrance of the Real "confuse[s] our confidence in seeing" and, in this way, in my own terms, serves as a core challenge to archism, which is above all a case of ruling by sight, a massive visual organization via the elements of representation that it controls.[68]

Aristodemou goes on to suggest that in Saramago's parable, people are struck by blindness because they suddenly see what they normally cannot: the blind spot, the part that cannot be represented, the excess that constitutes the Real. She further writes: "When Saramago's people are reunited with the bit that has been severed from them in order to be able to see, they see too much which in effect disables them from seeing at all . . . When the subject, like Oedipus, like Saramago's people, is reunited with the lost object, they see the gaze, that is, they cannot see at all."[69] To put this another way, the people of this city suddenly start to see the "real" archeon, the otherwise invisible basis of archist rule; that which forces itself into the world via representation suddenly comes into view. The subjects of *Blindness*—minus the doctor's wife—lose their sight because they see too much (everything is white). If representation itself becomes a basis of a failure to see—rather than what it normally is, a basis to force us to see in a particular way—in effect archism has succeeded all too well in its usual forms of self-authorization. Too much seeing becomes the same as too little, and so the very tools by which archism normally binds and controls us become, in Saramago's parable, a way to allow other forms of sight or at least to disallow the forms of vision that we are normally subjected to.

When everyone goes blind around her, including her husband, "the doctor," the doctor's wife assumes she will go blind too. She goes with her husband to a hospital, where the city leaders, in their panic to contain the contagion—it spreads from one person to another like a plague—put the newly blind. The hospital quickly becomes overcrowded and taken over by a group of men Saramago calls "the hoodlums."

The hoodlums hoard all the food that has been provided by the state. They set up a system where each group of residents, who are organized by wards, has to provide their women to be raped if they want to have any food at all. The other men quickly comply and the serial raping begins. The doctor's wife, who no one but her husband knows can still see, doesn't think she has any choice and gets raped along with the other women in her group in one of the most awful scenes in the book. After this, she says to her husband, "We are no longer the same women as when we left here, the words they would have spoken we can no longer speak," attesting once again to the violence and unrepresentability of the Real.[70]

After that, however, the doctor's wife decides she can't allow this to continue. She sneaks into the hoodlum's ward and, while they are engaged in raping another group of women, she kills the head hoodlum by stabbing him in the neck with a pair of scissors, subsequently punching her way out of the room and taking the other women with her.

The head hoodlum's assistant, an accountant who had been blind before the plague—and who therefore has better life skills than the others—grabs the dead leader's gun and brandishes it, trying to restore order. He makes everyone in the hospital get together and demands that the leader's killer be given over, but the doctor's wife's courage is contagious. An old man says that if anyone turns that person over, "anyone who gave himself up, I'd kill him with my own hands. . . . We, who have nothing, apart from this last shred of undeserved dignity, let us at least show that we are still capable of fighting for what is rightfully ours."[71]

Facing a full-on rebellion, the blind accountant is cornered and has only his gun to establish authority at this point. "After the tragic death of their first leader, all spirit of discipline or sense of obedience had gone in the [hoodlum's] ward, the serious error on the part of the blind accountant was to have thought that it was enough to take possession of the gun in order to usurp power, but the result was exactly the opposite, each time he fires, the shot backfires, in other words, with each shot fired, he loses a little more authority, so let's see what happens when he runs out of ammunition."[72]

Here, we see the most naked, violent face of archism winnowed down to its ultimate point: do what I say or I'll kill you. When it is so reduced, deprived of all its representational claims—the white blindness took care of that—archism is really nothing at all. In other words, the fact that it was always nothing becomes much more visible. With each shot fired, the blind accountant loses authority but, by the same token, each bullet he fires restores that authority to the community from which it was originally stolen.

Interestingly, the contagion of collective resistance might even have spread to the now dead leader of the hoodlums. Saramago says that the former leader, now poorly buried and rotting, "continues to be remembered, at least he makes his powerful presence felt by the stench."[73] Here, that leader's authority, what had once seemed nameless and invulnerable, becomes something all too human, mortal, and tangible, contesting that phantasmic power through its undeniable reeking materiality and undermining any sense that the blind accountant is offering anything but more death. In the absence of visuality, other senses necessarily come to the fore. Now that he is only a corpse, the leader of the hoodlums ceases to project one kind of authority and, via his bodily decay, begins to issue forth a different sort, akin to what Benjamin calls the "authority of the dead," which is counterprojective and anarchist.[74]

Seeing: The "Gentle Rebellion"

In *Seeing*, after 83 percent of the population of the unnamed city—Saramago tells us it is the capital of a country, possibly Lisbon, but also possibly not—turns in blank ballots, and not once but twice, the archons who run the election cannot understand what is happening. They immediately decide that there must be some kind of organized plot with leaders and cells because archism cannot imagine anything but more of itself. They are confounded above all by the lack of so much as a shred of paper suggesting this conspiracy. Because paper is how the archeon projects, records, and maintains its power into the world—or at least it used to be before it was replaced by virtual data—they assume that any challenge to them must also leave a paper trail.

The blank ballot may be particularly subversive in this regard; like the white blindness, its sheer blankness ruins any representational function that it might have been intended to serve. Since representation is the life's blood of archism, the way that people are led to believe their leadership is of and for them, not just set over them, the very blankness of the ballot suggests the erasure of that authority (and via the very instrument through which that authorization is normally made). This new preference for blankness is replicated by large demonstrations where the blankers all wave blank white flags. Here too, something that is normally meant to signify surrender—something archism understands very well—becomes a sign of its opposite, resistance and usurpation. Saramago tells us that even the patterns of speech among the blankers changes so that the word *blank* itself becomes scrupulously avoided in ordinary speech, perhaps reflecting that term's new and critical function.[75]

The archists' response to all this is to remove the government from the city and surround it with troops. They think this is the ultimate punishment because of course, in their understanding, a community cannot survive without its leaders. Yet in fact the community thrives without them; the expected crime wave and other forms of ruin the archists predict never happen (here, it is the archons who are disappointed!). Indeed, by having this level of "representation" removed, the city really comes into its own. More accurately, the anarchist community that the city has always been—albeit eclipsed by archist parasitism—comes to the fore, especially in terms of a kind of unplanned mass coordination that continually flummoxes the archons, who watch events from afar through their spy networks.

Beyond the widespread voting by blank ballots itself, this mass coordination becomes clear at the moment when the archons and their armies leave the city. They do so in the middle of the night under cover of darkness without any kind of prior announcement. As the top-secret convoy rolls out of town, the lights in the windows of all the houses along the streets they are traveling suddenly and simultaneously flick on and stay on until the convoys pass, at which point they simultaneously all flick off. This deeply unnerves the archons. Saramago adds that the worst part for them is that as these lights come on, there is no one at these windows, "as if the official convoys were foolishly fleeing from nothing, as if the army and the police, along with the assault vehicles and the water cannon, had been spurned by the enemy and been left with no one to fight."[76] If the blankers had jeered as the archons passed, if they had lobbed grenades at them, the archons would have known what to do. They could have mowed down the protestors and engaged with mass arrests. This simple act of turning the lights on and off, an act that normally passes without notice and which happens all the time, a simple part of ordinary life, suddenly becomes a moment of deep resistance.

Another example of ordinary life rising up to defeat archism happens when the archons arrange a garbage strike in the city to create—they hope—the chaotic conditions that they assume must accompany their withdrawal (they also explode bombs to sow confusion and mutual recrimination among the blankers, but no dice). In fact, however, on the first day of the strike, at precisely noon, groups of women come onto the street with brooms and clean everything up: "These women, were not just looking after their own interests, but after the interests of the community as well. It is possibly for this same reason that, on the third day, the refuse collectors also came out into the street. They were not in uniform, they were wearing their own clothes. It was the uniforms that were on strike, they said, not them."[77]

Here, to use Benjaminian language, a radical proletarian general strike has been undertaken, something that involves no negotiations with management (unlike the contrived garbage strike).[78] Here too, an ordinary act, sweeping with a broom, takes on a radical and subversive meaning. In both the examples of turning lights on and off and sweeping the sidewalks, in addition to saying no to archism in all its variants, these anarchist acts have a positive message. In saying no to the state, they are saying yes to the anarchist ferment, to ordinary nonarchist life—which includes sweeping and turning the light on among an infinite other myriad and ordinary acts—itself.

Saramago calls this a "gentle rebellion," a form of collective action that does not return the state's violence but simply abandons the state entirely.[79] The state of course thinks *they* have been the ones doing the abandoning by withdrawing from the city, but here they experience a key vulnerability of archism: namely, the way that archism needs its subjects to exist but the reverse is definitely not true. In a way, the archons are correct that this *is* a conspiracy, but it's not a top-down, planned conspiracy with leaders who make decisions and members who follow orders. Instead, it is a conspiracy of (almost) everyone, one that expresses a collective form of decision and action. That collective voice that is so rarely heard under conditions of archism—but which is always there in all its complexity and disharmony—becomes visible to itself and to the archons as well, although the archons do not have the capacity to understand or even to see what it is that they are facing.[80]

Spreading the Contagion of Anarchism:
The Doctor's Wife and the Superintendent

Because from the archon's perspective there has to be *a* leader, because there can be no movement without a head, the archons zero in on the doctor's wife, purely because she was the only one who didn't go blind during the previous plague. That single fact makes her exceptional and, bereft of any other potential candidates, they decide that it *must* be the case that she is guilty.

Archism, after all, is never really about reality per se but about its version of reality, and so the perceived guilt of the doctor's wife becomes increasingly a determined and required thing. In this way, it *does* become retroactively "true" in the same way that all archist truths function.

In order to expose her as the ringleader, the archons send in a man known only as "Superintendent" along with a team of assistants to gain her confidence and expose her for what she is (must be). Initially, the Superintendent is fully bought into an archonic logic. He tells his team during the investigation that the imagined conspirators, the doctor's wife and her husband, are "bound to make mistakes if they haven't reached some prior agreement about what they should say and what it would be best to stay quiet about, our job is to help them make those mistakes."[81]

Over the course of that investigation, however, the Superintendent becomes more and more anarchized (or maybe de-archized). In their first discussion, the doctor's wife offers the Superintendent a cup of coffee, which he refuses because "we don't accept anything when we are on duty," to which she replies, "Naturally, that's how all the great corruptions begin, a cup of coffee today, a cup of coffee tomorrow, and by the third cup, it's too late."[82] The doctor's wife appears to be sarcastic here, but in fact her words are prescient (even prophetic!). This is exactly the sequence by which the Superintendent is "corrupted," suggesting once again the power of ordinary actions: turning on the light, sweeping, and now serving—and drinking—a cup of coffee.

At their next meeting, the Superintendent accepts a cup of coffee and they have the following exchange:

> And [she asks] you're not afraid that the coffee I'm about to bring you will be a step along the road to corruption, Ah, [he replied] I seem to remember you saying that that only happens with the third cup of coffee, No, [the doctor's wife said] what I said was that the third cup of coffee completed the corruption process, the first opened the door, the second held it open so that the aspirant to corruption could enter without stumbling, the third slammed the door shut, Thank you for the warning, [he said] which I take as a piece of advice, and so I'll stop at the first cup.[83]

The Superintendent thinks he is tricking the doctor's wife, but it is clear that he is not as in control as he thinks he is. He is operating from an archist perspective on one level, but there may already be a suggestion that he really wants that cup of coffee precisely for the way it might corrupt him (or maybe he's just tired or thirsty).

Just as critically, the more the Superintendent talks to the doctor's wife, the more it is clear that there are no secrets to glean from her or her husband. She has nothing to hide because hers is not *that* kind—that is, an archist kind—of conspiracy. And since she has to be a grand conspirator according to archist logic, but clearly is not, the longer he is in her company, the more the Superintendent has no choice but to see things differently. The falsity of archist vision becomes unsustainable when faced with an ordinary person who fails to live up to its fantastic projections. Here the whole game, the tricks he has been trying to play on the doctor's wife, collapse on themselves.

> He had crossed the frontier [back into the city] in pure movie detective style, he had convinced himself that he had come to rescue his country from mortal danger, and, in the name of that conviction, had given his subordinates ridiculous orders for which they had been kind enough to forgive him, he had tried to hold together a precarious framework of suspicions that was gradually falling apart with each minute that passed, and now he was wondering, surprised by a vague anxiety that made his diaphragm tighten, what reasonably credible information could he, the puffin [his spy name] invent to transmit to an albatross [the code name for the minister of the interior who is monitoring his actions] who would, at this moment, be asking impatiently why he was so late in sending him news.[84]

In subsequent meetings, the Superintendent becomes more and more openly anarchist. He calls the doctor's wife to warn her that she is in real danger (shortly afterward, she is shot and killed by a sinister assassin known only as the man in the blue tie with white spots). As he is giving the doctor's wife these warnings, any pretense of his being a police superintendent investigating her is gone. Virtually the last thing they say to one another is that, after she tells him she thinks he helped her much more than he let on, he says, "That's just your impression, you're talking to a policeman, remember," to which she replies, "Oh, I haven't forgotten but the truth is that I no longer think of you as one."[85] He doesn't disagree with her; in fact, he thanks her for saying that. At this point, his metamorphosis into a blanker—and, I would add, an anarchist—appears to be complete. The contagion of anarchism has continued to spread, now among the archons themselves. The Superintendent is not the only convert at that point, and one suspects that many more will succumb in the near future too.

The Doctor's Wife as an Anarchist Prophet

In thinking about the prophetic power of the doctor's wife, it is certainly true that her vision is not unique in any way. As she tells one of the people she helps in *Blindness*, "I am simply the eyes that the rest of you no longer possess."[86] Her uniqueness comes from the way that she holds onto ordinary forms of vision when no one else does, but she does come to bear the weight and responsibility for everyone else in the process. In *Seeing*, the doctor's wife serves as an anarchist prophet because archism has singled her out to be one. That is, archism has set its focal point on a single person. It has picked the doctor's wife, perhaps arbitrarily, but she is picked nevertheless.

As such, the doctor's wife is forced, in a sense, to represent an anarchist conspiracy that she is only one small part of. Insofar as representation is a critical aspect of archism, the doctor's wife is herself not perfectly innocent of archism, even as she remains thoroughly anarchist. In *Blindness*, this doubleness is more apparent in that she is unquestionably the leader of the small band that she stays with throughout the plague. Yet even in *Seeing*, there is a way in which, demanded to speak on behalf of the conspiracy, the doctor's wife does so. But what she does or says is not some hidden truth or secret at the core of the conspiracy. Instead, she simply gives voice to one perspective among others, to one part of a collective that is feeling—and seeing!—itself as such for perhaps the very first time.

Representation is the life's blood of archism, perhaps a strange term to use for something that is dead and empty, but it conveys its importance. Archism cannot function without this pose of connectivity to those communities it sits parasitically atop. In fact, representation is the vehicle by which that parasitism is enacted; it is what transfers life from the community itself to this dead nonbeing in the guise of doing the opposite. It is here that we can see the greatest subversion that the doctor's wife performs. By becoming unique and even indispensable, the doctor's wife has smuggled ordinariness and a connection to actual—as opposed to faux—collectivity into the heart of representation. In doing so, she reverses the way that representation singles us out in order to isolate us, the way it makes us relate to the state and not to one another. This is not to say that the doctor's wife makes representation work but that she uses a false mechanism in ways that act against its intended purpose.

Here, we see once again the unexpected vulnerability of archism, wherein it is perpetually threatened by what it dominates and orders. As already noted in chapter 2, archism must live with and rely upon language that is, after all, an ongoing and collective set of decisions about meaning. It may pretend to control that process, but the truth is that it must accept the collective decisions its subjects make on an ongoing basis. In this one way at least, representation is never wholly a tool the archists control; taken as language itself, it always has this subversive aspect to it.

Although they are mistaken in the way that they characterize the doctor's wife, their mistake does allow the archons a sense of the existential threat that she and the other blankers pose to them. For some of them, like the Superintendent, their misunderstanding actually grants them access to the anarchist conspiracy itself. Yet for all her centrality, there is a way in which the doctor's wife also serves as a kind of decoy. While they are fixated on her, the conspiracy goes on apace. Killing her, we sense, is not going to stop the blankers; now that they have learned to see in a different way, a way that has no external source but is only about what they chose to see and how to see it, there is no stopping them. In this way too, the doctor's wife, for all her ordinariness—although not everyone would show the resolve that she showed during the plague of blindness—is doing a unique service for the anarchist community as a whole.

There is a way in which the doctor's wife understands her role as transitory. The job of any anarchist prophet is, after all, to make herself redundant. At one point in *Blindness*, she talks to someone in her group about what would happen if people remained blind forever. She says: "[There were] few [blind people] in comparison [before the plague], the feelings in use were those of someone who could see, therefore blind people felt with the feelings of others, not as the blind people they were, now, certainly, what is emerging are the real feelings of the blind, and we are still only at the beginning, for the moment we still live on the memory of what we felt."[87] This passage suggests that even if everyone goes blind and stays that way, the blind would adjust to their new form of vision, and the anarchist ferment of ordinary life would reestablish itself or would recognize the fact that it never went away but only changed its form. If anything, such an eventuality would deprive archism of visuality, which has always been its preferred and dominant sensory mode. Thinking in these terms means that there will always be a place for anarchist conspiracy, a force that is never going to stop hiding in plain sight even if there is no one to physically see it anymore. In a nutshell, as long as there is life, there is anarchism and there is nothing that archism can do about that.

The Earthseed Series

Moving on to Octavia Butler's Earthseed series, the two-book sequence *The Parable of the Sower* and *The Parable of the Talents* traces the life and work of a prophet named Lauren Olamina. Lauren is a young—and then not so young—Black woman who lives in a time set in the near future when the United States has completely fallen apart (these days, it is not so hard to imagine this, and the books seem prophetic in a more ordinary sense as well).[88] In the face of the abandonment of the kinder and gentler appearances of archism, we are left with its teeth: the state is overtly racist, classist, and aggressively violent. In the time when the novel is set—a time people call the "apocalypse"—the rich live in corporate enclaves and everyone else is left to suffer. In response to the myriad crises of this period, society itself has become more violent as well, and death swoops down on those who try to hold onto some form of "normal life."

Into this mix, Lauren develops her own religion, called "Earthseed," which is extremely anarchist in both its spirit and its practice. Yet Lauren herself often acts like any archist prophet would. She is often ruthlessly intolerant of dissent and disloyalty, and—as we see in the second book—she seems to be a deeply problematic parent. Yet, for all of her all-too-human—and archist—faults, we see that Lauren offers a way for her followers to resist the lures of archism and come to their own forms of sight, despite the fact that they live in a time of great danger, a time that usually makes people cling all the more desperately to archist promises.

There is something in Butler's work more generally that I find quite subversive, namely a way that she generalizes the Black experience to a larger population. Her main characters are almost always Black women, and the situations that her communities face include invasion—sometimes by extraterrestrials—slavery, domination, bullying, rape, and murder. None of this is science fiction; these are all a reflection of Black life in America. In this sense, Butler is not writing about the future but about the disaster that is already here, the disaster of archism. If Black and Brown people already know this disaster for what it is, Butler's books still offer resources of how to survive and even to thrive in the face of that ongoing catastrophe. Her characters evince a form of fatalism, but it's more in the spirit of Nietzsche's *amor fati* than any kind of passivity. They accept the world as it is rather than railing against the loss of what they are taught to expect it to be. In that acceptance, they find pathways for change that are not simply attempts to make archism be true after all.

Earthseed, Lauren's religion, is uniquely disappointing and, accordingly, radically anarchist. Unlike the Abrahamic God, Lauren's God is utterly indifferent to human affairs (making her more akin to Spinoza's God, who I discuss in the next chapter). The God that Lauren worships is nothing more than the vast anarchist materiality of the universe, a force of pure contingency. Put differently, it's not just that Lauren's God is an anarchist but that anarchism and this God are one and the same thing. This leads to what I think is the most critical aspect of Lauren's prophecy for the purposes of this book: by making the universe itself anarchist—including having human beings going out to live on other worlds, hence making the universe accessible and material rather than abstract and determining—Lauren deprives archism of one of its key architectural functions, its claim to be transcendent and all determining.

"A Pessimist if [She's] Not Careful"

In her own self-description, Butler calls herself "a pessimist if I'm not careful."[89] Just as optimism can be cruel—to cite Lauren Berlant—pessimism can be cruel as well, especially if it means giving up on trying to change a world full of violence and injustice.[90] The kind of bad fatalism that comes from such pessimism amounts to thinking, "I will be killed if I don't do x and y," an attitude that is critical for the perpetuation of archist rule even if it is not always a conscious thought. This is the great deception of archism, the fox telling the hens that they have no choice but to trust her because there are so many far worse things out there (better to be murdered by a fox than by a wolf! And anyway the fox said she *might* not kill you; she seems kind of nice sometimes, etc.).

The temptations of this kind of pessimism are very familiar to Lauren when the first novel starts. She lives with her father, stepmother, and siblings and a few other families in a cul-de-sac in Los Angeles, forming a community that has built up walls to keep out the killers and rapists who lurk outside. Her father is a preacher who holds the community together through the promise that things are bound to get better. But all his promises are in vain; he suddenly disappears one day, presumably killed on his way to or from the compound. Even before his death, Lauren refuses to pretend that everything is OK. At one point, her father tells Lauren that her ideas are scaring people. He tells her that she is wrong to make people look down into the abyss that stands before them. She replies, "Maybe it's time to look down. Time for some hand and foot holds before we just get pushed in."[91]

Here, we see two very different modes of seeing. Her father is still looking up, to heaven and the state, for rescue. Lauren is looking around for ways to live in this world, to live her life and not just hope that she doesn't die. This is a perspective that will serve Lauren well while so many people in her community, in their denial of what is really going on, fail to address the issues at hand and succumb to violence and exploitation.

The Religion of Earthseed

In a poem that she includes in *Earthseed: The Book of the Living*—the key scripture of her religion—Lauren writes: "We see what we're permitted to see," indicating that she is very aware of how archist vision is perpetuated.[92] It's not that Lauren doesn't see this way as well; it's just that Lauren *decides* to see things differently. Although she is not above using the language of truth at times, it would be more accurate to say that Lauren wants to give herself and her disciples a chance to see for themselves, to make decisions according to their own thoughts, experiences, and logics.

Speaking to the admixture of reality and resistance that characterizes her religion, at one point Lauren writes in her journal: "I've never felt that I was making any of this up—not the name, Earthseed, not any of it. I mean, I've never felt that it was anything other than real: discovery rather than invention, exploration rather than creation. I wish I could believe it was all supernatural and that I'm getting messages from God. But then, I don't believe in that kind of God. All I do is observe and take notes, trying to put things down in ways that are as powerful, as simple, and as direct as I feel them."[93]

In a conversation with a man named Travis, who becomes her first convert, he says:

> "But [Earthseed is] not a god. It's not a person or an intelligence or even a thing. It's just . . . I don't know. An idea."
>
> [Lauren] smiled. Was that such a terrible criticism? "It's a truth," [she] said.[94]

In both instances, Lauren is commenting on the nature of her truth. As I read these novels, the externality of truth for Lauren comes not because this truth is out there as an unchanging aspect of an eternal universal—that kind of truth is exactly what Earthseed makes impossible—but rather because it reflects the kinds of collective determinations that are outside any one individual, even an individual as singular as Lauren.

It may be that Lauren's insistence on speaking of God and calling Earthseed a religion is a way to give it legitimacy in an archist world where theology is the sine qua non of authority. Yet, not unlike as with Benjamin, Lauren describes a uniquely self-undermining God, one whose authority is swiftly subverted and which therefore immediately returns the focus to human agency. In this way, Earthseed may be one of the most radical versions of negative theology there is.

"God Is Change"

This can be shown more clearly by looking at one of the key doctrines of Earthseed that Butler uses to introduce one of the very first chapters of *Parable of the Sower*.

> All that you touch
> You Change.
> All that you Change
> Changes you.
> The only lasting truth is Change
> God is Change.[95]

If we take these tenets one by one, we can begin to better see the subversive possibilities inherent in Earthseed.[96] "All that you touch / You Change" suggests the impossibility of human nonagency. Even the most passive of persons cannot help but touch, and hence change, the world around them. While this might smack a bit of the liberal phantasm of the autonomous subject made famous by John Locke who goes out into the world and mixes a bit of themselves into the world, allowing him—and in the case of the liberal depictions, it is definitely a him that we are talking about—to control and dominate the world, we see that the second line, "All that you Change / Changes you," renders such a reading impossible.[97] Here the touchers and changers are themselves always being touched and changed, suggesting a plurality of intermingled and intermingling selves, a veritable anarchic stew of subjectivities both inside and outside the boundaries of each individual. Here, the contingent and ever-shifting bases of identity make precise delineations of selves—a prerequisite for liberalism—impossible.

This multiplicity of selves gets taken to the next level of generality by the following line, "The only lasting truth is Change." Insofar as archism, at least its Western form, tells us to think that something that is true is lasting by definition, to say the only "lasting truth is change" implies that everything else that we thought was true is not. If this is a way to universalize the ideas about personhood and subjectivity set down in the first two tenets, it does so in a way that actually ruins the very universe that such truths are projected onto. A universe marked by constants, by set principles and absolute laws, is precisely what Earthseed unravels. In a way, to say that "the only lasting truth is change" is to say that there is no truth at all, or at least that the truths that exist are always in the process of becoming, ensuring that no doctrine or form will last, hence making archism, which is all about lasting, about abstract universals and truths, impossible.

The final tenet, "God is Change," is the final blow to any archist readings of Earthseed. Such a statement determines that any attempt to circumvent this unraveling of all certainties by going straight to God—to the ultimate archon—is undone because God is brought into the maw of contingency, and indeed constitutes that maw. In a sense, "God is Change" is highly analogous to Hobbes's claim that "Jesus is the Christ." Both sentences are short and almost entirely devoid of content. Both create an irreducible pith that resists being further read into and fetishized. In this way, in both cases, these two simple statements engage in a form of derepresentation of their own, serving to ensure that every other statement, whether about Christianity in Hobbes's case or about Earthseed in Lauren's case, or about the universe more generally, is going to be nullified as a possible and self-sustaining truth. In this case, by saying that "God is Change," Lauren ensures that there is no higher authority from which to escape this general anarchization of the subject and the universe that subject occupies.[98]

Lauren explains: "Earthseed deals with ongoing reality, not with supernatural authority figures. Worship is no good without action. With action, it's only useful if it steadies you, focuses your efforts, eases your mind."[99] Here we see once again that the truth that Lauren sees is not some invisible and permanent truth that in some way supersedes the world around her. It works the other way around: her seeing of the world as being in constant flux and dynamism disallows her from seeing the stable icons that archism insists upon. It is up to her, and ultimately up to the community of Earthseed, to determine what she is going to take away from all that flux and change, as well as what she is going to do about it.[100]

Where archism tries to claim that the world can be understood, taxonomized, and dominated, Earthseed unravels the basis of that domination by giving the world back its own deeply aleatory aspects. Lauren's worship goes not outward to a godlike figure but back to herself via a God that is nothing but the anarchic quality of the universe, the way that all matter is entropic and always in flux.

It even appears that the people of the world can in fact change God, as Lauren acknowledges when she states: "The essentials [of Earthseed] are to learn to shape God with forethought, care, and work; to educate and benefit their community, their families, and themselves; and to contribute to the fulfillment of the Destiny [of human beings going to the stars]."[101] In a nutshell, if God is change, then God is also changed, and if human beings are changers, then they partake in that changing as well. Here, human agency is not so much lifted up in this way as it is connected to a much vaster universe. If saying God can be changed makes humans seem godlike, they can never be *that* godlike, they can never be as big and diverse as the universe itself.[102] They are only one set of players in a multitude of life—and nonlife—forms.[103]

Earthseed then propounds a kind of ultimate immanentism (in the next chapter, I discuss other modes of immanentist theologies), even as it retains some aspects that are usually considered to be transcendent. On the one hand, there is nowhere for this God to go or be that isn't part of the universe. The universe is only what it is (and that is always in flux). Nor is there any perch from which this God could judge or exempt herself from that judgment. In this way, God does not have to abandon this perch as she does with Benjamin, nor does she have to "die" as with Nietzsche. And yet this God is—at least as far as we are concerned—both omnitemporal and omnipotent and thus transcendent in this sense at least. Stuffed within our temporality, as it were, this deity defies any attempts by would-be archists to "wait her out" (she will be God for all of time) or find a space where she is not (she is everywhere).

Here we get a kind of "best of both worlds" situation, the human orientation of immanentism and the power and authority of transcendentalism in one. In terms of the former, insofar as this God has no set content of her own—like Hobbes's Holy Spirit, she is pure form—there is no danger of her becoming a basis for an occult reintroduction of archism, leaving human beings to their own devices. And in the latter case the very absolute conventions of archism—its very need to be everywhere and at all times—serve to defeat it since this God already occupies that space and denies it to them. So long as the tenets of Earthseed hold, this God, and hence those who follow her, is/are about as immune from archist theology as it gets.

Lauren as Prophet

In the same way that Earthseed embodies many elements of what seems like archist theology even as it is profoundly anarchist, so too, in examining Lauren's own bearing as a prophet, do we see a complicated and sometimes contradictory mixture of archist and anarchist elements. Lauren does not shy away from the respect and power that come with her prophetic functions, but does that in any way compromise her own role or the religion that she brings into the world?

The most troubling aspects of Lauren's career as a prophet become clear in the second volume, *Parable of the Talents.* Lauren has a daughter, Larkin, who is kidnapped early on in that novel and raised by a family of fundamentalist Christians. Lauren does not know where her daughter is until well into the novel, when Larkin is much older. In *Parable of the Talents*, Lauren's own narrative is juxtaposed with Larkin's so you can see things from both perspectives.

Although Lauren searches endlessly for Larkin, this does not stop her from continuing to focus on growing Earthseed, which becomes a huge and powerful movement. The very first sentence of *Parable of the Talents* is Larkin saying, "They'll make a God of her."[104] She writes: "I think that would please her, if she could know about it. In spite of all of her protests and denials, [Lauren]'s always needed devoted, obedient followers—disciples—who would listen to her and believe everything she told them. And she needs large events to manipulate. All gods seem to need these things."[105]

This already suggests the possibility that Lauren's own status—perhaps even as a god herself—might corrupt Earthseed, making it about her rather than her doctrines. Larkin also objects to her mother's preoccupation with Earthseed, which she sees as coming at her own expense. She comments that if her mother had found her earlier in her life, "How long would it have been before she put me aside for Earthseed, her other kid?"[106] She also writes: "I was her weakness. Earthseed was her strength. No wonder it was her favorite."[107]

We may read Larkin's criticisms of her mother through the lens of her own bitterness at feeling abandoned but, as she so often does in her writing, Butler does not give us an easy way to resolve this tension: Lauren had to pay a price for Earthseed and she did (and Larkin had to pay it too). While being a negligent parent—at least in Larkin's view—is not a requirement for archism, Lauren's choices do suggest a preoccupation with her own grandeur and status, a slow seduction into the pleasures of leadership and control.

The fact that anarchist forms of prophecy can come even from a partially archist person should not surprise us; archism is ubiquitous in our time, and we are all infected and formed by it. What is critical is to look for not pure anarchism but anarchist effects in the midst of an archist context and, more particularly in this case, anarchist sight in the midst of archist desires and projections. Lauren's example shows us exactly what this might look like.

The Destiny

Another complication around Lauren's form of prophecy is the idea of the "Destiny," her view that human beings must go out into the universe and colonize the stars. Not only is this very future oriented—the favored archist temporality—but it also smacks of the kinds of imperialism and colonization that are the hallmarks of archist practice more generally. Furthermore, in constantly evoking "the universe," another favorite archist trope, is Lauren sending her disciples right back into an archist phantasm?

In the same way that Lauren makes God into a radical and (largely) immanentist anarchist, she does the same thing to the concepts of the future and the universe, depriving archism of these critical foundations as well. At one point in speaking of the Destiny, she tells Travis, "After all, my heaven really exists, and you don't have to die to reach it."[108]

Here, Lauren is showing how the Destiny serves to push back the forms of archist phantasm by actually going out into the universe and experiencing it firsthand. The "afterlife," a place and time that archism normally uses to denigrate and dominate human life, becomes brought into the immanent, and available, universe; it can be accessed by the living and not just the dead. In this sense, the "Destiny," despite its capital letter "D," is the opposite of the archist destiny (whether capitalized or not). It offers a way to live while still alive, to have any rewards available within the universe instead of beyond it (in the next chapter, I describe the Melanesian immanentist viewpoint, which is similar in some ways). Such a life remains, as Lauren herself remains, fully in the present. Even if Lauren herself can't see life on other planets—she lives to see the assemblage of the first starship but no farther than that—that life will be real and tangible, that is, present, to those who will step onto those worlds. So while this is "future" and "destined," it does not serve as what Benjamin calls "homogenous, empty time" (the time of archism).[109] Lauren's Destiny takes the place of that other future, bringing it back to life, to change and to anarchism, instead of stasis and archism.

By creating a literal and tangible possibility of "heaven," Lauren disallows the metaphysical heaven and afterlife from competing with her own vision. Insofar as archism is ultimately based on the promise of immortality and the conquest of death, this is no small feat. Even a fully secularized and liberal version of archism is built on some conception of heaven, some transcendence of death, whether by exporting death to other people via racism and violence or by promising a kind of capitalist paradise where all cares are answered and life itself is assured, or even a future where "progress" takes us finally and utterly to some kind of happy culmination.

Earthseed's literalization of the afterlife also implicitly involves a secularized version of heaven, namely the universe itself. Instead of being a metaphysical space that represents perfection, omnipresence, and omnipotence, a kind of black box that archism can use to judge and rule the world from, the actual universe becomes a place to be visited. The vastness of the universe becomes a way to defeat human hubris rather than to bolster it; to actually go out into space is to experience its actual measure and its reach. Here again, as with the concept of heaven and the afterlife, Earthseed is displacing the metaphysical with the physical and the immanent and, by that connection, undermining once again some of the core tenets of archism—certainly of its liberal variants—in the process.

A final issue regarding the Destiny to think about is whether, despite all this, it becomes an opportunity for archist humankind to do to the universe what it has done to the Earth, namely colonize other beings, take over an area of space seen as "terra nullius," and make it available for plunder. If Earthseed is indeed an essentially colonizing mission, then no amount of anarchizing countertheology could serve to undermine this most archist of gestures based on the desire to dominate and control other spaces and other forms of life.

We don't get a lot of evidence one way or the other on this question. Toward the very end of *Parable of the Talents*, Lauren does note that the very first starship to go into the universe has been named the *Christopher Columbus*. Lauren comments: "I object to the name. This ship is not about a shortcut to riches and empire. It's not about snatching up slaves and gold and presenting them to some European monarch. But one can't win every battle. One must know which battles to fight. The name is nothing."[110] This could just be Lauren rationalizing. But here, once again, it is the doctrine of Earthseed itself that is the best defense against incipient archism. At one point, Lauren tells someone she is recruiting to Earthseed that with the Destiny "we can . . . become some combination of what we want to become and whatever our new environments challenge us to become. Our new worlds will remake us as we remake them."[111] This statement is very much in keeping with the idea that "God is Change." The archist premise that underlies colonization does not include the idea of the colonizers being altered by their encounter with new places and people. From its position of all knowing and all seeing—the stance of archist prophecy—it is the other peoples or worlds that will be changed, while the subject in question will remain constant and inviolable. The doctrine that "God is Change" removes that inviolable center, the very thing that gives the colonizer the supposed "right" to conquer, rape, and murder other communities in the first place. Without *that* kind of destiny, we get instead, once again, the "Destiny," which is less a guarantee of conquest and power and more a chance to live, to continue to change and adapt in new environments.

What Kind of Prophet?

Perhaps the most troubling issue to consider in the Earthseed novels is that of Lauren's indispensability for her followers. Without her, there would be no Earthseed and no alternative to the grinding misery that the world had become. Yet, just as with the prophet Zarathustra, Lauren does not truly change anyone. Instead, she restores them, as it were, to themselves, to their own power of decision and judgment. Her job, as with the other prophets I've looked at in this book, is not to tell them what to see or think but simply to disappoint them. She doesn't tell them anything they don't already know; she only takes away the archeonic position from which they are always and endlessly being judged and determined. Just as she tells us she didn't invent Earthseed but discovered it, so too does she merely reflect a larger conversation that envelopes her, even if, at times, she appears—because she is human too, after all—to take credit for it.

When her husband, Bankole, who is killed in the same raid that Larkin is kidnapped in, asks her about whether she has any doubts about Earthseed, Lauren says: "My doubts are personal. . . . You know that. I doubt myself, not Earthseed. I worry that I might not be able to make Earthseed any more than another little cult. . . . It could happen. Earthseed is true—is a collection of truths, but there's no law that says it has to succeed. We can always screw it up. I can always screw it up. There's so much to be done."[112] Here, Lauren tries not to make Earthseed all about her (contra Larkin's reading of her). Yes, she "discovered" it, but she is not *it*. Earthseed, whatever it is, is part of the universe, a collective response that works to undermine and deny the insights and truths and principles of any one person, even those of its greatest—and so far only—prophet.

While it might literally be true that Earthseed as such would not have happened without Lauren's vision, it is not the case that the insights of Earthseed would have been lost to the human race forever had she never existed. The insights that it has are based not on Lauren's own ideas but on the anarchic nature of the universe itself. The universe—normally that ultimate bedrock of archist authority and power—becomes the source of opposition to that very same thing. If the universe is in fact anarchic rather than archic, then Earthseed itself cannot depend on one person's sight; it merely needs to reflect the vast anarchic complex of people and things—with things infinitely outweighing the number of people—that it resonates with.

This anarchism is always there, to be stumbled on, to be encountered but never invented. By the same token, the planets that the Earthseed members will go to will be encountered as they are, having and affecting a material presence that is not up to human beings to determine or confer. That is one of the key insights that come from this kind of immanentism.[113]

The members of Earthseed may well consider themselves to have been lucky to have had Lauren as a prophet. She is indeed a most unusual kind of prophet, and Earthseed is a most unusual kind of religion, but it may just be that Lauren hastened but did not cause her follower's engagement with the world—and the universe—as it is. For all the gloom and harshness of the Earthseed series, I think its core message is very positive: The universe *is* anarchistic. God is change. No amount of archism can change that. People will continue to suffer from the temptations and predations of archism, but archism is not fated to rule the universe. That is not the Destiny that Lauren Olamina sees, and here, at least, the universe itself is in accord with her vision.

Making Anarchist Prophecy Redundant

Looking at the various examples that I have offered in this chapter—the Spanish and Rojavan Revolutions, the prophetic roles of the doctor's wife and Lauren Olamina—the common theme is that the kind of archist compromises that often come along with anarchism are not fatal to it and can in fact become a basis for greater and further resistance. Insofar as anarchism generally seems to find itself in archist contexts—although not always, as the next chapter attests—this is critically important knowledge. Even as the expression of anarchism in an open fashion always brings a violent archist response, as we see in the case of Spain in the 1930s and as we are seeing in Rojava today, it is clear that there are certain built-in advantages that anarchism has that archism can never overcome.

Archism's answer to anarchism, its only possible response, is violence. That response did succeed in destroying the Spanish Revolution, and has severely restricted and pressured the Rojavan Revolution as well. The violence that archism imposes is not only physical. Haiti, the site of perhaps the greatest rejection of archist power in history, became the subject of harsh economic sanctions, along with frequent invasion and occupation, long after it won its revolution. And we all live with yet another kind of violence, the violence of an imposed sense of reality, a demand to read the world in a certain way, what I have been calling appointing vision and Benjamin calls mythic violence.

Yet, as the blind accountant learned in *Blindness*, violence alone does not serve to perpetuate archism. Archism requires its disguise, its lies, its promises and seductions. It needs representation and other myths to assuage, confuse, and obfuscate its ultimate source of power, which is entirely stolen from the anarchist life that it predates. Here again, we see great vulnerability when all archism really wants us to see is its power and inpermeability.

The figures that I have looked at in this chapter, both actual and literary, are to a person imperfect beings infused with the archist contexts in which they lived. What all that imperfection and intermixing of archist and anarchist elements tells us is that anarchist vision does not need to come out of some pure form. If anything, it is precisely because they *know* archism and understand it from within and on its own terms that the anarchist prophets I have looked at here succeed. Ultimately the goal is not to have one anarchist prophet but to turn the entire community into a collectivity of prophets that will argue and struggle together over what they are seeing. Collective decisions and collective forms of vision can only come out of the ferment of anarchist life in all its variety and nonharmonious bases. The role of an anarchist prophet, if she is going to be singular, is simply to hold onto that sight, to allow for a transition from the requirement of one prophet to many; she can't have all those discussions and arguments by herself.

Any time the anarchist prophet goes beyond the simple act of holding onto collective forms of sight, she threatens—as Lauren Olamina might have threatened and as many of the leaders of the Spanish Revolution *did* threaten—to replace that collective with her own form of sight and, in that way, to reproduce archism even while trying to destroy it.

The anarchist prophet is thus in a very unstable position and it is not always even a necessary one. She will never be invulnerable to the temptation to make her vision only her own. She can never guarantee success, and indeed most anarchist prophets in real life anyway have ended in abject failure, if you use the archist norm of lastingness as your key principle of judgment. Yet for all this, anarchist prophecy remains a critical way for anarchist life to come to see itself. Above all, the form of anarchist prophecy allows the mechanics of archist subjectivity—wherein there must be one leader, there must be one form of sight given to others, and so on—to serve as a basis for their own undoing. Sometimes, then, from very bad (archist) sources, you can still get very good (anarchist) outcomes.

chapter six

can archism ever die?

THE PREVIOUS CHAPTERS have theorized in a context in which archism was an ongoing and ever-present challenge to anarchist forms of vision and politics despite the deep challenges such forms present to archism's power and authority. Neither the Spanish anarchists nor the democratic confederalists in Rojava (have) managed to eliminate archism entirely. Even in the literary treatments that I considered in the previous chapter, Butler's Earthseed series and Saramago's twin novels, archism is pushed to the vanishing point but doesn't actually vanish. Catastrophe is not in and of itself an existential threat to archism; it often merely exposes archism's most vicious and self-evident form.[1] Even in the previous chapter, where I suggest that the attack on key aspects such as universality, futurity, and representation might serve as existential threats to archist power, it is not clear that archism will actually die off when it is so threatened. We only get the sense that it *could* die under certain circumstances.

To take on archism wholesale, something else has to take place that goes well beyond the collapse of the state (since archism is not only a matter of states and sovereign authority), pandemics like the one the world is going through right now (since, being unattached to life except via its own parasitism, archism can survive even the death of much, albeit not all, of the community it predates upon), or other such forms of threat. To the saying that it is easier to imagine the end of the world than it is to imagine the end of capitalism, I think this might be even truer of archism.[2] Archism gets us to think that *it* is life, that is, realer and prior to the life it rules over, and so the end of archism is literally the end of the world.

Given the resilience, adaptability, and tenacity of archist forms of sight, given our own complicity with its lies and its seductions, are we therefore doomed to archism, or at least some form of struggle with archism, forever? Is anarchism itself always to be twinned with archism such that it can only ever be a rival for authority and forms of seeing? In this penultimate chapter, I argue that no, we are not so fated and that anarchism, for all its intertwining with archism, can readily survive the loss of its alter. Key to this realization is that archism relies, above all, on a sense of transcendent or nonimmanent space from which to draw its archeonic visions. The elimination or banishment of such spaces, or at least their redeployment as anarchist spaces, effectively deprives archism of its most basic source of power and authority. Archism can survive even the loss some of the aspects that are so central to it: representation, a sense of the future, the universe. It can retreat into a smaller, uglier and more openly violent center without these things, but it cannot live without the perspective that externality gives to it. It cannot live without the archeon, the king's head (or beak of the octopus), that interface between the transcendent and immanent realms.

Accordingly, in this chapter, I focus on two related questions. First, what are the conditions that make it possible for archism to "die"? This is a critical question not only in terms of the pragmatic issue of dispelling archism but also because one of the central conceits of archism is that it is itself immortal; the immortality that it promises to its subjects—even if only metaphorically or elliptically—simply serves as an extension of its own claim to be impervious to death. If archism can be shown to be mortal, or more accurately to be shown to have never been alive in the first place, then its avatars join its own subjects in ordinary humanness and archism loses its ability to offer them a viable, or at least seemingly viable, alternative after all.

Losing its false claim to transcendence, archism returns to the nothing that it has always been. In this way, archism dies a different kind of death than we do. Because we really do exist, our death is simply part of that existence, whereas archism, which never actually existed in the first place, loses even the pretense of that existence and vanishes utterly. How this state of affairs is possible and how it might be achieved make up the bulk of this chapter.

The second question that I explore here—which will be developed further in the book's conclusion—is to ask, what does anarchism look like when it is not so connected to archism? What form does it take and should we even still call this "anarchism," whose very name implies the connection that I am arguing is not foundational for anarchist practices? An anarchism without archism would be, in some sense, radically different from current practices, although it would not have to be reinvented out of whole cloth. Insofar as anarchism, in its own emphasis on direct action, on the local and the temporary, on the aleatory and the collective, on ordinary life itself, is already an effectively immanent political and social form, it would not have to begin anew because the world it is connected to would not itself begin anew. The deep connections that anarchism has to the world and the life that lives within it would remain, along with the deep connections that anarchist subjects, which in some sense is just about everyone, have with one another as a result of living and being in that world.

To make these points, I once again look from four vantage points. But here I reverse the order of presentation of the last chapter, beginning with the least powerful example and building up to the more ultimate manifestation of archism's death. The first case is taken from "real life" only in the sense that the subject of that example, Baruch Spinoza, was once alive. However, I look not at his actual life but at his writing, and, in particular, I look at his homegrown Western version of immanentism. Spinoza stands out for me because he, more than any other theorist I consider in this book, could be said to fully embrace a version of immanentism from within the edifice of Western philosophy. Although his *Ethics* takes the apparent form of a usual philosophical tractate, it uses that form to subvert and upend the form of transcendentalism that it is normally meant to deliver. Spinoza, who was recognized as a renegade in both his own time and ours, models the fact that even deep in the belly of the beast, as it were, immanentism is both possible and ongoing (and in Spinoza's case, it takes a purer form than we see with Hobbes, Benjamin, and Nietzsche, at least in terms of its cosmology). In this way, Spinoza offers a way to deny archism a perch from which to judge and rule the world. In so doing, Spinoza offers us a "what if" example of how archism might never have emerged in its virulent Western form in the first place.

My second example, which is the only case drawn from real-world experience as such, is a study of what has been called "Melanesian immanentism," a description of a worldview that has no place for transcendentalism and thus similarly no, or at least less, place for archism.[3] Unlike as with Spinoza, this was the "road that was taken" in Melanesia so we have a chance to see a form of thinking where archism is simply (or nearly) impossible. Here, I look at the cargo religious practices of Melanesia and, in particular, one area of Papua New Guinea—the Rai Coast—and a prophet named Yali to show that a way of seeing the world that affords no place for archism already exists. Indeed, given the ancientness of Melanesian practices and beliefs, I would readily say that it existed long before archism, certainly the archism that came out of the West, ever did.[4]

In looking at the case of New Guinea and the encounter that the people there had with Western colonialism, I am not trying to compare a "primitive" Indigenous people who foolishly believed that the "rational" West had something to offer them—namely cargo, or material riches—that they could not get on their own, causing them to imitate the West in ways that are often ridiculed by countless Western authors. Rather, I am arguing that the practitioners of the cargo belief systems correctly saw Western and archist promises for what they were; it was the white colonial administrators and missionaries who believed in things that weren't there, and hence, arguably, the ones who were—and are—the fools.

The large-scale turn away from Christian missionaries or, in some cases, the reappropriation of Christianity for anti-Christian belief structures in some areas of Melanesia that was afforded by the cargo beliefs is not unique by any means. In many colonized spaces, even Christian modalities became adapted for antihegemonic practices (witness the *pasyon* in the Philippines, where the passion play of Christ becomes an enactment of resisting colonialism).[5] It indicates that resistance to archist transcendentalism is possible as well as the even more critical point that archism is neither automatic nor even always successful. Even so, the case of Yali is perhaps unusually helpful in that it renders legible a dynamic with archist forms of colonialism wherein the subject implicit in the question "how could these people be so gullible?" turns from being a Melanesian prophet and his followers to Western colonizers themselves.

Finally, I look at two fictional depictions that help us think further about "the death of archism" within Western culture. The first of these explorations is the novel *Frankenstein* by Mary Shelley, wherein the monster is initially meant to be the triumph of archism in terms of its key promise, the conquest and defeat of death. Although the monster himself would very much like to fulfill this promise, his own hideous face, his murderous rage, and his general destructiveness ruin this promise from within, revealing—and (re) producing—the death that lies within the false life of archism, not unlike the stench of the dead leader of the hoodlums in *Blindness*.

The second and final fictional work that I look at is the book and television series *The Leftovers* (with a focus on the TV series). This work depicts what the death of archism would actually look like. An event called the "Sudden Departure" results in the destabilization of both religion and science, the two pillars of contemporary archism. In the aftermath of that event, the characters in *The Leftovers* grapple with the sudden absence of archist structure. One character in particular, a woman named Nora Durst, confronts the absolute failure of archism with an unusual single-mindedness that in effect renders her the one person who can see past and through archist lies (most of the other characters desperately try to reassert archism even though it is utterly broken). In this way, she can be read as a kind of singular anarchist prophet. More accurately, however, since anarchism doesn't need a prophet at that point—since archism has already died—we could say that Nora Durst is a sign of what it would be like to live in a world where prophecy itself is no longer needed, when collective forms of sight are the only kinds of sight that are left. She might point us, ever so slightly, to what might happen following our ultimate disappointment.

In what follows, I look at how archism can be attacked from two directions, from the transcendental (as my reading of *The Leftovers* and *Frankenstein* will show) and from the immanent (as the explorations of Melanesian immanentism and Spinoza suggest). Although I ultimately place anarchism within the immanentist tradition, in the present, the here and the now, I don't want to make it seem like immanentism is always good and transcendentalism is always bad.[6] In fact, archism can be considered, at the end of the day, to be a *very* bad form of immanentism that poses as transcendentalist but only as an excuse to project the archons' own desires. Yet archism's faux transcendentalism gives us another weapon in our arsenal because, by invoking and requiring such an externality, archism always risks, as Benjamin and Hobbes tell us, an interruption issuing from that realm, even if it doesn't actually exist. Such an interruption may give us not "true" immanentism but at least a form of atheism where God has canceled herself as a source of archist lies. This conspiracy, between immanentist and transcendentalist elements, in the various combinations that I look at, all serve to destroy and undermine archism both from within and from without. It allows us, as it were, to "traverse the fantasy" of archist transcendentalism, revealing it as utterly empty. Let me now begin this exploration with the case of Spinoza and the challenge his philosophy poses to archism.

Spinoza's Homegrown Western Immanentism

In terms of combatting archism in all its forms, those of us who live in the West may have a particularly hard job ahead of us, insofar as we live in the veritable belly of the beast, the maw of archist power and phantasm. The first part of this book was meant to show how archist vision could be combatted from within the Western system of thought, how an occult archist political theology can be countered by an anarchist form of vision. But I can also think of one thinker from the West, namely Spinoza—there are, of course, many others, but Spinoza is perhaps the purest example of what I am thinking of—whose cosmology works in ways that will accord very much with the Melanesian immanentists I speak of in the next section, despite his emergence from within a largely Western transcendentalist context.[7] Whereas the three thinkers that I looked at in part I—Hobbes, Nietzsche, and Benjamin, and I would definitely add Butler to this list as well—are all examples of negative theologists, I would call Spinoza more of a "positive" theologist.[8] For Spinoza, there is no negation; none is needed because the transcendental world that the other thinkers and writers are engaged in undermining doesn't exist—doesn't even not exist!—at all.

The reception of Spinoza as a radical immanentist has been clearly articulated by thinkers ranging from Antonio Negri to Gilles Deleuze.[9] These writers note Spinoza's exceptionality as someone who asserted a universe that was entirely and only material and existent, a form of materiality and existence that necessarily includes God. Such a view has drawn the attention of many who came to hate and attack Spinoza. Even in his lifetime, he was recognized for the threat that he posed to established, archist forms of authority. Above all, Spinoza's refusal of Western forms of transcendentalism—the ultimate void, the ultimate negation—is seen as leading to a radical and, I would add, anarchist politics, one that breaks entirely with the false positivisms of liberal and Western forms of ontology that are, as Nietzsche said as well, disguised forms of nihilism. As Deleuze writes in *Spinoza: Practical Philosophy*:

> In the reproach that Hegel will make to Spinoza, that he ignored the negative and its power, lies the glory and innocence of Spinoza, his own discovery. In a world consumed by the negative, he has enough confidence in life, in the power of life, to challenge death, the murderous appetite of men, the rules of good and evil, of the just and the unjust. Enough confidence in life to denounce all the phantoms of the negative. . . . In Spinoza's thought, life is not an idea, a matter of theory, it is a way of being, one and the same eternal mode in all its attributes.[10]

As Spinoza informs us in his *Ethics*, the very notion of a vacuum is anathema to the kind of cosmological immanentism that he expounds throughout that text. He writes:

> If corporeal substance could be divided in such a way that its parts are really distinct, why could not one part be annihilated whilst the other parts remain interconnected, as before? And why should all the parts be adapted in such a way that no vacuum exists? It is certainly true of things which are really distinct from each other that one can exist and remain in its state without the other. Since, therefore, no vacuum exists in Nature . . . but all its parts must agree in such a way that the vacuum does not exist, it follows also that there cannot be really distinguished; that is that corporeal substance, in so far as it is substance, cannot be divided.[11]

Spinoza's rejection of the concept of a vacuum stems from his argument that there is only one substance in the universe, namely that of God. All objects that we experience in the manifold of the universe are simply "extensions" of God. Insofar as God fills the universe, there is no absence of that substance. Thus Spinoza writes: "Besides God no substance can exist or be conceived."[12] And further he explains that "God is the immanent but not the transitive cause of things."[13] The upshot of this understanding is that, insofar as God is everywhere, everywhere is also God. While this might seem to raise all objects, including human bodies and pencils and other such things, up to a divine level, just as critically, it "lowers" God to the level of human bodies and pencils; God shares a state of immanence with all other objects even as God is the first and only cause of everything else. Yet, here again, by saying that such causation is immanent and not transitive, we see that in some sense God's causality is itself built into rather than directly affecting and controlling causality as such.

In this way, for Spinoza, there is a vast equalization of substance in his claim that denies the Western form of transcendentalism and its hierarchies. For Spinoza, the fact that God is the first cause also means that the universe is utterly determined rather than contingent.[14] Normally, an embrace of pure determinism seems to sit firmly in the archist camp because determinism ordinarily implies a direct and top-down command structure. Contingency certainly seems to be the more anarchic dimension. Yet this is where the truly subversive effect of Spinoza's thought becomes most apparent insofar as, in my view, Spinoza renders the distinction between contingency and determination completely moot. He explains, "Things could not have been produced by God in any other way, or in any other order, than that in which they were produced," showing that in effect even God is determined by her own determination.[15]

If God is included in what is determined—even if, in this case, God is a cause that also causes herself—then we are already a long way from the traditional Western archist reading of a God who determines everything from her utterly undetermined space (a model for the terrestrial archeon). But Spinoza goes even further than that by insisting that the universe God caused—which is itself only an extension of God—is quite different from the harmonious order that is often ascribed to determinism. Spinoza argues that when people see the universe in this way, they are placing their own desires for God to be serving them specifically. He says that they believe "there exists some governor or governors of Nature, endowed with human freedom, who have taken care of everything for them, and have made everything for their use."[16] Here, Spinoza tells us that human beings project onto God their own love of balance and harmony, assuming that because they love those things, God must love and seek those things as well, a great description of the archist tendency if I ever saw one.

In fact, however, Spinoza is very clear that the universe is radically imperfect from the human perspective. More accurately, he tells us that the very notion of what is perfect is not up to human beings to determine. Rather, "the perfection of things is to be estimated from their nature and power alone, nor are things more or less perfect on account of the fact that they delight or offend human senses, or that they assist human nature or are repugnant to it."[17]

Here, we get to the crux of the issue. Archism is, after all, about projecting falsities into the heavens, only to receive them back on Earth as "truths" that must be obeyed. In the end, archism isn't about God at all but uses the idea of God as a way to render certain all-too-human judgments and desires seemingly unimpeachable (because God "wills it" so). Here again, we see how archism is a form of disguised (bad) immanentism, one that is ruined when the built-in assumption that there is something better out there is replaced by the fact there isn't anything out there at all.

Spinoza makes mincemeat of this greatest of archist conceits. He makes it impossible for any human agenda to couch itself as divine or godlike because he has removed human volition from his view of that which orders—and disorders—the cosmos. God, in this case, can no longer vouchsafe for human beings and their desires because there is no correspondence between what any particular human or group of humans might want, which they then can claim comes from God rather than from them, and the universe itself. Here, the immanentism of the universe, its independent material presence, which does not exist to answer human wishes, defeats the desire to read human meaning and purpose into that universe.

Accordingly, we can begin to see that the difference between determination and contingency is negated because the qualities that both of those positions seek—the one order, balance, hierarchy; the other disorder, imbalance, horizontality—become indistinguishable, or perhaps, putting this point even more strongly, the universe that Spinoza depicts looks exactly like what a contingent universe would look like even if it is said to be fully and utterly determined. Another way to say this is that, whenever the archist agenda seeks to pack the universe full of its own principles, including those of human-determined order and hierarchy, they can find no place for that plan in Spinoza's version of determinism. In fact, by making it the enemy of human-based order, the very fixity of determinism becomes a way to ensure that such an order can never be imposed on the universe, much less on God. Here, as we've seen with other radical thinkers too, Spinoza takes one of the mainstays of archism and turns it against it, including its own (normally) transcendental elements.

Spinozan Immanentism

In saying all this, I am making something of a distinction between Spinoza and the three authors that I studied in depth in the first part of this book. Hobbes, Nietzsche, and Benjamin all seek to focus on the immanent world too, but they begin from a transcendental world and work their way out of it—another version of attacking archism from both directions—while Spinoza doesn't bother with that stage and skips directly to immanentism.[18] We can see how Hobbes, via his radical nominalism and the way he renders God effectively unknowable to human actors; Nietzsche, via his idea of the "death of God"; and Benjamin, via his depiction of a God who is anarchist as well as his related notion of a divine violence that works to undo the human fetishism attributed to God, all effectively hijack transcendentalism for their own purposes.[19] They all take advantage of the silence and opacity—or perhaps even the nonexistence—of the transcendental realm to reframe it and turn it against the nihilism that archism forces it to serve.

Spinoza is different. He doesn't remove God from an archist universe so much as cram God into an anarchist one. God and the material universe for Spinoza become one and the same thing (not unlike Butler). Accordingly, the problem for Spinoza is not to ask how we can unmake centuries of archist error but to ask how anyone could think along archist lines in the first place. In some ways then, Spinoza's approach is more in line with anarchist principles of direct action than the other thinkers I have treated in this work, insofar as he assumes that the conditions under which anarchism is possible already apply and asks us to act accordingly. At the same time, I have spent a lot more time with the thought of Hobbes, Benjamin, and Nietzsche because I think their theories are perhaps more pertinent to those of us who are stuck in a transcendentalist, archist logic; that is, they better serve the role of anarchist prophet to help us get out of an archist way of thinking (if that wasn't the case, then Spinoza is to be preferred because he shows us a way to think about a universe in which anarchist forms of thinking are the norm).

The Master's Tools

This may all come down to a question of "the master's tools," based on Audre Lorde's adage that "the master's tools will never dismantle the master's house."[20] Hobbes, Nietzsche, and Benjamin, it could be said, do see a value in seizing the master's tools, which in this case are largely transcendental in nature, as long as those tools are used against their original purpose (taking on the quality that Benjamin calls "pure means"[21]). They all offer ways to subvert archism by hijacking its main elements—its prophets, its language, its symbols of power and authority, and its deity—and turning them against that project, ruining it, as it were, from inside and by its own elements. Spinoza offers instead a model that may be more like a general strike, simply ignoring the lies of archism and acting accordingly (no tools at all). Perhaps we don't even need to take a side on this question; I see the value in both forms of approach. In fact, it makes sense, once again, to take these approaches, both negative and positive theologies, in tandem, both striking archism from deep within its maw and calling its very existence into question. And Spinoza is not the only thinker out of the West who offers a version of radical immanentism; many of the thinkers who take up Spinoza, like Negri and Deleuze, do much of the same thing. Even just in keeping with figures discussed in this book, I would say that Butler's depiction of a God who is only change is at least as radically immanentist as Spinoza's rendition, if not more so.

Of the three thinkers that I treated in part I, I would say that Spinoza is closest to Benjamin. This may reflect in part their shared heritage and interest in Jewish traditions that tend to be significantly more immanentist than many Christian-based systems of thought. There is a way in which Benjamin's God *is* entirely immanent insofar as every object in the universe is a manifestation of a divine violence that resists human fetishism (and perhaps, in particular, commodity fetishism). There is a kind of material democracy, an equality of all aspects of creation, that one finds in Benjamin and Spinoza alike.

Both thinkers also warn us not to impute too much to God. Benjamin does this by sternly policing the postlapsarian boundary between the divine and the human, and Spinoza does this by reducing human knowledge and agency to a tiny corner of the existing universe (although he complicates this with his understanding of reason). Yet, for all this similarity, Benjamin leaves us a bit more suspicious of our environs than Spinoza does and, in particular, in terms of our ability to really know and understand even our part of the universe. This may in part reflect the difference between a negative and a positive theology, but I also think that politically speaking, Benjamin may arm us a bit better against falsities posing as truths insofar as the very idea of truth or even an unproblematic reality is (now) anathema for him.

Here too we can see that the question of immanentism versus transcendentalism is not so much a matter of the former being good and the latter being bad. Instead, it makes more sense to speak of both archist and anarchist versions of each. The archist form of transcendentalism is false and empty; its immanentism is couched in that falseness and hence is false as well. The anarchist version of transcendentalism largely uses that device as a way to defeat the false transcendentalism of archism (here, as with Nietzsche, the question of whether God is alive or dead, existent or nonexistent, is almost beside the point in terms of the effect that the mere possibility of God has on archist theology). And anarchist immanentism is itself just a reflection of a life that takes place in a vast and interconnected material context.[22]

In any event, Spinoza shows us that even those of us who are raised in the West—or who live deep within its ideological shadow—are fully capable of rejecting the metaphysical bases of archism. Whether that is by fiat, as it is for Spinoza, or by careful and complex usurpation, as it is for Hobbes, Nietzsche, and Benjamin, we see in any event that archism is not only not immortal but that equally, not unlike the God that Nietzsche's madman describes in *The Gay Science*, mortal human beings can kill it too.

Yet, if Spinoza shows us a Western model that might have left archism behind had it become a prevailing practice, it seems clear that the reason that it has not and does not dominate is precisely because of the way that it is in disaccord with archism as such. It is not Spinoza but a thinker like Locke who articulates a modality of being that gives archism maximal access to life, to disguise its parasitism as reason and truth. Spinoza can and does deny this, but until and unless his philosophy becomes far more widespread, it is

Lockeanism that we must confront. Accordingly, we must leave the West entirely in order to find forms of immanentism that show not just the possibility but the actuality of resistant and anarchist systems, and for this reason I turn to the case of Melanesia in general and Yali the prophet in particular.

Melanesian Immanentism

In her Foerster Lecture at UC Berkeley in 2018, the British anthropologist Marilyn Strathern described a Melanesian cosmology that is radically different from Western models that are based on transcendental—and, I would add, archist—formulations. In that lecture, Strathern depicted Melanesian society—her focus in the lecture is on communities in New Britain and Papua New Guinea but could be extended to many other Melanesian communities as well—as having, as it were, two parallel economies, one of the human and one of the plants that those humans sow, tend, harvest, and eat.

As Strathern tells us, the two main diet staples of the Melanesians in question are taro and yams. In both cases, the crop is replenished by cutting off a piece of the tuber or root and planting it back into the ground, whereby it forms a new tuber or root that is genetically a clone of the original. By this formulation, it could be said—and this is indeed how the local communities think of these foods—as if they are only ever eating one continuous, immortal taro and yam.

Strathern tells us that the Melanesians think of themselves along the same lines. They have a concept of "replacement" wherein a given person, upon dying, gets recycled and comes back to life in a continuous cycle that is bolstered and made possible by collective rituals. This coming and going in and out of life thus serves as a form of collective and ongoing immortality precisely as is the case with the plants they eat.

This should not be taken to mean that life in the Melanesian cosmos is entirely static. As Strathern tells us, human intervention—the aforementioned series of rituals—is thought to be required to perpetuate these long chains of being. Accordingly, the possibility of change and difference is present in each iteration of the transmission of being across time. As Strathern puts it: "Taro soul is like a stalk. It has to be replenished but, properly replenished, it exists in perpetuity. A fractal entity, each particular soul is also part of generic soul. The same is true of human beings if one thinks for example of the perpetuity of matrilineal clan groups."[23]

In speaking of "taro soul," Strathern is describing the dual nature of material objects in Melanesian understandings, wherein there is a physical body and an equally physical soul. In this case, the body is the conduit for the soul and the soul is that which animates the body. Although from our own Western/transcendental perspective, the soul is normally the immortal part of us and the body falls away, in Melanesian understandings, both body and soul are equally potentially immortal.[24] By the same token, both body and soul are subject to a final death if the proper rituals and tasks of perpetuation are not adhered to. In this way, she explains that "the only life that can be lived is life everlasting. . . . The flourishing of people is there in the antecedent generations that brought them into being and the future generations that will replace them."[25]

Strathern cautions that there is nothing mystical for the Melanesians about any of this. She tells us that the Western dichotomy of material versus transcendental or immaterial has no analogue in Melanesian culture. Instead, the main divide is between "what is seen and what exists unseen."[26] Gods, ghosts, and other phenomena that would be considered "supernatural" in the West are often unseen in Melanesian considerations, but they are thought to be just as real and present as human beings are.

Immanentism and the Cargo Beliefs

In terms of this immanentist form of vision, it can perhaps already be surmised that archism would have a very difficult time in finding a purchase in such a worldview. There is no "outside" from which to order and hierarchize human communities. There is no special perch that is not itself part of the world, no site for an archeon to view and judge the world even as it exempts itself from that vision. A further exploration of the way that this highly developed form of immanentism manifests itself, particularly in terms of the way that such cosmologies came into contact with Western views starting with the colonial era, demonstrates the degree to which archism can be resisted, even undermined, by this refusal of exteriority.

The cargo belief systems in Melanesia exemplify a form of that resistance. As James Leach explains, in "rejecting missionism," these communities—his focus is the Rai Coast and the Madang District in Papua New Guinea—engaged "in re-interpretations and creative engagements with colonial rule that go under the name of 'Cargo Cult' in the Pacific" (because the term *cargo cult* has a pejorative connotation, Leach and others tend to refer to these systems as cargo beliefs or use other terms).[27] The broad-scale subversion and rejection of Christian doctrine—at least in terms of its orthodox, Western mode—largely reflected the fact that the local communities understood Christian doctrines through the lens of their own particular form of immanentism and, from that lens, rejected the false promises of transcendentalism in favor of actual, material benefits. Leach tells us that "the damnation/salvation binary [of Christianity] was immediately interpreted in immanentist, not in transcendentalist, terms—that the damnation or salvation that was talked about was the current and practical inequality between whites and Rai Coast people. That salvation would be 'cargo' as the material of recognition and power."[28] The Melanesians of the Rai Coast—but elsewhere in Melanesia too, of course—felt that the promises of heaven and fulfillment in the afterlife that missionaries made to them could only be understood as promises of material plenty or "cargo" (*kako* in Tok Pisin). They fully expected to be granted the same wealth and power as the white colonists, and, when they realized that this was not about to happen—for their form of immanentism also meant that they expected this plenty immediately rather than in some far off and utopian future—they took it upon themselves to get that cargo in their own way.

As Leach further explains, one way that they did this was by imitating the Europeans' forms of knowledge, which they assumed was a key part of how they acquired their own wealth. Leach writes:

> The circulation of paper was central to the project of achieving this "salvation." Paper was employed in direct mimicry of western bureaucracy, and as the medium in which to convey claims to the colonial and independent state. We cannot possibly read their enthusiasm for an anthropologist writing about their *kastom* [that is, their resistant practices often connected to their own Indigenous rituals] and history in any other context than this perception of the power of paper and documents in engaging with new manifestations of the power of life and death that they always claim was and is theirs. That is, in immanentist rather than transcendentalist terms.[29]

Here we see, as was also the case in *Seeing*, the centrality of paper records for archism, at least in a slightly earlier time. For Leach, the community's use of paper and writing was often purely symbolic, as literacy was not all that widespread. But this was not the point. The local communities adapted this form of writing to their own traditional practices, wherein the doing of a thing became part of its perpetuation. Thus, in the same way that they "cultivated" one single crop of taro and yams over the millennia, and similarly cultivated themselves to achieve a form of collective intergenerational immortality, so too did they begin to cultivate documents as a way to enhance and perpetuate their own rival sources of power and the accumulation of wealth to their Western overlords.

Often the practitioners of cargo beliefs are portrayed as ignorant Indigenous people totally misunderstanding the nature of Western power, fetishizing the symbols of that power and, in so doing, having none of it themselves. Even Peter Lawrence's classic text about the cargo beliefs, *Road Belong Cargo*, has this tone at times (although to be fair to him, he was also trying to explain its inner logic to those who might make light of it). From my own point of view, however, something very different is afoot. It is not once again that the Melanesians are too primitive to understand the reality of wealth and power. They understand it quite well, actually much better than their colonial masters do. It is in fact the westerners who misunderstand their own wealth and power. It is they, after all, who worship invisible and nonexistent things. It is they who put themselves under the spell of such nonexistence in ways that drive them toward acts of maximal destruction to other communities through the institutions of capitalism, slavery, and imperialism. They also do this within their own communities through savagely enforced hierarchies and the suppression of any and all forms of collective politics (although those forms survive nevertheless). While Western archism is ultimately a form of immanentism as well, albeit a bad one, its feint in the direction of transcendentalism is critical for the way that archism is constructed and supported, hence the requirement to believe in what doesn't exist at all.

In light of this, I would say that it is the Melanesians who are being the realists. They refused the lies of the missionaries and either rejected or reappropriated Christian doctrine in order to find their own pathway to material plenty. In phenomenology, they speak of the *hyle*, the material basis that is to be shaped into something else, without ceasing to be what it is.[30] In this case, the Melanesians recognized the *hyle* of paper and writing, its symbolic power being prior and more important than its actual content. Accordingly, we can see that the use of paper and documents by Western imperialists is no less ritualistic and formulaic than the Melanesians' imitation of that activity. The real power of documents lies in their connection to some unseen and secret place of judgment and ordering, a manifestation of a belief system.

But note a critical difference: for the westerners that the Melanesians imitated through the cargo beliefs, the endless documents that they produced were—and are—associated with the archeon. They are seen as emanating from that place and that time and, as such, could be read as emissaries from a mystical beyond that supported the power and material domination of the colonial administration more generally. For the Melanesian occupants of the Rai Coast, by contrast, their practices in terms of paper were entirely decentralized, having no one place or special status. In this way, the communities in question actually took the archeon and tore it into its tiny component shreds, democratizing its power and giving it back to the people from whom it was stolen. In other words, the Melanesians simply took the site of the archeon and put it entirely within the world, turning it from something that was clearly unavailable to them—that is the message that the West ultimately had for them—into something that was tangible and available and above all collective after all, hence the value and challenge of the cargo beliefs.

Although the cargo beliefs were long suppressed by their various colonial powers—in New Guinea, that power was Australia for much of the early to mid-twentieth century, the time pertinent to the story of Yali—Leach shows that even to this day, there is an immanentist logic that is active in the communities that he engages with. Working alongside a colleague, Gilles Lane, who is an artist and a designer, Leach helped create a rubric for local people to make booklets that reflected their relationship to their own culture, history, and local politics.[31] These booklets were often marked by drawings of plants and animals and very often repeated the same images and ideas over and over again with no concern about reduplication. Leach also notes:

> Most, if not all [of these booklets], however careful, are *incomplete* in some way. Booklets are more often than not *indicative* of a story or process than a complete rendering of it. Even those who are most vocal advocates of the booklet project have not used it to make a comprehensive record of knowledge that is in "danger" of being "lost." Most records are of things that are quite well "known." There has been no systematic effort to use them with frail old people, nor seemingly to prioritise rare or esoteric knowledge. Perhaps this reflects the fact that there is no sense of an existential need to document *knowledge as such*. The desire for documentation does not come from the same aesthetic of knowledge as that of a transcendentalist tradition.[32]

Because of their particular form of immanentism, for this community, there is no danger of losing knowledge that is entirely held within the world. The point of writing and drawing and other symbolic forms of representation for this community therefore lies, once again, in the way that it cultivates and perpetuates knowledge precisely by the act of reproducing and inscribing it. In this way, rather than transmitting some esoteric truth into the world from somewhere beyond, as is the case with the archeon, here, the members of the community are simply reproducing that knowledge, over and over, to keep it going, possibly forever.

Those acts of cultivation—of writing, of bodies, of souls, and of plants—are all interconnected. Collectively these acts constitute the life that I have been calling anarchism (again with a decidedly small *a*). Perhaps most critically of all, they show us that even representation, that workhorse of archism, need not always and only lead to archist outcomes (when it comes to the anarchist nature of language as a whole). In this case, the writings and drawings of a community serve to further the collective knowledge that is constantly changing even as it remains part of a long and transgenerational continuity.

Yali the Prophet

To give a clearer sense of how Melanesian immanentism connects to the question of prophecy, I turn to Peter Lawrence's depiction of one key and perhaps the most famous incident in the history of the cargo beliefs. In doing so, I will try to show that the movement to resist Western power and to recode its nominally transcendental aspects into immanentist ones demonstrates the way that archism, far from being inevitable and universal, can be, if not always utterly defeated—in the sense that New Guinea remains to this day within the orbit of Western colonialism and now neocolonialism—at least radically decentered, unmade, in a sense, by its very own tools of control.

In Lawrence's book, the central figure of the cargo beliefs is Yali, a man who was born in the early twentieth century and raised on the Rai Coast, and who in his own way became a prophet of resistance to Western power and control. Describing the context into which Yali was born and raised, Lawrence explains that the Indigenous political structure of the Rai Coast of New Guinea had "no political unity within, or single authority over, the whole area or even one of its component societies. . . . Leadership was democratic and limited in scope."[33] This horizontality also applied to the local cosmology. Lawrence writes, "Not only the whole mythology but even individual myths reflected the absence of the idea of time depth [i.e., progressive and chronologically ordered time]."[34] In this way, "events of antiquity were events of the present and would be events of the future as well."[35]

Lawrence concludes his summation of the cosmological context that Yali grew up in by stating: "By the same token, the body of knowledge was conceived to be as finite as the cosmic order within which it was contained. . . . The whole visible world—annually ripening crops, fertility of pigs, success in hunting—far from allowing it an aura of mysticism, proclaimed that it was solidly based on verified and empirical fact. There was no need—in fact no room—for an independent human intellect."[36]

Lawrence describes four waves of the cargo belief movement, spanning the late nineteenth and early to mid-twentieth century (the latter period corresponding to that of Yali himself). These movements produced a syncretic mixture of Christianity and traditional religions wherein God was merged with Kilibob, a local deity now named God-Kilibob (another key deity was Jesus-Manup; Manup was traditionally seen as Kilibob's brother).

These movements reflected a great deal of unrest and discontent within the Indigenous communities. Prophets and doctrines came and went in swift succession as individuals and communities tried to grapple with the tangible difference in wealth, power, and authority between Indigenous people and their colonial overlords. One slightly earlier prophet, Tagarab, emerged during World War II and the Japanese invasion and occupation of New Guinea. Tagarab argued that the missionaries and colonial administrators were liars and supported the Japanese invasion, creating an anticolonial rebellion in Madang in the process. Kaum, another prophet from this period, similarly supported the Japanese. Most of the prophets throughout this period were men, but there was at least one well-known female prophet, Polelesi.[37]

Through these prophetic interruptions, the basic cast of cosmological characters was continually being recast and reconsidered (in some places, Kilibob and Manus were seen as corresponding to Cain and Abel). Here, the same narrative material was being worked over and over again to produce very different results that were adapted to local beliefs and requirements. Insofar as this myriad of theologies served as ongoing sources of resistance, especially during the war, these movements were strongly suppressed by the missionaries and colonial administrators, but they proved impossible to completely eliminate.

In terms of his initial interactions with Australian missionaries and colonial administrators, Yali himself was far from a rebel. He worked for the colonial regime and tended to take on its views, expressing a disinterest or even skepticism in the cargo beliefs.[38] As he rose in status as a "native administrator," Yali nonetheless became a figure of religious devotion for other Indigenous people in and around his home district.

During the Japanese occupation, Yali remained loyal to the Australians. He survived a harrowing escape, which was widely seen as only being possible through divine intervention. He also made several trips to Australia, which hugely expanded his spiritual value to others. In an immanentist cosmos, there was no "heaven" that stood outside the world. It was therefore assumed that heaven was a place on Earth full of riches and that Sydney—sometimes conflated with Rome—was often considered to be that place.

Paradoxically, his trips to Australia also helped renew Yali's interests in his own Indigenous religion; whereas the missionaries taught him that traditional ritual objects belonged to "Satan," he saw them being displayed in a museum in Brisbane and reasoned that the Australians had stolen the New Guineans' magic items and were using them for their own sake, suggesting that they were a source of power and authority after all.[39]

Much of the lore about Yali that was spread by his fellow Indigenous people came independently of Yali's own desires or actions, especially at first. Lawrence recalls, for example, a speech made by "cargo enthusiasts" in which it was said:

> It was not to be thought that Yali was a mere human being: he was a spirit of the dead. He had been killed at Hollandia [the site of his miraculous escape] and had gone from there in spirit form, to Australia, where he had seen not only the King, but also God himself in heaven. God had told him that he had been wanting to "open the road of the cargo" for the natives for a long time and would do so now if they would reorganize their way of life along European lines. He ordered Yali to return to New Guinea and urge the natives to build large "camps," see that the population increased and eradicate abortion, infanticide, and polygyny [as ways to bring on the cargo].[40]

We see in this kind of talk a peculiar admixing of Western and Indigenous elements that is very characteristic of cargo beliefs more generally. Some of the Western prejudices against local practices—like polygyny—were preserved and endorsed, and westerners remained at the top of the social and political pyramid. And yet, for all this apparent acquiescence to Western rule, these kinds of beliefs constituted a subversion and reappropriation of Western deities and an attempt to beat the West at its own game.

Yali himself was slowly but surely brought over to these kinds of belief systems and was eventually led to practice a more sustained form of resistance against the Australian administrators he worked for. Given that during World War II he had refused to join the widespread rebellion against Australian colonialism, after the war, Yali was rewarded by being appointed a foreman in the Madang District, making him the highest-ranking Indigenous person in the area. He set out, as he was ordered, to set up a system of laws that would mix Western values with some degree of toleration of local practices. However, Yali became increasingly angry as his own hopes to get cargo by following orders and faithfully executing his job didn't pan out. Lawrence explains that as Yali became more bitter and resentful, "he regarded all Europeans as liars and cheats, but the main force of his fury was turned on the missionaries. They had deliberately deceived the people. They had hidden from them the truth about human origins [and the basis for the Europeans' material wealth]; and if they were prepared to be dishonest about so simple and basic a matter, it was hardly likely that they would ever reveal the really important secret they possessed—the ultimate source of the cargo."[41] Describing Yali's mindset at this point, Lawrence writes:

> Although convinced of the duplicity of the missionaries, he did not believe that the Christianity practiced by the white men had no basis of truth. He assumed that there were two separate religions in New Guinea, each constituted in roughly the same way and each powerful in its own sphere. First, there was Christianity, with its two deities (God and Jesus Christ), spirits of the dead and multiple totems. God and Jesus Christ were responsible for the material and social culture of the Europeans; in fact everything that he had seen in Australia. This was the European's secret. They would never reveal more than its externals to outsiders and would resent any attempt to purloin it—as, for example, by means of cargo ritual. . . . Second, there was the native religion, which had its own deities, spirits, and totems. These deities were responsible for the New Guinea material and social culture, to which he would now encourage his people to return.[42]

Here, we see how even as Yali broke from Christianity and formal allegiance to the West, he continued to include Western beliefs within his own immanentist belief system. In this way, even his own devotion to obtaining cargo led him inexorably toward an increasingly open break with the West. Simply put, it was inconceivable to him that the Europeans didn't have access to secrets about the source of their own plainly evident wealth and power, which they refused to share with the Indigenous people of New Guinea. Insofar as their promises were not bearing fruit—Yali felt, for example, that he had distinctly been promised cargo in exchange for continuing to back the Australians during World War II—the only possible response was to rebel against Western values as such.

Yali's rebellion mainly took the form of his establishing his own independent power base in Madang. He organized a series of "boss boys" who worked as his lieutenants throughout the area.[43] He also took over most of the police and juridical functions in the district, although that was not part of his job description. Under the cover of doing "patrols" of the region, Yali was able to spread his own influence and ideas.[44] As a result of these actions as well as the fact that he was almost automatically deferred to by a population that considered him to be a powerful prophet, Yali effectively had built up his own political apparatus. As Lawrence explains: "Although his charter was to continue the work of [postwar] reconstruction he had begun in 1945 and stabilize native life . . . for a very large part of 1948 practically nothing was done to define the geographical sphere of his authority or supervise his activities . . . He was, in fact *the* Administration, as far as [the local people] were concerned."[45]

Perhaps most critically, the power that Yali had amassed allowed a large-scale return to traditional culture and religion, particularly the Kabu Ceremony, which was a vital part of how these communities perpetuated their own collective forms of immortality. Missionaries had been speaking against and even forbidding the Kabu Ceremony for decades at this point, but Yali allowed it to be practiced openly. Even so, this did not constitute a return to some "authentic" earlier precolonial form of religion. The desire for cargo, the urge to imitate—or perhaps more accurately purloin the secrets of—the Europeans was always a primary motivator. It is perhaps this mixture of Western transcendentalist form and Melanesian immanentist content that was Yali's greatest strength. It allowed him to "hide in plain sight," as it were. He was allowed, albeit only for a brief time, to run this (non)state within a state, something that looked formally like a colonial society but which in fact had usurped its power without the colonial administrators initially recognizing what had happened.

Although, especially with his system of "boss boys," Yali's appropriation of Western models may have actually given him some of the trappings of archism himself, he never abandoned the form of immanentism that was peculiar to his community and which disallowed a strong version of archism to take hold. In practice, the Madang District when Yali was in charge reverted, at least in part, to a looser, more decentralized and locally based form of social, political, and economic life.

Eventually the archists got their revenge. The missionaries, particularly the Lutherans, deeply resented Yali's attacks on Christianity, and they browbeat the colonial administrators into first publicly denouncing him and then ultimately putting him in jail for what was seen as his abuses of power. His time in jail pretty much ended Yali's "reign," although not his status among his fellow Indigenous people.

Disappointed Vision

In thinking about Yali as an example of Melanesian immanentist—and anarchist—prophecy, we see that Yali's rise and fall represent not so much an absolute elimination of archism but an example of one set of visions that lies within another. In some sense, that is the condition for all of us who live under archism insofar as our life is always held apart from archism itself. Yet Yali's example expresses a more powerful break with archist projection than many other examples of this coexistence, insofar as he, and Melanesian immanentism more generally, denied archism the ability to represent itself as some all-powerful externality. Simply put, the Melanesian's own belief structure guaranteed that archism as such was literally incredible. The series of uprisings and countertheologies that came out of this whole period of time was a sign that Melanesian society was not accessible to the standard lies and faux realities of Western archism as such.

The kind of anarchism that I am attributing to the community that Yali was a part of was able to hide in plain sight for a time because archist vision is quite bad at recognizing that there could be another way to think or perceive the world (as Saramago's *Seeing* also suggests). There was no vocabulary for the archists to understand what they were facing except as a kind of "madness" or foolish fetishism.

Even the term *animism*, which is often a blanket term used to describe many non-Christian belief systems, Melanesian ones very much included, is sorely inaccurate to describe what transpired in Yali's world. As Strathern tells us, the name *animism* suggests a belief in a spirit that lives within material objects, whereas the spirit for the Melanesians is as "real" and existent as the body. The name *animism* represents a way that Western archism sees this nonarchist form of vision, projecting its own insistence on transcendental objects—spirits, anima—onto systems that do not recognize such things. Here again the real fetishists are not the Melanesians but the Europeans who worship invisible things that don't actually exist.

It could be argued that the success of Yali—if this story can be deemed a success, as I think it should—comes from the way that he is able to go deep within the apparatus of the Australian colonial state, albeit in a way that was strictly limited due to his race, and remain relatively impervious to the seductions and allures that generally constitute archist forms of vision. Yali looked at what he was directed to see, but he didn't take in what the colonial administration wanted him to. Whereas, in *The Castle*, we can note how K. was trained to see what he was told to see, for Yali, there was no equivalent mode of educating him because he failed to share the most basic premises that allowed such an enforced form of seeing in the first place. In this way, rather than being dazzled into quiescence by his trips to Australia or the time he spent being trained in Port Moresby, the colonial capital, Yali never lost his own form of immanentist perspective. In this way, he could be said to hold on, not just to his own particular form of sight but to the sight of his entire community and, in this way, preserve and even facilitate a more unencumbered form of that sight on a widespread basis.

In terms of that vision, it could be said that in Yali's case, we are seeing a different kind of disappointment. As someone who lived outside the European envelope of (faux) transcendental thought, he didn't need to be disappointed about the nonexistence of a transcendent heaven and all the rest; he was never going to believe in such places and things because his cosmology afforded no purchase for such ideas to take hold. His disappointment, and the disappointment of the community that he lived amid, was of a strictly pragmatic sort; they were told to expect a material reward and, when they figured out that it wasn't coming—wasn't imminent—they quickly got resentful and responded in kind.

In the Melanesian cosmology, sight and visuality played a much smaller role in terms of value and importance than it did in an archist context. In Yali's world, just because something could not be seen did not mean that it wasn't there. By the same token, just because something could be seen didn't mean that it was what you thought it was. Strathern tells the story of a man who saw someone who he thought resembled a dead relative of his and went up to him and asked, "Are you alive?" in all sincerity.[46] When the distinction is between visible and invisible instead of transcendent and immanent, a very different kind of political order results.

While it is true that Yali was not a perfect leader and did sometimes take advantage of his community, his "power" over them, such as it was, mainly just reflected the way that he allowed the people to readopt their own form of immanentist vision. The cargo beliefs constituted less a kind of materialist frenzy—which is how they are often depicted—and more a way to make sense of colonialism, a way to demand equal treatment from a system that was inherently, and archically, unjust.

Insofar as, as James Leach shows us, an ongoing devotion to immanentist forms of vision remains intact in at least some parts of Melanesia to this day, we can see the resilience of such forms of sight even without the concentrating aspect afforded by a figure like Yali. This also reveals once again the critical role of the archeon in Western forms of archism, the fact that it needs some place to issue from, a holy of holies from which it can regulate and judge the rest of the world. Since the deities of New Guinea are forced to share the Earth with the humans, plants, and animals who live there and since there is no magical space or time that is higher and better and truer than here and now, not even as a false screen that merely reflects the desires of the archon, archism once again itself has no secure place to issue from. Accordingly, it can rule and dominate but it can't insinuate itself into local communities the way that it can in many other places.

This difference can perhaps be seen most readily in the way that Nietzsche, for example, has to work so hard to achieve disappointment in the Western subject—raising and dashing hopes not just once and for all but over and over again—whereas such realizations come much easier and quicker in a place like New Guinea. Even if local people are initially attracted to the promises that are the hallmark of archism—promises of freedom, wealth, independence, even immortality—they are swiftly and readily let down when they see the obvious fact that the colonial regime (in this case) has no intention whatsoever of sharing its power or resources with Indigenous people.

Perhaps even more critically, the Melanesians' own cosmology meant that the greatest promise that archism makes, that of immortality, has no effect on them because, on their own terms, they already *are* immortal! Their own form of immortality, however, is not something bestowed on them by an almighty God or priest (or state) as with archism. It exists only in real space and in real time. It is up to the community itself, in this case, to carefully steward that immortality as a collective and anarchist practice; they need no externality to make this possible or to tell them how to do this. They must collectively see to their own intergenerational transmission of life, making their immortality their own, under their own control and responsibility and not subject to archist parasitism. Here, the greatest gift that archism promises has no seductive value. In this case, in trying to pitch a doctrine of immortality, the archists are engaged in the veritable act of trying to sell coal to Newcastle (only their "coal" is fake, while that of the Melanesians is very tangibly real).

Without the veil of archist transcendentalism, the Melanesians of Madang District and elsewhere in the Pacific were able to see quite clearly what archism is and what archism does. Is it any wonder then that their response to it is not "how can we subject ourselves to this?" but "how can we make this work for us, so that we can have what they have?" And, when that disappointment inevitably follows, it does not lead to thinking, "There is something wrong with me, I am not worthy of these rewards, apparently." Instead, the thinking is "I've been tricked. This is illicit power," with the requisite responses and results.

The case of Melanesian immanentism tells us that human beings, far from being fated to archism for all time, already have the means not to believe in its lies. While it may be the case that those of us who are not blessed with the belief systems of the Melanesians have a harder time escaping from archist logics, the very fact that there *is* an alternative, not just in theory but materially and on the Earth in real and ordinary time, suggests that we do not have to despair about archist power being as immortal as it claims to be. The Melanesian example shows that archism is in fact limited and not actually universal; in fact, it is not even global. And, insofar as one of the greatest conceits of archism is its omnipresence and eternity, the very fact that Melanesian immanentism—among other forms—represents a kind of island within the supposedly unbroken fabric of archist vision shows once again how vulnerable and parochial that power really is.

Frankenstein

Turning now to my literary treatments of the death of archism, in terms of the idea that immortality, archism's one greatest (and falsest) promise, can actually be achieved, we see a great contrast between Melanesian practices and what Mary Shelley describes in *Frankenstein*. Whereas the former is a practice of collective immortality making, akin to the forms of collective prophecy that I have been discussing throughout this book, in the latter we see Shelley, as it were, calling archism out on its bluff. That is, she looks directly at the challenge of making the archist promise of immortality come true and shows that even if that were technically to be achieved—as it is in that text—it would lead to nothing but more death and destruction, reflecting the violence, emptiness, and nothingness of archism itself. To challenge archism in this way is, I claim, to pose a challenge that goes beyond the kinds of threats that I detailed in the previous chapter. Those threats certainly take away key aspects of archist authority, but they do not cause its death (as the anarchist prophets that I described in that chapter have to live with the ongoing presence and threat of archism).[47] But to take away the promise of a life that surpasses ordinary human life is to show that archism really offers nothing at all, nothing, that is, that can't already be found in the world independently of its power and spectacle (as the Melanesian example suggests). Without this ultimate promise, archism can simply no longer survive, making the challenge of *Frankenstein* an exceptional and fundamental one.

The power of *Frankenstein* comes in part from the fact that it poses this ultimate threat while appearing to benignly and merely be part of a genre (one that Shelley arguably created, namely horror fiction). While *Franken-stein* is certainly a highly entertaining and suitably thrilling tale, for my own purposes what this novel achieves over all is the depiction of a catastrophic failure. This failure constitutes an inability to make the lies of archism, lies about transcendence, lies about immortality, and lies about the human ability to surpass their fleshy and mortal limits become true. The creature that lies at the heart of the novel may be a body that has been newly animated by science and technical wizardry, but it does not represent the kind of life beyond death that archism always promises. Or, perhaps more accurately, it *is* the achievement of that promise, and in that very "success" we see the death and faux existence of archism as such. While our attention might be drawn to the spectacular and dramatic aspects of that failure due to the power of Shelley's plot and writing, the failure itself is the key to understanding how this is a very subversive and radical text.

Maybe the first, albeit obvious, thing to say about *Frankenstein* is that it is a book about a monster. The Latin root word *monstrum*, from which the modern English term *monster* is derived, means a divine omen, a portent or sign similar to the modern French verb *montrer* (to show).[48] Although this term is often taken—as is usually the case with archist deities—as something terrifying and dangerous, portents do not have to be entirely caught up with such displays of overwhelming violence, power, and authority. Taking the concept of the monster in another sense, we could say that even as he is an avatar of archism, Frankenstein's monster is also a portent, that is, a prophet (and an anarchist one at that).

As such, for all the ways that the monster shares the fervent wish of his creator—Victor Frankenstein—to become immortal, thus fulfilling a promise of archism that had always in fact been a lie, and retroactively making it true after all, his very being betrays that wish. The monster's violence and ugliness may be horrible, but they also serve to dispel our own tendencies as archist subjects and readers to worship what we think is life but is actually only death. Manifesting the death that poses as life in the heart of archist phantasm, the monster shows, regardless of his own desires, how the path he represents is not only futile but disastrous. The monster is a warning; he is an avatar that reveals a fundamental truth about archism, that in its desire to export death to others, archism only ever becomes death itself. Insofar as even in its most secular guises, archism suggests the possibility of living forever if only by attachment to the undying—but also unliving—body of archism itself, the threat and the warning posed by the monster help us think further about both the vulnerability and, indeed, the mortality of archism along with the possibility of human life without its parasitic presence.

A Creature Who Wants Immortality

Frankenstein is a set of narrations, told mostly by Victor Frankenstein to Robert Walton. Walton is a man who is exploring the arctic wilderness and who stumbles upon Victor and thereby saves his life (at least for a moment). Near death, Victor recounts his whole life, including the fact that he was pursuing the monster he had brought "to life" in the first place into the wilderness for the purpose of destroying the creature once and for all. Victor tells Walton that when he first conceived of making a creature that would be immortal, he was full of joy. He felt that he was on the verge of making a radical departure from what had until then been an unavoidable human fate. He tells Walton: "Life and death appeared to me ideal bounds, which I should first break through, and pour a torrent of light into our dark world. A new species would bless me as its creator and source; many happy and excellent natures would owe their being to me. . . . Pursuing these reflections, I thought that if I could bestow animation upon lifeless matter, I might in the process of time (although I now found it impossible) renew life where death had apparently devoted the body to corruption."[49] This dream of a new race—one that is devoted to Victor—that has transcended death is not just Victor's. The monster too, even in the depth of his abjection, wants above all for Victor to make him a mate and to thereby inaugurate this new race (even if they can't procreate in the usual way that ordinary living humans can).

The conquest of death is critical to archism because death is seen in Western thought as the ultimate limit on human power and agency. As such, the promise of overcoming death literally (whether via Christian promises of an afterlife or, as we see today, with certain billionaires who want their brains frozen so that they can someday be revived) or metaphorically (partaking in some ongoing historical eschatology or taking part in some sovereign or national body politic) serves as the key by which archism both distinguishes itself from ordinary human life—at least in the West, which, unlike as with the Melanesians, does not see itself as being able to confer immortality—and shows that it has something indispensable to offer its subjects.

In making his creature, Victor chose only the most perfect body parts so that he would be both beautiful and superhuman. This fantasy held fast until the moment that the monster finally stirred to life, at which point Victor says: "I saw the dull yellow eye of the creature open. It breathed hard and a convulsive motion agitated its limbs."[50] It is as if, when the monster opens his eyes, Victor can finally see with his own eyes what he has done.

Horrified, Victor runs off, leaving the monster to his own devices and setting off a bitter struggle that occupies a great part of the book. The monster, searching for his lost father/creator, turns into a serial killer, first encountering and killing Victor's beloved younger brother and then framing a girl who is a dear family friend with the crime, before embarking on yet more murders, which include victims such as Victor's fiancée and his best friend, Henry Clerval. Those murders comprise the basic plot of the novel, culminating in the wild chase across the frozen arctic wilderness, which is when Victor meets Walton and narrates his tale.

In one of their few and unhappy conversations, the monster attests to his own inner goodness, as when he tells Victor, "Believe me, Frankenstein, I was [once] benevolent; my soul glowed with love and humanity."[51] He also speaks of his own servitude, his willingness to be an instrument of Victor's will if only Victor would treat him as he deserved: "I am thy creature, and I will be even mild and docile to my natural lord and king if thou wilt also perform thy part."[52]

A creature who is, in effect, made from death, the monster perhaps understands the desire to live, the basic promise that, in exchange for giving up your freedom, archism offers you the promise of life, possibly forever, more tangibly and palpably than others do. He therefore wants just what Victor wants, but he proves to be unable to fulfill their collective dream.

There are some basic aspects of the monster that make his fulfillment of this dream impossible. For starters, the monster is hideously ugly. Although Victor chose beautiful individual body parts, collectively they demonstrate not life but, in their very unnatural mismatching, the death that each of these body parts comes out of.[53] In a sense, the monster's face is a visual manifestation of the failure of the archist dream. His face is deeply disappointing precisely because it is real, tangible, and present, as opposed to the dreams that Victor conjures in his head. Perhaps more accurately, the monster's face is the true face of archism. It is not something of its own but a stitched-together hodgepodge of (once) living elements. It is not alive but more like undead, a parasitical and zombified characterization of life just as archism is more generally. The monster's ugliness is thus the ugliness of archism as such.

Through the monster, the various characters of the novel get to see a face that archism never wants to actually present. It is the greatest irony of this novel that the presentation of archism's true face only comes about through the attempt to make archism's lies real and tangible once and for all. This attempt has led to the subversion and ruin of precisely what it most sought to convey; the horror that the monster's face incites in others is the mark of their own inability to conquer death, their own submission to mortality. What was meant to be the proof of archism's power over life becomes instead the proof that life can never be more than it already is. The people who encounter the monster want to see *anything but that*.

In addition to being hideously ugly, the monster is also a murderer. As the murders pile up, the reader is increasingly disgusted and repelled by the monster despite his own beautiful and moving eloquence. And yet for all its horribleness, this repulsion also serves a function. It helps stop a tendency that we as readers might have to think, "If only Victor had somehow made a more beautiful monster. If only he had treated him differently." According to this logic—which is inherently archist—if we only got things right, then archism wouldn't be a lie after all (and everything that *does* go wrong isn't therefore archism's fault but only Victor's). By making it impossible for us to feel too much sympathy for the monster—and thus imagine that he deserves better than he gets—death becomes all too real, readily legible not only in his face but also in his murderous comportment, regardless of what he thinks or says.

In this way, once again the monster can't help but be a sign and avatar of death. The fact that he kills not just once but over and over again seems to be a reflection of this most basic fact of the monster's existence. Like the objects Benjamin discusses that are in constant rebellion against the categorizations that humans would put on them, the monster's murderousness defies any attempt—even on the monster's own part—that would signal anything but the death that he personifies and produces.

The Monster's Agency

Another way in which the monster suggests a subversion of fundamental archist norms comes from the fact that he is an agent in a way that Victor simply is not. More accurately, the monster is an agent at Victor's direct expense and, in fact, they appear to share a single agency that only one of them can exercise—almost always the monster—at any given time. Although the monster often complains that Victor holds all the cards and that he himself is a pure victim, we see that from the moment the monster opens his eyes, there is an effective transfer of agency from Victor to the monster himself. Victor's passivity from that moment on is itself monstrous. He does nothing except watch helplessly, albeit with a lot of fuming and self- and other recrimination, as the monster destroys his life as well as the life of his entire family.

One example of Victor's inordinate passivity comes when the monster kills his little brother and frames a family friend, Justine, for the murder. At her trial, which goes very badly, Victor watches in agony and does nothing, thinking, "The tortures of the accused did not equal mine; she was sustained by innocence but the fangs of remorse tore my bosom and would not forgo their hold."[54] The idea that Victor's suffering at this moment is worse than Justine's is grotesque, to put it mildly!

Another instance of this passivity comes when the monster, upon seeing Victor destroy his intended mate on the verge of bringing her to life, tells him, "I shall be with thee on thy wedding night."[55] Obsessed with himself as he is, Victor thinks this is a threat to his own life, whereas it is quite obvious—and the monster follows through on this—that the threat is to his fiancée, Elizabeth. Part of this portrayal of Victor's self-obsession may be Shelley's own vengeance against self-regarding men in her life (the introduction to *Frankenstein*, where she describes the origins of the story, wherein her husband, Percy Bysshe Shelley, and his close friend Lord Byron treat her as a junior partner—at best—is itself a masterpiece of subtle subversion of male privilege and ego). But I think this also speaks to the way that the monster and Victor share a single agency. Most of the time, it is Victor who is the passive one watching the monster blaze a trail of destruction, but at least at one moment, when Victor decides to destroy the female monster, it is the monster who watches helplessly in horror, who can do nothing but fume and feel sorry for himself.

If you think of Victor and the monster as sharing one self, one agency, you can see that whether the agent is Victor or the monster, they are always working to destroy the possibility of transcending death. That is, when the monster is the agent, he kills and destroys, rendering it impossible for the reader to see him as a source of hope for immortality. When Victor is the agent, he uses his agency to destroy the monster's mate, similarly ruining the dream of making archism truly transcendent and immortal.

If this argument is convincing, it amounts to using agency for a radically different purpose than what archism usually employs it for. The concept of human agency normally epitomizes the way that archism colonizes each of us with a kind of internal commander in chief who dominates all the variety of voices that constitute our interior self. As far as that agent relates to other external persons, they are said to be entirely autarkic, venturing into the world to extend their internal colonization outward to encompass other, lesser people. In the case of *Frankenstein*, however, we see that agency serves to unmake that very conquest, particularly when it comes to the all-important conquest of death. Even the idea of two persons sharing one agency is a subversion of the notion of the autonomous self that Locke—a supreme archist if anyone is—promotes. Rather than determining, as an archist standpoint would insist, who is the master and who is the slave, we can see *Frankenstein* as an anarchistic subversion of this kind of contest so that in effect the question is rendered moot.

If the monster and Victor share one agency, then they also in effect share one prophetic function. In terms of how they respectively see things, it is worth repeating that Victor's archist phantasm of defeating death ended the moment the monster opened his eyes. Victor was, in effect, seeing through the monster's eyes, as it were, what he had actually created, not a life beyond death but only more death, as archism is wont to do.

Even as he serves to undermine it, Victor is never quite released from the spell of archism, although he does come to recognize it for what it is. When he first meets Walton and hears of Walton's own desire to conquer the Arctic, his response is "Unhappy man! Do you share my madness? Have you drunk also of the intoxicating draught? Hear me: let me reveal my tale, and you will dash the cup from your lips!"[56] In this way, Victor's shared vision with the monster puts him in a worst of both worlds situation; he seeks the delusion but he also sees it for what it is and what it costs him.

Victor's insight affords the reader some insight as well. Because the novel is dictated retroactively, we always see Victor's archist phantasms as just that, a form of mania. In this case, his mania lies in insisting that what is clearly false is actually true (even when he knows better, the precise condition of archist subjugation).

By planting a self-proclaimed madman at the heart of the archist project—not to mention as the one who is nominally responsible for its ultimate fulfillment—Shelley has, in effect, had her revenge on a system that would relegate her to the sidelines.[57] Perhaps just as powerfully as producing a vision of God—as Nietzsche, Benjamin, and Butler have done—who is an anarchist and who unravels the archist phantasm from its theological roots, Shelley has set science and its claim to empirical reality against itself. The man who conquers death is also the one who shows that this conquest, even if "real" in a technical sense—that is, real within the bounds of the story, real as a phantasm among other phantasms—serves to undermine a deeper form of perceived reality, the claim to ontology and the reconfiguration of temporality that would finally render archism (retroactively) natural and eternal.

In ruining that possibility, at least in the confines of this story, Shelley has offered us a vision of how archism can be defeated at its very heart, how it might be able to die—or, more accurately, to show that it has never been alive—once and for all.

The Leftovers: The End of Archism and the "Sudden Departure"

If *Frankenstein* shows that archism can be robbed of its chief feature, the promise of immortal life—that is, the achievement of transcendence after all—another literary and filmic treatment, *The Leftovers*, goes a step further and imagines the end of archism altogether.

The Leftovers, which is the title of a book by Tom Perrotta and a television series of the same name on HBO—the latter of which extends the narrative well past the confines of Perrotta's original novel—offers us a unique vision of the ultimate demise of archism, at least as ultimate as possible within a system that does not necessarily allow things to stay dead forever.

Let me begin an exploration of *The Leftovers* by giving a sense of its basic plot. The premise of both the novel and the TV show is that on one particular day, at one particular moment (October 14, year not specified), 2 percent of the world's population—140 million people in all—suddenly disappeared on the spot in what comes to be called the "Sudden Departure." People were there one moment and in the next they were gone. There was no forewarning of the Sudden Departure and definitely no explanation that followed. It just happened.

The advent of the Sudden Departure does more than just pose an existential threat to archism. In a sense, it simply does archism in. On the secular side of things, there is no way to understand this event. There is no possible scientific explanation for what happened. Worse yet, scientists of the day—it is set in contemporary times—can't promise that this mysterious force won't return to carry off others, or perhaps even get rid of everyone.

By the same token, religion has nothing to say about the Sudden Departure either, although this is not for a lack of trying. There are multiple attempts by Christians to read this event as the rapture, for example. Yet it seems quite clear that this is *not* the rapture; good people and bad people alike are taken away indiscriminately (celebrity departures range from Jennifer Lopez to Pope Benedict to Gary Busey). The Sudden Departure makes no sense from a theological perspective. It cannot be explained away as some mysterious plan of God; it is just too awful, too devastating, and too random to be something that any deity would actually do (even one who works in mysterious ways).

Without these bases in secular and theological power, archism loses it spectacular authority. It's as if the great eye that has watched over the world all this time has withdrawn itself, no longer holding the rest of us in its gaze. To be sure, the power of archism doesn't disappear all at once. In *The Leftovers* there are still states and political systems and laws, but they are all depicted as being on the verge of collapse.

The show focuses on the effect of the Sudden Departure on one family originally based in the town of Mapleton, New York. The father, Kevin Garvey, is the sheriff (in the book, he's the mayor). His children, Jill and Tommy, are lost and broken and his wife, Laurie, leaves him to join a cult. As paterfamilias and as representative of the law, Kevin affords us a unique point of view, an eyewitness account of the collapse of so many of the assumptions that come with having an archeon.

In the absence of the normal assurances of archist forms of authority, numerous cults spring up. The most significant cult in *The Leftovers* is called the Guilty Remnant, a group devoted to pointing out to others that the world—in other words, archism—has already ended (this is the group that Laurie joins, although she later turns against them). The members of the Guilty Remnant wear only white, smoke cigarettes constantly—by mandate; nonsmoking is not tolerated—and don't speak. Members of the GR, as they are known, plot endlessly to ruin any attempts to lead a normal life. The whole idea of a "new normal" is palpably impossible. How can anything ever be normal ever again after what happened?

One key target of the Guilty Remnant is Nora Durst, who is infamous for having lost all three members of her family (her husband and two kids). This is considered to be exceptionally unlucky since the number of departed is relatively few and randomly distributed. Nora is initially depicted as a deeply broken woman. She neurotically replaces over and over the exact same paper towels, cereal boxes, and other quotidian items that her family was using the day they disappeared. She hires a prostitute to shoot her in the chest while she is wearing a bullet-proof vest, and she carries a gun in her purse. She seems desperate to feel things but is not sure what those feelings could or should be.

At one point, Nora becomes Kevin's love interest, and together they try to forge a new family and a new way of life that reproduces as much as possible whatever normal means for each of them. In a way, Nora and Kevin are a perfect couple insofar as they are equally broken, but they end up taking very different paths to try to come to terms with what has happened.

Many Ways of Seeing

After the Sudden Departure, the human population as a whole is subjected to a vast breakdown in belief structures, leading to a radical instability in their forms of vision. At one point, Nora, who is employed by the Department of Sudden Departures—an agency that gives compensation to people who lost relatives—goes to a conference on the Sudden Departure in New York City. There, she hears a priest, who is giving a talk, describe what he calls the "Prophet's Dilemma." He says:

> For most of humankind's existence certain individuals have come across as self-professed interpreters of the world's mysteries. But what happens when those conversations with God go wrong? Following a catastrophic event or circumstance, let alone one that defies scientific explanation, the incidents of prophetic delusion rise dramatically. It's not just megalomaniacs who make the news for a week. This is happening to our friends, our neighbors, our own families. This belief that a higher power is speaking to us whether through dreams or science, even voices, is a powerful coping mechanism and, if left unchecked, is a very dangerous one.[58]

Here, we see that in effect, in the wake of the Sudden Departure, everyone has become a prophet and in so doing, prophecy itself has become a dangerous and destabilizing form of sight. Rather than ordering and preserving hierarchy—by returning that community to "purity" and "truth"—such acts of prophecy are a sign of the breakdown of all those things. This could be seen as a kind of transition stage from archism to anarchism as a dominant mode of seeing and thinking because it has elements of both. It is at once collective and divided; it represents both the requirement to see *something*, to be authorized by *someone*, even as it breaks that authorization and sight into an infinite number of mutually contradictory pieces.

In a way then, the world described in *The Leftovers* is the worst of both worlds in the sense that it still requires determination but finds none at all (not unlike the position that Victor Frankenstein finds himself in). Yet, for all of this, in the morass created by the Sudden Departure, collective and anarchic networks, increasingly unburdened by archist competition, start to become a bit more visible. It is certainly true that the communities of the world—at least those depicted in Mapleton, New York, and later in Jarden, Texas, where the family moves in season 2 of the TV show—are not in the habit of recognizing their own collective and horizontal forms of authority, not to mention other, more local, forms of law and life practices. But even if it is not recognized, we see that, despite their best effort, these characters fail to reproduce the old "normal," which suggests that new forms of seeing lead to new forms of life as well. These other forms require some time to fully emerge from their deep interconnection with archism. Yet, bereft of the overall guidance provided by *the* point of view afforded by archism, there is in some sense no avoiding the novelty and experimentation of form that archism always warns and guards against.

Kevin: Law and the Collapse of Archist Perspective

In all this chaos and madness, the law suffers along with everything else in the post-Departure world. Like a dinosaur that dies but takes a long time to realize it, the law continues to function—at least sort of—well after the Sudden Departure (the TV series begins three years after the event). Even in the beginning of the show, when Kevin is the sheriff of Mapleton, New York, it is easy to see that he is losing his grip on things very quickly. Like the blind accountant in *Blindness*, Kevin has to resort more and more to pulling out his gun to get order. The usual deference to a person in uniform seems to be increasingly becoming a thing of the past.

As already noted, with Kevin as a central character, and thereby serving to some extent as the foil for the audience too, we get a sense of the collapse of the archeon and the perspective that it offers, not just for the subjects who live in its shadow but from within the archeon itself, among its employees and enforcers. Kevin is the chief of police, but he *knows*—and so the viewers know as well—that the power of the law is entirely hollow.

There is a theological dimension to this exposure of hollowness as well. As the TV series progresses, it becomes weirder and more mystical, perhaps because the sense of what is normal and ordinary, a major aspect of sustaining archism, has started to unravel. Kevin appears to die on three separate occasions over the course of the series, each time being magically revived. Toward the end of the series, he is considered a messianic figure by a small band of devotees (in their frenzy to be saved by a man who can be raised from the dead, they kill another sheriff who also happens to be named Kevin, a horrible case of mistaken identity gone awry). Yet, even as he knows that the law is empty, Kevin also *knows* that he is not a messiah (at one point, he tells his would-be followers, "I'm not fucking Jesus").[59] Rather than being someone who fulfills the law and the expectation for salvation, Kevin occupies that position and renders it—and we see him rendering it by sharing his viewpoint—null and void.

Even Kevin's experience of the afterlife reinforces this disappointment. The afterlife looks like an anodyne hotel complete with muzak and his-and-her guest bathrobes. There's nothing special about the transcendent realm. Indeed, it isn't really different from the Earth itself; at one point, while he's "dead," Kevin leaves the hotel and drives home, suggesting that "heaven," if that is what it should be called, is an exact duplicate of ordinary life.

This is another marker of the radical nature of this show; as with Nietzsche's idea of eternal recurrence, in *The Leftovers* too, the afterlife, other worlds, or any other way to transcend or replace our all-too-human life is rendered equally mortal, fallible, and ordinary and thus no escape at all. To the transcendent worlds that archism imagines, *The Leftovers* answers with a healthy dose of its own peculiar brand of immanentism.

The Leftovers undermines all these possibilities even as it also undermines our sense of the authority of narration itself. Many of the strangest things that happen in the show occur after Kevin goes to sleep (for a while, Nora takes to handcuffing him to her in order to keep him from wandering around in his sleep). We are never 100 percent sure if the fugue states that Kevin falls into are actually happening, if he really did die and really did get resurrected, not to mention the visions of the afterlife that we are shown.

While it is true that a great many works of film and literature use this device—the unreliable narrator is one version—these depictions generally occur in a universe where the larger norm, the archist position, remains intact. Accordingly, any transgression of orthodox boundaries generally pertains only to that character or to her context. In *The Leftovers*, the destruction of that archeonic perspective makes this unreliability infinitely more transgressive because there is no longer a "big other" to guarantee the order of the universe in the face of these kinds of subversions, making the resulting disappointment all the stronger.

We see a very similar dynamic afoot in terms of the authority of the law in ways that go beyond Kevin's own perspective. Throughout the series, we occasionally get a glimpse of higher-up workings of the law and how it is rapidly deteriorating. Kevin's superiors are utterly uninterested when he is accused of killing Patty, one of the local leaders of the Guilty Remnant. They take him in for questioning but even when he admits his crime, he is told to go home and forget about it. The police as a whole simply mow down members of this cult, among others, whenever and wherever they encounter them.

This might not, at first glance, look like a good thing, much less a subversive one; after all, police favoritism toward their own, vigilantism, and a disregard for the very laws that authorize them are hardly new practices. The incessant killing of unarmed Black and Brown people in the United States by police is one key example of how the practice of law is always far more violent, racist, and chaotic than the law imagines or purports itself to be. Yet it shows that when the police, and in particular the higher-ups who deal with law on a national level, stop believing in the law—don't recognize the way that the law has never been anything but their whim and their personal exercise of power—law's ability to sustain itself becomes highly unstable.

While the concept of rule of law is almost entirely empty, as with other aspects of archism, its mere symbolic existence has a critical effect on its constituents. Even the most corrupt, violent, and racist of police might believe that even if *they* aren't practicing the law properly, somewhere in the world—or more accurately outside the world—there *is* law, there is the transcendent truth that the archeon instantiates. It is in fact that belief that might allow them to violate the law in the first place, because if the law exists somewhere else—even if only in the noumenal realm—then it isn't their duty to uphold it; the law as such exists independently from human actions so their own corruption can't ruin it. Without such a position for law, it becomes each person's and each collectivity's responsibility to not only uphold but to determine the law (or not), and in this way, law changes from an archist to an anarchist formulation.

Accordingly, whether in terms of the practice of law or the narrative structure of the TV show, or pretty much any other way that authority and human relationships are narrated, the dissolution of the archeon depicted in *The Leftovers* changes everything (and it furthermore changes things whether the persons involved like it or not, and they definitely do not).

Nora: Choosing Disappointment

Kevin's descent into madness and passivity suggests the death of archism unleashed by the Sudden Departure. But what about the anarchism that follows? To discuss this in more detail, I need to shift focus from Kevin to Nora. Ultimately, it is she and not he who shows us a way beyond archism. Nora starts out in *The Leftovers* as a deeply wounded and lost person. When she begins to date Kevin, his daughter, Jill, is instantly suspicious. She thinks Nora is a liar—she lies about having a gun in her purse, for instance—and a phony more generally. And Jill is onto something. Nora's whole life is based on a lie, the idea that somehow if she does everything exactly the same way she did when her family was still with her, if she leads a small, rigid, and entirely circumscribed life—with occasional visits to an armed prostitute—she might just win her family back.

But Nora is also desperate and, as such, she is not immune to the lures of the many cults and belief systems that are flooding the world. At one point, she pays a lot of money to a prophet named "Holy Wayne," who "hugs your pain [i.e., the pain inflicted by the Sudden Departure] away" (she does feel relieved, but the effect only lasts for a short while). Toward the end of the series, Nora begins to get calls from a group of people claiming that they can reunite her with her family. This is not the first such call that she has received; every past call turned out to be a ridiculous hoax. The viewer can tell that Nora is highly skeptical of this new invitation as well. Yet she wants her family back so badly that all her rationalism can't prevent her from wanting these frauds to turn out to be true after all.

When this particular group asks her to turn up in a hotel in Melbourne, Australia, with $20,000 in cash, she says yes right away. She convinces her highly skeptical boss that the purpose of her trip is to bust a ring of scam artists (that is part of her job as well). At the last minute, Kevin asks to come with her to Australia and she allows it, setting into motion the events that lead to the ending of *The Leftovers*.

Once in Melbourne, Nora meets with the people who've been calling her. They seem relatively harmless and very much on the level. They say they have the means to pass her over to whatever other dimension or space the departed now find themselves in. Over time it becomes clear that Nora fully intends to take them up on their offer. She is prepared to risk even death if there is a chance that she might "go through," as they put it, to wherever her husband and children have gone. The actual process involves being potentially drowned in a small chamber that fills with some sort of fluid. She goes into the capsule and screams as the fluid fills up beyond her head.

That is all we know for a while, but in the final episode of season 3, the finale for the whole series, all is explained—at least sort of (what follows is definitely a spoiler). We see an older version of Nora who looks really sad and worn, living a very lonely and isolated life in the middle of nowhere in Australia. Kevin somehow manages to track her down, and after much reluctance, she tells him everything.

As Nora and Kevin sit down to finally talk, she begins one of the most compelling narratives that I have ever seen on television as she explains what happened to her after she entered the chamber. She tells Kevin that after she "went through," she came out in the same parking lot that she went into but there were no cars there. The same landscape was there but most of it was derelict. After a lot of wandering, she came to a house with a man and a woman inside and this is what she found: "They were kind and they told me . . . that seven years earlier he was in a supermarket and every single person disappeared except for him. And the woman told me she lost her husband, her three daughters, and all eight of her grandchildren, and that's when I understood. Over here we lost some of them but over there they lost all of us."[60]

Here, we finally learn the big secret of what happened to the departed. For them, the same thing happened at the same exact time but in vastly bigger numbers. It turns out that the world we have been experiencing, Kevin and Nora's world, is the lucky one. The other world, where all but 2 percent of the human population (that is, 98 percent of everybody) vanish in an instant, is virtually, but not entirely, wiped out.

The beauty of this answer is that it is not an answer at all. We now know what happened to the departed, but it doesn't in any way address the bigger question of how or why it happened. Furthermore, by appearing to figure out what happened, Nora effectively blocks any chance for a fuller resolution exactly because her "going through" to the other side and finding only more of the same—not unlike Kevin's explorations of the afterlife—shows us a version of Nietzsche's eternal recurrence, where other worlds and lives are just like the one the subject is trying to escape from (in this case, the "other world" is actually quite a bit worse). Without hope for some big solution or discovery, Nora is forced to reckon with the situation at hand.

And reckon she does. Others in the show have also "gone through" (among other people, the actor Mark Linn-Baker of *Perfect Strangers* fame is also said to have done so). But Nora *is* unique in one way. As far as we know, she is the only one who went to another world and then came back to her own.[61] In her discourse with Kevin, Nora explains that after great effort, she made her way from Australia back to the Mapleton, New York, of the world of the departed. Finally she came to her house, the house that she lived in with her husband and two children. At that point, she describes the following:

When I got there, I stood by a tree and waited because I was too scared to go up there and knock. And after a while the door opened. At first I didn't recognize them. A tall teenage boy with curly hair and a girl, maybe eleven. They were my children. And then my husband came out and he was with a woman. She was pretty. She was pretty and they were all smiling.

They were happy. And I understood that here in this place they were the lucky ones. In a world full of orphans, they still had each other. And I was a ghost. I was a ghost who had no place there. And that, Kevin, is when I changed my mind.[62]

What does Nora mean when she says she changed her mind? In changing her mind, she finally accepts that archism, that salvational perspective, is no more, along with all the disappointment that such a realization creates for her. In fact, I would go further and say that Nora *chooses* her disappointment, something else no other character on the show is able to do. This too has a Nietzschean aspect to it, akin to *amor fati*, the love of one's fate. Rather than continuing to rail against a universe that seems to have wronged her, Nora chooses to be what she is: disappointed, abandoned, bereft. Having gone through to the other side—in an almost perfect rendition of what Lacan calls traversing the fantasy to discover its ultimate emptiness—Nora knows for sure that that is all she'll ever get, and she makes her peace with such a realization.

Having come back, Nora doesn't necessarily know what to do with her newfound freedom. She tells Kevin that she thought of him often but was worried that after so much time had passed—time seems to move at the exact same speed on the other world as it does on ours, and she spent years there before she was able to return—he wouldn't be able to forgive her. She also says she was afraid that he wouldn't believe her, to which he replies:

"I believe you."
"You do?" she asks.
"Why wouldn't I believe you? You're here."
"I'm here," she agrees, with tears streaming down her face (and his), the last line of the series.[63]

When Nora first heard Kevin was looking for her, she was terrified and spoke to him only with the greatest reluctance. It seems clear that she doesn't want to go back to her earlier life if it would destroy her new resolve, if it would get her to change her mind back again and begin to hope and regret—and worst of all be moved once again to pity, mostly of herself—all over again. In other words, the thought of having to go back to being a subject of the archist gaze has gone from being a comfort to a source of terror; now she sees that gaze for what it is, what it has always been. As sad and lonely—and disappointed!—as her new life is, she still clearly prefers it to the old life that was all based on lies.

We don't know what is going to happen next. Perhaps she will return with Kevin to Jarden. Perhaps she won't. But what we do know is that Nora is perhaps the first and so far only member of the human race who looked heaven in the eye and turned the other way; in a sense, at least among Western subjects of archism, she is the first true a-theist (and maybe, by the same token, the first full-on an-archist, the first to fully break with what anarchism has long struggled with). It's possible that Kevin will follow suit and perhaps many others as well, but I'm not sure that this makes Nora an anarchist prophet so much as it suggests that the need for such prophecy has finally ended since people and communities now have no choice but to see what they see and decide upon what that sight means for themselves.

The End of Externality

What Nora has finally given up on—and we can see the huge cost and struggle that such a giving up entails—is externality itself as a source of validation and truth. In some sense, you could say that externality, the black box that has supported illicit forms of authority throughout the history of archism, is suddenly shown to have a mind, and an agenda, of its own. From that very void comes an event that effectively deauthorizes everything that has ever been done or said in its name, as if the void itself is getting revenge for the endless personifications that it has been forced to endure.

In this way, it could be said that the Sudden Departure is the ultimate anarchist event. If I were going to picture what a Benjamin-style act of divine violence might look like in our own time, the Sudden Departure would be a great example. It is an act that destroys all false authorizations, but in doing so it also ensures that its own manifestation does not lead to new myths that would otherwise inevitably follow such a visible act of supernatural power. If there is a God in *The Leftovers*, that deity is determined to rule herself out of the world, or perhaps more accurately—like the Melanesian deities and Spinoza's God—to rule herself *only* within the world and share its materialism and determination along with the rest of us. If there is such a God, she is definitely an anarchist. Radically withdrawing her viewpoint from the world so that it becomes unavailable for human actors to hijack it and claim it as their own, this God serves to actualize and enable all those perspectives that are normally eclipsed and superseded by archist forms of vision, allowing for other forms of visuality, as well as other senses more generally to come into their own.

If Nora's own disappointment seems unbearable to us, that might be because we still haven't given up on the dream that archism promises us.

Nora has given up on that dream; it was offered to her—she was given a chance, not only to "know" the truth but also possibly to join that other worldly realm—and she refused it. She shows that such a refusal can be done *voluntarily*—not just accidentally as it is for the other characters in *The Leftovers*—and perhaps that is all we need to know in the end in order to be able to challenge archism at its very core.

Life without the Archeon

In the various descriptions that I have made in this chapter, we see different iterations of the possibility of life without the archeon, that is, an anarchist life that is freed, at last, from its archist parasite. While, despite Ramnath's excellent advice, it might still seem strange to apply the word *anarchism*, for example, to a form of Melanesian life that predates Bakunin and others by several thousand years, I want to recognize a pattern of living that is oriented not toward the beyond, the transcendental, the unknown—that is, at least in its Western form, an orientation toward nothingness, toward nihilism and death with a commensurate focus on violence and destruction—but toward the kind of immanentism that I have been discussing here: the present, the local, and life itself. A focus on life instead of death recuperates what I have been calling the anarchist life that we are already living (or perhaps, in the case of Melanesia, the immanentist life that they have always led).

We see elements of this life in all the works that I have studied in this book but maybe particularly so when the end of archism becomes *imaginable*, when, rather than having to learn how to live with it, we can think of life without it. We see it in Spinoza's understandings of bodies and of a God who lives only inside our own universe and thus shares a quality that all things share. We see it too in the robust life of the inhabitants of the Rai Coast of New Guinea that were able to some extent to stand up to the predations of archist colonization and rearrange the elements of archist phantasm to come up with their own understandings and explanations that were antithetical to the archist projection of reality. We see this quality even in as horrible a story as *Frankenstein*, in small moments such as the famous scene where the monster meets De Lacy, a blind man who treats him well and humanely—at least until his sighted family comes in, sees him, and starts to scream—or even in the strange intimacy and shared agency that develop between the monster and Victor despite their deep hatred of one another. We see this finally, in *The Leftovers* too, in the sad but free life that Nora lives once she chooses to turn her back on archist promises.

Although anarchist life happens all the time, I think it changes when it is relieved of its archist entanglements, experiencing what Benjamin would call a "slight adjustment."[64] To return to the question of law as one example—thinking again of Kevin Garvey and his experience as a sheriff in a world that survives the death of archism—law under archist conditions is always referring itself to externalities, whether nature, God, or the stance of a "rational actor," but in fact it is always practiced at the ground level. This is why Benjamin says the police are always a manifestation of law that is far more violent and arbitrary than law imagines itself to be.[65] Part of that violence might be due to the fact that those who "lay down the law" can do so in the comfort of knowing that no matter how much they kill and brutalize in the name of the law, the law itself remains safely ensconced in its noumenal form. It can't be threatened even by the most egregious violations of actual legal violence even though "the law" as such only actually exists via those practices.

But if that safeguard is removed, then law becomes something else entirely. Law becomes only its practice (a "pure means"), and, as such, the responsibility for creating the law rests on each practitioner, both as individuals and as members of a community. This is something that Benjamin anticipates when he writes that even the Commandment "Thou Shalt Not Kill" cannot be taken as an absolute—and hence transcendent—command insofar as "it exists not as a criterion of judgment, but as a guideline for the actions of persons or communities who have to wrestle with it in solitude and, in exceptional cases, to take on themselves the responsibility of ignoring it."[66]

Benjamin's passage tells us what law *always* is, even when it is practiced under archist conditions. Law is never actually about some absolute outside as much as it insists that it is. As long as it is deemed to be so, it continues to invite the privileged to interject their own agenda into the place of the archeon. But without that device, the question of law ceases to be "what does the law command me to do?" and it becomes instead "what will I, along with my fellow community members, decide to do?" People can no longer kill because they believe that they are commanded by God, nature, the state, or a "reason" to do so. That judgment and responsibility is on each of us and on all of us together, and, as such, it becomes something radically different.

Another major change without the archeon comes in the nature of subjectivity. In a previous writing, I speculated that the self at our core is itself anarchist, that there is not one true self to organize the rest of us but rather a plethora of selves, a vast and overlapping anarchist interiority that also binds us to a much larger set of anarchist selves that form the basis of horizontal forms of collective authorization.[67] This is the self that Nora has encountered and has chosen to be, not an "authentic" or true being but someone who sees from her own multiple perspectives. Having turned her back on archism—and, in the original German of the passage cited above, Benjamin does not say that we "ignore" the Commandment but that sometimes we actually turn our back (*abzusehen*) on it as well—Nora is no longer determined by what she is not and can begin to be what she is, whatever that may be.[68] And, although Nora seems radically alone, she is herself containing multiple selves and many voices. Nora holds within herself, therefore, that vast anarchist network that can always be extended to others, although I would hasten to add that an anarchism consisting of just one person operates more on the psychic than on the political level. And Nora is just one example of this possibility. While the example of a shared agency between Victor and the monster might seem horrible, we can say that when archism is removed, such overlapping of selves may look—and feel, sound, smell, and taste—quite different as well.

I would suggest that without the colonizations and interpellations that archism foists on us, we would occupy our own anarchic selves in utterly different ways. Without the burden of finding out who we "really are" or having to follow a moral law that is really just, as Lacan notes, a form of sadism, we have the distinct pleasure of "becoming who we are," as Nietzsche so beautifully put it. And not just who we are as a separate person but also who we are as a person among other persons. This in turn suggests a radically different form of politics, not so much in the sense that we would have to start all over again—because as I've been saying throughout this book, we are already all living anarchist lives whether we realize it or not—but more in the sense that our experience and occupation of that form of life would be radically changed, given the critical shifts of perspective that it would entail.

The Leftovers does not definitively answer the question for us of what life is when it is relieved of its archist parasite, but even by giving us a scenario where such a thing is possible, it suggests a direction for thinking further. And the fact that this planet has myriad traditions—Melanesian immanentism very much included—that are, if not anarchist in the usual, Eurocentric sense of the term, then at least not archist, shows that human life is not fated to be always determined and read by and through archist forms of vision. Maybe the most important fact in this regard is to think that *archism didn't need to happen at all*. To say that we are not fated to always bear it means that its own origins are equally unfated. Archism as we know it—that is, the virulent Western model that took over much of the rest of the world—can be seen as a horrible accident of history rather than as a fated manifestation of progress. In this way, we can without danger return it to the void from which it came and the sooner, the better!

conclusion

beyond
anarchist prophets

HAVING LAID OUT A SERIES OF ARGUMENTS for and examples and imaginations of an anarchist politics, as well as a series of anarchist prophets to help facilitate its visibility to the rest of us, the most pressing question of all still remains: What does all of this have to do with contemporary politics, with the question of what is possible or, to cite Vladimir Lenin, "What is to be done?"[1]

In order to think more specifically about this question, I focus in this concluding chapter on the advantages that anarchism already has over its archist parasite. Chief among these is the fact that anarchism is simply another word for life in all its complex, nonharmonious, messy, and ordinary glory. Accordingly, unlike archism, which must always be reinventing itself as it engages with and mimics what it parasitizes, anarchism is continually engaged in a practice of self-development that is part and parcel of itself. It does not need to learn anything from beyond itself. It does not need to reinvent human nature or start from scratch. It must instead come to see itself for what it is—even as it also sees archism for what it is—in order to realize the full extent of its own power. In thinking further about Benjamin's understanding of a "slight adjustment" as a mode of revolutionary—and messianic—change, merely shifting focus from archist to anarchist forms of vision and judgment brings us a long way toward realizing how much power already lies with the anarchist community, and how little power actually lies with the archons themselves. This is not to say that this adjustment is easy; the real-life examples that I have supplied show the intense violence and exploitation that archism practices against anarchist life. But this is where anarchist prophecy comes most into the fore; as I see it, insofar as archism has stolen our power, our voice, our very life from us, anarchist prophets are the ones who can help us steal it back.

Even so, in addition to sketching out the way that anarchist prophets can help us take advantage of the asymmetries that favor anarchism over archism, I also focus on the ways that we can and must move on from the requirement of anarchist prophecy at the end of the day. If it is possible for archism to die, then it is also not only possible but necessary to move on from anarchist prophecy to make way for the anarchism of the living, of whom the anarchist prophet is just a small part. It is possible for the anarchist prophet to overstay her welcome. When she becomes a risk of further incipient archism, the anarchist prophet cannot remain (just as Moses once again was not, in the end, allowed to go to the promised land).

To think further about these questions, this final chapter is also in four parts. I look first at the question of authority: where it comes from and how it can be reappropriated from archism. I then turn to an elaboration of my earlier claims that the universe itself is anarchist in some sense, offering how archism is always swimming against the stream in its attempts to control and dominate the world. Then I look at the ubiquity of anarchist life, offering three more brief examples of anarchist practices and prophecy in the works of José Carlos Mariátegui, Emma Goldman, and Frantz Fanon and their own enmeshment within a larger form of anarchist life. Finally, I turn to a consideration of the role that anarchist prophecy plays in the life of anarchism, how it both partakes of that life and how it is, in some sense, set apart, as well as how we can and must ultimately dispense with it so that it does not itself become an agent for the reintroduction of archism (a possibility that we can never assume out of existence).

Authority and Trust

In terms of thinking about the possibility of an untrammeled anarchist life, one of the chief stumbling blocks that archism puts before anarchism is that of authority. In Machiavelli's telling of Numa's story of fabricating an encounter with a goddess who gave him the laws for Rome, we see a claim—one that Machiavelli may actually be challenging by revealing the law's false origins—that people can't believe in something of their own devising. Trust in one another can only come, this (archist) theory holds, when some externality holds everyone in its gaze, favoring—the story goes—no one and thus serving as an objective and neutral criterion for judgment. The fact that this arrangement is patently false does not in and of itself suggest that there is an alternative. Liberalism's answer has always been, yes, our society is unfair, but that is not liberalism's fault. Racist cops are bad apples, the poor are lazy, some billionaires are jerks (but most aren't), and so on. The gaze, the source of the archeon itself, is never at fault—how could it be? it is transcendent and perfect by definition!—it is always the all-too-human practitioners who dole out its authority who must be the problem. This conclusion in turn only reinforces the basic premise of archism, that human beings are hopelessly flawed and generally incompetent—even the ones who represent the state/the law, etcetera—and thereby require the very transcendence that archism promises but never delivers. Archism in all of its forms will always peddle what might be called a human deficiency model, the idea that people as themselves are always inadequate, untrustworthy, and fickle, requiring and justifying the plethora of administrators, managers, elected (and nonelected) representatives, and so forth that archism so readily supplies. And, when we see ourselves through archism's eyes (as we are commanded to do), we too take on this model, assuming our own deficiency, our own untrustworthiness, without the guidance of those who are above us.

The key question then becomes, how can people learn to trust themselves after all? How can we see that authority can come from within a community as well as without? One perhaps unexpected source for the claim that communities produce their own versions of authority can be found once again in Hobbes. In *Leviathan*, Hobbes famously tells us that the people are authors of sovereign power. He writes: "Of Persons Artificiall, some have their words and actions *Owned* by those whom they represent. And then the Person is the *Actor*; and he that owneth his words and actions, is the AUTHOR: In which case the Actor acteth by Authority. . . . So the right of doing any Action, is called AUTHORITY and sometimes *warrant*. So that by Authority, is always understood a Right of doing any act: and *done by Authority*, done by Commission, or Licence from him whose right it is."[2] As Hanna Pitkin notes, many readers, probably most, have read this claim, thinking it is somehow a trick.[3] The assumption here is that Hobbes doesn't really mean what he says, that he is only telling us that people are authors so that people can't complain when the sovereign does whatever it pleases, exercising a public authorization that cannot be revoked or altered. Hobbes does in fact go on to write, "From hence it followeth, that when the Actor maketh a Covenant by Authority, he bindeth thereby the Author, no lesse than if he had made it himselfe; and no lesse subjecteth him to all the consequences of the same," seemingly confirming this impression.[4]

Even so, based on some of the arguments that I made in chapter 2, I think it is possible to argue that this is not a trick after all (Pitkin makes a nuanced claim to this effect herself). Or, perhaps more accurately if it is a trick, the joke may just be on the sovereign rather than on the rest of us. After all, it is Hobbes himself who demonstrates the way that it is human beings in all their variety and number who produce the bases of meaning and judgment, which effectively bind the sovereign before it can come to its own "decision."[5] This prior form of authorization is, just as Hobbes suggests, the basis for any authority that the sovereign itself may lay claim to.

In thinking about this situation, it might seem as if there are at least two kinds of authority to go with two kinds of power, archist and anarchist, already described. There seems to be vertical authority, that which is ascribed to the sovereign and to archism more generally, and horizontal authority, that which is generated by the people themselves. However, there is in fact only one kind of authority. Archist forms of authority are merely stolen aspects of collective authority. Archism is unable to truly generate its own authority because it is not alive; it does not partake in the deep-rooted and rich variety of human life and so cannot generate anything out of that life either. It can only rule with an authority that it has stolen from the true "authors," the people in all their variety. Yet, in doing so, archism takes care to delegitimize the true source of its power and claim that it and it alone holds that kind of authority. This is one of the ways that Hobbes can be really subversive because even his claim that the people are "authors" comes dangerously close to acknowledging this basic fact of politics. For this reason, when its own form of authority is put into any kind of question, archism quickly turns to violence, a sign of its own inherent illegitimacy.

Archism is always telling us that were it not for itself, we would all be running amok. It is very easy in liberal Western society to conjure up the specter of what would happen if the state should fail (Mad Max! Lord of the Flies! Anarchy!). But if you think of authority as having only one source, you begin to see that to the extent that people generally refrain from murdering each other, it is not because of the state or other archist modalities. Indeed, archism is itself the source of the chaos and violence that it seeks to project out beyond itself and onto its captive population.

Hobbes explains the lopsided arrangement that archism has attempted to foist onto the rest of us when it comes to the issue of civil rest and unrest. While the subject population is expected to hold itself back from the kind of violent acts that archism claims they would do in its absence, it is in fact archism itself, or more accurately the archons, that is/are enabled to run amok. Hence the police killing of Black and Brown people, hence the unchecked theft and transfer of property to the rich and the white via capitalism, hence the hierarchies based on race, gender, class, sexuality, and other criteria.

While Hobbes suggests that the "state of nature" is endemic to all persons, its only contemporary manifestation is in the sovereign who is uniquely not bound by the social contract and who therefore remains a wild and dangerous creature in our midst. Here, Hobbes is making visible the very transfer of authority that archism generally seeks to cover over. He readily admits that it is sovereignty that is wild and dangerous under conditions of the social contract.

Whether Hobbes wanted us to look at this state of affairs and think that we were lucky to have such an arrangement or not, the clarity with which he describes this relationship, along with his claims that people are the "authors" of the political authority of the sovereign, combine to suggest that people have a power to retract this arrangement regardless of what he formally states in *Leviathan*. As I explained in chapter 2, Hobbes shows us that people in their collectivity have their own resources, their own form—actually, once again, the only form—of authority that they are already exercising; it is they and they alone who are the authors, after all. The social peace that this collective form of authorization (usually) produces is precisely what archism steals credit for; here again, it projects its own chaos and violence onto the community that it parasitizes and then claims that it is the only thing standing between the people and that very same violence.

Instead of arguing that Hobbes saying that the people are authors effectively colonizes them with archist authority, I argue that it returns that authority to the people as such. I would not make the same claim about the term *sovereignty*. Calling the people "sovereign" does indeed affect this colonization by giving people a false title of power that belongs entirely and only to archism. Authority is something different from sovereignty, the latter of which I see as an entirely archist construction. Whereas authority comes from the people and properly belongs to them as an expression of their own multivaried and dynamic anarchist life, sovereignty—at least the Western version of this concept—is the name for the parasite that draws its strength from their life.[6]

In this way, we can see that even taking Hobbes on his own terms, it is not the case that archism holds all the cards. In my thinking, besides archist-manufactured manifestations of collective violence like Kristallnacht or the racist destruction of Black Wall Street, or more recently the assault on the US Capitol by white supremacists, whenever people do riot, it tends to be in response to some particularly awful manifestation of archist power and hence it is not "unauthorized" so much as following a different concept of authority. A riot, in my view, represents not the breakdown, but the recapturing of authority from the archons who have stolen it. These actions reflect the kinds of collective networks that sustain and shape human interaction in that vast anarchist sphere that the state and other archist models barely touch on. When a community decides to cease acting peacefully, that decision is its own; it's never all about the state and what it can and can't do.[7]

In my view, the fact that authority is inherently collective, and actually anarchist, is the answer to the problem of trust that I've been describing throughout this book. Recognizing that this is actually what authority *is*, that it doesn't have to be manufactured out of thin air (that is the condition of false archist authority, after all), and that it doesn't therefore share that same vulnerability and anxiety as to the sources of its own legitimacy shows that people not only can but already do follow their own collective forms of judgment, even when they don't recognize that they are doing so. When authority reverts to the people who are its authors, it looks, to be sure, messier and less harmonious (but then again, archism's form of harmony is simply the mask that hides its naked predation); this doesn't *look* like what we are taught systems of authority are meant to look like, but that only reflects the way archism draws our eye away from what properly belongs to the people as a whole, part of what it means to "see like a state."

The fact that authority ultimately comes from the anarchist ferment itself explains why, whenever communities do find themselves freed of archist parasitism, whether that is via some kind of natural disaster (as Rebecca Solnit records) or the temporary absence of archism due to war (the conditions that led to the Paris Commune and the Rojavan Revolution) or even from their own revolutionary action (like the situation in Spain in the 1930s, or the events in Tahrir Square or Gezi or Zuccotti Park, or the liberated zones that sprang up in Seattle and New York in the last year), people know what to do.[8] Although the stereotype of anarchism is a bunch of people all shouting and arguing for hours on end and getting nowhere, when anarchists have had actual power, they have radically reconstituted their societies virtually overnight.[9] As James Scott suggests too, these communities have, in effect, been rehearsing for such moments for their whole lives.[10] Under-standing this, it may be possible to begin to forsake that almost automatic response—at least among those of us who have been conditioned to desire or require archism—of conflating archism and authority and to think about anarchist authority in new and untrammeled ways.

Treating authority as an anarchist production allows us to think differently about a whole plethora of social and political forms. For example, when responding to the fact that someone has committed a crime, in our usual archist vocabulary, we would say that they did something that was *against the law* or also against the state, as if it is the law or the state that suffered the grievance. In fact, such actions go against the community within which the person who committed the crime is embedded (all of this is, of course, complicated by the fact that under conditions of archism, crime itself is defined by and through archist logics). Here, the injury—if that is what it is—has been dealt to the authority of the collective rather than the archist power that seeks to dominate that community.

When one takes this perspective, the resolution to this situation changes radically. If someone does something against the law, the only recourse is punishment through legal means. The law doesn't like competitors for its authority; it is inherently punitive because this is the way that it polices its boundaries. Furthermore, as Benjamin shows, the law *needs* to punish and to kill not for the community's sake but for its own (so that it can, as he so elegantly puts it, "jut manifestly and fearsomely into existence").[11] An act deemed to be criminal helps give the state its justification for engaging in violence; it can serve to displace entire populations deemed dangerous, as is the case with the de facto extension of Black slavery into the twentieth and twenty-first century via the prison carceral and police violence. State punishment is a parasitical act that helps only itself in maintaining the state's parasitism, its preferred systems of rule and controls.

If you think instead of a kind of anarchist form of authority and law, you come to different kinds of conclusions about how to respond to a given crime. If the community considers that it has been wronged—a decision that it must make itself—it seeks not punishment but reparations, actions that serve to make the community whole once again. This could perhaps include punishment sometimes, but punishment is not the automatic recourse that it would be in a "criminal justice" system, where there is no way to repair the state except to punish the offender.

Another example that might show what it would look like when authority is returned to the community that it is normally stolen from can be seen in the way that the state engages with the economy. Here again, the claim is that the state is doing us a big favor when it does so, serving to adjudicate disputes and even rein in the markets when it gets too "exuberant" (a claim that actually presupposes capitalism). Yet here again, the state does this not for the sake of the people it pretends to serve but for itself because capitalism as a whole is what determines why we need a state in the first place. Capitalism is one of the key pillars of archism in its contemporary form, and even the idea that you find on some of the libertarian fringes that you could somehow have a market without a state—or maybe just a very tiny state—is an example of how archism can disguise itself in a million forms, even forms that seem to be "antistate" (leading to one of the worst oxymorons that I know: the notion that there is or could be something called "anarcho-capitalism").[12]

Thinking about economic authority as a form of anarchism allows us different insights as well. Exactly as with the political model, in economic life, owners, shareholders, managers, and administrators exert a parasitical power over workers, an example of what Foucault calls "governmentality."[13] And, just as with our collective political life, economic authority is produced only among workers, something that is expressed by and through their working process.[14] Collectively, the workers know everything there is to know about their job. The managerial elite only knows what they are told to know; all the rubrics and spreadsheets in the world are no substitute for deep collective forms of knowledge that these managers depend on to actually get the work done. Without a way for the workers to talk to one another, a concrete expression of their collective life, it appears as if it is the workers who are ignorant. However, the issue isn't their ignorance but the fact that their collective knowledge has no outlet (is replaced by the manager's "knowledge," which is limited, oriented only to its own self-perpetuation, and stolen).

This explains the value of the economic models that come out of the Spanish Revolution, which shows what happens when workers take control of their own environment and working conditions. Management as a whole is *not* an economic but a political activity. It is a way to "supervise" workers, that is, to watch over them and control them. They are, just like archism in general, disconnected from the economic and social life that they rule over, and their only role is to dominate, sponge off of, and interfere with that life.

Academia, my own profession, is a perfect case in point. At universities across the globe, my own very much included, the number of highly paid administrators grows while the number of faculty stays flat (or, if it raises at all, it does so only by employing more lecturer faculty, who are inherently and by design more vulnerable to the market). The administrators must prove that they deserve to be there and that they have earned their extraordinarily high salaries. This is done by treating the faculty as the enemy, a set of employees who can't be trusted—because trust must only come from above!—and hence watched over, judged, and ordered to the satisfaction of this growing army of bureaucrats who know nothing about teaching or learning.[15]

These bureaucrats pump out mountains of data, buying expensive platforms that are imposed on the faculty to do everything from giving out essay prizes to making sure that faculty don't "cheat" when they put in any kind of claim for travel to a conference, for example. Multiple levels of proof are required for even the smallest expenditure that is to be reimbursed. Student learning outcomes (SLOs), which in my school as in most others must be displayed on every syllabus, are not for students. Students themselves learn what their class is about from the minute class begins. No, SLOs are for bureaucrats who don't understand the subject matter but need some easily digested and oversimplified bullet points so that they can hold them over the faculty member to "prove" that they are actually teaching something. The truth is that universities don't need *any* administrators. They are just a parasite on the body of the students, faculty, and staff alike. Budget crises, which come fast and furiously, are always taken as an opportunity to render the faculty more precarious and less in charge of their own professional life.

More generally, archist entities like the state and capitalist corporations take advantage of the fears and self-doubt on the part of the workers to convince them that economic life would grind to a halt without them. This claim is the economic analogue to the political claim that we would all run amok without the state. When we think in this way, we see how capitalism and the state offer nothing whatsoever to the communities they prey upon. The forms of knowledge and consensus that emerge between workers are usually overshadowed and denied by the capitalist mode of economic organization, but they cannot be read out entirely because they and they alone produce the knowledge and the authority to keep worksites functioning. The archist managers and administrators (the "experts") parasitize that authority and claim it as their own so that the workers experience their own production of authority as an alienated and alienating thing. In this sense, authority itself can be seen as a form of material production that, along with other material forms, becomes alienated and expropriated.

For all these reasons, we can see that the question of how a community can come to trust itself does not require inventing new forms of authority. Here again the community already possesses all the resources that it requires to "trust" itself. After all, authority comes out of collective experience. In the same way that we all "trust" that the word *cat*, for those of us who speak English, refers to a four-legged animal that some of us keep as pets, we can trust other collective decisions as well. This trust does not come from some imagined absolute connection between the letters *c*, *a*, and *t* and that animal (that is more in the style of stolen, archist renditions of authority). The association between the word *cat* and the animal it claims to represent only comes from a pattern of association that we have decided among ourselves. Language does change all the time, and it might be that in the future, the English-speaking community decides to call this animal something else, but in the meantime, we can rest assured in our own participation in a collective process that delivers ongoing and publicly known and produced sets of decisions. This is in and of itself a form of trust.

Rather than being a matter of trust, to restore authority to the community that it is initially stolen from, we need to steal it back. Anarchist prophets can be critical in this endeavor, depending on the circumstances, because, by taking on the form of an archist prophet, they readily elicit our trust. The anarchist prophet betrays this initial and false archist model of trust ("trust me because I'm wiser than you, because my information is coming from a superior source than yours," etc.), but in doing so, she effectively redirects that trust to where it properly belongs. In this way, the prophet can maximally exploit a permanent vulnerability of archism: the fact that it cannot generate authority on its own, something that Hobbes once again says outright, even if he is not usually read that way.

Yet, at the same time, if we need the anarchist prophet to trust ourselves, then we are really only trusting her. For this reason, we can't ultimately rely on the anarchist prophet to trust ourselves; we must trust ourselves only as ourselves. The anarchist prophet is a transitional figure but she must, in the end, become absorbed into the community itself, just one of many. In the end, we must all accept our role as collective prophets. Only then does the final piece of archism fall away (at least for that moment, at least in that place).

The Universe Is Anarchist

Another key realization of already existing advantages that anarchist life has over its archist overlords comes in thinking further about the anarchist qualities of the universe itself. The fact that archism has always been in the business of manufacturing reality suggests that they are fighting, as it were, an upstream battle, insisting on an existence that the universe simply doesn't provide. That is precisely why archism is so invested in inventing other false universes, or projecting onto the actual universe some fake "universal" qualities; it needs somewhere else to draw its reality and judgment from because it can't find any of its own reality and judgment in the world—and universe—as we experience it.

Anarchism is different. In my view, the fact that even under conditions of the most dire archism, all of us practice, even if we don't always recognize it, anarchist forms of life and politics means that anarchism cannot and will never be read out of the world. Insofar as I have been arguing throughout this book, that anarchism is about life and archism is about death—albeit in the latter case, not the death that is part of life but a death that is unto itself, unconnected to life altogether—anarchism has a link to a world and a universe that archism simply does not. For that very reason, archism is vulnerable, as Butler shows, to having its subjects call its bluff and go out into a universe that until now has simply stood as a void onto which archist power is projected and reflected back.

I wouldn't go so far as to say that anarchism is more natural than archism in part because that term has been utterly appropriated by archism itself. Nor would I say that anarchism is truer or realer than archism once again because these terms are slippery slopes back into archist forms of thought. Instead, I would say that anarchism has certain advantages that come from its own form of practice, its own multivaried, contingent, and collective aspects that align in many ways with the way that we experience materiality and the universe more generally.

In the last few years, a few really good books have come out that have suggested what could be considered some anarchic aspects of the universe or, perhaps more accurately, a way to read the universe in a way that dispels archist lies and agendas. Two books, in particular, stand out for me. First, Karen Barad's *Meeting the Universe Halfway* looks at quantum physics, especially as it comes to us from Niels Bohr, as offering a universe that is far more anarchic than we usually consider it to be.[16] The so-called laws of physics in this view, normally serving as an epistemological anchor that undergirds archism, turn out to be much more fluid, aleatory, and infinitely complex. Barad speaks, for example, of a "crucial ontological shift [in Bohr's work] from 'observation-independent objects' to physical phenomena."[17] Here, the question of correspondence between what we observe and what must be understood is far more complex than what a more archist-oriented scientific view would demand. Barad writes: "Bohr points to the failure of representationalism on which correspondence theories of truth are premised. Likewise 'description' cannot have the same valence it has in representationalist theories, since in

Bohr's account theoretical concepts are not mere ideations but are materially embodied in apparatuses that produce the phenomena being described. That is, there's an important sense in which Bohr's framework offers a proto-performative account of the production of bodies."[18] Barad goes on to say that this does not mean that the phenomena in question are not real but that our science has to be humbled in the face of that reality; it is not ours to control and determine but to observe and to respond to. Here, human activity, including science, is reimmersed into the larger material context that it is always part of.

Samantha Frost's *Biocultural Creatures* makes a similar argument about biology, also a field that archism has borrowed heavily from to make its case for its own groundedness in empirical reality (and, as such, it liberates to some extent the life that I think anarchism also is). In Frost's account, rather than render us into the autonomous and predetermined creatures that correspond to Cartesian concepts of subjectivity, a careful study of biology shows us that "the porosity and responsiveness of a biocultural creature to its own modes of persisting in its habitats entails, first, that we not conceive of living matter as impenetrable, and second, that we do not think of the traffic of habitats into biocultural creatures as a deposit, an imprint, or a sedimentation that is determinative of what they are."[19] As I read this, Frost offers a biological equivalent to the kind of overlapping, radically contingent, and anarchist forms of selves that I have been arguing for in this and other works. These selves overlap and are intertwined but also remain in some sense distinct.

As a longtime student of Walter Benjamin, I hesitate to say that these books "prove" that the universe is anarchist—because in his view, any kind of certainty is itself an artifact of mythic violence—but I would say that at the very least they suggest a kind of empirical agnosticism that is fatal to archist claims but which anarchism is entirely compatible with. In their own way, both Barad and Frost steal away physics and biology from archist sensibilities and offer it back to anarchist forms of understanding and vision.

It may be too that we don't have to make such an absolute claim (i.e., the universe either is or isn't anarchist); we don't need to know what is real but we do need to know what isn't. Archism insists that the universe is real in a way that it is not. Anarchism as a lived practice—that is, as life—only needs to concern itself with how individuals and collectivities function, how they work together and apart, how they interact with plants and rocks and pencils and bagels, along with all the other things that collectively compose the material universe.

The anarchist anthropologist James C. Scott has presented us with many examples of how archism is not a condition that comes readily into being. He also shows how it is not easily maintained. In *The Art of Not Being Governed*, for example, Scott looks at the history of the founding of the kingdoms of Burma and Thailand in order to show that, as these archist entities began to form, the would-be subjects of those regimes fought back mightily to keep themselves free from archist entanglements.[20] In particular, these people resisted the demand to pay taxes and fight in their would-be leaders' wars. As Scott tells us, those twin primary demands of archism are immediately recognized by its intended subjects for what they are, usurpations of local and collective power and authority. They are both effectively forms of thievery, whether of lives or of money, and people rebelled by running away, moving to remote hills and making themselves as "primitive" as possible to get these nascent states to leave them alone. Scott explains that the archist entities in question had to frequently resort to finding and kidnapping people to make them their subjects. It was only over a very long time that the habits of archism became engrained in people in these territories. Only then can one begin to speak of political "subjects" in anything but a literal sense.

If Scott's account is credible and if it can be generalized, it suggests once again that it is not anarchism but archism that has to swim against the current of a universe given to entropy and diffusion rather than to stasis and control ("God is change"). Archism in this view has to work very hard to keep itself in power, and anarchism has the advantage of being a political form that requires no coercion, no mythic violence, and no spectacularity, none of that extra effort that archism must ceaselessly engage in to be able to "exist" at all.

Even so, for all of this, it is undoubtedly the case that archism has found a way to insinuate itself into its subjects' lives and imaginations such that many of them have come—once again as demonstrated in Kafka's parable "The Refusal"—to desire it, to think that they are nothing without its authority, to even find that their existence depends on archism's own, whereas the exact reverse is true. Perhaps most critically of all, over time, political subjects have come to *see* through the lens of archism, to understand it as being not only part of reality but the basis for it as well.

Much of Scott's work is about the way that communities are always resisting archism, how various rituals and actions are in fact forms of collective counterpower and dress rehearsals for the possibility of revolt and (sometimes) revolution. Acknowledging and agreeing with this view, I would add something just as critical; as I've been arguing throughout this book, collectivities do not only engage in resistance. They also engage in collective forms of politics in their own right; whenever they speak to one another, whenever customs arise, whenever collective judgments are engaged with, whenever people have a chance to experience themselves as a collectivity, even—or maybe especially—one marked by disharmony and disagreement, some kind of alternative form of political power is being exercised and created as well. This too is anarchy.

This doesn't mean that all things that people do collectively are automatically good. A lot of really horrible things have been done by and justified through the collectivity, and I don't think anarchism is immune from this aspect by any means. It's very important to stress once again that even if archism isn't fated, that doesn't mean that it cannot and will not come back over and over again (in the same way that God may not stay dead forever).

Having said that, I do think that collectivities that exist under the aegis of archism more deeply reflect the politics of division and conquest that archism requires to continue itself. Racism, classism, misogyny, homophobia, transphobia, ethnic nationalism, and ableism are all diseases of archism; anarchism may not be the "cure" to these diseases in the sense that there are all these problems in contemporary anarchist communities too—taking that term more in its "Circle-A brand" sense—but I think that without the aggressive and projective violence of archism, these forms of hatred would not have the same purchase, the same centrality, that they currently have.[21]

This is not to suggest that even if they were free from archism, anarchist communities would never engage in forms of prejudice or long-held practices of oppression would magically disappear if archism went away.[22] I do, however, think it would be a mistake to assume that nothing would change. We ought not to take the current form of collective politics, which is a hybrid of anarchist and archist forms of power, and use that as a basis for thinking about what a more untrammeled anarchism would look like (or has looked like because there are many instances of anarchic practices rising up to rival archism in both our past and our present times).

When a community is entirely disenfranchised from politics—as communities are under conditions of archism—people are much more prone to the kinds of manipulations and political phantasms that keep them divided and subjected. With no outlet of their own, no way to express to themselves and their fellow community what they think and what they see, there seems to be nothing but archist sight. More accurately, archist sight is always mottled by its interaction with anarchist forms of sight, but the archist form usually predominates.

There is, of course, no guarantee—only archism offers guarantees and they are always lies—that an untrammeled anarchist world would lead to an absolutely better politics. Yet, as Benjamin points out, we already *do* practice a nonviolent form of relationality in our collective lives, and that is under conditions of archism.[23] When you remove archism's anxiety, its projection and fetishism, the way it is always trying to assert a life and an existence that it doesn't have, always trying to divide and conquer, always trying to protect and rationalize the gross inequalities that are part and parcel to and of it, I think anarchism has more than a fighting chance to be something entirely different and infinitely better.

Here again, anarchist prophecy has a role to play in this situation. If the universe is inherently hostile to archist predations, the anarchist prophet does not have to do much more than align herself with its currents, or more accurately to remind us all that we are all similarly aligned. Once again this does not mean that we align ourselves with the universe as it really is but more in the sense that Benjamin offers us too, of understanding that we are surrounded by a real universe and that it is not up to us to determine what it is and what it means in truth (the pose of archism). We can only collectively decide what we think it means—or doesn't—and go from there. An anarchist prophet can facilitate this kind of sight; if she tries to tell us "the truth" about ourselves and the world around us, she immediately slips back into archist forms of sight and, for that reason, once again, cannot be a permanent institution but only a waystation for the community to come fully, and only, into its own.

Anarchist Prophecy Is Everywhere

Another advantage that anarchism has over archism is that it is everywhere—everywhere, that is, where there is life and maybe even further if you include, as I would, the "life" that exists in all objects, even in the so-called vacuum of outer space, all corresponding once again to Benjamin's idea of "the magic of matter." I would even go further and say that anarchism includes the dead too, those who once partook in life and remain as matter, as memories, and as coconspirators to the living. The vastness of anarchism may seem like a real irony because archism, which is devoted to being everywhere, is nowhere, and anarchism, which is relegated to being nowhere, is everywhere. But I do not think this association is accidental. Instead, it illustrates once more how archism steals from whatever it has in its grip, transferring the reality of anarchist life to itself and derealizing that life in the process. Since it is nowhere, archism steals the form of being everywhere from anarchism itself, just as it steals the sense of being organized, of having a voice, of being authoritative, from anarchism when it is itself only a force of chaos and nihilism. But here too that theft is not an actual and full transfer of reality to itself but only a symbolic version of the same, and this too is a point of vulnerability.

To demonstrate a bit more of this ubiquity in purely terrestrial and human terms, I would like to add to my considerations of anarchist politics beyond what I've already described in Spain in the 1930s, New Guinea in the 1940s, and Rojava today. Let me give three more fairly brief examples to show the ubiquity of this form in places and in persons that are not always associated with the word *anarchism*" Here again I am cognizant of Maia Ramnath's admonition that if we are going to use the word *anarchism* to apply broadly, it has to be with a distinctly small letter *a*. In looking at these three further examples, Mariátegui, Goldman, and Fanon, I focus not just on their own acts of prophecy but also on the way that each of them demonstrate their own ensconcement in a particular community and a particular history. Whereas they all diverge in their temporal focus (for Mariátegui, the focus is on the past, for Goldman on the present, and for Fanon all of temporality), these thinkers demonstrate the way that anarchist prophets emerge out of their context and draw all their strength, all their insight from that context, from anarchist life itself. Here too then, the focus is not only what these thinkers and writers do and see but also how they can effectively expand that doing and seeing via an engagement with the community as a whole, making themselves, once again, effectively redundant.

Another Non-Western Example: The *Ayllu*

One important example of anarchist prophecy from the non-West involves José Carlos Mariátegui and his reading of what he calls Inca communism. Mariátegui considered the Incan civilization to be the basis for a pure communist form in precolonial Peru, one that far antecedes any possibility or even thought of communism in the West. This idea in and of itself constitutes a major break with more orthodox Marxist thought by scrambling and reversing Marxist teleologies.[24] Although Mariátegui was himself a student of Western Marxism—as well as being the founder of the Peruvian Communist Party and also an inspiration for the Sendero Luminoso (Shining Path) many decades later—his basis for Inca communism corresponds very highly with the kind of anarchist collective and horizontal forms of power and authority that I have been talking about in this book.

For Mariátegui, the *ayllu* (a local, family-based collective) was the basic unit of an agrarian Inca communism. Although he acknowledges that "the Inca regime was unquestionably theocratic and despotic," for Mariátegui, the true basis of this society was not the small political and theocratic elite but the vast network of *ayllu* that organized and collectivized the entirety of the Inca world at that time.[25] Thus Mariátegui tells us that despite its imperial form of organization in ancient Peru, "the *ayllu*—the community—was the nucleus of the empire. The Incas [here meaning the imperial authorities] unified and created the empire, but they did not create its nucleus. The legal state organized by the Incas undoubtedly reproduced the natural pre-existing state. The Incas did not disrupt anything."[26] In a sense, Mariátegui is arguing that the Inca empire was effectively not really archist, or rather that its mode of archism was much weaker and smaller than the Western model, permitting a form of collective communism that was largely left to its own devices (the Incan archons "did not disrupt anything") in a way that has yet to happen in the West. In saying this, Mariátegui also centers Peru, rather than Western Europe, as the focal point of radical politics, making a second major break with traditional Marxist forms of thought (his interest in agricultural and rural life versus industrial and urban may be a third, although here he shares that feature with many other radical traditions, including Maoism).

Mariátegui also notes that whereas colonialism and capitalism in Peru have reduced the country's interior to a feudal economy—another example of the way that Mariátegui scrambles European temporal narratives—the *ayllu* have survived even this disastrous event and remain as the possible basis for a revived communism that by definition will look nothing like the European model.[27]

In claiming that the vision of Inca communism based on the *ayllu* that Mariátegui offers here is inherently anarchist—he himself always used the word *communism*—I am not trying to force a one-size-fits-all model onto all political modalities in the world but, on the contrary, to once again open up the meaning of anarchism—and, by extension, archism too—so that no one model gets to determine what it is or how it works.

Although Mariátegui focused on a communist, Incan past, his understanding that the *ayllu* form survived into his own time means that he recognizes the ongoing nature of organized anarchist life. His influence on radical movements in Peru is unmistakable, making his own recognition of the power and resilience of the *ayllu* a way for that life to also recognize itself.

To show the ongoing power of this model, a much more recent book by Raul Zibechi, *Dispersing Power*, takes up the question of the *ayllu* in the modern setting, focusing here not on Peru but on Bolivia, which was historically part of the traditional sphere of Incan authority. Zibechi describes a city called El Alto that is largely, although not entirely, dominated by Indigenous people, principally the Aymara, and which is marked once again by the *ayllu* form as a way to thwart and resist all governmental incursions.

What is striking about both Mariátegui's and Zibechi's descriptions is the way that there really are no leaders in these movements. In the Incan case, the formal political leaders were set apart from the true "nucleus" of the society. In modern-day Bolivia, Zibechi offers a similar understanding. He describes, for example, an uprising in El Alto in 2003:

> For ten or twelve days in October 2003, residents of El Alto, organized through neighborhood councils and other means, operated as a neighborhood government that supplanted the delegitimized and absent state. Descriptions of the insurgency all indicate that there was no single organization or leadership, and that actions were carried out directly by the residents of the neighborhoods, overriding all other institutions and organizations, even the ones created by them beforehand. Even the local councils, the most "grassroots" organizations of the EL Alto movement, did not lead the mobilization but acted as "structures of territorial identity within which other kinds of loyalties, organizational networks, solidarities, and initiatives are deployed in an autonomous manner above and, in some cases, outside of the authority of the neighborhood council."[28]

Here we see something that is indicative of anarchistic forms of power more generally, the way that they operate despite, and sometimes even in opposition to, the formal representative structures that persist in these respective communities (thus they work against "leaderism" even in their own ranks).

If we are to consider Mariátegui himself to be an anarchist prophet, he is mainly a retrospective one (as is appropriate in a Benjaminian sense). He tends to use his authority, at least in his written work, mainly to turn the attention back to those who are the true basis of that collective and horizontal form of authority. If his narrative about the *ayllu* is correct, the communities in question act from a thoroughly horizontal and collective position, and so their forms of collective sight are not as readily eclipsed by archist forms of vision as they might otherwise be (a form of action that corresponds to what Mariátegui considers to be a form of material rights).[29] The legibility and duration of the *ayllu* structure may make something like anarchist prophecy as a kind of separate category either unnecessary or immediately redundant. Perhaps the (relative) dearth of Abrahamic logics and its specific forms of archist prophecy in the Peruvian context make the need for an answering anarchist form of prophecy less critical, even into modern times.[30]

Even so, I would consider Mariátegui's own function to be important. Although the *ayllu* form functions with or without the kind of self-consciousness that he brings to it, Mariátegui allows for a kind of transmission of the inherent knowledge of the *ayllu* from past to present. This transmission is not purely determined by ethnic origin or cultural practices; as Zibechi shows us, the non-Aymara people in El Alto who were not raised with the tradition of the *ayllu* nonetheless often cooperated with that community organizational structure and shared in its tactics and responses to archism. Anarchist life always persists in all its beautiful variety, but when it is aware of itself as such, when one part can speak to another part, the threat that it poses to archism is that much more powerful and effective.

Back to the West: Emma Goldman and the Anarchist Tradition in the United States

In the West, where the influence of Abrahamic modes of vision and organization and also the models of statecraft that stem from those modes of seeing are much stronger, the question of anarchist prophecy perhaps becomes more prominent. In considering Emma Goldman and the anarchist tradition in the United States as a prime example of Western anarchism, we are directly considering the "brand" of anarchism with a capital *A* that Ramnath describes. We should be aware, accordingly, of the hegemony of this model vis-à-vis other forms of what I have been calling anarchism as well (arguably this is also true of my analysis in chapter 5 of the Spanish Revolution).

Yet, even within the confines of this "brand," we see how anarchist life acts back against its own archist tendencies. In thinking specifically about Goldman, who may be a paragon amid the examples of "brand" anarchism, one thing that is particularly striking about her is the way that Goldman allowed the community she was engaged with to affect her as much as she affected them, that is, the way that she permitted horizontal and collective conversations to be expressed in and through her own relationship to anarchism.

In her superb book *Emma Goldman: Political Thinking in the Streets*, Kathy E. Ferguson captures this tendency very well. She considers Goldman to have a political theory that is "ectopic" or "out of place."[31] She explains that Goldman is also "untimely in Nietzsche's sense, that is, out of joint with the prevailing conceptions of history and thus open to new thinking about how things might happen."[32]

Yet, even as Goldman is out of place and time as those terms are normally understood, Ferguson notes that Goldman is also deeply rooted in local practices, in the rhythms of her anarchist life, the schedules of printing anarchist newspapers, the cadence of her speeches, and above all her interactions with other people. For Ferguson, Goldman is at once unique and deeply ordinary, taking the latter word in the nonpejorative sense of being very much located in horizontal currents of discourse, relationship, power, and authority that disrupt archist geographies and temporalities in order to offer a place and a time of their own.

Interestingly, Goldman herself suggests that when she was a girl, she was tempted by the model of archist prophecy. In *Living My Life*, her autobiography, Goldman writes: "At the age of eight I used to dream of becoming a Judith and visioned myself in the act [of] cutting off Holofernes' head to avenge the wrongs of my people. But since I had become aware that social injustice is not confined to my own race, I had decided that there were too many heads for one Judith to cut off."[33]

In *Living My Life* more generally, Goldman gives us a sense of what turned her into an anarchist as well as the particular way that she experienced and related to this form of politics. In particular, she shows how she herself came under the spell and influence of certain key male anarchist leaders and furthermore how, in engaging with these influences, Goldman did not ultimately succumb to the temptation to model herself after these figures, a move that would have reinstated a kind of archist relationship inside of an anarchist one. Instead, Goldman chose her own path, often by recognizing the way that she herself was deeply connected to the larger anarchist community. In doing so, Goldman models a way not to model, to allow influence to move in many directions instead of just one.

Initially, Goldman's relationship to anarchism began with her admiration for the anarchists who were executed after the Haymarket incident in Chicago. Goldman explains that after their trial and execution, and after much emotional suffering on her own part as a result, "I had a distinct sensation that something new and wonderful had been born in my soul. A great ideal, a burning faith, a determination to dedicate myself to the memory of my martyred comrades, to make their cause my own, to make known to the world their beautiful lives and heroic deaths."[34] She further notes that the slain anarchists' "death gave me life," suggesting both her own immersion into anarchist life as well as the thought that the life she had—just like the life that the Haymarket martyrs had had—was not hers alone but required a complicated and ongoing set of negotiations with other people.[35]

At that point in her life, Goldman left her loveless marriage behind in Rochester, New York, and moved to New York City. Once there, in addition to meeting Alexander (Sasha) Berkman, who would be one of the great loves of her life and a major influence on her politics, Goldman fell under the spell of Johann Most, the editor of the German-language anarchist paper *Freiheit*. She writes, "Most became my idol. I worshipped him."[36]

Yet, for all the ways that she was heavily influenced by these male anarchist figures, there is a way in which Goldman rebelled against them as well. She tells a story early on in her autobiography that she began, at Most and Berkman's insistence, to give public speeches, a first for a woman in the German-speaking anarchist community in the United States.

Due to her lack of experience and insecurity, Goldman initially tried to parrot the points that Most wrote out for her, drawing upon him and Adolph Spies (one of the anarchists killed after Haymarket) for inspiration. Giving a speech in Buffalo, New York—her second speech ever—Goldman began by hectoring the working-class audience for their small ambitions, for the way that they were begging for scraps from their capitalist overlords. Much of the audience responded positively to this, but one old man said he would probably not live to see the end of capitalism and why was it so wrong for him to ask for some small concessions if they made his life materially better? Goldman writes:

> I realized I was committing a crime against myself and the workers by serving as a parrot repeating Most's views. I understood why I had failed to reach my audience. I had taken refuge in cheap jokes and bitter thrusts against the toilers to cover up my own inner lack of conviction. My first public experience did not bring the result Most had hoped for, but it taught me a valuable lesson. It cured me somewhat of my childlike faith in the infallibility of my teacher and impressed on me the need of independent thinking.[37]

When Goldman speaks of "independent thinking," she is not referring merely to her own thoughts. Rather, she is once again allowing the knowledge of the collective to inform her own knowledge, to think and act collectively, as it were. Although she continued to admire a figure like Most, Goldman realized that to be consistent with anarchist politics meant that one could not speak down to the community from a high perch (the stance of the archon, although this is not a word that Goldman used). Instead, she drew her power from shared visions, from things that were collectively known but not necessarily collectively recognized or acted upon. It is this horizontality, I think, that is Goldman's great gift, not a personal charisma but a marker of what charisma always really is: a way to recognize and reflect those collective decisions and authorities that are normally stolen from a community and used to lord over it.

This is not to say that Goldman always perfectly stuck to this mode of being and thinking in concert; of course, she had her own responses and thoughts and even her own reveries and ambitions, but she characterizes a way of being anarchist that aligns with that collective generality in a way that makes her own role in this situation much more of a conduit than an obstacle to that ongoing and contingent collective political life that she came to love and appreciate so much. And, of course, there is a tendency to think of Goldman as one of a kind, as someone who had special sight that no one else did. But I think her own emphasis on overcoming any sense of specialness helped mitigate, although certainly not eliminate, the archist forms of interpretation that seemingly inevitably come with anarchist challenges to its power (including effectively dismissing Goldman and her politics, ironically by turning her into a unique and nonrepeatable hero, which had the effect of delegitimizing that larger stream of collective thinking and acting that she was part of).

Fanon and the Black Power Movement

A final critical figure I include in this list of modern-day anarchist prophets is Frantz Fanon. Like Mariátegui and Goldman, Fanon was not just a writer but also an activist and a revolutionary. Fanon is well known for having radically altered the way that colonized people thought about colonialism and about their own roles as colonial subjects. Homi K. Bhabha writes in his foreword to *The Wretched of the Earth*:

> In 1966, Bobby Seale and Huey Newton read *The Wretched of the Earth* in a house in Oakland, and—so the story goes—when they were arrested some months later for "blocking the sidewalk," the text provided foundational perspectives on neocolonialism and nationalism that inspired the founding of the Black Nationalist Party. . . . In the early seventies, Steve Biko's room in the student residence of the University of Natal became . . . the intellectual center of the black consciousness movement. That dorm room in Durban was the place where Biko, "the person who brought ideas," first circulated *The Wretched of the Earth* to his friends and comrades—writers, activists, community workers, actors, students—who were also conversant with the poetry and the politics of the Black Panther movement.[38]

In his own accounting of what could be called his achievement of prophetic insight, Fanon famously recounts an encounter that he had with a young white boy in Lyons while he was a student there. Born and raised in Martinique, Fanon had thought—even though on some level he knew this not to be the case—that he was a Frenchman through and through, a true subject of the (French, white) universal. The white boy's act of pointing to Fanon and saying to his mother, "Look, a negro," came as a shock to Fanon.[39] Although he tells us that he had until then been aware of racial difference as an "intellectual understanding," he had not yet felt this difference viscerally, the way it connected him to the very physical body that Cartesian rationalism told him wasn't "really him."[40]

Fanon writes "And then the occasion arose when I had to meet the white man's eyes. . . . In the white world the man of color encounters difficulties in the development of his bodily schema. Consciousness of the body is solely a negating activity. It is a third person consciousness."[41] Focusing on this experience as a visual engagement (he meets the "white man's eyes"), Fanon suddenly can't continue to see things the way that he had been taught to see them; he knows now that the white man's eyes (unlike as with the townspeople in "the Refusal" and the colonel's eyes) are not his own. He is, one could say, bitterly disappointed by a universal that he had thought included him but markedly did not.

Like many forms of prophetic sight, this insight is initially unwanted; for Fanon, it means giving up on the promise of being "French," of being a universal subject, equal, free, and perfect in every way. The entirety of *Black Skin, White Masks*, the book in which Fanon recounts this experience, is given over to the shock and also the mourning of what he feels he is forced to give up. But it is also a celebration of the fact that he was able to give up this melancholic stance along with gaining a determination to see and experience himself, his identity as a Black man, and his relationship to the world differently.

By the time we get to *The Wretched of the Earth*, that period of doubt and confusion is definitely over. Fanon uses his own changed sense of sight to revisit the way that reality itself is entirely constructed by colonialism, arguing that "it is the colonist who *fabricated* and *continues to fabricate* the colonized subject."[42] Here, Fanon zeroes in on the double vision of the colonial subject, exposing the way that one kind of (archist, colonial) vision is superimposed over another (anarchist, Algerian, in this case) one. Arguably, Fanon's calls to violence in *The Wretched of the Earth* serve as ways to kill off not just the colonial oppressor but also the way that the vision of that oppressor has insinuated itself into the psyche—and vision—of the colonial subject herself.

And Fanon did not just write these ideas in his books; he lived them as an actual practice insofar as he took a very active role in fomenting the

Algerian Revolution against French colonial rule. Part of the reason that he was such a major influence on the entire anticolonial movement is precisely because he was able to emphasize a way to contend with the apparent power of colonialism by unseeing its false authority, opening up a space for those collective forms of vision that existed under the surface of colonial rule.

By lending his expertise as a practicing psychiatrist to the question of colonial subjectivity, Fanon found a way to get at archism's deep insinuation into the psychic landscape of the colonial subject. As he explains in *Black Skin, White Masks*: "I believe that the fact of the juxtaposition of the white and black race has created a massive psychoexistential complex. I hope by analyzing it to destroy it."[43]

Finally and most critically, Fanon located this other form of sight not in some mythological and authentic past—since, in his view, colonialism had stolen the past for its own nefarious purposes—but in collective forms of struggle. In doing so, Fanon jettisoned the content of colonized life—which he thought was thoroughly corrupted by colonialism itself—but saved the form, the way that decisions are made, the way that nonharmony and differentiation are integrated into the process by which anarchist life expresses itself. Fanon's focus on struggle is a perpetuation of the way that anarchist life always works; it struggles externally against archist predations and it struggles internally within each subject and between subjects.

Accordingly, for Fanon, struggle is the only possible basis for collective knowledge and decision. In this way, the collectivity itself is the foundation for new forms of anticolonial identity and subjectivity, a different form of seeing, of collective forms of prophecy. This too helps mitigate the tendency to read Fanon as unique or possessing special sight; he used his position as author and revolutionary to turn the focus onto the collective itself, using an archist platform once again to introduce an anarchist and collective form of vision to the anticolonial movement.

Fanon inspired so many movements that followed in his wake, including his emphasis on collective versus individual action. One of the key movements in this regard was the Black Power movement in the United States in the late 1960s and early 1970s. The Black Panthers were the most prominent of the groups involved in this movement (and for that reason suffered the most violent forms of repression). Although the Black Panthers are most famous for the way they openly defied the white police state—taking advantage of California's open carry laws at the time to do so—they also were pioneers in creating an entire network of schools, health centers, and other social institutions that were not offshoots of the white supremacist state or the capitalist economy. From the outside, leaders like Huey P. Newton, Bobby Seale, and Ericka Huggins understood what they were doing as creating an alternative social, economic, and political space that was entirely based in the Black community.

Although the Black Panthers were not avowed anarchists and did have a more formal leadership model, the focus on social programs served as a way to politicize and make visible the collective processes that undergirded their movement. It also shows an attention to Black life as such, allowing Black life to thrive under its own conditions and its own authority. The creation of the Oakland Community School, the Free Breakfast for School Children, a community news service, and other community-based endeavors gave a shape and a form to that collectivity and that life.

To be sure, there was a division in the movement between those who favored this approach and those who followed Eldridge Cleaver in seeking mainly military approaches to Black Power, but insofar as the social institutions were not only created but began to take on a life of their own, there were long-standing repercussions of this approach that resonate to this day in the Black community in the United States.

This very much includes Black Lives Matter, a movement that has in some ways inherited Fanon's mantle and is itself in many ways a continuation of the Black Power movement. Black Lives Matter, which was formed by Alicia Garza, Patrisse Cullors, and Opal Tometi in 2013, is a loosely organized, anarchistically structured organization. It has a list of guiding principles that it asks its chapters to honor but is otherwise quite decentralized. Black Lives Matter is a movement as much as it is an organization, and its name is invoked by many who are not affiliated with any of its chapters. It has demands such as police abolition but it is not interested in policy negotiations. It definitely has more of the form of a general strike than a normative political organization.

Since the murder of George Floyd, the movement has seen a renewed energy. White-led institutions have been falling over themselves to declare that "Black Lives Matter" (or to explain the intricacies of Juneteenth), and the City Council of Minneapolis—where George Floyd was murdered—was at one point considering a version of police abolition. This extraordinary moment when the usual invocation of "thugs" and "terrorists"—Trump and his allies used both terms for describing the insurrection that followed Floyd's murder—did not work the way that they were usually expected to suggests exactly how quickly the archist model, based on lies and projections, can dissipate, losing at least some of its compelling force.

Clearly, the entirety of the archist production of white supremacy remains more or less intact in this moment, but the ease by which it keeps itself perpetuated has suddenly been interrupted in a way that is inescapable. A racist figure like Aunt Jemima, which had lasted for more than a century, was suddenly deemed unacceptable—by the white corporate leaders who run the company anyway; most Black and Brown folk have always recognized it for what it was all along—and was eliminated as a brand name. Princeton University removed the name of that avowed racist and Ku Klux Klan supporter Woodrow Wilson from the policy center that had until then borne that name. The State of Mississippi removed the confederate symbol from its state flag after decades of refusing to do so under any circumstances.

None of these actions are even remotely revolutionary; they merely reflect the judgment by the neoliberal authorities that control these names that it is in their prudent interest to change these symbols. But there is a more radical form of this disassociation too; statues honoring the confederacy have been torn down during this period by protestors, thereby skipping the lengthy process of review that often served in the past to effectively preserve these statues. And this kind of action has not just been confined to the United States but has spread to Britain and France and other founding members of the regime of white supremacy and colonial rule.

At the time of this writing, in a post-Trump era, it seems that reformism, rather than revolt, is the contemporary tempo. But even so, things are not the same as they were. Black Lives Matter is not going anywhere. Each new murder of a Black person by the police leads to demonstrations and widespread outrage. The recent decision to convict the police officer who murdered George Floyd came amid an atmosphere of intense anticipation and a readiness to hit the streets. I would love it if this kind of insurrection remains and spreads, an expression of Black life rising up against the reign of death that archism has only ever offered to it, in this case quite literally. Yet even if the insurrectionary stance beginning in the summer of 2020 and continuing into our own post-Trump moment does not sustain itself for much longer, we see the thin ice that archism is always skating upon. Insofar as many revolutionary moments tend to be preceded by a period of reform, what may be seen as empty symbolism—Black Lives Matter signs in every window, sold-out copies of *White Fragility*, and so forth—could just as easily presage something quite a bit more radical.

In the present moment, we can more clearly see how forms of vision switch in an instant. There are always those who see things differently from how they are told; white supremacy has been attacked throughout its entire long history. Yet, for entrenched institutional racism and white supremacy to truly falter, that opposing form of vision has to become contagious—these days we might say viral, although that word has recently taken on a whole new and very negative connotation—hence the role both of an anarchist prophet like Fanon and also of the community that he was writing in connection with and in response to.

The Black Power movement has had so many of these kinds of prophets; Angela Davis, Assata Shakur, Fred Hampton, and Huey P. Newton all come immediately to mind. The three founders of Black Lives Matter and other figures like Melina Abdullah in Los Angeles, Janaya Khan in Toronto, Assa Traoré in Paris, and Imarn Ayton in London, to name just a few examples, are all engaged in similar forms of organizing and allowing the expression of Black life to be visible to itself and to the world. The main point, however, is perhaps that when collectivities are allowed a kind of political life of their own, the community as such more readily takes on the role of prophecy for itself. While we tend to think of the civil rights era as the high-water mark of popular protest in the United States, in fact the current Black Lives Matter movement is the biggest in US history. When an entire community gets into the business of deciding exactly what they are seeing and why, the function of that prophecy shifts from specific to collective forms of sight, and that is all for the better.[44]

In addition to his influence on political activism, Fanon also continues to have a major and ongoing impact on the realm of theory and philosophy. Here too, as with his influence on political movements, the focus is not on theory, and not even on practice per se—at least in the way that it is usually understood—but on life, and in particular on Black life as such. The Afropessimism movement, as articulated by thinkers like Frank Wilderson III and Jared Sexton, owes a great deal to Fanon's insight that Black people have been shut out of ontology (here referring not to reality as such but the false reality superimposed by colonialism and white supremacy).[45] Other thinkers like Saidiya Hartman and Hortense J. Spillers also reflect this legacy.[46] For Wilderson, a key insight of this lack of ontology is, as he puts it, that "no Blacks are in the world, but, by the same token, there is no world without Blacks."[47] In other words, the exclusion of blackness from the ontological realm is a founding act that creates all other forms of identity, that creates what I have been calling the archist form of reality itself.

Fred Moten, who is connected to but not a part of Afropessimism per se, has written a great deal about the meaning and possibility of this lack of ontology as a way to think about resisting the falsities of white supremacy.

He asserts that "black life—which is as surely to say *life* as black thought is to say *thought*—is irreducibly social; that, moreover, black life is lived in *political* death or that it is lived, if you will, in the burial ground of the subject by those who, insofar as they are not subjects, are also not, in the interminable (as opposed to the last) analysis, 'death-bound.'"[48] Here, Moten is involved in a recuperative project: just as in Zarathustra's dream where he saw that "life overcome regarded me from glass coffins," Moten too sees life in what archism—my word, not his—has relegated to death.[49] In some sense, Moten sees the exclusion of blackness from ontology as an advantage, albeit an advantage that Black people have paid a hideous price for, insofar as, in being so denied, blackness isn't subject to the lies of ontology—and hence, archism—as such. This is why he explains that "life" means Black life and "thought" means Black thought. These forms of life and thought are the effect of living and thinking outside the realm that archism has carved out for itself. Although Black life for this reason is subject to an unprecedented degree of violence, Moten sees its ongoing vitality nonetheless. Hartman's work points to this as well, a recuperation of Black life even from its ongoing relegation to (social) death.

Even in the hold of the ships in the Middle Passage, Moten insists, there is life, not just surviving but inventing and creating, a life that could not be reduced entirely to death. Given this insight, Moten asks: "What if (the thinking and the study of) blackness is an inhabitation of the hold that disrupts the whole in which the absolute, or absolute nothingness, is structured by its relation to its relative other? What if the nothing that is in question here moves through to the other side of negation, in 'the real presence' of blackness, in and as another idea of nothingness altogether that is given in and as and to things?"[50] Here, for Moten, the vitality of Black life shows that the negation of life that is intended by white supremacy, far from succeeding, has instead created pockets of radical resistance that can "disrupt . . . the whole." In his thinking about what he and Stefano Harney call "the undercommons," Moten sees this as a stage for a larger and more general form of resistance, a continuation of the struggle that Fanon himself sought in his own grappling with European colonialism and white supremacist phantasms of authority and power.[51]

Whether it is demonstrated through protests on the streets of US cities by Black Lives Matter activists or in the thought, writing, and advocacy of authors like Wilderson, Hartman, and Moten, the legacy of Fanon is very present in our time. The focus, as always, is not on these figures per se but on Black life itself, on resisting the reduction of Black life to nothing but death and on recognizing that in Black life there is the means for a radical and revolutionary overturning of ontology—and, I would add, archism—itself.

In thinking about all three figures—Mariátegui, Goldman, and Fanon—we see that what they share is precisely their wish and even ability to have their vision merge into and effectively reflect the vision of the community, not in the usual, archist sense, wherein they all learn to see the way these singular prophets see, but the opposite, wherein their own particular vision merges into the larger collective of which they become only a part (albeit a much renowned part). Just as Fanon makes struggle, and not this or that ideological position, central to his work, so too do Mariátegui and Goldman focus more on the collective envelope than on any specific thought or action, the latter of which would just be grist for the mill of further archism.

Moving beyond Anarchist Prophecy

Understanding the various ways that anarchism has some clear and vital advantages over archism, for all the violence and spectacularity the latter engages in, we see the helpful role—at least at times and for a time—for anarchist prophets too, to take advantage of those advantages, as it were, and communicate them to the larger population. Yet that role cannot become permanent, lest it itself becomes a way to reintroduce the very archist logics, the very focus on singularity and uniqueness that it is the role of the anarchist prophet to do away with in the first place.

If the role of the anarchist prophet is to allow a community access to its own authority and knowledge as we see in the above examples, how does the shift from anarchist prophet to that community actually work? How do we facilitate this shift and how can we ensure, as best we can, that that transition actually occurs, that the anarchist prophet doesn't overstay her welcome, becoming an obstacle to rather than a facilitator of anarchist and collective forms of vision?

By way of an answer to this question, I am reminded of what Foucault said about the role of intellectuals such as himself. One of Nietzsche's greatest disciples, Foucault grappled with precisely this problem when it came to the question of whether people on their own can figure out their own situation or whether they require the aid of specialists or experts, akin to the question of prophecy that I have been discussing throughout this book. Foucault's answer to this was to say that each of us is an expert in whatever we do in life.[52] People who work at McDonald's are experts at McDonald's. People who work in factories are experts at their particular production processes.

Each person knows and sees what they need to know and see and collectively they know everything; knowledge is power. The job of each of these experts, in Foucault's view, is to use their knowledge to destroy and dismantle the basic structure of whatever overarching regime they serve. The role of the intellectual, by analogy to the prophet, is to destroy the architecture of the meta-regimes that hold these other disciplinary modes together. Their knowledge is not *required* per se but it helps combat archism at its most abstract, metalevel.

By extending the power and role of the intellectual or the expert, Foucault is partaking in the same kind of thinking that Benjamin sought to engage with as well, the decentering of knowledge, the dissemination of the power of interpretation and experience to everyone so that the very concept of expertise—and the stolen authority that comes with it—becomes radically transformed and redistributed.

In thinking further about this question of expertise, it may be the case that politics has a unique status because it is one field where I think not only *can* everyone be an "expert" simply by being allowed to engage in it—rather than supplanting one's political life with sham engagement through acts like voting once every few years or partaking in polling or "listening tours" or what have you—but also that it is something that everyone *must* do to safeguard the collective's own horizontal forms of authority and anarchist power.

Whereas from a Rousseauvian perspective any one of us can hold onto the collective because the collective will is single and unitary, I would say the opposite is the case (here, I adhere to both Fanon and Arendt's understanding). The collective needs us all because it is created by interaction, by conflict, by multiplicity, and that *can't be represented*; it can only come into existence by actual conflict, actual political expressions coming together and working things out (or not).

We are often told that those who engage in politics are somehow better at it than the rest of us, but I would argue that you can't exclude 99.99 percent of the population from politics and then use that exclusion as a way to "prove" that only the political elite is capable of engaging in political life. As soon as politics is ceded to others, collective forms of authority are undermined and archism gets the upper hand. The idea of professional politicians knowing something that no one else knows and doing something that no one else can do is the very epitome of archist hierarchy, and it is this conceit perhaps more than anything else that must be struggled against.

Perhaps the proof, if you need any, that anarchist models of politics and economics are inherently stronger and more viable than archist ones, and that therefore people in general are "better" at politics than a select group of archons, comes once again from Max Tomba's observation that it is not necessary to actually overthrow the state or the market. He tells us that when real alternatives are created, as was the case in the Paris Commune and in the Spanish Revolution, and arguably in Rojava and Chiapas today, just to give a few examples, the anarchist version readily supplanted and bypassed the state formations, rendering the latter empty or useless. It is precisely for this reason that such formations are inevitably met with intense violence by archist forces. Even a small anarchist network poses an existential threat to archist power (whereas the reverse is not true) and must be stamped out, as was the case with the Communards and the Spanish Revolution, or at least isolated and hemmed in, as is the case with Rojava and the Zapatistas today.

Given my understanding of political life as an unrepresentable process—unless by representation you mean something like what I described in the previous chapter about the way Melanesians had their own take on paper and inscription, a process that is itself collective and multitudinous—something that can only be engaged with at the collective level, it is especially critical to note that anarchist prophecy itself cannot provide this most crucial function of collective forms of vision. While I've been arguing that the anarchist prophets I have looked at hold that vision for the larger community, I only mean that in a very basic sense, as a kind of placeholder. But the actual content of that vision cannot come from these prophets, and, if they supplant that content with content of their own (a very strong temptation, as I have shown), then they are no longer serving as anarchist prophets. This built-in constraint on anarchist prophecy certainly cannot guarantee that anarchist prophets will give way to the communities that they seek to preserve and enhance, but it does at least give us a criterion by which to determine when that prophet is continuing to serve an anarchist function and when she is not.

Insofar as there is always a kind of archist element to anarchist prophecy, at least under the conditions of modern archism that I have been describing in these pages, and because anarchist prophets must look like archist ones in order to successfully steal into the heart of archist power and ruin that sight from within, they can never really be more than a transitional figure; the role of the anarchist prophet is to make herself redundant. Having said that, however, given the fact that the defeat of archism, even if it can be achieved, is never utterly secure, given that archism can come springing back to life quite readily, even if it is at odds with an anarchist universe, the potential role for anarchist prophecy itself can and should never be entirely abandoned. Whenever archism reasserts itself, as and if needed, anarchist prophecy comes up to meet and overturn it once again.

Building the Anarcheon

In thinking about what anarchism might look like beyond its struggle with archism and even beyond its need for anarchic prophecy, it seems to me that an entirely different vocabulary might be useful. There are so many words in the English language that suggest the predominance of archism. Words like architecture, archdiocese, archetypes, archipelago, and archenemy all speak to the pervasiveness of archism, whereas the word *archism* itself is relatively absent. In general, these words speak to the usual meaning that is derived from *arkein*: the most, the original, the best, the strongest, the highest. The architect, for example, is the master builder, the archbishop, the highest bishop of them all, and so on.

To build up a countering vocabulary, we can see that some of these designations, like the term *anarchism* itself, already exist (although it does not come without its own baggage). Furthermore, there is already the idea of anarchitecture as articulated by Gordon Matta-Clark, who along with others formed a group by that name in the early 1970s that was more about creating voids than creating buildings.[53]

In keeping with some of the ideas already expressed in this book, I would like to think of this additional "an"—or "a," depending on the word in question—not simply as the negation but as an entirely alternate way of being. So, for example, you could say that just as an architect builds an archeon, an anarchitect—if I may borrow that word from those who originally coined it—can work to build the anarcheon. If the archeon is the place that judgment and rule come from, the anarcheon is the redistribution of that site back to everyone in the community.[54] Whereas the archeon must be in a particular and unique place, the anarcheon is everywhere. Without the archeon—or putting this in a positive language once again, with the anarcheon—space and time become (re)anarchized; every place becomes as important or special as every other place, and every time is as special as every other time. Here, the house of the archon is no longer better and higher than any other house or place, and the future and the ancient past are no longer the only times that matter. Where Carl Schmitt famously says, "Sovereign is he who decides upon the exception," we see that when we cease to privilege certain points of time and space, the exception is removed entirely; nothing is exceptional anymore, nothing stands outside space and time to rule over the rest, everything is in play.[55] More accurately still, since space and time are *already* anarchist, the role of anarchitecture is simply the expression of that basic concept.

The idea of an anarchitect might seem to allow us a way to speak of anarchist prophets without recourse to theological language, which many leftists simply can't and won't abide. Similarly, to make one last neologism, through this act of anarchitecture, perhaps we can speak of them as being anarchons too, the unmakers and unseers of the power of the archons. Yet I would hold off associating either term with anarchist prophecy per se or, rather, I would say that their relationship to these terms cannot be total, so that *only* the anarchist prophet can be the anarchitect or the anarchon. As a transitional figure, the anarchist prophet might well engage in some of these activities, serving to unbuild the structures of archism itself (as an anarchitect) and occupying and subverting the position of the archon (as an anarchon), but I think that ultimately we should reserve these terms for the community itself. There is only one architect, one master builder, but everyone must be an anarchitect to keep that building from being reassembled. Similarly, there is only one archon but everyone must be an anarchon, a term that refers to everyone when their power and authority are returned to them.

These neologisms allow me to be a bit more specific about answers to some of the basic questions this book has raised. What does the anarchist prophet see, what is the disappointing vision that she has? She sees the anarcheon, the empty throne of power redistributed and dissipated in the vastness of the world. She sees, in other words, the anarchons that we all are. In this way, her seeing these things helps us unsee their archist opposites. When we see the anarcheon, we no longer see the archeon itself (arguably this is what happens in Saramago's novel *Blindness*). When we recognize ourselves as anarchons, then our habit of giving our authority to the archons necessarily gets disrupted. The anarchist prophet then can *see* these things but she cannot *be* these things. Like the doctor's wife in Saramago's novels, she can participate as an anarchon, not in her special unique function as prophet but only insofar as she is one of many.

Double Vision

Given the inherent risk of the anarchist prophet becoming seduced by her own unique status, and given too that she does not actually possess special vision at any rate, what is her own "expertise"? What does she bring as herself versus what she brings in terms of the status that archism has lent her? I think her expertise, if I can use such an archist word to refer to something that is so anarchist, is that she knows how to navigate the kind of double vision that we all have but, in her case, if she succeeds, such double vision leads not to acquiescence but subversion and disruption. Perhaps this is the thing that she can teach the rest of us. By "double vision," I mean the way that we all see simultaneously with our anarchist eyes, wherein we already know everything there is to know, or unknow, and see everything that there is to see, or unsee, even as, at the same time, we also see with our archist eyes, those eyes that belong to an external "higher, better" self that seeks to obey our wish to be annihilated by salvation, a self that hates itself, its mortality, and its fellow subjects. With these other eyes, we see an entirely alternative and alienated universe, one that is superimposed over the world itself.

This duality is something that the anarchist prophet shares with us all. As we saw with Zarathustra and the angel of history, even the anarchist prophets are not immune to the lures and temptations of archism: Zarathustra falls for those lures over and over again; and the angel of history would like to save the world, but an anarchist God won't let him.

In the real-life examples I looked at too, you can see this same struggle; Buenaventura Durruti was always worried and vigilant about his own engagement with "leaderism," and some of his comrades clearly succumbed to that temptation. Similarly, Yali the prophet wanted "in" very badly; he was willing to give up his own culture and become associated with Western archism and only retreated from that stance when he realized that the West had no intention of sharing its treasures with him.

The literary figures that I looked at in this book are no less conflicted by their double vision. Lauren Olamina has a messiah complex (at least her daughter thinks so). Frankenstein's monster is a 100 percent archist wannabe who is only "saved"—if you can call it that—by his hideous face and violent and vengeful actions. The doctor's wife certainly doesn't want the position she has been put into by the "twin plagues" of blindness and blanking. Nora Durst would have given anything to return to an archist world. When she goes to the world of the departed, she realizes that that world isn't archist anymore either. Only by realizing that there's no getting away from the death of archism—akin to her experiencing eternal recurrence in a very literal way—does Nora finally accept and even choose her place in the world.

Perhaps the only "pure" anarchist prophet that I looked at in this book was Hobbes's Holy Spirit. This spirit is reduced nearly to the vanishing point so that it cannot have any wishes or desires of its own, whether of the archist or the anarchist variety. It holds a critical space—the space of the archeon—and has no ability of its own to fill that space with itself, leaving it effectively empty for the rest of us (thus allowing us to see the anarcheon a bit more clearly).

What the anarchist prophets I am discussing here do, even for themselves, is teach us how to navigate this double vision by turning the lies of archist vision against itself. This process is far from easy; we see how readily Zarathustra fails in his mission. He only convinced one person throughout the length of *Thus Spoke Zarathustra*—the tightrope walker we meet in the prologue—and that person was dying and then dead when their conversation happened. But the fact that it can happen at all—that the anarchist prophet can help dislodge the grip that the archist sense of reality has on the rest of us, even as they, like all of us, remain mesmerized by archist seductions—is a critical and precious gift, albeit a gift based on removal rather than handing something over. The rest of us don't need their intervention or insight to be anarchists. We already *are* all anarchists—and anarchons!— but these prophets help defeat our own archist viewpoints from within the archist apparatus; they defeat archism on and by its own terms. Let's compromise and say that we don't *need* anarchist prophecy, but it helps us in our own struggle to decide what there is to see and stop seeing what isn't there.

The Living

Whether we need anarchist prophets or not, this book is not ultimately about them but about the much larger group that I have been calling by various names, ranging from the people to the community to the living (and sometimes the dead as well). The notion of the living in particular is important because it offers us a way to speak of a group of persons (actually everyone) with a language that recognizes the temptations of archism—because the living would presumably like to stay alive—as well as its connection to a larger anarchist universe. To get at this other sense, let me reiterate a quote from Benjamin to think about the nature of the living and their relationship to anarchism. In "Critique of Violence," Benjamin famously writes, "Mythic violence is bloody power over mere life for its own sake; divine violence is pure power over all life for the sake of the living."[56] Who are the living as distinct from those who possess mere life? It seems to me that we are talking about the same group of persons, depending on whether we read them as subjects of mythic violence (mere life) or as objects of divine violence (the living). Here again we see a simultaneous doubleness. As long as there is archism, we are all mere life *and* we are all the living.

Archism, while it has living human representatives—the archons—is not itself alive. In some sense, it isn't really dead either, insofar as it has never been alive. It is a parasite, a vampire that feeds off the life it oversees. Maybe using the term *undead* is (therefore) the best term for what archism is. When an undead thing becomes the center of our life, we become merely (or barely) alive. In the false transfer of substance and reality that lies at the basis of archism, our own life becomes derealized, so that archism itself can appear to be larger—and realer—than life. Accordingly, our life becomes almost beside the point; it ceases to be "our" life at all and becomes instead a source of authority and power for the archons to reflect those things back upon us as alienated power and authority.[57] It is not that we cease to be the living; it is just that our life has become a source of power and vitality for a select few.

When, on the other hand, we resist archism and put ourselves—or find ourselves, depending on how you read it—in the stream of divine violence, we are returned to our status of the living, or more accurately we find that we have been the living all along. Normally the very idea of "the living" threatens to offer the worst possible generalizations and is a trope used endlessly by archism itself. Yet Benjamin helps us conceptualize what we mean by the living in a way that avoids that kind of grand narrativization. If we think of the living as he does, we see that even when we are "merely" alive, subject to the phantasms of archism, we are also always (and still) living, afforded the opportunities to defy that effect. As described in chapter 4, divine violence isn't a once-in-a-long-while or long-ago event; it is always happening via the "magic of matter," a vast anarchist conspiracy that occurs throughout the universe and throughout time. As participants in that conspiracy, we the living—and the dead as well—can never be totalized by the shadows of archism.

It is our identity as the living that we must seek to recover or perhaps more simply acknowledge. We must not just see it but hear it, smell it, touch it, taste it; all our senses are involved in this most basic and human of attributes. This is the reason that I have spent so much time discussing ordinary life, daily interactions, speech communities, collective decision-making, and other things that are effectively and relatively free from archist interference. It would make sense that archism would want to control every aspect of this life— Foucault's notion of biopolitics seems to be an explanation of how it is going about doing so in our own time—but I think it is critical to note that archism can't ultimately succeed in reducing life to what it is itself, to something that is undead.[58] Since it is not itself alive, archism needs some *life*, something outside itself to draw from. If it totalized our life, if there was no space for anarchism at all, archism would fail by succeeding—in much the same way as the plague of blindness Saramago describes can be read as representation succeeding all too well—dragging us into its own nothingness once and for all. Archism can, of course, kill us all. It threatens to do so on a fairly regular basis via the twin specters of nuclear war and global warming and other forms of environmental devastation. Yet this would mean the end of archism too, although at a price that is too horrible to contemplate.

The part of life that remains outside the clutches of archism is not merely a holding pen for archism to draw upon, however. It is also something that is of itself; life has its own rhythms, its own connections that are utterly independent of archism. If archism were ever to actually end, this anarchist life would go on; unlike archism, which can't exist without it, anarchist life doesn't need archism at all. This is perhaps the ultimate asymmetry that means that in the end, unless all life and the world itself is destroyed, anarchism will or at least can survive archism.

This does not mean that all we have to do is "wait it out," until archism collapses from its own contradictions. I don't think that will ever happen (if it did, it would have happened already). And further, even if it did, archism is not a system that we can "learn to live with" or seek to moderate while we live in its shadow. The point is that there is literally no "living" with archism at all. It does not allow or condone life that it does not control. While this is clearer for Black and Brown communities who are assaulted daily by white supremacy, it is true at the end of the day for all life under conditions of archism (and racism itself is a mechanism that helps disguise that fact).

I have no doubt whatsoever that archism would readily destroy the world and kill us all rather than face the threat of its elimination; perhaps that is why it is already poised to do so. In a very real sense, we the living, therefore, have nothing to lose in challenging archism. It seeks only our death and we seek only our life (the latter in all its richness and contradiction).

Perhaps most critically, this life, and the anarchism it manifests, is in tune with the universe in a way that archism simply cannot be. If the universe is itself anarchic, that is, multivaried, dynamic, and every changing—the universe Lauren Olamina describes in the Earthseed series by Octavia Butler— that matches the condition of the living as well. This connection is a source of sustenance and power even as it is also a source of resistance to archist rule. This is another way to say what Benjamin tells us: that the objects of the world—and by extension the objects of the universe as well—are in perpetual revolt against mythic violence. But it's more than revolt; it's also a vast ferment, an interactive dynamic that is positive just as much as it is resistant to archist phantasm.

This is not to say that life as such is real and empirical versus the lies of archism. I think we get into trouble when we say things like that; the archist maw immediately reappears whenever we try to cite something empirical and true to definitively assert something. But if we think of reality as being contingent, undetermined, and affected by multiple connections across space and time, what Benjamin refers to as the "now-time," I think we can say at the very least that anarchism is real*er*, more material than archism, and that reality itself, whatever that means, conspires with life to avoid the certain unrealities, the determinations, and the taxonomizations of archist parasitism.

This is all a long-winded way to say that small *a* anarchism gets us to think about ordinary, daily life in a way that is the opposite of what archism tells us. For archism, daily life is boring. It's unglamorous and banal. It's mere drudgery. Who cares what you, your friends, and your family have to say compared to what Kim Kardashian, Mark Zuckerberg, or Queen Elizabeth have to say? What do you, as a private individual or a member of some local community, know compared to the experts? Who are you to have an opinion (unless it is solicited by some leading polling agency or unless you get the earnest, nodding looks of someone doing a "listening tour")? Although modern liberal forms of archism run a kind of counternarrative to this way of thinking (Your opinion counts! You are somebody! Anybody can succeed if they really try!), people tend to see this for what it is—a lie—that really serves to bolster the idea that only the better among us get to do important things and think important thoughts. And of course, under conditions of modern biopolitical archism, racism, misogyny, and other cleavages further reduce the living by designating whole populations whose life is not deemed worthy. This is one of the reasons why I think the name *Black Lives Matter* is so powerful—it speaks against a reduction of Black life to nothingness. Or, perhaps more accurately, to reiterate Moten's way of thinking, it shows that inside that nothingness is a whole lot of life.

My definition of the living is what people are when they are not (only) the subject of archist interference. This accords with Benjamin's view that nonviolent relations, acts, and speech—that is, action that doesn't sustain mythic violence—happen all the time between private citizens, between diplomats, between those not bound up by contracts and determination of what is true. I much prefer Benjamin's vision of the living to that of Arendt, who seems to discount—depending on how you read her, of course—the ordinary aspects of life: brushing your teeth, talking to friends, and so forth, in favor of a more idealized notion of political life. I think that in a way Arendt has insufficiently questioned the association of ordinary life with banality (and in fact banality becomes a very negative term for her when she associates it with Adolf Eichmann).[59] In the end, I think she is looking for the same model of politics as Benjamin but can't quite eliminate these archist overlays in doing so (perhaps in part because she is so attracted to the idea of arche as a form of origin and not only as a basis for ruling).

In Benjamin's view, which I share, ordinary life is where it is at. This is the repository of a political life that survives even the starkest of archist contexts. This is where a connection to the larger anarchist network of the universe comes to the fore. If we can think of life at this level and in these ways, we are indeed thinking in accordance with the insights of anarchist prophecy. We can see from the perspective of where we are rather than where we are not—just as Lauren Olamina advised her father to do—and not just alone but in community with other persons (and other things too). From this perspective, it seems, we can think and do things that are not only unimaginable—because archism forbids us from imagining things outside itself—but that we have already long been practicing. This is possible not via some externality, some kind of god or state or whatever else archism has foisted on us, but entirely and only on our own and only by treating and connecting with one another. When we think of ourselves as joining up with an anarchist universe, aligning ourselves with the contingency of everything that exists as Butler so clearly lays out, the key point perhaps is that there is no externality. There is nothing but what is, and that, it turns out, is more than enough.

This concept of the living helps show why we can eventually move on from the need—at least for a time—for anarchist prophets. While we are all the living at all times—and I would definitely include a link to the dead in this concept as well—we are also mere life under conditions of archism and hence once again we live a kind of double life, partially alive and partially not. When our existence as the living takes priority over mere life, then we have no need at all for anarchist prophets. They remind us of our life when we don't quite have it, but only we can actually live it for ourselves.

This last point is especially important for the kinds of political agendas that come out from thinking about the distinction between the living and mere life. For all my admiration of James Scott and his work, I for one am not satisfied with the way that he finds resistance in ordinary life as a good unto itself. For me, and I think for Benjamin too, it is not enough that by living, talking, and acting in anarchist ways, we are in fact defying the archism that reduces us to mere life. Yes, there is rebellion in every act and gesture; yes, the universe itself conspires against archism, but as long as archism is busily preying upon the living, this is more of a potential than an actuality. We always have the ability to resist, we are always practicing it—which is no small thing; it means that when we revolt, we already know what to do—but to really change things, to lose our double vision, we need something more. We need revolution, we need overt resistance, we need, at least some of the time, anarchist prophets in order for us all to be able to "become what we are"—to cite Nietzsche once more—that is, the living.

She Unnames Them

By way of final conclusion, I turn to one final inkling of a radically different way to go about the question of trust and community, a very different and in some ways potentially much deeper vision of anarchism and its relationship to materiality. This comes from Ursula K. Le Guin's very short (one page!) story, "She Unnames Them."[60] The "she" in question is Eve, although she is resolutely unnamed in the story. After Adam goes about naming all the things in the Garden of Eden, the one who is no longer called Eve comes by and takes all the names back. Almost all the animals are only too happy to let them go (a few pets and speaking birds object, along with the yaks, who like the sound of their name). She tells Adam, "You and your father lent me this [name], gave it to me, actually. It's been really useful, but it doesn't exactly seem to fit very well lately. But thanks very much! It's really been very useful." Adam barely pays attention and then says, "O.K., fine, dear, When's dinner?"

Once she takes the names away, the one who is no longer called Eve notes the following:

> NONE were left now to unname, and yet how close I felt to them when I saw one of them swim or fly or trot or crawl across my way or over my skin, or stalk me in the night, or go along beside me for a while in the day. They seemed far closer than when their names had stood between myself and them like a clear barrier: so close that my fear of them and their fear of me became one same fear. And the attraction that many of us felt, the desire to feel or rub or caress one another's scales or skin or feathers or fur, taste one another's blood or flesh, keep one another warm—that attraction was now all one with the fear, and the hunter could not be told from the hunted, nor the eater from the food.

It seems as if once the name has been removed, so has the distance between human beings and the world they are part of. We get an image here of what life would be like without any form of representation—or even presentation!—at all. Here, the distances between persons and between animals, the taxonomies and the hierarchies that are the stuff of archism, seemingly melt away. Benjamin's entire opus is devoted to seeking to deal with the loss of Adam's power of naming, but Le Guin suggests that this might not be the terrible loss we think it is. "She Unnames Them" suggests an even more radical form of self-trust than what Benjamin proposes, not so much using a *pharmakon*, a way to use fetishism against itself as he suggests, but a trusting in our own materiality, seeking to rejoin that vast material communion with no sense of human particularity or uniqueness whatsoever. As long as we seek a name, any name at all, as long as we remain creatures of language, or at least this kind of language, we will continue to distance ourselves from the world that we are part of. Surely archism itself would not be possible without the insistence on (over)naming, on some form of representation after all.

The one who is no longer named Eve in this way can be seen as offering something beyond the scope of anarchist prophecy entirely. She is calling us away, not only from the archist forms of seeing but even from those collective forms of seeing that involve only human beings. In his own telling of the story of the Fall, Benjamin barely mentions Eve, which indicates the degree to which this possible outcome really comes out of left field for an Abrahamic-based source of resistance to archism (even as it keeps the centrality of the Fall as an Abrahamic origin story).

I do think there are resources in Benjamin for precisely this reappraisal of humanity's position vis-à-vis the material world. Yet I also think from a Benjaminian perspective that we might get a concern that what is being proposed here looks suspiciously like the promises of archism itself, a kind of unity and connection to "the things themselves" that hides an ongoing form of domination.[61] Or, if it isn't that—because in some sense it is the opposite of what archism wants—it would be hard to tell the difference between a full post- (or even pre-) nominal universe and one that just pretended to be real and authentic.

Depending on what you think about these last few issues, the one who is no longer named Eve, as rendered by Le Guin, is perhaps the ultimate response to archism, renouncing both the need for and even the possibility of prophecy, of the value and necessity of human sight entirely. And given the fact that even if archism can die (as *The Leftovers* shows), it can also come back to life (as Nietzsche explains to us), it might be good to have a "Plan B," a different way to oppose archism than perpetually seeking its death, just as it seeks ours, within and by its existing structures, through language itself.

For my own way of thinking, I hesitate to go too far down this path, not only because it could in some ways be hijacked for a more obscure form of archism after all—a kind of ultimate transcendentalism in immanentist clothing—but also because I don't think there is anything wrong with being human centric so long as we recognize our relationality to the rest of the universe. That is, since we all are humans, it makes sense for us to see the universe through human eyes, through our connections to and conflicts with one another, through our myriad perspectives. This is actually a problem that I have with an idea like object-oriented ontology; I just think it makes sense to acknowledge where we are coming, and looking, from.[62] To do otherwise denies or obscures the very kinds of ordinary and engaged ways of life that for me are crucial to a kind of admittedly human-based anarchism in the first place. To conspire with an anarchist universe doesn't mean that we have to leave ourselves behind or merge with everything else, and in fact I don't think we either could or necessarily should do so, just as I don't think or expect rocks or bagels or pigeons to give up their rock, bagel, or pigeon orientation.

Having said this, thinking along with Le Guin does show that, at the very least, there are always options beyond our options and choices beyond what we actually choose. The universe is vast and anarchic, and our place in it, as Butler shows so well, is but a tiny corner of it all. Perhaps we can learn how to occupy that corner differently, whether that be in ways that are shaped by and in response to the Abrahamic legacy of archist prophecy or in ways that accord with other human traditions and styles of politics. Or perhaps we can reoccupy our position in ways we have not yet imagined, ways that are even unimaginable but still very much remain in the realm of what can and is to be done.

notes

Introduction

1 In this way, liberal capitalist parliamentary systems, fascist and authoritarian systems, and any other system with a top-down hierarchy is an example of archism. Political systems that are predominantly anarchist are much rarer, especially in the contemporary world. At the same time, as I will argue further in this book, every polity has a huge array of anarchist aspects insofar as anarchism corresponds to human life itself, to that body of interactions, mutuality, and decision that archism preys upon.

2 Kafka, "The City Coat of Arms," in Kafka, *Parables and Paradoxes*, 37.

3 Kafka, "The City Coat of Arms," 39.

4 Kafka, "The City Coat of Arms," 39.

5 Kafka, "The City Coat of Arms," 39.

6 Kafka, "The Refusal," in Kafka, *Parables and Paradoxes*, 165.

7 Kafka, "The Refusal," 171.

8 Kafka, "The Refusal," 171.

9 Kafka, "The Refusal," 173–74.

10 Kafka, "The Refusal," 161.

11 Kafka, "The Refusal," 173.

12 In *Textual Conspiracies*, I discuss at length "The City Coat of Arms" as well as *The Castle*. In these Kafka works, and especially in *The Castle*, the possibility of the nonexistence of the power that the villagers obey and desire is constantly dangled before us (and them).

13 However, as I will argue throughout this book, this could never happen. Being a parasite, archism requires some form of collective sight to prey upon and draw from.

14 See Arendt, *The Human Condition*, 22.

15 Cedric J. Robinson, quoting Otis Madison, notes that "the purpose of racism is to control the behavior of white people, not Black people. For Blacks, guns and tanks are sufficient." Robinson, *Forgeries of Memory and Meaning*, 82. I think this is a fundamental insight that explains a lot of the working mechanisms of archism. I first encountered this quote when it was cited by Robin Kelley in a talk that he gave at the American Political Science Association's annual conference on September 1, 2017.

16 Monmouth University Polling Institute, "Protestors' Anger Justified Even if Actions May Not Be."

17 Fanon, *Black Skin, White Masks*, 110.

18 Here I recognize that Fanon himself did not use the term archism.

19 Fanon, *The Wretched of the Earth*, 21.

20 Fanon, *The Wretched of the Earth*, 51.

21 Later in this book, I will show how the anarchist prophets I am interested in use these founts of archist authority to ruin and expose these very same forms of power.

22 See Foucault, *Discipline and Punish*.

23 In fact, I'm not so sure that this reading of the gaze is so discordant with Foucault's model. After all, he recognizes the way that people internalize the guard tower into their own minds so that they are in effect guarding themselves. The next step, to see themselves from that tower, doesn't seem such a stretch.

24 W. Benjamin, *The Origin of German Tragic Drama*, 70. In the original German, it is "Der purpur muss es decken." Slavoj Žižek cites Lacan, who talks about something similar when it comes to the idea of the "emperor's new clothes." See Žižek, *The Sublime Object of Ideology*, 29.

25 In practice, this distinction is not always so neat. The doctor's wife in Saramago's two novels is both an anarchist prophet and a member of her community. This is true of the other figures that I look at as well, although in the case of the doctor's wife, the special markers that make her seem to stand out from the community are entirely absent.

26 In speaking of vision in the sense of having eyesight, it may seem that I am saying that only sighted people can participate in either archist or anarchist vision, but as I'll argue when speaking of Saramago's *Blindness*, blind people are just as susceptible to archism and are just as capable of anarchist sight as the sighted. The visuality that I am talking about is not strictly speaking in accordance with the possibility of visual sight per se but is more a matter of organizing and composing reality as a lived experience and read through a visual metaphor, something that can be conveyed to the sighted and the blind alike.

27 Goodrich, "Proboscations," 361. I am indebted to Jonas Rosenbrück for pointing out the dominance of vision in the concept of archist prophecy and the possibility of alternatives to thinking/seeing in that way.

28 In *The Trial*, for example, K. gets overcome by an overheated and stinking court of law that doubles as a lived-in attic space. A woman says to him, "You're a little dizzy, aren't you? . . . Don't worry, . . . there's nothing unusual about that here, almost everyone here has an attack like this the first time. . . . The sun beats down on the attic beams and the hot wood makes the air terribly thick and stifling. . . . Then if you take into consideration that a great deal of wash is hung out here to dry as well—the tenants can't be entirely forbidden from doing so—it will come as no surprise that you feel a little sick. But in the end people get quite used to the air." This is K.'s real initiation into the law. Kafka, *The Trial*, 73–74.

29 See the chapter on atheism in Aristodemou's *Law, Psychoanalysis, Society*.

30 W. Benjamin, "On the Concept of History," 392. For an excellent investigation of the various sorts of negativity that are out there, see Kramer, *Excluded Within*.

31 A more accurate term might be anti-gnostic since the anarchism that I am describing here is always and positively oriented toward human life as such. I am indebted to Andrew Benjamin for the way he connects this attitude in Walter Benjamin to anti-gnosticism.

32 Aristodemou, *Law, Psychoanalysis, Society*, 108.

33 It should be added that the Abrahamic religions do not have a monopoly on the institution of prophecy.

34 Ramnath, *Decolonizing Anarchism*, 6. I am grateful to Simmy Makhijani for referring me to Ramnath's work.

35 Ramnath, *Decolonizing Anarchism*, 7.

36 Karen Barad's *Meeting the Universe Halfway* helps me think of an anarchist universe as well.

Chapter One. Appointing Prophets

An earlier version of part of chapter 1 appeared as "Why Does the State Keep Coming Back? Neoliberalism, the State and the Archeon," *Law and Critique* 29, no. 3 (November 2018): 359–75.

1 Machiavelli, *"The Discourses,"* 147. Machiavelli offers a countering image of anarchist prophecy in the form of Appius Pulcher. In describing a Roman ritual where sacred poultrymen threw grain to a group of chickens as an augury to predict victory in battle—if the chickens pecked at the grain, the battle would be won; if they didn't, it would be lost—Machiavelli contrasts two consuls, Papirius and Appius Pulcher. In Papirius's case, the chickens didn't peck, but Papirius lied and said they had (and had the head poultryman killed by "friendly fire" to silence him). Pulcher's chickens also didn't peck, and Pulcher said, "Then let us see whether they will drink," having them thrown

into the sea, where they all drowned. Machiavelli, *"The Discourses,"* 158. Here, Pulcher risks the disappointment of the augury in order to assert human self-determination, making him more of an anarchist prophet, while Papirius, who does what he needs to preserve the lies that give him power, is more in the mode of an archist prophet.

2 See Althusser, "Ideology and the State."

3 Kafka, *The Castle*, 1.

4 Kafka, *The Castle*, 8.

5 I owe Nick Doliber for the insight that the castle in Kafka's novel may not exist at all.

6 Kafka, *The Castle*, 8. For the German version, see Kafka, *Das Schloss*, 17.

7 Kafka, *The Castle*, 9. My italics.

8 Kafka, *The Castle*, 98–99.

9 In fact, just about every Abrahamic variant has an ongoing version of prophecy, even if it is not always called so by name. Thus, for example, in Mormonism (which some consider a fourth branch of Abrahamic religion rather than a subset of Christianity), prophecy is an ongoing and active feature. Similarly, in Shiism, active prophecy is possible in a way that it is less evident in the Sunni Muslim tradition. In Judaism, you have, for example, the case of Chabadism, which has designated (at least some strands of it) Menachem Mendel Schneerson as the messiah (*moshiach*). Fundamentalist forms of Protestantism also have a very active relationship with God, reflecting some of its original and potentially radical basis in the Reformation; for some sects, especially, everyone is potentially a prophet.

10 An excellent book on this subject is Shulman, *American Prophecy*.

11 In *Emergency Politics*, Bonnie Honig notes how Rosa Parks, for example, is seen as having spontaneously refused to go to the back of the bus, whereas she was part of a larger protest movement and the act was planned very deliberately. Portraying someone like her as a one-off is a way to make it seem that her act was personal and not political, not coming from a strong and organized challenge to the status quo, weakening the radical implications of her act. See Honig, *Emergency Politics*, 128. For an extended reading of this same situation, see Kramer, *Excluded Within*.

12 Isaiah 1:4, in *Holy Scriptures*, 563. Page numbers of further citations from this source are given parenthetically after the verse number.

13 Isaiah 1:14 (564).

14 Isaiah 1:19–21 (564).

15 Isaiah 2:3–4 (565).

16 Isaiah 2:17 (566).

17 Jeremiah 1:11–13, (662).

18 Johnston, *Ancient Greek Divination*, 13.

19 Johnston, *Ancient Greek Divination*, 13.

20 Johnston, *Ancient Greek Divination*, 34.

21 Johnston, *Ancient Greek Divination*, 34.

22 Johnston, *Ancient Greek Divination*, 56.

23 Derrida, *Archive Fever*, 2.

24 I am indebted to Tiffany MacLellan for alerting me to the concept of the archeon.

25 Kantorowicz, *The King's Two Bodies*.

26 In *Archaeology of Babel*, Siraj Ahmed makes the argument that when various scriptures from the Arabic, Persian, and Hindu traditions were translated into English by Sir William Jones in the 1770s, this began a transformation of those traditions from a loose and local interpretation of their own histories into a highly regimented and absolutist form of legal and political authority. In this way, these traditions become the basis of an exported and colonial archism, very much in keeping with the way that Fanon understood the appropriation of colonized history and reality by colonial forces.

27 Foucault, "Truth and Power," 121.

28 Against this false form of discontinuation between cause and effect, as I argue further in chapter 4, Benjamin counterposes the idea of "pure means" as a way to actually, rather than phantasmically, sever this link.

29 Althusser, "Ideology and the State," 118.

30 Althusser, "Ideology and the State," 116.

31 See Foucault, *The Birth of Biopolitics*.

32 See Martel, *Unburied Bodies*. See also Baldwin, "Going to Meet the Man."

33 Baldwin, *The Fire Next Time*, 92.

34 However, my discussion of the Melanesian prophet Yali, in chapter 6, shows that this promise does not work the same way on everyone.

35 Benjamin, "On the Concept of History," 395.

36 In a somewhat unrelated conversation with our reading group, Richard Joyce called this a form of "sneaky retroactivity."

37 W. Benjamin, "Fate and Character," 201.

38 See, for example, W. Benjamin, *The Arcades Project*, 66 (B2,4); 544 (S1,5); 548 (S2a,3); 842–43 (G17).

39 W. Benjamin, "Critique of Violence," 248.

40 Arendt, *The Origins of Totalitarianism*, 298.

41 Birmingham, "The An-Archic Event of Natality," 766.

42 Birmingham, "The An-Archic Event of Natality," 766–67. Arendt further complicates this when she acknowledges that the right to have rights is effectively empty unless communities make a political decision to enforce those rights. Arendt, *The Origins of Totalitarianism*, 298.

43 Birmingham, "The An-Archic Event of Natality," 766.

44 See, for example, Derrida, "Force of Law," 27. I am grateful to one of my anonymous reviewers for suggesting the link to Arendt and Derrida in terms of the question of *arche*.

45 Kamuf, "From Now On," 207.

46 The opposite can also be true wherein something that appears anarchist can actually be archist. If Ahmed's argument is convincing, the entirety

of humanism in Western thought, arguably the basis for continental philosophy and other leftist forms of writing and thinking, is actually derived from the colonizing project of William Jones, a key philologist who sought to break the spell of Hebrew and the sense of it being an original and true language that determined all of human life. By introducing (and translating) the Arabic, Persian, and Hindu tradition to the West, Jones sought to immanentize those cultures and make claims for specific, local, and all-too-human practices. The purpose of this endeavor, however, was not to actually introduce a radical degree of anarchist-style immanentism but to displace other traditions in order to subject them all to a secularized and ruthless form of Western transcendentalism, the basis for colonialism itself. His claim that scholars ranging from Nietzsche to Edward Said (!) have been prey to this ruse is a powerful and disturbing one. This argument is evidence for a claim I make later in the book, based on the work of Barad, that there are good and bad forms of transcendentalism and immanentism alike. Archism is a form of fake (bad) transcendentalism and hence fake (bad) immanentism too. See Ahmed, *Archaeology of Babel*. I also can't help but note the connection between Ahmed's discussion of Babel and Kafka's.

47 Hobbes, *Leviathan*, 128 (2.18). Citations to *Leviathan* provide the page number, followed by the part number and chapter number in parentheses.

48 Although I will argue that in some sense we are *all* anarchist prophets.

49 See Martel, *Unburied Bodies*.

50 Critically, the coconspiracy works both ways, for the sake of the living and the dead. After all, as Benjamin writes: "*even the dead* will not be safe from the enemy if he is victorious. And this enemy has never ceased to be victorious." W. Benjamin, "On the Concept of History," 391.

Chapter Two. Hobbes and the Holy Spirit

1 Hobbes, *Leviathan*, 287–88 (3.36). For other readings of Hobbes and prophecy, see Hoekstra, "Disarming the Prophets"; and Coleman, "Hobbes's Iconoclasm." For more general views of Hobbes and theology, see Botwinick, *Skepticism, Belief, and the Modern*; Curley, "The Covenant with God in Hobbes' Leviathan"; Springborg, "Leviathan and the Problem of Ecclesiastical Authority"; Springborg, "Hobbes on Religion"; Pocock, *Politics, Language, and Time*; and Eisenach, *Two Worlds of Liberalism*.

2 Hobbes, *Leviathan*, 288 (3.36).

3 Hobbes, *Leviathan*, 288 (3.36).

4 Hobbes, *Leviathan*, 293 (3.36).

5 In an earlier work, *Subverting the Leviathan*, I argue more generally for the way that Hobbes subverts his own overt political message in texts like *Leviathan*. In that text, I focus less on prophecy and more on his political theology more generally, as well as his rhetorical style. For more on Hobbes's rhetoric, see Skinner, *Reason and Rhetoric in the Philosophy of Hobbes*.

6 Botwinick, *Skepticism, Belief, and the Modern*, 11.

7 Hobbes, *Leviathan*, 120-121 (1.17).

8 Hobbes, *Leviathan*, 120 (1.17).

9 Hobbes, *Leviathan*, 245 (2.31).

10 Hobbes, *Leviathan*, 120 (1.17).

11 Hobbes, *Leviathan*, 322-23 (3.40).

12 Hobbes, *Leviathan*, 323 (3.40).

13 Hobbes, *Leviathan*, 323 (3.40).

14 Hobbes, *Leviathan*, 324 (3.40).

15 Hobbes, *Leviathan*, 324-25 (3.40). This is a critical moment for Botwinick in his own genealogy of Hobbes's understanding of the covenant.

16 Hobbes, *Leviathan*, 325 (3.40).

17 Botwinick, *Skepticism, Belief, and the Modern*, 11.

18 Hobbes, *Leviathan*, 271 (3.34).

19 Hobbes, *Leviathan*, 24 (1.4).

20 Hobbes, *Leviathan*, 25 (1.4).

21 Hobbes, *Leviathan*, 25 (1.4).

22 More accurately, it *can* be done by just one person if they are literally the only person on Earth, such as was the case with Adam. Then, with the addition of Eve and then their families, that linguistic community necessarily grew.

23 Hobbes, *Leviathan*, 30 (1.5).

24 Gregory S. Kavka tells us that for Hobbes, injustice is "'somewhat like' absurdity, which involves contradicting what one earlier maintained." Absurdity then is the danger of violating the decisions about speech and meaning that have come out of the collective process of language and meaning making. Kavka, *Hobbesian Moral and Political Theory*, 306.

25 Hobbes, *Leviathan*, 290 (3.36).

26 Hobbes, *Leviathan*, 290-91 (3.36).

27 Hobbes, *Leviathan*, 291 (3.36).

28 Hobbes, *Leviathan*, 293 (3.36).

29 Hobbes, *Leviathan*, 293 (3.36).

30 Hobbes, *Leviathan*, 293 (3.36).

31 Hobbes, *Leviathan*, 297 (3.36).

32 Hobbes, *Leviathan*, 297 (3.36).

33 Hobbes, *Leviathan*, 298 (3.36).

34 In *De Cive*, Hobbes revisits the notion of judging prophets by whether they can accurately predict the future. He complicates this question, asking "whether the events . . . do truly answer [the predictions] or not, may admit many controversies; especially in predictions which obscurely and enigmatically foretell the event." Hobbes, *De Cive* (in *Man and Citizen*), 318. In such cases, he argues, "we cannot judge, otherwise than *by the way of natural reason*; because that judgment depends on the prophet's interpretation, and on its proportion with the event." Hobbes, *De Cive*, 318. Here again, human judgment remains the only basis for engagement with what is ascribed to God.

35 Hobbes, *Leviathan*, 291–92 (3.36).

36 Hobbes cites Scripture as saying *"the Magicians of Egypt did like by their Enchantments."* Hobbes, *Leviathan*, 303 (3.37).

37 Hobbes, *Leviathan*, 292 (3.36).

38 I make another version of this argument at some length in Martel, *Divine Violence*.

39 Hobbes, *De Cive*, 317.

40 Hobbes, *De Cive*, 317–18. While it is true that Hobbes sometimes speaks of humans setting these notes and marks and sometimes he says it is God who does this, the idea that God sets these marks is itself a human interpretation and a human decision about what those marks are and what they convey.

41 Hobbes, *De Cive*, 319.

42 Hobbes, *De Cive*, 320.

43 Hobbes, *Leviathan*, 325–26 (3.40).

44 Hobbes, *De Cive*, 321.

45 Hobbes, *De Cive*, 322.

46 Hobbes, *De Cive*, 322.

47 Hobbes, *De Cive*, 323.

48 Hobbes, *Leviathan*, 479–80 (4.47).

49 Hobbes, *De Cive*, 323.

50 Hobbes, *De Cive*, 323.

51 Hobbes, *De Cive*, 324.

52 Hobbes, *De Cive*, 324.

53 Hobbes, *De Cive*, 324–25.

54 Hobbes, *De Cive*, 325.

55 Hobbes, *De Cive*, 325.

56 Hobbes, *De Cive*, 325–26.

57 Hobbes, *De Cive*, 326.

58 Another example of Hobbes leaving out a direct reference to popular interpretive power comes when addressing the question of the king's own interpretive power and right to judge vis-à-vis the clergy (a pressing question in his own time as well). Hobbes writes that just because a king might not be as well schooled in liturgy as a priest, this does not mean that the king can't judge on theological questions (Hobbes, *De Cive*, 326–27). He says the king can get advisors to advise him in religion and all other matters. But here too the same argument applies: if kings do not need "expertise" to be able to make judgments, then neither do the people who in their plurality contain much more knowledge and complexity than the king and any set of advisors.

59 Hobbes, *De Cive*, 327.

60 Hobbes, *De Cive*, 327–28.

61 Hobbes, *Leviathan*, 10.

62 There are exceptions to this understanding, however. Both the Shiite tradition within Islam and the Mormon tradition within Christianity, for example, hold to the ongoing possibility of prophecy.

63 Hobbes, *Leviathan*, 334 (3.41). I also develop this argument about Hobbes and the Holy Spirit in Martel, *Subverting the Leviathan*, particularly in chapter 6, "The Fellowship of the Holy Spirit."

64 Hobbes, *Leviathan*, 339 (3.42).

65 Hobbes, *Leviathan*, 342 (3.42).

66 Hobbes, *Leviathan*, 343 (3.42).

67 Those who read Hobbes here as favoring sovereign over ecclesiastical authority include Patricia Springborg (although her view is more nuanced than most). See Springborg, "Hobbes on Religion"; and Springborg, "Leviathan and the Problem of Ecclesiastical Authority."

68 Hobbes, *Leviathan*, 345 (3.42).

69 Hobbes, *Leviathan*, 345 (3.42).

70 For some of these criticisms, see Bowle, *Hobbes and His Critics*.

71 Hobbes, *Leviathan*, 348 (3.42).

72 Hobbes, *Leviathan*, 354 (3.42).

73 Hobbes, *Leviathan*, 355 (3.42).

74 It is worth noting that Hobbes's understanding of the Holy Spirit was markedly different from both the Puritan and Orthodox Anglican views on this figure. For the Puritans, at least some of them, and for the Quakers too, the Holy Spirit was a unifying force, sending the same interpretation into all minds. For the Anglicans, the Holy Spirit is purely metaphorical and nothing else. For Hobbes, it is something different. For a good overview of the politics of the Holy Spirit during this time, see Nutall, *The Holy Spirit in Puritan Faith and Experience*. See also Burgess, *The Holy Spirit*.

75 Hobbes, *Leviathan*, 279 (3.34).

76 For an interesting take on the relationship between idolatry and politics in Hobbes, see Coleman, "Hobbes's Iconoclasm." See also Pye, "The Sovereign, the Theater, and the Kingdome of Darknesse."

77 Hobbes, *Leviathan*, 451 (4.45).

78 Hobbes, *Leviathan*, 341 (3.42).

79 Hobbes, *Leviathan*, 112 (1.16). See also Pitkin, *The Concept of Representation*, for a commentary on the question of Hobbes's claim that we are all "authors" of sovereignty.

80 Hobbes, *Leviathan*, 291 (3.36).

81 In this sense, I am using the term *prophecy* here in a way that accords with the work of George Shulman. See Shulman, *American Prophecy*.

Chapter Three. A Most Disappointing Prophet

An earlier version of part of chapter 3 appeared as "Nietzsche, Revelation, and the Materiality of Metaphor," *Theory and Event* 24, no. 1 (January 2021): 220–39.

1 Nietzsche, *The Genealogy of Morals*, 157.

2 Nietzsche, *Thus Spoke Zarathustra*, 39.

3 Nietzsche, *Thus Spoke Zarathustra*, 39.

4 Nietzsche, *Thus Spoke Zarathustra*, 39; see also 333.

5 In *The Nietzsche Disappointment*, Nickolas Pappas discusses Nietzschean disappointment in a way that is different from what I am focusing on here. For Pappas, what is perhaps primary is the question of Nietzsche's own psychology, his contention with his readers, his aggression, and also the failure of many of his goals. He concludes his book by writing: "You read Nietzsche valorizing his person's uniqueness and also taking up his claims and theories as communicable: you digest them: as if you did no more than overhear the words . . . and now you think 'What shall I do with these ideas?': *take them and run*—and it appeals to your vanity to appeal to his because you reading Nietzsche are a philosopher too, disappointed in philosophy but always hopeful" (252). See also Safranski, *Nietzsche*.

6 See Martel, *The Misinterpellated Subject*. See also Martel, "Nietzsche's Cruel Messiah."

7 Nietzsche, *Thus Spoke Zarathustra*, 161.

8 For more on Nietzsche's cruelty and its uses, see Soll, "Nietzsche on Cruelty, Asceticism, and the Failure of Hedonism." See also Higgins, "Suffering in Nietzsche's Philosophy."

9 Nietzsche, *Thus Spoke Zarathustra*, 163.

10 Nietzsche, *Thus Spoke Zarathustra*, 159.

11 Nietzsche, *Thus Spoke Zarathustra*, 161.

12 See Berlant, *Cruel Optimism*.

13 Nietzsche, *Thus Spoke Zarathustra*, 82.

14 In "Of the Despisers of the Body," Zarathustra speaks of an archist element within each of us called the "Self." He says the body as such is a "great intelligence" (Nietzsche, *Thus Spoke Zarathustra*, 61). But the Self is the body's would-be ruler. He likens the Self to "a mighty commander" (62). He says, using the same visual language of archism itself: "The Self seeks with the eyes of the sense, it listens too with the ears of spirit. The Self is always listening and seeking: it compares, subdues, conquers, destroys. It rules and it is also the Ego's ruler" (62).

15 I am indebted to Jonas Rosenbrück for his commentary on parts of this book that I presented as a paper at Northwestern University. He asked whether there is an epistemic equality between some of these authors in their relationship to archism, allowing me to think about how these authors are distinct from one another, not all doing the same thing. He and many other interlocutors at that meeting were extremely helpful in honing especially the work on Nietzsche and Benjamin. In particular I would point out Marc Crépon, Sam Weber, Mick Dillon, Jacob Levi, Jackie Stevens, and Mauricio Oportus Preller.

16 Robert Gooding-Williams discusses this in *Zarathustra's Dionysian Modernism*, 193. In the original German, the title of this section is "Der Wahrsager," which means something like fortune or truthteller, i.e., a soothsayer. Nietzsche, *Also Sprach Zarathustra*, 110. Calling him a soothsayer may suggest his falseness from the start. However, in the following chapter, I will be arguing that

the difference between prophet and soothsayer is not so significant since in effect all prophets are necessarily false for both Nietzsche and Benjamin—necessarily including Zarathustra—if the definition of the prophet is one who sees absolute and eternal truths. Since no such truths are available to human actors for either of these thinkers, the difference between a true and a false prophet is based on whether they recognize that absence, at least some of the time.

17 Nietzsche, *Thus Spoke Zarathustra*, 155.

18 Nietzsche, *Thus Spoke Zarathustra*, 156.

19 Grace Neal Dolson writes that Nietzsche accepts Schopenhauer's "pessimistic premises" but denies "the conclusions drawn from them." Dolson, "The Influence of Schopenhauer upon Friedrich Nietzsche," 247.

20 Nietzsche, *Thus Spoke Zarathustra*, 156.

21 Nietzsche, *Thus Spoke Zarathustra*, 156.

22 Nietzsche, *Thus Spoke Zarathustra*, 157; Nietzsche, *Also Sprach Zarathustra*, 111.

23 Nietzsche, *Thus Spoke Zarathustra*, 157.

24 Nietzsche, *Thus Spoke Zarathustra*, 157.

25 Nietzsche, *Thus Spoke Zarathustra*, 157.

26 Nietzsche, *Thus Spoke Zarathustra*, 157.

27 Nietzsche, *Thus Spoke Zarathustra*, 158.

28 I'm grateful to Shalini Satkunanandan for several observations about Zarathustra's behavior including that he does not agree with his disciples' interpretation of his dream. As a rule, Satkunanandan is more charitable toward the Higher Men than I am prone to be (and she also sees Zarathustra as being more charitable to them as well). I am convinced by her argument and have made some tweaks in what I say here to reflect that.

29 See, for example, Fink, "The Subject and the Other's Desire."

30 Nietzsche, *Thus Spoke Zarathustra*, 255.

31 Nietzsche, *Thus Spoke Zarathustra*, 255.

32 Nietzsche, *Thus Spoke Zarathustra*, 255.

33 Nietzsche, *Thus Spoke Zarathustra*, 256.

34 Nietzsche, *Thus Spoke Zarathustra*, 256.

35 Nietzsche, *Thus Spoke Zarathustra*, 256.

36 Nietzsche, *Thus Spoke Zarathustra*, 257.

37 Nietzsche, *Thus Spoke Zarathustra*, 257.

38 Nietzsche, *Thus Spoke Zarathustra*, 258.

39 The Higher Man is the same figure that the prophet in the previous section claimed was uttering a cry of distress. This cry motivated Zarathustra to look for the Higher Man in the forest, coming upon this road, these kings, and their donkey.

40 Nietzsche, *Thus Spoke Zarathustra*, 261.

41 Kafka, "Before the Law," in Kafka, *Parables and Paradoxes*, 61–65.

42 Nietzsche, *Thus Spoke Zarathustra*, 289.

43 Nietzsche, *Thus Spoke Zarathustra*, 290.

44 Nietzsche, *Thus Spoke Zarathustra*, 292.

45 Nietzsche, *Thus Spoke Zarathustra*, 293.

46 Nietzsche, *Thus Spoke Zarathustra*, 293.

47 Nietzsche, *Thus Spoke Zarathustra*, 293. Although, of course, Zarathustra is an archist too so whatever he is smelling from the Higher Men is something that he is emitting as well.

48 Nietzsche, *Thus Spoke Zarathustra*, 322. Actually, I'm not so sure the donkey really talks. In the original German, it does not say "Yea-a" or its German equivalent. It merely says "I-A," which is the way Germans write down the sound that donkeys make (in English, it is Hee-Haw). So the donkey in this instance isn't strictly talking at all, a further sign of the way that it gets increasingly fetishized. Nietzsche, *Also Sprach Zarathustra*, 254.

49 Nietzsche, *Thus Spoke Zarathustra*, 323.

50 Nietzsche, *Thus Spoke Zarathustra*, 325.

51 Nietzsche, *Thus Spoke Zarathustra*, 329. This turn to the dead as being re-deemable, albeit in a Nietzschean sense only, also reminds me once again of Benjamin's claim that *"even the dead* will not be safe from the enemy if he is victorious. And this enemy has never ceased to be victorious." W. Benjamin, "On the Concept of History," 391.

52 Nietzsche, *Thus Spoke Zarathustra*, 325–26. Shalini Satkunanandan said this to me while I presenting a reading of *Thus Spoke Zarathustra* based on this chapter for her class on November 18, 2021 at University of California, Davis. Satkunanandan has a forthcoming book titled *Passing By* which describes this reading, among other interpretations of *Thus Spoke Zarthustra*. It is from her that I got the idea of reading *Thus Spoke Zarathustra* like a novel with a plot, something that she brings out wonderfully in her own work.

53 Nietzsche, *Thus Spoke Zarathustra*, 333. The night before, he tells them directly, "You do not understand me" (330).

54 Nietzsche, *Thus Spoke Zarathustra*, 331.

55 Nietzsche, *Thus Spoke Zarathustra*, 336.

56 Nietzsche, *Thus Spoke Zarathustra*, 336.

57 Then again, part IV may not be the actual "end" of the book. Paul S. Loeb argues that it is an anachronistic part of the book that comes before the end, as it were (with the end of part III being the true end of the book). See Loeb, *The Death of Nietzsche's Zarathustra*, 90. I am indebted to Shalini Satkunanandan for this reference.

58 Once again, the dead are often better resisters of archism than the living.

59 Nietzsche, *Thus Spoke Zarathustra*, 51.

60 Nietzsche, *Thus Spoke Zarathustra*, 103; Nietzsche, *Also Sprach Zarathustra*, 65.

61 Fanon, *Black Skin, White Masks*, 232.

62 Kafka, "The Refusal," 173.

63 See Nietzsche, *Ecce Homo* (1993), 68.

64 Nietzsche, *Thus Spoke Zarathustra*, 324.

65 Nietzsche, *Thus Spoke Zarathustra*, 324.

66 Nietzsche, *The Gay Science*, 167 (section 108).

67 Nietzsche, *The Gay Science*, 181 (section 125).

68 Nietzsche, *The Gay Science*, 181 (section 125).

69 Arendt, "Willing," 195.

70 Fanon, *The Wretched of the Earth*, 51.

71 I think, for example, that the entire opus of James Scott is devoted to uncovering precisely these kinds of instances. See, for example, Scott, *Domination and the Arts of Resistance*.

72 Nietzsche, *Ecce Homo* (1992), 71.

73 Nietzsche, *Ecco Homo* (1992), 69, 72.

74 Nietzsche, *Ecco Homo* (1992), 72. Nietzsche, *Ecce Homo* (2005, German), 49.

75 Nietzsche, *Ecce Homo* (1992), 72.

76 Nietzsche, *Ecce Homo* (1992), 73.

77 Nietzsche, *Ecce Homo* (1992), 73.

78 W. Benjamin, "On the Concept of History," 72.

79 I don't think Hobbes is at this other extreme pole, although he is closer to it than either Benjamin or Nietzsche.

80 Foucault, *The History of Sexuality*, 93.

81 Nietzsche, *Thus Spoke Zarathustra*, 40.

82 Nietzsche, *Thus Spoke Zarathustra*, 40.

Chapter Four. A Prophet Who Can't See the Future

An earlier version of part of chapter 4 appeared as "Walter Benjamin and the General Strike: Nonviolence and the Archeon," in *The Meanings of Violence: From Critical Theory to Biopolitics*, ed. Gavin Rae and Emma Andrea Ingala Gomez (New York: Routledge, 2018), 13–30.

1 W. Benjamin, "The Work of Art in the Age of Its Technical Reproducibility," 252.

2 Theodor Adorno and Max Horkheimer have a similar take on the dilemma of postlapsarianism, although the Fall doesn't feature quite as much for them as it does for Benjamin. In *Dialectic of Enlightenment*, they write that the "Jewish religion allows no word that would alleviate the despair of all that is mortal" (23). Here, Judaism is favorably contrasted to some other religions in its stringent policing of God as a concept that cannot be known. The prohibition "on pronouncing the name of God" is, the authors state, the basis of a form of critique and negation, a kind of negative theology of their own (23). In this way, they argue, Judaism "associates hope only with the prohibition against calling on what is false as God, against invoking the finite as the infinite, lies as truth." (23). See also Weber, *Benjamin's -abilities*, 301.

3 For an excellent series of books engaging with Benjamin's strategies in general, see Weber, *Benjamin's -abilities*; Fenves, *Arresting Language*, 251–61; Fenves, *The Messianic Reduction*; Hamacher, "Afformative, Strike"; and A. Benjamin, *Working with Walter Benjamin*.

4 This isn't entirely true, of course. For example, in "On the Concept of History," Benjamin includes this quote from "an eyewitness" to the July Revolution in France: "Who would have believed it! It is said that, incensed at the hour, Latter-day Joshuas, at the foot of every clocktower, were firing on clock faces to make the day stand still" (395). Benjamin also compares Joshua to Baudelaire in a way that specifically hives him off from a prophetic function when he writes: "To interrupt the course of the world—that was Baudelaire's deepest intention. The intention of Joshua. [Not so much the prophetic one: for he gave no thought to any sort of reform.] From this intention sprang his violence, his impatience, and his anger; from it, too, sprang the ever-renewed attempts to cut the world to the heart [or sing it to sleep]. In this intention he provided death with an accompaniment: his encouragement of its work" (W. Benjamin, *The Arcades Project*, 318 [J50,2].

5 For a good overview of Benjamin's relationship to prophecy and other related issues, see Britt, *Walter Benjamin and the Bible*. For a distinction between Benjamin's notion of theology and the idea of religion, see A. Benjamin, *Working with Walter Benjamin*.

6 W. Benjamin, "On the Concept of History," 397.

7 W. Benjamin, "On the Concept of History," 392.

8 W. Benjamin, "Paralipomena to 'On the Concept of History,'" 407.

9 W. Benjamin, "Paralipomena to 'On the Concept of History,'" 405.

10 W. Benjamin, "Paralipomena to 'On the Concept of History,'" 405. Søren Kierkegaard, who is a major influence over Benjamin—albeit a rarely cited one—says something very similar. Citing Karl Daub, he writes: "Whoever apprehends the past, *historico-philosophus*, is therefore a prophet in retrospect." Kierkegaard, *The Portable Kierkegaard*, 171. I am grateful to Max Tomba for pointing this out to me.

11 W. Benjamin, "Konvolute K: Dream City and Dream House, Dreams of the Future, Anthropological Nihilism, Jung," in W. Benjamin, *The Arcades Project*, 390 (K1a,2).

12 This was something that Gershom Scholem found highly objectionable about his close friend. He resisted what he called Benjamin's "Janus face" in trying to reconcile such discordant traditions. Scholem, *Walter Benjamin*, 209.

13 For an excellent analysis of political theology as a general category of modern times and its relationship to questions of reason, interpretation, accountability, responsibility, and other basic building blocks of politics, see Miguel Vatter's two superb recent books, *Living Law* and *Divine Democracy*, about, respectively, Jewish and, to a lesser extent, Islamic and then Christian political theology.

14 W. Benjamin, "On Language as Such and on the Language of Man," 65.

15 In "The Animal That Therefore I Am," Derrida discusses Benjamin's essay on language and the sadness of objects to have lost their name but explains, "I am not (following) Benjamin when I find myself naked under the gaze of the animal" (389; he is talking about his cat who saw him when he was

undressed). Here, Derrida seems to critique Benjamin for offering that the power to name is, in a sense, inherently aggressive and human centric, not offering for ways that the animal's gaze could disrupt as much as it seems to affirm human domination. I think he may have a good point here, although it seems that Derrida does not entirely avoid this charge himself since the cat mainly stands as a site upon which Derrida can project his own disruptive insights, which ultimately are not for the sake of the cat at all.

16 W. Benjamin, "On Language as Such and on the Language of Man," 72.

17 W. Benjamin, "On Language as Such and on the Language of Man," 73.

18 In the conclusion, I discuss a wonderful very short (one-page) story by Ursula K. Le Guin in which Eve undoes Adam's job of naming the animals in Eden. See Le Guin, "She Unnames Them."

19 W. Benjamin, "On Language as Such and on the Language of Man," 67.

20 For more on this aspect of Benjamin's materialism, see Martel, *Textual Conspiracies*.

21 Karen Barad's work is once again very helpful in conceiving of an anarchist universe where even the iron-clad "laws of physics" subvert rather than reinforce dominant archist hierarchies.

22 This discussion is an example of the collective thinking I refer to in the acknowledgments. In this instance, I am indebted to Max Tomba, Karen Barad, Daniela Gandorfer, and Isaac Jean-François for their help in thinking this out. The word *confront* comes from Julia Ng, who is also a member of my Benjamin reading group; she recently published a superb new translation of the "Critique of Violence," along with other works, with Peter Fenves. See Fenves and Ng, *Toward the Critique of Violence*.

23 Fitzpatrick, *Modernism and the Grounds of Law*, 12.

24 I am grateful to Isaac Jean-François for this insight.

25 W. Benjamin, "On Language as Such and on the Language of Man," 66; W. Benjamin, "Über Sprache überhaupt und über die Sprache des Menschen," 146.

26 W. Benjamin, "On Language as Such and on the Language of Man," 67; W. Benjamin, "Über Sprache überhaupt und über die Sprache des Menschen," 146.

27 W. Benjamin, "Konvolute H: The Collector," in W. Benjamin, *The Arcades Project*, 206 (H2,3).

28 W. Benjamin, "On the Concept of History," 395.

29 See W. Benjamin, *The Arcades Project*, 66 (B2,4); 544 (S1,5); 548 (S2a,3); 842–43 (G17).

30 On hearing a version of this chapter at a conference, Samuel Weber suggested that both Nietzsche's idea of eternal recurrence and Benjamin's notion of reproducibility serve to unmake the idea not only of progress but even the possibility that one thing, time, or place could be different, higher, or better than another place. For more on this, see Weber, *Benjamin's—abilities*.

31 See Nietzsche, *The Genealogy of Morals*, 149.

32 W. Benjamin, "On the Concept of History," 395.

33 W. Benjamin, "On the Concept of History," 396.

34 W. Benjamin, "On the Concept of History," 397.

35 In this conversation, I am indebted to Karen Barad for their notion that entanglement, an idea that comes out of quantum physics, links up seeming unrelated and distant objects both spatially and temporally. See Barad, *Meeting the Universe Halfway*. See also Barad, "Troubling Time/s and Ecologies of Nothingness"; and Barad, "What Flashes Up."

36 Britt, *Walter Benjamin and the Bible*, 138.

37 In reconciling the fact that after the Fall, truth is impossible (except in glimpses and flashes), with the apparent moments of revelation during the Hebrew prophetic tradition as such, Britt tells us that for Benjamin, "if Genesis is the Biblical text of language before the Fall, then prophetic lament applies after the Fall" (*Walter Benjamin and the Bible*, 97). In this way, the ancient Hebrew prophets may, in Benjamin's view, constitute a series of largely failed attempts to discern and grasp at a lost connection to both the divine and the material. Benjamin's focus on the modern prophets over those figures from the Hebrew tradition may reflect this understanding. The prophets as such for Benjamin may not have anything more to tell us (except as a form of lamentation) than those subjects whose times and histories were of more interest to him (such as Kafka and Baudelaire).

38 W. Benjamin, "Letter to Gershom Scholem on Franz Kafka," 325.

39 W. Benjamin, "Letter to Gershom Scholem on Franz Kafka," 325.

40 W. Benjamin, "Letter to Gershom Scholem on Franz Kafka," 326.

41 W. Benjamin, "Letter to Gershom Scholem on Franz Kafka," 326.

42 W. Benjamin, "Franz Kafka," 815.

43 W. Benjamin, "Franz Kafka," 805.

44 W. Benjamin, "Franz Kafka," 805-6.

45 Here is an example of how another sense can sometimes link us to what the visual field, mastered as it is by archism, cannot.

46 W. Benjamin, "On the Concept of History," 392.

47 W. Benjamin, "On the Concept of History," 392.

48 Although it would be incomplete without including a discussion of Satan, it honestly had not occurred to me to do so. I am grateful to Mick Dillon for reminding me of this other angel.

49 W. Benjamin, "Konvolute S: Painting, Jugendstil, Novelty," in W. Benjamin, *The Arcades Project*, 544 (S1,5).

50 W. Benjamin, "Agesilaus Santander (Second Version)," 716.

51 W. Benjamin, "Agesilaus Santander (Second Version)," 714.

52 W. Benjamin, "Agesilaus Santander (Second Version)," 714.

53 W. Benjamin, "Agesilaus Santander (Second Version)," 714-15. This story resembles the Muslim story wherein, when God created Adam, he demanded that all angels worship what he had created. The angels did so except for Satan, who loved God so much that he refused to praise anyone or anything

but God, leading to his fall (presumably he got his vengeance on Adam a bit later). Another version has it that he said that since he was a superior being, made of fire instead of clay, he would not bow before Adam.

54 W. Benjamin, "Agesilaus Santander (Second Version)," 715.

55 W. Benjamin, "Agesilaus Santander (Second Version)," 715.

56 W. Benjamin, "Agesilaus Santander (Second Version)," 715.

57 W. Benjamin, "Agesilaus Santander (Second Version)," 715.

58 W. Benjamin, "Agesilaus Santander (Second Version)," 715.

59 W. Benjamin, *The Origin of German Tragic Drama*, 230.

60 W. Benjamin, *The Origin of German Tragic Drama*, 230.

61 W. Benjamin, *The Origin of German Tragic Drama*, 232.

62 W. Benjamin, *The Origin of German Tragic Drama*, 232.

63 W. Benjamin, *The Origin of German Tragic Drama*, 232.

64 W. Benjamin, "Agesilaus Santander (Second Version)," 715.

65 Or rather, yes, they are anarchist prophets in the sense that we all are, via our daily life, our interactions, etcetera. But not in their capacity *qua* prophets, not as "experts" who know what others do not know.

66 W. Benjamin, *The Origin of German Tragic Drama*, 183. This comes from his description of how the baroque dramatists managed to allegorize even Jesus Christ, showing "examples of birth, marriage, and funeral poems, of eulogies and victory congratulations, songs on the birth and death of Christ, on his spiritual marriage with the soul, on his glory and his victory" (183). Benjamin writes, "It is an unsurpassably spectacular gesture to place even Christ in the realm of the provisional, the everyday, the unreliable" (183). Here, allegorizing the ur symbol has a devastating and massive effect on the normative power of Christian dogma. With Satan, I think, something similar is at foot (arguably, this could make Christ an anarchist prophet as well, of course).

67 W. Benjamin, "Critique of Violence," 250.

68 W. Benjamin, "Critique of Violence," 250.

69 W. Benjamin, "Critique of Violence," 250.

70 W. Benjamin, "Critique of Violence," 250.

71 W. Benjamin, "The Meaning of Time in the Moral Universe," 286.

72 W. Benjamin, "The Meaning of Time in the Moral Universe," 286.

73 W. Benjamin, "The Meaning of Time in the Moral Universe," 287.

74 Once again, I am indebted to Karen Barad for suggesting that the angel of history may not himself be a historical materialist.

75 When Benjamin writes in "On the Concept of History" that the historical materialist "regards it as his task to brush history against the grain" (392), I see him as referring to the false directionality of archism, not to the direction of (anarchist) time itself.

76 W. Benjamin, "On the Concept of History," 394.

77 W. Benjamin, "The Work of Art in the Age of Its Technical Reproducibility," 267.

78 Nietzsche, *The Genealogy of Morals*, 159.

An earlier version of part of chapter 5 appeared as "An Anarchist Power amidst Pessimism: The Overcoming of Optimism in José Saramago's *Blindness* and *Seeing*," *The Comparatist* 43 (October 2019): 125–46.

1 As a rule of thumb, being a leftist does not make one immune from archism, although I do not think that being a Marxist or a communist more generally automatically means one is an archist; far from it, in fact. As with all political forms—and here I very much include "brand A" anarchism itself—communism can have an archist form. The distinction lies not in the ideology per se—although some ideologies like liberalism and fascism are purely archist—but once again the mode of transmission of that thought. If leaders are thought to have some unique vision that their followers simply accept, the system is archist. If they merely share that vision with their communities, are not in fact leaders at all, then a form of anarchism is what ensues.

2 Aristodemou, *Law, Psychoanalysis, Society*, 108.

3 Arendt, *On Revolution*, 249.

4 Tomba, *Insurgent Universality*, in particular chapter 3 on the Paris Commune, 71–119. This of course does not eliminate the violent response from archist forces but, by the same token, I don't think it renders the resultant anarchist community any more vulnerable to such threats than a full overthrow does. In some cases, it might even buy time as the degree of threat such a movement poses may be less evident at first to the archists.

5 Bookchin, "An Overview of the Spanish Libertarian Movement," 10.

6 I discuss the anarchist nature of the Haitian revolution in Martel, *The Misinterpellated Subject*.

7 Bookchin, *The Spanish Anarchists*, 12.

8 Bookchin, *The Spanish Anarchists*, 2. Note that the term *libertarian* was the anarchists' own name for themselves (*libertariano*) and has nothing whatsoever to do with libertarianism as we know the concept in English.

9 Richards, *Lessons of the Spanish Revolution*, 45.

10 It is not literally the case that all anarchists were also anarchosyndicalists or that anarchosyndicalism was ubiquitous across Spain. One prominent anarchist, Federica Montseny, stated along with two comrades that "especially in agricultural villages, where the syndicalist solution is not appropriate, even in a traditional sense, I reserve the right to pursue the revolution from the moment that we proclaim free communes throughout Spain, on the basis of the socialization of the land and of all the means of production, placed in the hands of producers." Here, the traditional Spanish basis for anarchism—the communal village—becomes itself a basis for organizing. Acklesberg, *Free Women of Spain*, 44.

11 Mintz, *Anarchism and Worker's Self-Management in Revolutionary Spain*, 56. Mintz also mentions a related problem of "followerism."

12 Gómez Casas, *Anarchist Organization*, 61–62.

13 Mintz, *Anarchism and Worker's Self-Management in Revolutionary Spain*, 49.

14 Mintz, *Anarchism and Worker's Self-Management in Revolutionary Spain*, 37.

15 Richards, *Lessons of the Spanish Revolution*, 68.

16 Richards, *Lessons of the Spanish Revolution*, 69–71.

17 Mintz, *Anarchism and Worker's Self-Management in Revolutionary Spain*, 38–40.

18 However, as Martha Acklesberg points out, there were limits to the degree to which gender equality was put into effect. For one thing, equal pay for men and women on the anarchist collectives was not always practiced. More generally, gender norms about the division of labor on these collectives was also widely (but not exclusively) practiced. Acklesberg, *Free Women of Spain*, 107.

19 Pestaña, always a critic, first inside and then outside the CNT, states, "Officially we have no paid officials today, but the editors of *Solidaridad Obrero* are paid. Off the record, under the table, so to speak, there are two paid and permanent posts on the National Committee; one or two—more often two than one—on the Regional Committee of Catalonia, etc." Quoted in Mintz, *Anarchism and Worker's Self-Management in Revolutionary Spain*, 54.

20 Mintz, *Anarchism and Worker's Self-Management in Revolutionary Spain*, 48.

21 Jane Macalevy similarly states, "There are only two sides, the owners and the rest of us." Macalevy, "How Unions Can Still Win Big."

22 Paz, *Durruti*, 212.

23 This radically open style began to suffer as the struggle with Franco reached its culmination. Over time, and especially toward the end of the struggle that would effectively destroy the Spanish Revolution, the tone of the anarchist newspapers—especially the official ones—changed and began to move from frank candor to sounding more like the communist and socialist newspapers, full of triumphalism and the party line. Richards, *Lessons of the Spanish Revolution*, 187.

24 Quoted in Gómez Casas, *Anarchist Organization*, 95.

25 Gómez Casas, *Anarchist Organization*, 132–33.

26 Richards, *Lessons of the Spanish Revolution*, 99.

27 Richards, *Lessons of the Spanish Revolution*, 74.

28 Richards, *Lessons of the Spanish Revolution*, 188.

29 Richards, *Lessons of the Spanish Revolution*, 132.

30 Paz, *Durruti*, 191.

31 Durruti quoted in Paz, *Durruti*, 183.

32 Paz, *Durruti*, 183–84.

33 Paz, *Durruti*, 185.

34 Paz, *Durruti*, 184.

35 I am grateful to Diego Arrocha Paris for this suggestion about the mimetic nature of leadership.

36 "Victor Hugo, Lenín, reposan en el pantéon, en soberbios mausoleos. Nuestro camarada Durruti no está en el pantéon; era demasiado modesto y ofenderíamos su nombre y su obra, llevándole en un lugar de privilegio. Reposa al lado de aquel otro gran luchador, hermano suyo, hermano nuestro, también, el

gran Ascaso." *Boletín de Información*, no. 110, Barcelona, November 23, 1936, 3. All quotes from the Boletín de Información are my translation.

37 *Boletín de Información*, 3.

38 *Boletín de Información*, 3.

39 Acklesberg, *Free Women of Spain*, 136–37.

40 For Machiavelli, glory is a collective form of recognition. Even if it is oriented toward a leader, it is a reflection of that leader's embeddedness in that community. Thus he writes of Agothacles, the Sicilian tyrant: "it cannot be called virtue to kill one's fellow citizens, betray one's friends, be without faith, without pity, without religion; by these methods one may indeed gain power but not glory." Machiavelli, *The Prince*, 32.

41 See Öcalan, *Democratic Confederalism*.

42 Graeber, introduction to Öcalan, *Manifesto for a Democratic Civilization*, 12. See also *CrimethInc.*, "Understanding the Kurdish Resistance."

43 Biehl, "Kurdish Communalism."

44 One website addressing the issue of Bookchin's influence on Öcalan states: "Although Western leftists are fascinated by the Bookchin-Öcalan connection, it is not as if Kurdish militants are walking around with Bookchin under their arms in the region. Sure, Democratic Confederalism resembles libertarian municipalities, but pointing to Bookchin as the ideological forefather reeks of Eurocentrism." *CrimethInc.*, "Understanding the Kurdish Resistance."

45 Sabio, *Rojava*, 32.

46 Sabio, *Rojava*, 32.

47 As Ali B. writes in "Eroding the State in Rojava": "The revolution in Rojava is a women's revolution above and beyond anything else—exemplified most forcefully by the YPJ [Yekîneyên Parastina Jin, Women's Protection Units]—but it is not necessarily a feminist one. Kurdish women are currently advancing their own gender theory under the rubric of *Jineoloji* (*Jin* means women in Kurdish). This is beyond the scope of this article but among other things *Jineoloji* grapples with the incompatibility between western feminism and the Kurdish family structure, perhaps reminiscent of some of the earlier critiques levelled by Black feminists in the US."

48 Ali B., "Eroding the State in Rojava."

49 Öcalan, "Democratic Confederalism," 17.

50 Ali B., "Eroding the State in Rojava."

51 Sabio, *Rojava*, 66, quoting PhD candidate Ulrike Flader.

52 Sabio, *Rojava*, 66.

53 Sabio, *Rojava*, 66.

54 Sabio, *Rojava*, 67.

55 Ali B., "Eroding the State in Rojava."

56 Sabio, *Rojava*, 67.

57 Ali B., "Eroding the State in Rojava." Speaking of the Tev-Dem, Sardar Saadi, a Toronto-based activist and PhD student, said that this body was "responsible for implementing" the general principles of the Rojavan Revolution.

He also indicated that "in spite of its ideology [the Tev-Dem] recognized that the path to an ideal society would be a long one and would take time to build." Sabio, *Rojava*, 62, summarizing what Saadi said. Another Kurdish activist, Salih Muslim, is quoted as saying that people were still "learning how to govern themselves," indicating both a sense of the transition to effective full democracy as well as its (present) limitations. Sabio, *Rojava*, 67.

58 The term *Athenian* may be a reference to part of Öcalan's theory, which he in turn got from Bookchin, about various modes of culture, one choice between Athenian/ideological and Roman/Materialist. Öcalan, *Manifesto for a Democratic Civilization*, 164. See also Sabio, *Rojava*, 34.

59 Ali B, "Eroding the State in Rojava."

60 Ali B, "Eroding the State in Rojava." Bread has a very important cultural place in Kurdish society, so a bakery is of no small importance.

61 Ali B, "Eroding the State in Rojava."

62 Graeber, introduction to Öcalan, *Manifesto for a Democratic Civilization*, 12.

63 Sabio, *Rojava*, 32.

64 Öcalan, *Manifesto for a Democratic Civilization*, 30.

65 As Graeber notes, "Abdullah Öcalan seems to have done a better job writing with the extremely limited resources allowed him by his jailors than authors like Francis Fukuyama or Jared Diamond did with access to the world's finest research libraries." Graeber, introduction to Öcalan, *Manifesto for a Democratic Civilization*, 18.

66 However, I will be arguing via Aristodemou that the blindness in *Seeing* comes not from the absence but from a surfeit of phantasmic vision. See Aristodemou, *Law, Psychoanalysis, Society*.

67 Aristodemou, *Law, Psychoanalysis, Society*, 35.

68 Aristodemou, *Law, Psychoanalysis, Society*, 35.

69 Aristodemou, *Law, Psychoanalysis, Society*, 35. This demonstrates the power of seeing things that aren't there—quite literally in this sense; one sees one's own non-seeing in this sense—but also, it suggests the possibility of seeing and responding to things that are there if one thinks in terms of immanence. Oedipus was responding to phantasms, but there are also things out there that are not phantasmic, even if we don't necessarily know them in their full material presence.

70 Saramago, *Blindness*, 182–83.

71 Saramago, *Blindness*, 195–96.

72 Saramago, *Blindness*, 209.

73 Saramago, *Blindness*, 209.

74 W. Benjamin, "The Storyteller," 151. In *Unburied Bodies*, I make a much more extensive argument about the way that dead bodies can resist the powers and projections of archism far more readily than the living can.

75 Saramago, *Seeing*, 43–44. Although I am risking anarchizing Saramago's wonderfully anarchic forms of punctuation, I have turned the commas that he uses to end sentences into periods to aid comprehension.

76 Saramago, *Seeing*, 74.

77 Saramago, *Seeing*, 92–93.

78 W. Benjamin, "Critique of Violence," 245–46.

79 Saramago, *Seeing*, 100.

80 I say disharmony but in fact Saramago tends to portray it as very harmonious (and coordinated!), indeed suggesting something more like Rousseau's general will than the cacophonous forms that I have been describing until now.

81 Saramago, *Seeing*, 204.

82 Saramago, *Seeing*, 211.

83 Saramago, *Seeing*, 212–13.

84 Saramago, *Seeing*, 227–28.

85 Saramago, *Seeing*, 299.

86 Saramago, *Blindness*, 256.

87 Saramago, *Blindness*, 252.

88 This includes, in the second book, having the election slogan of the horrible racist candidate be "Make America Great Again." This book was published in 1998. Butler, *Parable of the Talents*, 19.

89 Butler, *Parable of the Sower*, 346.

90 See Berlant, *Cruel Optimism*.

91 Butler, *Parable of the Sower*, 65–66.

92 Butler, *Parable of the Talents*, 307.

93 Butler, *Parable of the Sower*, 78.

94 Butler, *Parable of the Sower*, 217.

95 Butler, *Parable of the Sower*, 3.

96 I remember when I first read this series simply as a work of science fiction; I didn't take these terms seriously and was often impatient during all the long explications of Earthseed as a religion. Now I have a greater appreciation for the way that Butler created an entire worldview, one with serious and radical implications.

97 See Locke, *Two Treatises of Government*.

98 In a conversation with me, Daniela Gandorfer noted here that the statement "God is Change" has two subjects and no object, no place for the Cartesian cut to take place.

99 Butler, *Parable of the Sower*, 219.

100 In many ways, I see Earthseed as a fictionalized version of what Fanon talks about in his own work; just as for Fanon, resistance is its own form of truth making, so too for Lauren do communities need to continually generate truth forms of their own devising. For both, the logic of flux and change is foundational (or maybe more accurately an antifoundational foundation).

101 Butler, *Parable of the Sower*, 261.

102 I am grateful to Karen Barad for this insight.

103 This strikes me as being very similar to Benjamin's notion of the idea, something he discusses in *The Origin of Tragic Drama*. He writes, "ideas are to

objects as constellations are to stars" (34). Rather than having the idea serve as an eternal truth that all material objects are subservient to (an archist view if there is one), for Benjamin the idea is only present in the physical manifestation (he also notes that the idea is "the objective interpretation of phenomena" [34]). As with constellations drawn between stars, we connect those objects and thereby constitute an idea (however much we might get that wrong).

104 Butler, *Parable of the Talents*, 1.
105 Butler, *Parable of the Talents*, 1.
106 Butler, *Parable of the Talents*, 294.
107 Butler, *Parable of the Talents*, 294.
108 Butler, *Parable of the Sower*, 222.
109 W. Benjamin, "On the Concept of History," 395.
110 Butler, *Parable of the Talents*, 406.
111 Butler, *Parable of the Talents*, 358.
112 Butler, *Parable of the Talents*, 180.
113 Karen Barad has argued convincingly with me that there may well be good and bad immanentisms and even good and bad transcendentalisms—an idea that I discuss further in the next two chapters. Accordingly, I don't want to make these categories absolute but rather note their contrast in terms as they are generally understood in the West (and sometimes in the non-West too, as my description of Melanesian immanentism in the next chapter attests).

Chapter Six. Can Archism Ever Die?

An earlier version of part of chapter 6 appeared as "Perspective," in *Research Handbook on Law and Literature*, ed. Peter Goodrich, Daniela Gandorfer, and Cecilia Gebruers (Northampton, MA: Edward Elgar Publishing, 2022), 64-80.

1 Rebecca Solnit argues that under catastrophes when the state must withdraw, local communities do a much better job of organizing themselves and, in fact, fiascos usually come when the state tries to reassert itself. See Solnit, *A Paradise Built in Hell*.
2 Fisher, *Capitalist Realism*, 1.
3 See Strathern, "Souls in Other Selves, and the Immortality of the Body." I am grateful to James Leach for introducing this concept to me at his keynote address at the Legal Materiality Research Network, concluding conference, Birkbeck College, University of London, London, UK, January 9-10, 2020, and for sharing some of his other work with me.
4 Throughout this book, I have been careful not to conflate the West with archism altogether. I do believe there are non-Western forms of archism, but the Western form has definitely predominated and subjected much of the rest of the world to its own particular forms of archist vision.
5 See Ileto, *Pasyon and Politics*.

6 Here again, I am indebted to Karen Barad for this insight.

7 Having said that, I think it is fair to say that Judaism, when it is divorced from the Hellenizing influence that it received in Europe, is a largely immanentist religion, so that it is perhaps understandable that a figure like Spinoza, with roots in Sephardic Jewish culture from the Iberian Peninsula, would be someone who had access to that form of thought and that form of resistance.

   I want to add that everything I have to say about Spinoza comes thanks to an extraordinary reading group that I have had the privilege to be part of: my great thanks to Daniela Gandorfer, Karen Barad, Zulaikha Ayub, Patricia Williams, Emanuele Edilio Pelilli, Isaac Alexandre Jean-Francois, Stephen Engle, and Gabriele Wadlig.

8 Actually, Butler is a complicated figure in this regard. Like Spinoza, she confines God to the actual universe, but she is less careful to shut out any transcendental elements than he is, so she is something of an in-between case. It may well be that when you get to one extreme of negative theology, a position that Butler ably occupies, you might see that one extreme leads to another and you are in a positive territory after all or as well.

9 See Negri, *The Savage Anomaly*; and Deleuze, *Spinoza*. See also Deleuze, *Difference and Repetition*.

10 Deleuze, *Spinoza*, 13.

11 Spinoza, *Ethics*, 88–89.

12 Spinoza, *Ethics*, 85.

13 Spinoza, *Ethics*, 93.

14 Spinoza, *Ethics*, 99.

15 Spinoza, *Ethics*, 102.

16 Spinoza, *Ethics*, 107.

17 Spinoza, *Ethics*, 112.

18 That is what, in my opinion, makes Spinoza more like the Melanesian immanentists, who similarly start in an entirely different place than Western transcendentalists do.

19 In Hobbes's claim that we use the concept of God to determine what we deem to be the highest and most valued, we see a kind of immanentism at work as well, but, whereas Hobbes focuses on human agency and leaves God out of it, Spinoza goes right to the source and offers that our views of what is best and truest are definitely *not* in accord with God's own desires and universe. His greater attention to immanentism, where God is absolutely and only in the universe, allows this.

20 Lord, "The Master's Tools Will Never Dismantle the Master's House."

21 W. Benjamin, "Critique of Violence," 245.

22 On immanentism versus transcendentalism, see Barad, "What Flashes Up."

23 Strathern, "Souls in Other Selves, and the Immortality of the Body."

24 Hobbes thought of the soul as completely immanentist as well. In fact, for Hobbes, the term *soul* is purely a figure of speech, a representation of the body

that was given an afterlife and became superior to the body, becoming a fetish concept.

25 Strathern, "Souls in Other Selves, and the Immortality of the Body."
26 Strathern, "Souls in Other Selves, and the Immortality of the Body."
27 Leach, "'Documents against Knowledge,'" 22.
28 Leach, "'Documents against Knowledge,'" 26
29 Leach, "'Documents against Knowledge,'" 26.
30 Buck-Morss, "Aesthetics and Anaesthetics," 28.
31 Leach, "'Documents against Knowledge,'" 27–29.
32 Leach, "'Documents against Knowledge,'" 29.
33 Lawrence, *Road Belong Cargo*, 11.
34 Lawrence, *Road Belong Cargo*, 32–33.
35 Lawrence, *Road Belong Cargo*, 33.
36 Lawrence, *Road Belong Cargo*, 33.
37 Lawrence, *Road Belong Cargo*, 161–62.
38 Lawrence, *Road Belong Cargo*, 119.
39 Lawrence, *Road Belong Cargo*, 132.
40 Lawrence, *Road Belong Cargo*, 160–61.
41 Lawrence, *Road Belong Cargo*, 176. The experience that Yali had here is for me very reminiscent of other moments when Western lies led to radical responses by communities under its subjection, all of which I would place under the common title of misinterpellation. One such moment is during the Haitian Revolution when the French "Declaration of the Rights of Man and Citizen" helped to inspired a successful slave revolt in Haiti even though Black Haitian slaves were the last people that the drafters of the Declaration had in mind when they wrote that document. Also, when Woodrow Wilson gave his fourteen-point speech at the end of World War I, declaring the self-determination of all nations, he had in mind only European nations shedding their hereditary empires, but colonized people from all over the world came to Versailles inspired by the promise of his words. When they realized that they were not included, they turned to increasingly radical liberatory politics as a result. I look at these stories more closely in Martel, *The Misinterpellated Subject*.
42 Lawrence, *Road Belong Cargo*, 177–78.
43 Lawrence, *Road Belong Cargo*, 210.
44 Lawrence, *Road Belong Cargo*, 213.
45 Lawrence, *Road Belong Cargo*, 204.
46 Strathern, "Souls in Other Selves, and the Immortality of the Body."
47 It's true that the Melanesians have to live with ongoing archism as well, but in their case archism didn't have to "die"; it was never born or alive in the first place, and its power over them is, for this reason, always deeply limited.
48 One book on monsters explains: "Enlightenment Europe, however, tried to banish monsters. Monsters were identified with the irrational and the archaic. Category-crossing beings were abhorrent to Enlightenment ways

of ordering the world; sometimes they were classified as things of the devil, the antithesis of godly purity." Tsing et al., *Arts of Living on a Damaged Planet*, 5–6. I am indebted to Daniela Gandorfer for bringing this quotation to my attention.

49 Shelley, *Frankenstein*, 52–53.

50 Shelley, *Frankenstein*, 56.

51 Shelley, *Frankenstein*, 96.

52 Shelley, *Frankenstein*, 96.

53 For more on the monster's ugliness, see Gigante, "Facing the Ugly."

54 Shelley, *Frankenstein*, 81.

55 Shelley, *Frankenstein*, 161.

56 Shelley, *Frankenstein*, 161.

57 For more on the question of Shelley and the way she came up against sexist constructions of women through her writing, see Ferguson Ellis, "Mary Shelley's Embattled Garden."

58 *The Leftovers* (TV series, HBO), season 1, episode 6, "The Guest." See also Perrotta, *The Leftovers*.

59 *The Leftovers*, season 3, episode 1, "The Book of Kevin."

60 *The Leftovers*, season 3, episode 8, "The Book of Nora."

61 *The Leftovers*, season 3, episode 8, "The Book of Nora." We know that Nora is the only one to go back to her original world because in the other world she travels to, she finds the man who invented the machine that transported her, a man who had gone through himself, and talked him into making another machine in this world and sending her back. She explains that the man who invented the machine "asked me if I'd come all that way, why in God's name did I want to go back, and I told him it's because I didn't belong there. So he built it and I came back through. I came back here." *The Leftovers*, season 3, episode 8, "The Book of Nora."

62 *The Leftovers*, season 3, episode 8, "The Book of Nora."

63 *The Leftovers*, season 3, episode 8, "The Book of Nora."

64 W. Benjamin, "Franz Kafka," 811.

65 W. Benjamin, "Critique of Violence," 243.

66 W. Benjamin, "Critique of Violence," 250.

67 See Martel, *The Misinterpellated Subject*.

68 W. Benjamin, "Zur Kritik der Gewalt," 201. I am grateful to Marc de Wilde for pointing this out to me.

Conclusion

An earlier version of part of the conclusion appeared as "Why Does the State Keep Coming Back? Neoliberalism, the State and the Archeon," *Law and Critique* 29, no. 3 (November 2018): 359–75.

1 See Lenin, "What Is to Be Done?"

2 Hobbes, *Leviathan*, 112 (1.16).

3 Pitkin, *The Concept of Representation*, 34.

4 Hobbes, *Leviathan*, 112 (1.16).

5 For a superb treatment of how language can be said to bind the sovereign as much as the people, see Feldman, *Binding Words*.

6 I should qualify this claim somewhat, insofar as many scholars of indigeneity make claims for sovereignty that are not caught up with Western and white supremacist forms of archism. See, for example, Simpson, *Mohawk Interruptus*; Coulthard, *Red Skin, White Masks*; and Bruyneel, *The Third Space of Sovereignty*.

7 For a history of political *dis*obedience, and a theory of riot, see Clover, *Riot, Strike, Riot*.

8 See Solnit, *A Paradise Built in Hell*.

9 This is one of the key insights of Max Tomba in *Insurgent Universality*.

10 See Scott, *Domination and the Arts of Resistance*.

11 W. Benjamin, "Critique of Violence," 242.

12 I know it is often said that one aspect of being an anarchist is that one cannot provide a proper definition for anarchism and that, as befits a system that does not seek to impose one-size-fits-all kinds of rubrics, anyone can call themselves an anarchist whenever and however they please. Yet to think that way is merely to accept uncritically the archist claim that anarchism is random and unorganized, which I fully reject (actually, I think it is archism itself that is random and unorganized). I think anarchism *does* mean something and can't be defined willy-nilly, and I think the idea, for example, that libertarians or "anarcho-capitalists" have anything to do with anarchism is just plain wrong.

13 See Foucault, *The Birth of Biopolitics*, 15.

14 This is one place where I strongly part company with Arendt. Although her model of politics is one that has long inspired me, when it comes to revolutionary practices, she tells us toward the end of *On Revolution* that the great fault of the workers' councils in, for example, the Russian Revolution was that they tried to apply the same democratic principles to their workplace as they did to their political life. Rather than letting "experts" manage economic and technical matters, they sought to do it themselves and so, she says, failed entirely, bringing down their political form with them. I think in saying this, Arendt is herself subscribing to a form of archist thought—an intrinsic faith in the wisdom of managers—that works against the anarchism that her own theory seeks to propagate.

15 An interesting phenomenon that, while not unique to academia, is nonetheless relatively rare in other professions is that very often the administrators themselves, especially those near the top, are drawn from the faculty. When this happens, you can see the transformation in forms of vision happen very quickly. These new administrators get drawn into the very same kind of "leaderism" that the Spanish anarchists were so concerned with, forgetting their own participation in collective forms of sight and becoming just another arm of neoliberal punishment (some people resist this better than others, but in

my experience, over time it's almost impossible to resist the transformation, and, for those few who do manage to hold onto their collective form of vision, they usually get fired and returned to the faculty from which they came, if they don't get booted out of academia altogether).

16 See Barad, *Meeting the Universe Halfway*. See also Barad, "What Flashes Up."
17 Barad, *Meeting the Universe Halfway*, 129.
18 Barad, *Meeting the Universe Halfway*, 129.
19 Frost, *Biocultural Creatures*, 151.
20 See also Scott, *Against the Grain*.
21 See Ramnath, *Decolonizing Anarchism*.
22 The specter of an anarchist community deciding to be racist or misogynist is one that is often held out by liberals. They hold that liberal notions of "tolerance"—which masks a great deal of intolerance and violence—are the only possible antidote to such a possibility, a reason to stay under the umbrella of liberal archism. This view is, I think, a pure fabrication, a projection of liberalism's own unacknowledged connection to racism and sexism. For more on this question, see Brown, *Regulating Aversion*.
23 I don't think that Benjamin's understanding of nonviolence means literally pacifism; it just means the absence of mythic, hence archist, violence.
24 To be fair to Marx, he himself is not always a teleological thinker.
25 Mariátegui, "The Problem of Land," 75. I am very grateful to my colleague and friend Kate Gordy for introducing me to Mariátegui, a singularly fascinating theorist.
26 Mariátegui, "The Problem of Land," 75–76.
27 In fact, Mariátegui tends to flip back and forth between a more standard Marxist vision for the future and an Indigenous-based vision of Inca communism; the two visions do not easily coagulate in his work.
28 Zibechi, *Dispersing Power*, 13, quoting García Linera, *Sociología de los movimientos sociales en Bolivia*, 606.
29 Mariátegui, "The Problem of Land," 31.
30 Of course, Peru was not just colonized but also proselytized by Catholic missionaries. However, as in many parts of the world that European missionaries sought to convert, in Peru too the church's influence is complicated and often allows for pre-Columbian cultural elements to be translated into Christian terms without fundamentally abandoning their own, non-Abrahamic origins.
31 Ferguson, *Emma Goldman*, 6.
32 Ferguson, *Emma Goldman*, 7.
33 Goldman, *Living My Life*, 206. Perhaps even more to the point, as an adult, she often wished for the kinds of archist visions that in her view were the basis of Soviet communism, as when she wrote, "Alexandra Shakol had once told me that she would forgo half her life to wake up a Communist, so as to give herself unreservedly to the party's demands and service. Now I understood what she had meant. I felt that I would also give anything to be able to take Vetoshkin's hand and say: 'I am with you. I see your cause with your eyes and

I will serve with the same blind faith as you and your sincere comrades.' Alas, there was no such short and easy way out of the mental anguish for those who seek life beyond dogma and creed" (46).

34　Goldman, *Living My Life*, 7.

35　Goldman, *Living My Life*, 18.

36　Goldman, *Living My Life*, 23.

37　Goldman, *Living My Life*, 30.

38　Homi K. Bhabha, foreword to Fanon, *The Wretched of the Earth*, xxviii–xxix. Nasser Hussain pointed this out to me.

39　Fanon, *Black Skin, White Masks*, 111.

40　Fanon, *Black Skin, White Masks*, 110.

41　Fanon, *Black Skin, White Masks*, 110.

42　Fanon, *The Wretched of the Earth*, 2.

43　Fanon, *Black Skin, White Masks*, 12.

44　I should add that Black Lives Matters has its critics even on the left.

45　See Wilderson, *Afropessimism*; Wilderson, *Red, White & Black*; and Sexton, *Amalgamation Schemes*.

46　See Hartman, *Wayward Lives, Beautiful Experiments*; Hartman, *Scenes of Subjection*; and Spillers, *Black, White, and in Color*.

47　Wilderson, *Afropessimism*, 40.

48　Moten, "Blackness and Nothingness," 739.

49　Nietzsche, *Thus Spoke Zarathustra*, 157.

50　Moten, "Blackness and Nothingness," 751.

51　Moten and Harney, *The Undercommons*.

52　At one point Foucault says in an interview: "My position is that it is not up to us to propose. As soon as one 'proposes'—one proposes a vocabulary, an ideology, which can only have effects of domination. What we have to present are instruments and tools that people might find useful. By forming groups specifically to make these analyses, to wage these struggles, by using these instruments or others: this is how, in the end, possibilities open up. But if the intellectual starts playing once again the role that he has played for a hundred and fifty years—that of *prophet*, in relation to what 'must be,' to what 'must take place'—these effects of domination will return and we shall have other ideologies, functioning in the same way" (emphasis mine). Here, by prophet, I am reading Foucault as speaking of prophecy in its normative, archist form. Foucault, "Confinement, Psychiatry, Prison," 197. See also Foucault, "The Political Function of the Intellectual"; and W. Benjamin, "The Author as Producer."

53　See Matta-Clark, "Splitting the Humphrey Street Building." See also Lebbeus Woods, *Anarchitecture*; and Evans, *Translations from Drawing to Building and Other Essays*. I am indebted to Zulaikha Ayub for these references.

54　I think anarcheon is a much better word than utopia for what I'm talking about. Utopia means "no place," and the very name signifies the way that it too is tied up with phantasm, with what isn't, and with hopes and dreams for a future that does not, nor ever will, exist.

55 Schmitt, *Political Theology*, 1.

56 W. Benjamin, "Critique of Violence," 250.

57 I recognize that in saying this I am running against a very well-developed school of interpretation by figures like Giorgio Agamben (and maybe especially him) who read "mere life" in a more positive way, as a basis to resist the false dichotomy between *zoe* and *bios*. See, for example, Agamben, *Homo Sacer*. I am basing my own point on the contrast between mere life as a reflection of mythic violence and the living as the subject of divine violence, arguing that whatever the virtues of mere life, the concept of the living is worth treating as a separate category.

58 See Foucault, *Society Must Be Defended*.

59 See Arendt, *Eichmann in Jerusalem*.

60 I am grateful to Ellen Peel for mentioning this story to me.

61 See, for example, Hannsen, *Walter Benjamin's Other History*.

62 See, for example, Harman, *Object-Oriented Ontology*.

bibliography

Acklesberg, Martha. *Free Women of Spain: Anarchism and the Struggle for the Emancipation of Women*. Oakland, CA: AK Press, 2005.

Adorno, Theodor, and Max Horkheimer. *Dialectic of Enlightenment*. Translated by John Cumming. New York: Continuum, 1997.

Agamben, Giorgio. *Homo Sacer*. Translated by Daniel Heller-Roazen. Stanford, CA: Stanford University Press, 1998.

Ahmed, Siraj. *Archaeology of Babel: The Colonial Foundation of the Humanities.* Stanford, CA: Stanford University Press, 2018.

Althusser, Louis. "Ideology and the State." In *Lenin and Philosophy and Other Essays*, 85–126. New York: Monthly Review Press, 2001.

Arendt, Hannah. *Eichmann in Jerusalem: A Report on the Banality of Evil.* New York: Penguin Classics, 2006.

Arendt, Hannah. *The Human Condition*. Chicago: University of Chicago Press, 1958.

Arendt, Hannah. *On Revolution.* New York: Penguin Books, 1986.

Arendt, Hannah. *The Origins of Totalitarianism.* New York: Harcourt, Brace, Jovanovich, 1951.

Arendt, Hannah. "Willing." In *The Life of the Mind.* New York: Harcourt, Brace, Jovanovich, 1978.

Aristodemou, Maria. *Law, Psychoanalysis, Society: Taking the Unconscious Seriously.* London: Routledge, 2014.

B., Ali. "Eroding the State in Rojava." *Theory and Event* 19, no. 1 (2016).

Baldwin, James. *The Fire Next Time.* New York: Vintage Books, 1993.

Baldwin, James. "Going to Meet the Man." In *Going to Meet the Man*, 227–49. New York: Vintage, 1995.

Barad, Karen. *Meeting the Universe Halfway: Quantum Physics and the Entanglement of Matter and Meaning.* Durham, NC: Duke University Press, 2007.

Barad, Karen. "Troubling Time/s and Ecologies of Nothingness: Re-turning, Re-membering and Facing the Incalculable." *New Formations: A Journal of Culture/Theory/Politics* 92 (2017): 56–86.

Barad, Karen. "What Flashes Up: Theological-Political-Scientific Fragments." In *Entangled Worlds: Religion, Science and New Materialisms*, edited by Catherine Keller and Mary-Jane Rubenstein, 21–88. New York: Fordham University Press, 2017.

Benjamin, Andrew. *Working with Walter Benjamin: Recovering a Political Philosophy.* Edinburgh: University of Edinburgh Press, 2013.

Benjamin, Walter. "Agesilaus Santander (Second Version)." In *Walter Benjamin: Selected Writings*, vol. 2, *1927–1934*, edited by Marcus Bullock, Howard Eiland, and Gary Smith, 714–16. Cambridge, MA: Belknap Press of Harvard University Press, 1999.

Benjamin, Walter. *The Arcades Project.* Cambridge, MA: Belknap Press of Harvard University Press, 1999.

Benjamin, Walter. "The Author as Producer." In *Walter Benjamin: Selected Writings*, vol. 2, *1927–1934*, edited by Howard Eiland and Michael W. Jennings, 768–82. Cambridge, MA: Belknap Press of Harvard University Press, 1999.

Benjamin, Walter. "Critique of Violence." In *Walter Benjamin: Selected Writings*, vol. 1, *1913–1926*, edited by Marcus Bullock and Michael W. Jennings, 236–52. Cambridge, MA: Belknap Press of Harvard University Press, 1996.

Benjamin, Walter. "Fate and Character." In *Walter Benjamin: Selected Writings*, vol. 1, *1913–1926*, edited by Marcus Bullock and Michael W. Jennings, 201–6. Cambridge, MA: Belknap Press of Harvard University Press, 2004.

Benjamin, Walter. "Franz Kafka: On the Tenth Anniversary of his Death." In *Walter Benjamin: Selected Writings*, vol. 2, *1927–1934*, edited by Michael W. Jennings, Howard Eiland, and Gary Smith, 794–818. Cambridge, MA: Belknap Press of Harvard University Press, 1999.

Benjamin, Walter. "Letter to Gershom Scholem on Franz Kafka." In *Walter Benjamin: Selected Writings*, vol. 3, *1935–1936*, edited by Howard Eiland and Michael W. Jennings, 322–29. Cambridge, MA: Belknap Press of Harvard University Press, 2002.

Benjamin, Walter. "The Meaning of Time in the Moral Universe." In *Walter Benjamin: Selected Writings*, vol. 1, *1913–1926*, edited by Marcus Bullock and Michael W. Jennings, 286–87. Cambridge, MA: Belknap Press of Harvard University Press, 1996.

Benjamin, Walter. "On Language as Such and on the Language of Man." In *Walter Benjamin: Selected Writings*, vol. 1, *1913–1926*, edited by Marcus Bullock and

Michael W. Jennings, 62–74. Cambridge, MA: Belknap Press of Harvard University Press, 2004.

Benjamin, Walter. "On the Concept of History." In *Walter Benjamin: Selected Writings*, vol. 4, *1938–1940*, edited by Howard Eiland and Michael W. Jennings, 389–400. Cambridge, MA: Belknap Press of Harvard University Press, 2003.

Benjamin, Walter. *The Origin of German Tragic Drama*. New York: Verso, 1998.

Benjamin, Walter. "Paralipomena to 'On the Concept of History.'" In *Walter Benjamin: Selected Writings*, vol. 4, *1938–1940*, edited by Howard Eiland and Michael W. Jennings, 401–11. Cambridge, MA: Belknap Press of Harvard University Press, 2003.

Benjamin, Walter. "The Storyteller: Observations on the Work of Nikolai Leskov." In *Walter Benjamin: Selected Writings*, vol. 3, *1935–1938*, edited by Howard Eiland and Michael W. Jennings, 143–66. Cambridge, MA: Belknap Press of Harvard University Press, 2002.

Benjamin, Walter. "Über Sprache überhaupt und über die Sprache des Menschen." In *Gesammelte Schrhfiten*, vol. II.1, 140–57. Frankfurt: Suhrkamp, 1991.

Benjamin, Walter. "The Work of Art in the Age of Its Technical Reproducibility." In *Walter Benjamin: Selected Writings*, vol. 4, *1938–1940*, edited by Howard Eiland and Michael W. Jennings, 251–83. Cambridge, MA: Belknap Press of Harvard University Press, 2003.

Benjamin, Walter. "Zur Kritik der Gewalt." In *Gesammelte Schriften*, vol. II.1, 179–203. Frankfurt: Suhrkamp, 1980.

Berlant, Lauren. *Cruel Optimism*. Durham, NC: Duke University Press, 2011.

Biehl, Janet. "Kurdish Communalism." Interview with Ercan Ayboga. New Compass, September 10, 2011. http://new-compass.net/article/kurdish-communalism.

Birmingham, Peg. "The An-Archic Event of Natality and the 'Right to Have Rights.'" *Social Research* 74, no. 3 (2007): 763–76.

Boletín de Información. No. 110. Barcelona, November 23, 1936.

Bookchin, Murray. "An Overview of the Spanish Libertarian Movement." In *To Remember Spain: The Anarchist and Syndicalist Revolution of 1936*, 8–56. San Francisco, CA: AK Press, 1994.

Bookchin, Murray. *The Spanish Anarchists: The Heroic Years, 1868–1936*. New York: Free Life Editions, 1997.

Botwinick, Aryeh. *Skepticism, Belief, and the Modern: Maimonides to Nietzsche*. Ithaca, NY: Cornell University Press, 1997.

Bowle, John. *Hobbes and His Critics: A Study in Seventeenth Century Constitutionalism*. London: Jonathan Cape, 1951.

Britt, Brian. *Walter Benjamin and the Bible*. New York: Continuum, 1996.

Brown, Wendy. *Regulating Aversion: Tolerance in the Age of Identity and Empire*. Princeton, NJ: Princeton University Press, 2008.

Bruyneel, Kevin. *The Third Space of Sovereignty: The Postcolonial Politics of U.S.-Indigenous Relations*. Minneapolis: University of Minnesota Press, 2014.

Buck-Morss, Susan. "Aesthetics and Anaesthetics: Walter Benjamin's Artwork Essay Reconsidered." *October* 62 (Autumn 1992): 3–41.

Burgess, Stanley M. *The Holy Spirit: Medieval Roman Catholic and Reformation Traditions.* Peabody, MA: Hendrickson, 1997.

Butler, Octavia. *Parable of the Sower.* New York: Grand Central, 1993.

Butler, Octavia. *Parable of the Talents.* New York: Grand Central, 2000.

Charter of the Social Contract of Rojava (Syria). Accessed November 29, 2021. https://www.kurdishinstitute.be/en/charter-of-the-social-contract/.

Clover, Joshua. *Riot, Strike, Riot.* New York: Verso, 2016.

Coleman, Frank. "Hobbes's Iconoclasm." *Political Research Quarterly* 51, no. 4 (1998): 987–1010.

Coulthard, Glen Sean. *Red Skin, White Masks: Rejecting the Colonial Politics of Recognition.* Minneapolis: University of Minnesota Press, 2014.

CrimethInc. "Understanding the Kurdish Resistance: Historical Overview and Eyewitness Report." September 23, 2015. http://www.crimethinc.com/texts/r/kurdish/.

Curley, Edwin. "The Covenant with God in Hobbes' Leviathan." In *Leviathan after 350 Years*, edited by Tom Sorrell and Luc Foisneau, 199–216. Oxford: Oxford University Press, 2005.

Deleuze, Gilles. *Difference and Repetition.* Translated by Paul Patton. London: Bloomsbury, 2014.

Deleuze, Gilles. *Spinoza: Practical Philosophy.* San Francisco, CA: City Lights Books, 1988.

Derrida, Jacques. "The Animal That Therefore I Am (More to Follow)." Translated by David Wills. *Critical Inquiry* 28, no. 2 (2002): 369–418.

Derrida, Jacques. *Archive Fever: A Freudian Impression.* Chicago: University of Chicago Press, 1996.

Derrida, Jacques. "Force of Law: The Mystical Foundation of Authority." In *Deconstruction and the Possibility of Justice*, edited by Drucilla Cornell, Michel Rosenfeld, and David Gray Carlson, 3–67. New York: Routledge, 1992.

Dolson, Grace Neal. "The Influence of Schopenhauer upon Friedrich Nietzsche." *Philosophical Review* 10, no. 3 (1991): 241–50.

Eisenach, Eldon J. *Two Worlds of Liberalism: Religion and Politics in Hobbes, Locke and Mill.* Chicago: University of Chicago Press, 1981.

Evans, Robin. *Translations from Drawing to Building and Other Essays.* Cambridge, MA: MIT Press, 1997.

Fanon, Frantz. *Black Skin, White Masks.* New York: Grove, 1994.

Fanon, Frantz. *The Wretched of the Earth.* New York: Grove, 2004.

Feldman, Karen S. *Binding Words: Conscience and Rhetoric in Hobbes, Hegel, and Heidegger.* Evanston, IL: Northwestern University Press, 2006.

Fenves, Peter. *Arresting Language: From Leibniz to Benjamin.* Stanford, CA: Stanford University Press, 2001.

Fenves, Peter. *The Messianic Reduction: Walter Benjamin and the Shape of Time.* Stanford, CA: Stanford University Press, 2011.

Fenves, Peter, and Julia Ng, eds. *Toward the Critique of Violence: A Critical Edition.* Stanford, CA: Stanford University Press, 2021.

Ferguson, Kathy E. *Emma Goldman: Political Thinking in the Streets*. New York: Rowman and Littlefield, 2011.

Ferguson Ellis, Kate. "Mary Shelley's Embattled Garden." In *The Contested Castle: Gothic Novels and the Subversion of Domestic Ideology*, 181–206. Urbana: University of Illinois Press, 1989.

Fink, Bruce. "The Subject and the Other's Desire." In *Reading Seminars I and II: Lacan's Return to Freud*, edited by Richard Feldstein, Bruce Fink, and Maire Jaanus, 76–97. Albany: State University of New York Press, 1996.

Fisher, Mark. *Capitalist Realism: Is There No Alternative?* Washington, DC: Zero Books, 2009.

Fitzpatrick, Peter. *Modernism and the Grounds of Law.* Cambridge: Cambridge University Press, 2001.

Foucault, Michel. *The Birth of Biopolitics: Lectures at the Collège de France, 1978–79.* New York: Picador, 2008.

Foucault, Michel. "Confinement, Psychiatry, Prison." Interview by David Cooper et al. In *Politics, Philosophy, Culture: Interviews and Other Writings, 1977–1984*, edited by Lawrence D. Kritzman, translated by Alan Sheridan, 178–210. New York: Routledge, 1988.

Foucault, Michel. *Discipline and Punish: The Birth of the Prison.* New York: Vintage Books, 1995.

Foucault, Michel. *The History of Sexuality: Volume 1.* New York: Penguin, 1973.

Foucault, Michel. "The Political Function of the Intellectual." Translated by Colin Gordon. *Radical Philosophy* 17 (Summer 1977): 12–14.

Foucault, Michel. *Society Must be Defended: Lectures at the Collège de France, 1975–1976.* New York: Picador, 2003.

Foucault, Michel. "Truth and Power." In *Power/Knowledge: Selected Interviews and Other Writings, 1972–1977*, edited by Colin Gordon, 109–33. New York: Pantheon, 1980.

Frost, Samantha. *Biocultural Creatures, Biocultural Creatures: A New Theory of the Human.* Durham, NC: Duke University Press, 2016.

García Linera, Álvaro. *Sociología de los movimientos sociales en Bolivia.* La Paz: Oxfam-Diakonía, 2004.

Gigante, Denise. "Facing the Ugly: The Case of Frankenstein." *ELH* 67, no. 2 (2000): 565–87.

Goldman, Emma. *Living My Life.* Mineola, NY: Dover, 1970.

Gómez Casas, Juan. *Anarchist Organization: The History of the FAI.* Montreal: Black Rose Books, 1986.

Gooding-Williams, Robert. *Zarathustra's Dionysian Modernism.* Stanford, CA: Stanford University Press, 2001.

Goodrich, Peter. "Proboscations: Excavations in Comedy and Law." *Critical Inquiry* 43, no. 2 (Winter 2017): 361–88.

Graeber, David. Preface, *Manifesto for a Democratic Civilization*, vol. 1, *Civilization: The Age of Masked Gods and Disguised Kings*, by Abdullah Öcalan, translated by Havin Guneser, 11–20. Coppell, TX: New Compass Press, 2020.

Hamacher, Werner. "Afformative, Strike: Benjamin's 'Critique of Violence.'" In *Walter Benjamin's Philosophy: Destruction and Experience*, edited by Andrew Benjamin and Peter Osborne, 110–38. London: Routledge, 1994.

Hannsen, Beatrice. *Walter Benjamin's Other History: Of Stones, Animals, Human Beings, and Angels*. Berkeley: University of California Press, 2000.

Harman, Graham. *Object-Oriented Ontology: A New Theory of Everything*. New York: Pelican Books, 2018.

Hartman, Saidiya. *Scenes of Subjection: Terror, Slavery, and Self-Making in Nineteenth-Century America*. New York: Oxford University Press, 1997.

Hartman, Saidiya. *Wayward Lives, Beautiful Experiments: Intimate Histories of Riotous Black Girls, Troublesome Women, and Queer Radicals*. New York: Norton, 2019.

Higgins, Kathleen Marie. "Suffering in Nietzsche's Philosophy." In *Reading Nietzsche at the Margins*, edited by Steven V. Hicks and Alan Rosenberg, 59–72. West Lafayette, IN: Purdue University Press, 2008.

Hobbes, Thomas. *Leviathan*. Edited by Richard Tuck. New York: Cambridge University Press, 1996.

Hobbes, Thomas. *Man and Citizen ("De Homine" and "De Cive")*. Edited by Bernard Gert. Indianapolis, IN: Hackett, 1993.

Hoekstra, Kinch. "Disarming the Prophets: Thomas Hobbes and Predictive Power." *Rivista di Storia della Filosofia* 59, no. 1 (2004): 97–153.

Holy Scriptures. Philadelphia, PA: Jewish Publication Society of Philadelphia, 1917.

Honig, Bonnie. *Emergency Politics: Paradox, Law, Democracy*. Princeton, NJ: Princeton University Press, 2009.

Ileto, Reynaldo Clemeña. *Pasyon and Politics: Popular Movements in the Philippines, 1840–1910*. Manila: Ateneo de Manila University Press, 1997.

Johnston, Sarah Iles. *Ancient Greek Divination*. Malden, MA: Wiley-Blackwell, 2008.

Kafka, Franz. *The Castle*. New York: Schocken Books, 1998.

Kafka, Franz. *Das Schloss*. Frankfurt: Fischer Taschenbuch, 1981.

Kafka, Franz. *Parables and Paradoxes*. New York: Schocken Books, 1961.

Kafka, Franz. *The Trial*. New York: Schocken Books, 1998.

Kamuf, Peggy. "From Now On." *Epoché* 10, no. 2 (2006): 203–20.

Kantorowicz, Ernst. *The King's Two Bodies: A Study in Mediaeval Political Theology*. Princeton, NJ: Princeton University Press, 1957.

Kavka, Gregory S. *Hobbesian Moral and Political Theory*. Princeton, NJ: Princeton University Press, 1986.

Kierkegaard, Søren. *The Portable Kierkegaard*. Edited by Simon Yee. Vancouver, BC: Emerald Knight, 2009.

Kramer, Sina. *Excluded Within: The (Un)Intelligibility of Radical Political Actors*. New York: Oxford University Press, 2017.

Lawrence, Peter. *Road Belong Cargo: A Study of the Cargo Movement in the Southern Madang District, New Guinea*. Prospect Heights, IL: Waveland, 1971.

Leach, James. "'Documents against Knowledge': Immanence and Transcendence and Approaching Legal Materials." *Law Text Culture* 23 (2019): 16–39.

The Leftovers. TV series based on the book by Tom Perrotta. HBO, 2014–17.

Le Guin, Ursula K. "She Unnames Them." *New Yorker*, January 21, 1985, 27.

Lenin, Vladimir Ilyich. "What Is to Be Done?" In *Essential Works of Lenin: "What Is to Be Done?" and Other Writings*, edited by Henry M. Christman, 53–176. New York: Dover, 1987.

Locke, John. *Two Treatises of Government*. Cambridge: Cambridge University Press, 1965.

Loeb, Paul S. *The Death of Nietzsche's Zarathustra*. New York: Cambridge University Press, 2010.

Lorde, Audre. "The Master's Tools Will Never Dismantle the Master's House." In *Sister Outsider: Essays and Speeches*, 110–14. Berkeley, CA: Crossing, 1984.

Macalevy, Jane. "How Unions Can Still Win Big: Excerpt from 'A Collective Bargain: Unions, Organizing, and the Fight for Democracy." January 19, 2020. https://janemcalevey.com/writing/how-unions-can-still-win-big-excerpt-from-a-collective-bargain-unions-organizing-and-the-fight-for-democracy/.

Machiavelli, Niccolò. *"The Prince" and "The Discourses on the First Ten Books of Livy."* New York: Modern Library, 1950.

Mariátegui, José Carlos. "The Problem of Land." In *Seven Interpretive Essays on Peruvian Reality*, translated by Marjory Urquidi, 31–76. Austin: University of Texas Press, 1988.

Martel, James. *Divine Violence: Walter Benjamin and the Eschatology of Sovereignty*. New York: Routledge, 2011.

Martel, James. *The Misinterpellated Subject*. Durham, NC: Duke University Press, 2017.

Martel, James. "Nietzsche's Cruel Messiah." *Qui Parle* 20, no. 2 (2012): 199–223.

Martel, James. *Subverting the Leviathan: Reading Thomas Hobbes as a Radical Democrat*. New York: Columbia University Press, 2007.

Martel, James. *Textual Conspiracies: Walter Benjamin, Idolatry, and Political Theory*. Ann Arbor: University of Michigan Press, 2011.

Martel, James. *Unburied Bodies: Subversive Corpses and the Authority of the Dead*. Amherst, MA: Amherst College Press, 2018.

Matta-Clark, Gordon. "Splitting the Humphrey Street Building." Interview with Lisa Béar, May 21 and 25, 1974. http://avalancheindex.org/interviews/gordon-matta-clark-splitting-the-humphrey-street-building/.

Mintz, Frank. *Anarchism and Worker's Self-Management in Revolutionary Spain*. Oakland, CA: AK Press, 2013.

Monmouth University Polling Institute. "Protestors' Anger Justified Even if Actions May Not Be." June 2, 2020. https://www.monmouth.edu/polling-institute/reports/monmouthpoll_us_060220/.

Moten, Fred. "Blackness and Nothingness (Mysticism in the Flesh)." *South Atlantic Quarterly* 112, no. 4 (2013): 737–80.

Moten, Fred, and Stefano Harney. *The Undercommons: Fugitive Planning and Black Study*. New York: Autonomedia, 2013.

Negri, Antonio. *The Savage Anomaly: The Power of Spinoza's Metaphysics and Politics*. Minneapolis: University of Minnesota Press, 2000.

Nietzsche, Friedrich. *Also Sprach Zarathustra*. Munich: Goldmann, 1996.

Nietzsche, Friedrich. *Ecce Homo: How One Becomes What One Is.* New York: Penguin, 1992.

Nietzsche, Friedrich. *Ecce Homo: Wie Man Wird, Was Man Ist.* Project Guttenberg, 2005.

Nietzsche, Friedrich. *The Gay Science.* New York: Vintage Books, 1974.

Nietzsche, Friedrich. "The Genealogy of Morals." In *"The Birth of Tragedy" and "The Genealogy of Morals,"* translated by Francis Golffing, 147–299. New York: Anchor, 1956.

Nietzsche, Friedrich. *Thus Spoke Zarathustra.* New York: Penguin Books, 1969.

Nutall, Geoffrey F. *The Holy Spirit in Puritan Faith and Experience.* Oxford: Basil Blackwell, 1947.

Öcalan, Abdullah. *Democratic Confederalism.* Coppell, TX: Transmedia, 2020.

Pappas, Nickolas. *The Nietzsche Disappointment: Reckoning with Nietzsche's Unkept Promises on Origins and Outcomes.* New York: Rowman and Littlefield, 2005.

Paz, Abel. *Durruti: The People Armed.* Montreal: Black Rose Press, 1976.

Perrotta, Tom. *The Leftovers.* New York: St. Martin's, 2014.

Pitkin, Hanna. *The Concept of Representation.* Berkeley: University of California Press, 1967.

Pocock, P. G. A. *Politics, Language. and Time: Essays on Political Thought in History.* New York: Atheneum, 1973.

Pye, Christopher. "The Sovereign, the Theater, and the Kingdome of Darknesse: Hobbes and the Spectacle of Power." *Representations* 8 (1984): 85–106.

Ramnath, Maia. *Decolonizing Anarchism.* Oakland, CA: AK Press, 2011.

Richards, Vernon. *Lessons of the Spanish Revolution.* London: Freedom Press, 1983.

Robinson, Cedric J. *Forgeries of Memory and Meaning: Blacks and the Regimes of Race in American Theater and Film before World War II.* Chapel Hill: University of North Carolina Press, 2007.

Sabio, Oso. *Rojava: An Alternative to Imperialism, Nationalism and Islamism in the Middle East (An Introduction).* Coppell, TX: Lulu, 2020.

Safranski, Rüdiger. *Nietzsche: A Philosophical Biography.* New York: Norton, 2002.

Saramago, José. *Blindness.* London: Harvill, 1997.

Saramago, José. *Seeing.* London: Random House, 2006.

Schmitt, Carl. *Political Theology: Four Chapters on the Concept of Sovereignty.* Cambridge, MA: MIT Press, 1985.

Scholem, Gershom. *Walter Benjamin: The Story of a Friendship.* New York: Schocken Books, 1981.

Scott, James C. *Against the Grain: A Deep History of the Earliest States.* New Haven, CT: Yale University Press, 2018.

Scott, James C. *The Art of Not Being Governed: An Anarchist History of Upland Southeast Asia.* New Haven, CT: Yale University Press, 2010.

Scott, James C. *Domination and the Arts of Resistance: Hidden Transcripts.* New Haven, CT: Yale University Press, 1992.

Scott, James C. *Seeing like a State: How Certain Schemes to Improve the Human Condition Have Failed.* New Haven, CT: Yale University Press, 1998.

Sexton, Jared. *Amalgamation Schemes*. Minneapolis: University of Minnesota Press, 2008.

Shelley, Mary. *Frankenstein*. New York: Singlet, 1983.

Shulman, George. *American Prophecy*. Minneapolis: University of Minnesota Press, 2008.

Simpson, Audra. *Mohawk Interruptus: Political Life across the Borders of Settler States*. Durham, NC: Duke University Press, 2014.

Skinner, Quentin. *Reason and Rhetoric in the Philosophy of Hobbes*. New York: Cambridge University Press, 1996.

Soll, Ivan. "Nietzsche on Cruelty, Asceticism, and the Failure of Hedonism." In *Nietzsche, Genealogy, Morality: Essays on Nietzsche's Genealogy of Morals*, edited by Richard Schacht, 168–92. Berkeley: University of California Press, 1994.

Solnit, Rebecca. *A Paradise Built in Hell: The Extraordinary Communities That Arise in Disaster*. New York: Viking, 2009.

Spillers, Hortense J. *Black, White, and in Color*. Chicago: University of Chicago Press, 2003.

Spinoza, Baruch. *Ethics*. New York: Oxford University Press, 2000.

Springborg, Patricia. "Hobbes on Religion." In *The Cambridge Companion to Hobbes*, edited by Tom Sorell, 346–80. New York: Cambridge University Press, 1996.

Springborg, Patricia. "Leviathan and the Problem of Ecclesiastical Authority." *Political Theory* 3, no. 3 (1975): 289–303.

Strathern, Marilyn. "Souls in Other Selves, and the Immortality of the Body." Foerster Lectures on the Immortality of the Soul, UC Berkeley, April 17, 2018. https://gradlectures.berkeley.edu/lecture/souls-in-other-selves-immortality-of-body/.

Tomba, Massimiliano. *Insurgent Universality: An Alternative Legacy of Modernity*. New York: Oxford University Press, 2019.

Tsing, Anna, Heather Swanson, Elaine Gan, and Nils Bubandt. *Arts of Living on a Damaged Planet: Ghosts and Monsters of the Anthropocene*. Minneapolis: University of Minnesota Press, 2017.

Vatter, Miguel. *Divine Democracy: Political Theology after Carl Schmitt*. New York: Oxford University Press, 2021.

Vatter, Miguel. *Living Law: Jewish Political Theology from Hermann Cohen to Hannah Arendt*. New York: Oxford University Press, 2021.

Weber, Samuel. *Benjamin's -abilities*. Cambridge, MA: Harvard University Press, 2008.

Wilderson, Frank B., III. *Afropessimism*. New York: Liveright, 20202.

Wilderson, Frank B., III. *Red, White & Black*. Durham, NC: Duke University Press, 2010.

Woods, Lebbeus. *Anarchitecture: Architecture Is a Political Act*. London: Academy Editions, 1992.

Zibechi, Raul. *Dispersing Power: Social Movements as Anti-state Forces*. Oakland, CA: AK Press, 2010.

Žižek, Slavoj. *The Sublime Object of Ideology*. New York: Verso, 1989.

index

authority from community, 17, 22, 55, 60, 77, 134, 211, 258, 260, 266; stealing credit from anarchism, 21, 160, 213, 271; subversion of, 60; as source of violence, 260; theological basis for, 34–41, 67, 116–17, 170, 217; theological subversion of, 23, 68, 242; trans people and, 21; transfer of reality and, 13, 19, 44, 198, 240, 271; "truth" of, 6, 10, 203; vulnerability of, 10, 53, 55, 61, 77, 84, 189, 195, 198, 211, 235, 237, 266, 292; Western, 23, 25, 62, 85; white people and, 8; women and, 8, 21; working class, poor people and, 8, 21; undead nature of, 237, 260, 291; undocumented people and, 8; uphill struggle to exist, 158, 269. *See also* universe, universal

archons, 23, 36, 41, 50, 115, 146, 191, 216, 235, 261, 288, 291

aristocracy, 66

Aristodemou, Maria, 1, 22, 23, 170, 191, 194–97, 199, 301n29, 319n66; atheism and, 22, 170

Arkein, 39, 43, 51, 52, 288

ark of the covenant, 45

Arendt, Hannah, 7, 52, 171, 286, 294, 303n42, 303n44, 325n14; and the absolute, 52; and concept of "a world," 7; and elementary republics, 171; natality and, 52; and *On Revolution*, 171, 325n14; and *Origins of Totalitarianism*, 303n42; on right to have rights, 52

Armenians, 184

Arrocha Paris, Diego, 317n35

Ascaso, Francisco, 168, 179, 180, 181

Assyrians, 184

atheism, 22, 23, 25, 93, 170; anarchism and, 170

Athens, 42

Athenian, 185

Aunt Jemima, 8, 282

Australia, 44, 227, 229, 231, 249, 250

authority, 12, 22, 43, 51, 54, 62, 66, 74, 113, 127, 156, 181, 193, 259–61, 286; alienation of, 22; authors and, 259; charisma and, 181; community as source of, 21; ecclesiastical, 86; redistribution back to community, 156, 159; transmission from God to human kings, 66

Ayboğan, Ercan, 183

Ayton, Imarn, 283

Ayub, Zulaikha, 327n53

B., Ali, 184, 185, 186, 318n47; and "Eroding the State in Rojava," 184, 186

Babel, tower of, 1, 3–4, 6, 7, 14, 78, 133, 303–4n46

Babha, Homi K., 278

Babylonian captivity, 83

Baldwin, James, 47; and "Going to Meet the Man," 47

Bakunin, Mikhail, 25, 26, 172, 253

Barad, Karen, 267–68, 301n36, 313nn21–22, 314n35, 315n75, 320n102, 321n113, 322n6

Baudelaire, Charles, 142, 158, 312n4

Benedict, Pope, 243

Benjamin, Andrew, 301n31

Benjamin, Walter, 16, 19, 20, 36, 43, 50, 56, 61, 68, 94, 102, 116, 121, 122, 125–60, 167, 193, 195, 205, 214, 216, 217, 220, 221, 222, 242, 253, 254, 263, 268, 270, 271, 286, 291–92, 293, 294, 295, 296, 297, 304n50, 310n51, 312n4, 315n75, 320–21n103, 326n23; *Agesilaus Santander*, 149, 150–51, 152, 153; *Angelus Novus*, 147, 150; *Arcades Project*, 137; "Authority of the dead," 193; baroque, 152, 153; baroque dramatists, 153; communism of, 26; cosmology of, 126; "Critique of Violence," 126, 154, 156, 157, 291; divine violence and, 23, 126, 146, 149, 155, 156, 221, 252, 291, 292; "The Dreaming collective" 130; expertise, 159; homogeneous, empty time, 128, 141; the Fall, 121, 126, 131, 141, 149; false prophecy and, 131, 135, 142; fashion, 138, 139; "Fate and Character," 50; fetishism and, 126, 129, 131, 134, 135, 144; "Foreseeing the present," 129, 142, 144; "Franz Kafka: On the Tenth Anniversary of His Death," 143; God as anarchist, 126, 153; historian, 128, 129, 130, 137, 138, 139, 140–41, 157, 158; Hell and, 51, 138, 152; Kafka as prophet,

Benjamin, Walter (continued)
143–46; last Judgment, 156, 157; "Living,
The" and, 16, 159, 291–93, 294; magic
of matter, 132, 159, 271, 292; material
resistance, 135, 240; "Meaning of Time
in the Moral Universe," 156, 157; mental
[geistigen] being, 135; Messianic time,
141; "muteness of" objects and, 121, 132;
mythic violence, 51, 118, 121, 127, 129, 138,
153, 291, 293, 294; mythic violence and
archism, 121, 125, 127, 135, 152, 157; now-
time (Jeztzeit), 137, 139, 140, 156, 294; "On
Language as Such and On the Language
of Man," 130, 135; "On the Concept of
History," 127, 129, 138, 140–41, 157, 158;
overnaming, 131; Origin of German Tragic
Drama, 142, 151, 153, 154; phantasm and,
130; phantasmagoria, 144; police violence
and, 254; "Pure means," 221, 254; "Real
state of emergency" and, 23; revelation
and, 135–36; Satan, 149, 150, 151, 152, 154,
157, 230, 314n53, 315n66; seat of Judgment
and, 148; the Seer, 128; "Slight adjustment" and, 254, 257; soothsaying (vs.
prophecy), 127, 128, 134, 135, 137–38, 139,
146; storms and, 102; struggle (kampf), 133;
"Thou shalt not kill," 155, 254; Trauerspiel
and, 19, 142; "Useless for the purposes of
fascism," 125, 126, 134, 151; waiting, 150
(see also Nietzsche: waiting and; Zarathustra: waiting and); "The Work of Art in the
Age of its Mechanical Reproducibility,"
159. See also Adam; Angel of History
Berkman, Alexander (Sasha), 27
Berlant, Lauren, 99, 201
Berlin, 150
Bible, 35, 36, 38, 39, 58, 87, 109
Biden, Joseph, 9, 46
Biko, Steve, 278
Birmingham, Peg, 52
Black people, 8, 11, 21, 47, 48–49, 200, 248,
261, 263, 282; communities, 172; police
carceral and, 263
Black life, 46, 200, 281, 282, 283, 283–85
Black Lives Matter, 8, 281–83, 284, 293,
327n44

Black Nationalist Party, 278
Black Panthers, 278, 280
Black Power Movement, 17, 280, 283
Black Skin, White Masks. See under Fanon
Black Thought, 283
Black Wall Street, 261
Bland, Sandra, 56
blindness, 1, 40, 98–99, 253, 290, 292
    (see also under Saramago: Blindness)
Bohr, Niels, 267–68
Bolivia, 273–74; Aymara, 274, 275; El Alto,
274, 275
Bolsonaro, Jair, 24
Bookchin, Murray, 168, 171, 172, 173, 183,
318n44
Botwinick, Aryeh, 61, 67, 305n15
Bouazizi, Mohamed, 56
Braudel, Fernand, 183
Brazil, 24
Brisbane, 230
Britt, Brian, 142, 314n37
Brown, Michael, 56
Brown people, 8, 21, 47, 248, 261, 282
Buddhism, 24, 93
Buffalo, New York, 277
Burma, 269
Busey, Gary, 243
Butler, Octavia, 16, 26, 36, 133, 161, 167, 169,
200–210, 212, 221, 242, 267, 293, 294, 298,
320n96, 320n8; apocalypse and, 200;
Earthseed religion (see under Olamina,
Lauren: Earthseed religion); Lauren
Olamina (see Olamina, Lauren); The
Parable of the Sower, 169, 200, 212; The Par-
able of the Talents, 169, 200, 205, 208, 212;
pessimism and, 201
Byron, Lord, 241

Cain, 229
Calderón, Pedro, 153
California, 280
capitalism, 9, 10, 18, 138, 140, 171, 186, 207,
226, 264–65, 277, 299n1
Caribbean, 172
Casas, Juan Gómez, 173, 175
Catholic Church 170, 172

materialism, 129, 130, 131 (*see also* Benjamin, Walter: historian)

Matta-Clark, Gordon, 288

Melanesia, 162, 214, 215, 216, 217, 223, 238, 253, 255, 287, 323n47; cargo beliefs and, 224–29, 287; immanentism and, 162, 207, 214, 216, 223–32, 235, 252, 255; Yali (*see* Yali)

Melbourne, 249

messiah, messianic 16, 23, 98, 106, 130, 140, 141, 142, 145, 151, 246, 257, 290, 302n9; "negative messianism," 142

metaphor, 121, 238

metaphysics, 135, 208, 222

Middle East, 183, 187

Middle Passage, 284

Minneapolis police, 8–9, 281

miracles, 75, 77, 78

Miriam, 34, 72, 91, 142

misogyny, 270, 293

Mississippi, 282

misrecognition, 45; *see also* Althusser, Louis

Modi, Narendra, 24

monarchy, 43, 66; *see also* kings

monster (Frankenstein's), 161, 215, 237, 238–41, 247, 255. See also *Frankenstein*

Montseny, Federica, 180, 181, 316n10

Mormonism, 302n9, 306n62

Moscow, 173

Moses, 14, 58, 65, 72, 73, 74,77, 78, 90, 91, 147, 154–55, 258; as "God's lieutenant," 65, 78; as person of God, 85; death of, 66; pledge of the Israelites to, 65, 78

Most, Johann, 277

Moten, Fred, 283–84, 293; nothingness and, 284; *The Undercommons,* 284

Mount Sinai, 72

Myanmar, 24

nature, 12

negation, 22, 23; as void, 22, 23; negation of, 23

Negri, Antonio, 217, 221

neocolonialism, 227

neoliberalism, 24, 43

Netanyahu, Benjamin, 24

New Britain, 223

New Castle, 235

New Guinea, Papua, 17, 161, 214, 223, 227, 228, 235, 253, 272; Rai Coast, 17, 161, 214, 225, 227, 253; Hollandia, 230; Madang district, 224, 229, 230, 231, 232; Port Moresby, 234

Newton, Huey, 278, 280, 283

New York City, 245, 262, 275

Ng, Julia, 313n22

Nietzsche, 16, 22, 36, 43, 56, 61, 94, 95–124, 125, 126, 129, 137, 156, 158, 160, 161, 167, 205, 214, 217, 220, 221, 222, 242, 250, 255, 275, 285, 296, 297, 303–4n46; as anarchist, 109, 118; as fascist, 109; as one who disappoints, 95, 104; on becoming who we are, 255; collectivity and, 99; on cycles of disappointment and hope, 95, 112; death of God and, 22, 115–18, 119, 124, 126, 205, 220, 222; donkey and, 104, 109–11, 310n38; *Ecce Homo,* 119–24; externality and, 100, 118, 123; on future as a lure to the present, 139; *Gay Science,* 116, 117, 222; *Genealogy of Morals,* 161; God and, 109, 115–18, 222; on kings, 105, 106, 107, 230; on kingdom of earth, 109, 112; on kingdom of heaven, 109; and mishearing the twelve strokes of noon, 139; nihilism and, 97, 101, 102, 103; redemption and, 119; revelation and, 119–24, 129, 132, 135 (*see also under* Benjamin, Walter); and the Higher Man/Men 104–12, 309n28, 309n39, 310n47; and The Prophet (character), 101–4, 107–8, 113; and The Wanderer, 109; *Thus Spoke Zarathustra,* 95, 97, 99, 101, 103, 104, 109, 111, 112, 113, 119, 120, 149, 291; on the tightrope walker, 111, 112, 291; waiting and, 106 (*see also* Benjamin, Walter: Satan); Western philosophy and, 97. See also Zarathustra

nihilism, 48, 101–2, 103, 253, 272

North America, 172

Noumena, 48, 248

Numa, 30, 33, 258

Oakland, California, 278, 281

object, 121, 122

rape, 192, 200, 201, 208
rapture, the, 243
Reagan, Ronald, 46
reason, 73
Reichstag, 43
representation, 44, 48, 53, 63, 68, 89, 125,
    143, 194, 198, 286, 292, 296; archism and,
    53, 63; derepresentation, 90, 137; failure
    of, 143; as life blood of archism, 198;
    transfer of power to archists via, 198;
    unrepresentability of, 286
revelation. See under Nietzsche; Benjamin,
    Walter
Richards, Vernon, 174, 177
revolution, 16, 46, 94, 138, 140, 142, 257;
    Spanish (see Spanish Revolution); Roja-
    van (see Rojavan Revolution)
Road Belong Cargo, 226
Robinson, Cedric, 300n15
Rochester, New York, 275
Rojava, 168, 182, 184, 185, 186, 187, 210, 272,
    287
Rojavan Revolution, 16, 168, 181, 182–90,
    210, 212, 262; anarchism and, 168, 169,
    181–87, 212; "Charter of the Social
    Contract of Rojava (Syria)," 185, 186;
    Jineolojism, 183, 318n47; KCK (Union of
    Communities in Kurdistan), 184, 187;
    Mala Gel (People's Houses), 184; peace
    and consensus committees, 185; PKK
    (Kurdish Workers Party), 183, 185, 187;
    PYD (Democratic Union Party); Tev-
    Dem, people's assemblies, 185, 187; YPG
    (People's Protection Units), 183
Rome, Roman, 29, 39, 138, 230, 258
Rosenbrück, Jonas, 301n27, 308n15
Roosevelt, Franklin Delano, 46
Rousseau, Jean-Jacques, 185, 286, 320n80
Russia, 24, 25
Russian Revolution, 171, 325n14

Saadi, Sardar, 318–19n57
Said, Edward, 303–4n46
Samuel, 72, 75, 92
Sánchez, Saornil Lucia, 181
Sanders, Bernie, 46

Saramago, José, 16, 55, 161, 167, 169, 190–99,
    212, 233, 289, 292, 300n25, 320n80; Blind-
    ness, 16, 55, 162, 167, 169, 190–92, 193, 198,
    199, 211, 212, 216, 246, 289, 300n25; The
    Doctor's Wife (see Doctor's Wife, The);
    plague of anarchism and, 16; Seeing, 16,
    55, 90, 162, 167, 169, 190, 193–99, 212, 233
Satan. See Benjamin, Walter: Satan
Satkunanandan, Shalini, 111, 309n28, 310n52
Saul, 75, 77, 85
Shakol, Alexandra, 326n33
Shia, 184, 302n9, 306n62
Schlegel, Friedrich, 128
Schmitt, Carl, 288
Schneerson, Menachem Mendel, 302n9;
    Chabadism, 302n9
Scholem, Gershom, 143, 312n12
Schopenhauer, Arthur, 101; pessimism of,
    101
Scott, James C., 18, 262, 268, 291, 311n71; The
    Art of Not Being Governed, 268; becom-
    ing "primitive" to avoid the state, 269;
    Seeing Like a State, 18, 19, 64, 262; positive
    forms of resistance, 269; unnaturalness
    of archism, 269
Scripture, 59, 69, 72, 87; see also Bible
Seale, Bobby, 278, 280
Seattle, 262
Secularism, 12, 22, 23, 30, 34, 39, 43, 60, 62,
    63, 64, 65, 74, 92, 133, 207, 243; as disguise
    for theology, 25
senses, 20, 255; sight (see under vision);
    smell, 20, 109, 114, 145–46, 193; sound,
    109, 114, 143
Sexton, Jared, 283
Shakespeare, William, 153
Shakur, Assata, 283
Shelley, Mary, 17, 215, 236, 237 (see also
    Frankenstein); and subversion of male
    privilege, 241, 242; and subversion of
    science, 242
Shelley, Percy Bysshe, 241
Shulman, George, 307n81
signs, signification, 19, 41, 50, 59, 70–71,
    77, 82
sight. See vision

Sikhism, 93
slavery, 200, 226, 263
Social Contract, 62, 64
Solnit, Rebecca, 262, 321n1
Solomon, Temple of, 42
South America, 172
South Asia, 26
sovereignty, 54, 59, 61, 63, 64, 66, 72, 86, 88, 90, 170, 212, 261, 288, 325n6; as final decider, 69; earthly sovereign vs. an active God, 77; interpretive power of, 66–69, 74, 82–84, 91; forced to recognize collective decisions about language, 69, 91; right to judge, 81; speaking as God, 68; vs. authority, 261; vs. archism, 170, 261; vs. popular judgment of false prophecy, 74; vulnerability of, 94
Soviet Union, 171; and collectivization, 175; and worker's councils, 171
Spain, 168, 169, 170, 171, 172, 187, 210, 272; Andalusia, 177; Aragon, 177; Barcelona, 177; Caciques and, 172; Catalonia, 177; Indigenous anarchism of, 172; Léon, 178; Levant, 177
Spanish Civil War, 171, 172, 176; and Francoists, 172; and Republican government, 172, 174
Spanish Revolution, 16, 162, 167, 168, 170–82, 187, 210, 212, 275, 287, 317n23; anarchist takeover, 171; *Boletín de Información*, 180; CNT (National Workers Confederation), 168, 172–81; collectivization and, 175–76; crushing of, 171; decentralized planning and, 174; Direct Action, 175; diverse practices of, 175; Durruti, Buenaventura (*see under* Durruti, Buenaventura); FAI (Iberian Anarchist Federation), 173, 175, 176, 178; Forums for popular authority, 176, 177, 181; confederal structure of, 175; Generalitat, 177; general strike, 178; ignoring of, 171; *Iniciales*, 175; *La Revista Blanca*, 175; Mujeres Libres (Free Women), 181; newspapers, 174–75; piecemeal nature of, 187; popular front and, 173, 181; *Redención*, 175; solidarity of, 174; success of, 171; *Solidari-*

dad Obrera, 174, 175; Telephone Exchange (takeover of), 178; *Tierra y Libertad*, 175; UGT (General Union of Workers), 173; vs. civil war 172; women and, 175
Spies, Adolph, 180, 277
Spillers, Hortense I., 283
Spinoza, Baruch, 17, 201, 214, 216, 217–23, 253, 322n7, 322n18, 322n19; anarchism of, 221; Benjamin and, 221–22; contingency and, 218, 220; decentering of human perspective and, 219; determinism and, 218, 220; *Ethics*, 217; general strike and, 221; nonharmonious nature of the universe, 218; positive theology and, 217; refusal of transcendence and, 217; Spinoza's God, 201, 217–23, 252; Western immanentism and, 214, 217–21
Spinoza: Practical Philosophy, 217
Sri Lanka, 24
State, 13, 18, 45, 54, 114, 212, 264; failed, 44; "reining in" the economy, 264
Stoics, 40
storms, 102, 103, 147, 156, 158; expiation, 155, 156; out of paradise, 147; storm of forgiveness, 155–56
Strathern, Marilyn, 223 (*see also* Melanesia: cargo beliefs and; Melanesia: immanentism and); Foerster Lecture, UC Berkeley, 223, 233, 234
subjects, subjectivity, 122, 269
Sunnis, 184, 302n9
Sydney, 230
Sympatheia, 40
synagogue, 87
Syria, 183, 184, 185, 187
Syriac, 184

Tahrir Square, 262
Taylor, Breonna, 8, 56
Terra Nullius, 208
Thailand, 269
theology, 17, 22–24, 31, 60, 61, 74, 170; countertheology, 31, 34, 170; materialism and, 130; "negative theology," 61, 66–69, 86, 87, 93, 142, 156, 202, 217; political, 76, 126
Thessalonika, 87

Thus Spoke Zarathustra. See under Nietzsche

Zadok, 81

Zachariah, 83

Zapatistas, 287

Zarathustra, 16, 96, 120, 141, 148, 150, 157, 163, 167, 188, 209, 284, 290, 291, 308n14, 308-9n16; abandonment and, 115; "a cripple at this bridge," 97, 119; *amor fati*, 115, 200; archist seductions and, 97; as archist prophet, 96, 97, 99, 104; as assister, 119; as one of us, 119; as pharmakon, 119; as redeemer, 97; as subverter of archism, 96; cave and, 106-9; cruelty of, 98; cry of distress and, 103, 108, 109; disciples and, 102, 114; disappointment and, 96, 98, 102, 108, 113; dream of, 101-2; friend and, 99; followers of (or lack therein), 113; future and, 98; hermit and, 124; hill fortress of death and, 101; hunchback and, 98; "I too—am a prophet," 104, 111; nonharmony and, 100; noontide, 112; pity (ultimate sin), 103-4, 112; readers and, 124; redemption and, 99, 106, 108; redundancy of, 113; ruining archism from within, 100; salvation and, 15, 98, 106, 113; seduction by archism and, 100; seeing the present and, 99; speech to the sun, 96; storm and, 102, 103; trust and, 118; waiting and, 106 (*see also* Benjamin, Walter: Satan)

Zeus, 40

Zibechi, Raul, 273

Zion, 37

Žižek, Slavoj, 300n24

Zuccotti Park, 262

Zuckerberg, Mark, 294